First Impressions

Photos and Reflections of a Danube River Cruise

Eric Allen Jacobson

Copyright © 2019 Eric Allen Jacobson
www.ericallenjacobson.com

ALL RIGHTS RESERVED.
ISBN: 9781083084286

DEDICATION

This book is dedicated to my mother for checking off an item on my wife's bucket list (The only item on her bucket list.)

To my wife Joy, my travel companion.

Please visit www.EricAllenJacobson.com for information about the author and his other publications.

INTRODUCTION

In April 2019 my mother told us that she wanted to give my wife the gift of a cruise for her birthday. A cruise had been on my wife's bucket list for many years. It was a perfect storm of opportunity and preparedness, except that we weren't quite ready for a trip so soon. Yet three months later we started our journey.

It appears that Germans will do anything to stay on schedule. We flew with Lufthansa Airlines. They were ultra-organized, and even kept serving meals during some turbulence, unlike the wimpy American airlines we typically fly.

The cruise was the experience we hoped it would be. My wife has issues with her stomach, and the month before the trip it was acting up. We weren't sure if she would be able to take the trip, however it settled down and we made the journey. We had asked for low fat meals for her and hoped that she'd be okay on the ship. The first day the Maître' D came to our table to review the menu and let Joy know what items they could modify for her diet and what she shouldn't eat. The next morning, he found us at breakfast and reviewed the lunch and dinner menu with the same objective. We can report that my wife didn't get sick once on the 8-day trip and is still off her stomach medicine over a month later.

Our cabin was in what I call the dungeons. That is the lowest level of three on the ship. Since we sailed most often at night a balcony view wasn't missed. The cost savings was substantial and we spent so little time in the cabin that we were okay with the accommodations. The mattress on the ship was left over from the Spanish Inquisition. It was in stark contrast to the hotel mattress we slept on during the Budapest pre-trip vacation. Our friends on the upper level felt the same about their mattresses.

The first evening of the cruise we sat with two couples in the back of the dining room. There is no assigned seating and to our delight we hit it off with the couples we met for the first time. Our age differences spanned 20 years, however we got along well. So well that for the remainder of the trip we had dinner together, and often sat together at other meals. We were protective of our table and our time together, turning other people away who wanted to join us even if the other couples hadn't yet arrived. We also had lunch together in a pub-like restaurant in Vienna.

Most evenings the ship sailed, and in the morning we would be in a new city. The excursion guides were well informed and organized. It was a fast pace and as I expected, we could have used more time to see sights in each town or city. We didn't do the paid excursions (except Joy did the concert in the evening in Vienna) so we had that time to explore on our own. The only time we sailed during the day was after stopping in Krems, Austria, when we passed through the Wachau Valley.

The off-ship excursions were not overly challenging for the average walker, however a few easy options were offered for those who needed them. In my opinion, these cruises are not for people who have a challenge walking. There are many cobblestones in the small towns and hills to walk. The bus portions that were on some of the tours are fine, but don't provide the best way to see the sights. They go by too quickly to enjoy, and if you are on the wrong side of the bus you can't see the sites at all.

The on-board entertainment was geared toward an older crowd. Local talent got on the ship and sang, played instruments, or offered similar entertainment. My wife, a singer in a church choir, was in her element and sang along with gusto. A fun aspect of river cruises is that you are exposed to people from many cultures and countries. We heard the phrase, "in the nip" for the first time from the program director when talking about the thermal baths in Budapest. It means to be naked. No, they don't go naked in the baths. We laughed about it for the rest of the trip.

The coffee experience in Europe is different than here in the States. It is served with a small glass of water. (See the photo in the Passau section of the book.) You can find to-go coffee in most of the towns; however, it isn't as common as here. Coffee is meant to be an experience rather than just to fill a need.

The ship had one piano player on board who played most evenings and sometimes during the day. He was from Budapest and was one of the most positive and smiling people I've ever met. Many of the staff were from nearby countries. The Maître' D was from Slovakia. Both he and the piano player were married and their families both included several children. The men wouldn't see their respective families for 6 months while they worked on the ship. I found out that they don't switch ships or rivers, so they go back and forth between Budapest and Passau (or similar Danube itineraries.)

On the morning of our last day most people were gone by 8:30am. We, along with another couple, took the shuttle from Passau to the Munich airport.

Now I know why they drive so fast on the Autobahn. It's because they are looking for a bathroom! The trip to the airport was 2 hours. Our driver was German and didn't speak English. This presented a problem when I had to go to the bathroom halfway to the airport. When I expressed a heightened sense of urgency the driver thought I was saying that we were going to miss our plane and to drive faster. However, we had plenty of time until our flight. I spotted what looked like a truck stop. When we approached the next rest stop, I said, "Achtung!" and pointed to the rest stop. The driver got the hint and I was able to use that rest stop bathroom. I said the only other German word I know, "Danka," when I got back on the shuttle and we then proceeded to the airport.

After 10 days away from Pennsylvania we were ready to go home. A few people added an extension to Prague to the end of the cruise. While I would love to see Prague, I think we may make that a separate trip in the future. The time in Budapest was special because it's somewhere we wouldn't have planned on going ourselves.

We are thinking about taking another river cruise. There are so many great people to meet and places to see. A river cruise provides an easy way to get a taste of different countries, cultures, and food. So, come along and see some of the highlights from our trip. Each chapter starts with a brief overview of what we saw and our impressions of that stop. The views are strictly ours, and others who travel to those towns may have a different experience.

Our journey started in Budapest, Hungary.

BUDAPEST, HUNGARY

We opted for a two-day pre-trip extension so that we could explore the city with greater depth. The people were extremely friendly and helpful. English appeared to be spoken everywhere we went. The currency there is the forint. The exchange rate was around 288 forints to the dollar. We found most prices there reasonable.

The Hungarian Parliament building is one of the most visible and impressive sights in Budapest. Its size is dramatic during the day, but at night the soft yellow glow of the lights that illuminate the structure transform the cold white building into a warm presence on the river. The 59,000 square foot building was built in the late 19th century. We were taking photos of the building at night and a young man was standing near us taking photos. We started talking to him and it turned out that he was from Pittsburgh! He worked for Disney cruises and was on a brief vacation. He lent me his tripod so I could get a good photo of the Parliament building. I ended up using that photo for a canvas print when we returned home. It is the first photo in the Budapest chapter in this book.

Another beautiful nighttime sight is the Fisherman's Bastion and Buda's Castle. The Buda side of the river is quiet and peaceful at night, but if you want some nightlife stay or visit the Pest side.

Buda's Castle (Royal Palace or the Royal Castle), the large baroque-style structure to the left of Fisherman's Bastion as you look up the hill, was built in the late 1700's. There are several guard stations where you can see guards standing at. There is also a section of the grounds where excavation is taking place to uncover portions of the original castle that was built in the late 1200's.

As we waited outside of the Dohány Street Synagogue (built in the mid 1850's) for our tour of the Jewish district our guide told us that the many steel pylons that stood like soldiers between the street and the concrete sidewalk were erected as a security measure against terrorists. It was a stark reminder of the challenges Jews continue to face today. The synagogue is the largest synagogue in Europe. The interior looks like a church and can seat 3,000 worshipers. In the large building complex are also Heroes' Temple, a graveyard, the Memorial and an impressive Jewish Museum. The sight of the yellow fabric Star of David in the museum with the word "Jood" (Dutch word for 'Jew') was a sober reminder of the horrors of the Holocaust and the great number of Hungarian Jews killed during the Nazi regime. During the Holocaust the Synagogue was part of the border of the Budapest Jewish Ghetto.

In front of some of the doorways in the Jewish quarter are copper and stone plaques on the ground. They are called stumbling stones. Inscribed on the blocks are the names of people who lived in that house during the Second World War before the Nazis removed the people to send them to concentration camps.

Another reminder was the "Shoes on the Danube" memorial sculpture. The metallic shoes spread out on the concrete represent the Jews who were killed in the second World War by the Hungarian far-right "Arrow Cross" party members. Jews were directed to remove their shoes before they were shot next to the river, and their bodies were swept down the Danube.

Our second night we took the metro three stops north to a small town in the Obuda section of Budapest. The town where the restaurant was located had a quaint square, but it was clearly a place for locals. We were seated in an outdoor garden section of the restaurant. Our waiter was friendly and helpful. At the end of the meal I ordered palinka. Palinka is a fruit flavored brandy-like drink. I tried the plum palinka and the waiter brought himself one and we did a shot together.

The two times I had chicken paprika it was sweet rather than spicy. Most of the food throughout the river cruise and on land was heavy, leaning toward pork, dumplings, red cabbage or sauerkraut, etc. The goulash was excellent.

We visited Matthias Church in Castle Hill. The large church is a Roman Catholic church which was originally built in 1015. In the 1900's the church was named after King Matthias. At different times during World War II the church was used by the Soviets and Germany. The majolica (ceramic in bright colors and glossy surfaces) roof tiles make for a beautiful and unique roof pattern.

The Chain Bridge was built in the 19th century and connects Buda and Pest. The other major bridge is called Liberty Bridge, built in the late 1800's, and named after Emperor Franz Joseph. Nazi troops blew up the original bridge, which was rebuilt in 1945.

We heard a lot about the ruin bars in Budapest. Ruin bars are buildings that were about to be condemned that people bought and fixed up enough to occupy. We stopped by Szimpla Kert (Simple Garden) around 11:30 am, thinking we would have lunch there. The place was fun to walk around, with many rooms with eclectic decorations. I think these places are more for nighttime activities because it didn't appear that many people were there for lunch, and no one came out to ask us if we wanted to eat.

Budapest is known as a major thermal bath destination. We selected the Széchenyi Baths because they were near Heroes' Square and other sights we wanted to explore. The Széchenyi Baths receive over a million bathers each year. Once we checked in and got our bracelet to open our locker we changed and entered the baths.

There are multiple indoor and outdoor pools, and each has a different temperature. The experience was more fun than either of us expected and we spent about two hours there.

Heroes' Square is a large outdoor square with a bunch of stoic statues to fallen Hungarian heroes. Statues include the 7 chieftains of the Magyars and the Memorial Stone of Heroes. In the center is the Millennium column. Some of the statues reminded me of the Crusades.

Városliget in nearby City Park was built in the late 1900's to commemorate the anniversary of the Magyar conquest of Hungary in 895. The area is beautiful, and the architecture is well done.

St. Stephen's Church (there seems to be a church with that name in every town,) has an imposing exterior and beautiful interior that is decorated with fifty varieties of marble. The shops and area around the church were more upscale than the average shopping in Budapest.

The Millennium Museum is an underground museum located at the crossroads of several metro lines. It's meant to showcase the history of the metro in Budapest. It's a definite need to miss attraction. Two older women sat in the ticket booth. My wife and I were the only visitors. It seemed like something out of a Wes Anderson movie. There were some historical photos and two trolley cars with mannequins placed inside to represent the conductor and some passengers. It is somewhat common in museums to pay an additional fee if you want to take photos. I overpaid for this museum (and it wasn't expensive.)

We visited the Museum of Fine Arts which has a fantastic Egyptian artifacts section. Their paintings were also well done.

I had read about Kerepesi Cemetery before our trip and I was excited to visit. The cemetery exceeded my expectations. I realize it isn't a typical tourist attraction, however, the statues that marked many of the gravesites were as intricate as sculpture in any museum. There was a small museum (hard to find) on the property and the exhibit was interesting. When we walked into the room someone came out and put on the English video presentation for us to watch. It's around 3 metro stops away from downtown, and then a 5-minute walk, however on a nice day it is well worth a trip. We spent about an hour and a half but could have easily spent twice that.

This book is called First Impressions because the reflections and photos are based on our first impressions of the cruise and the cities and towns we visited. I realize that had we more time to explore each area we may have come away with different opinions of the towns and the people. Let the journey begin!

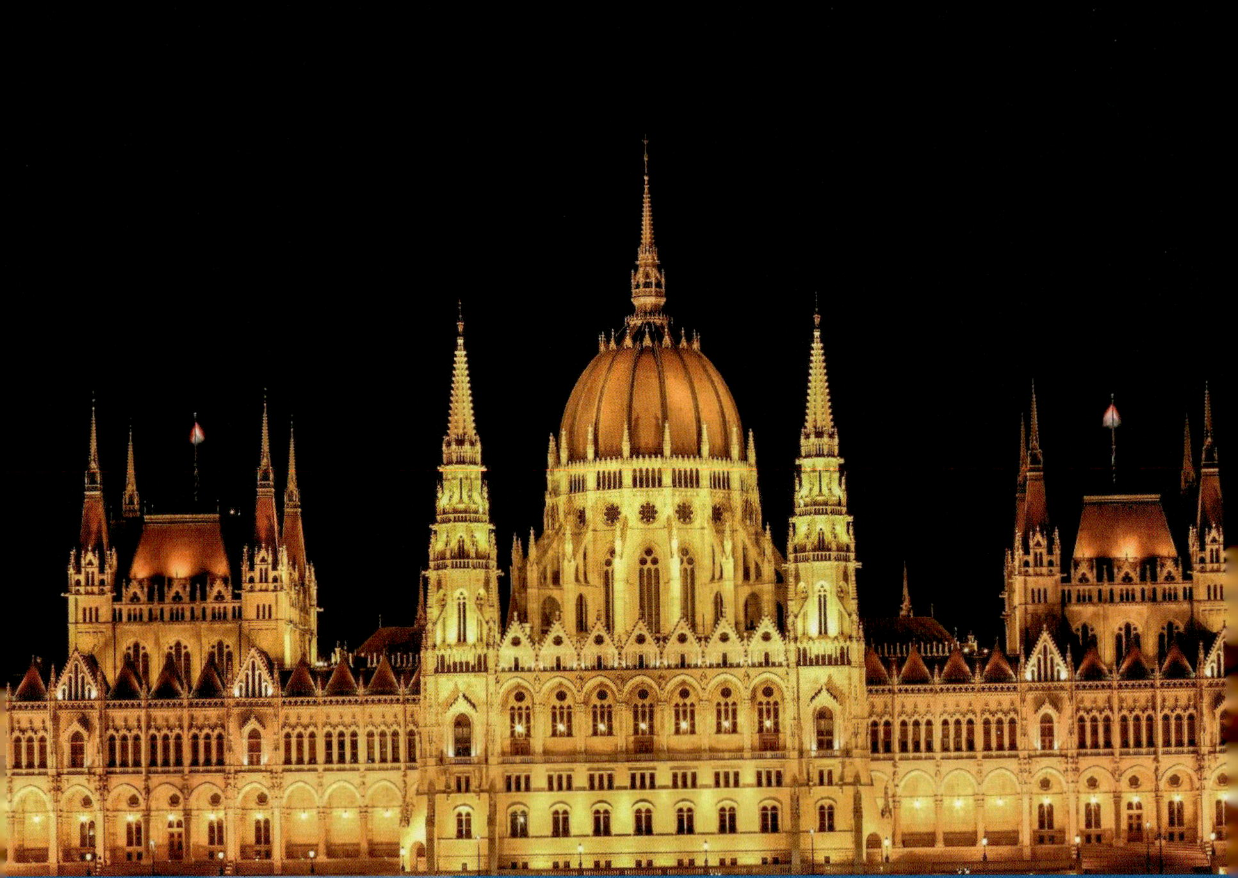

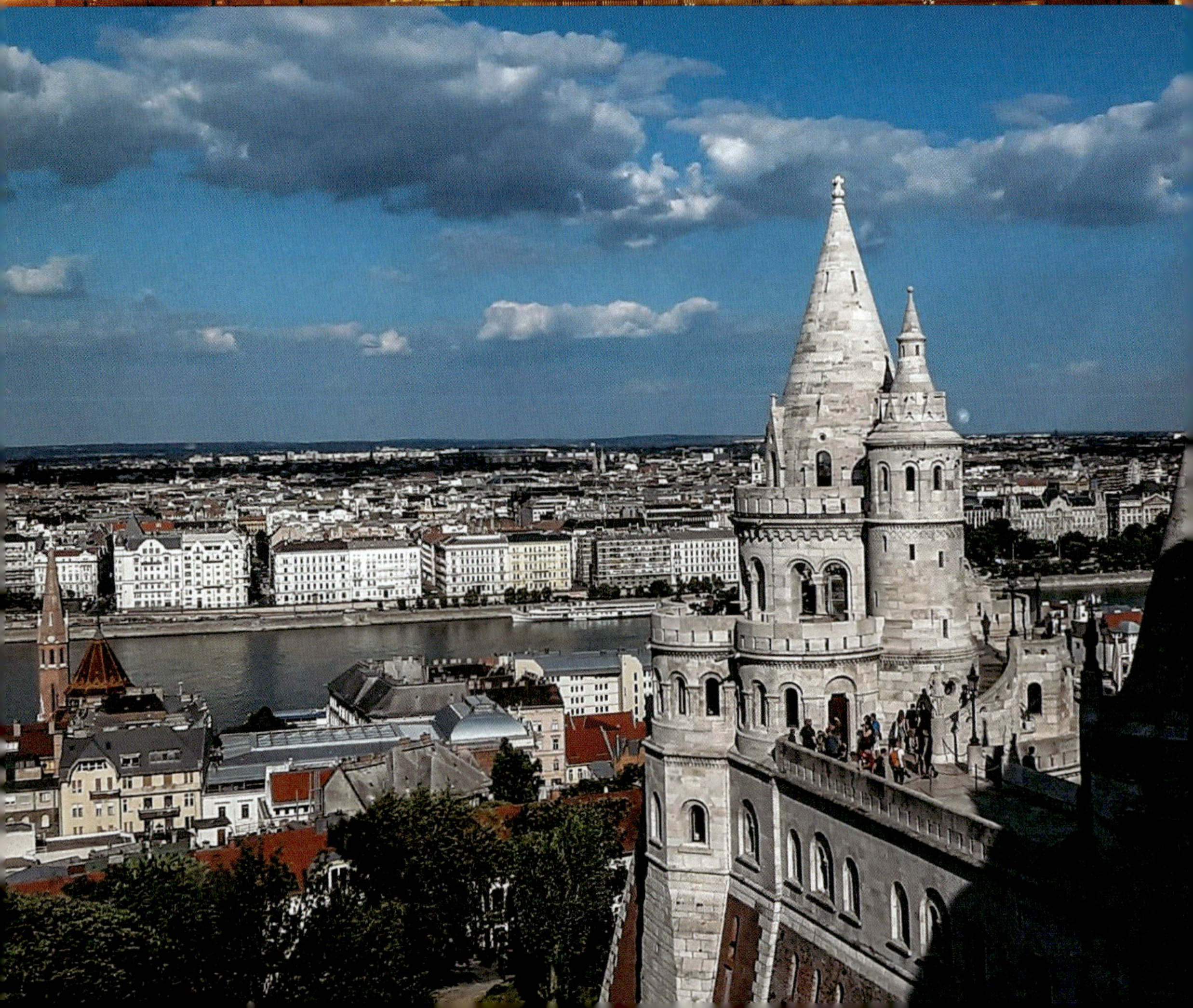

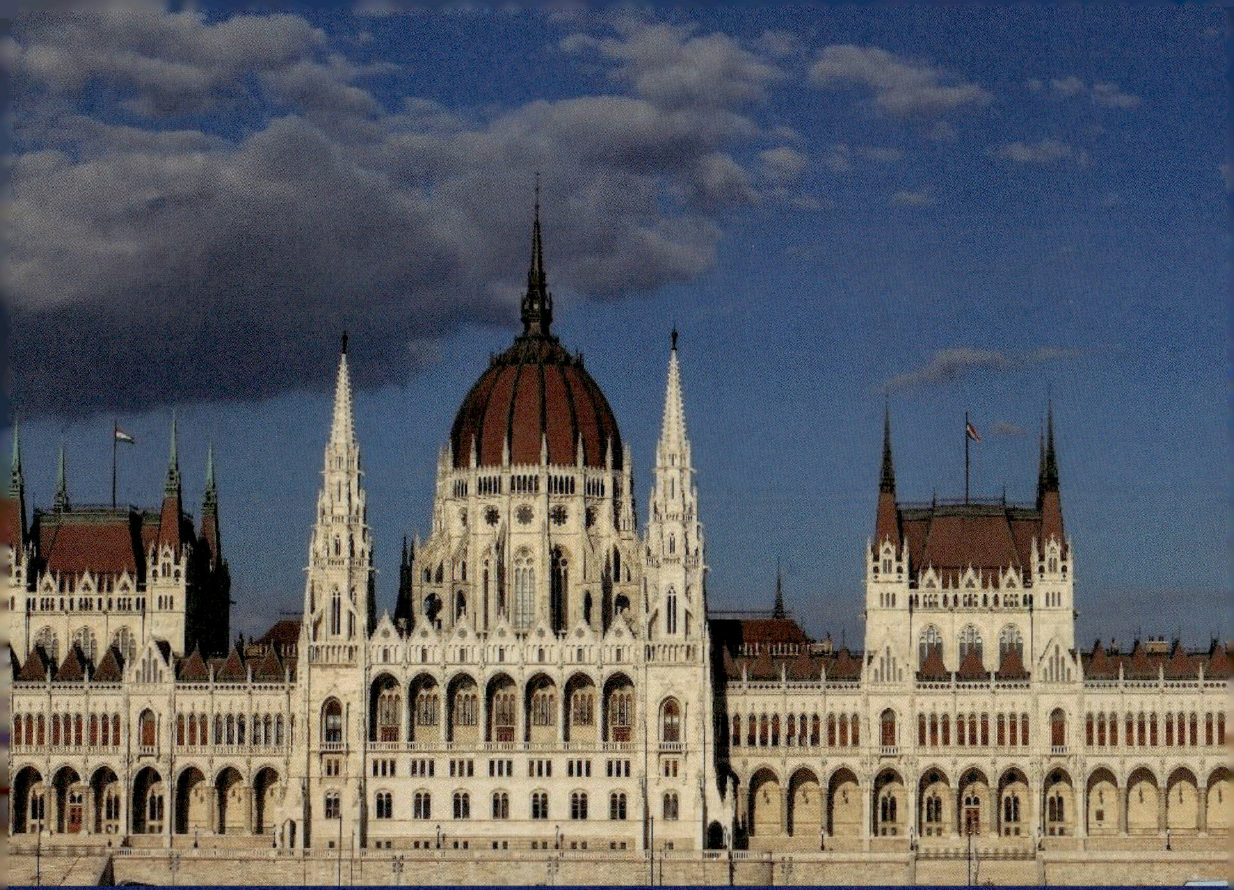

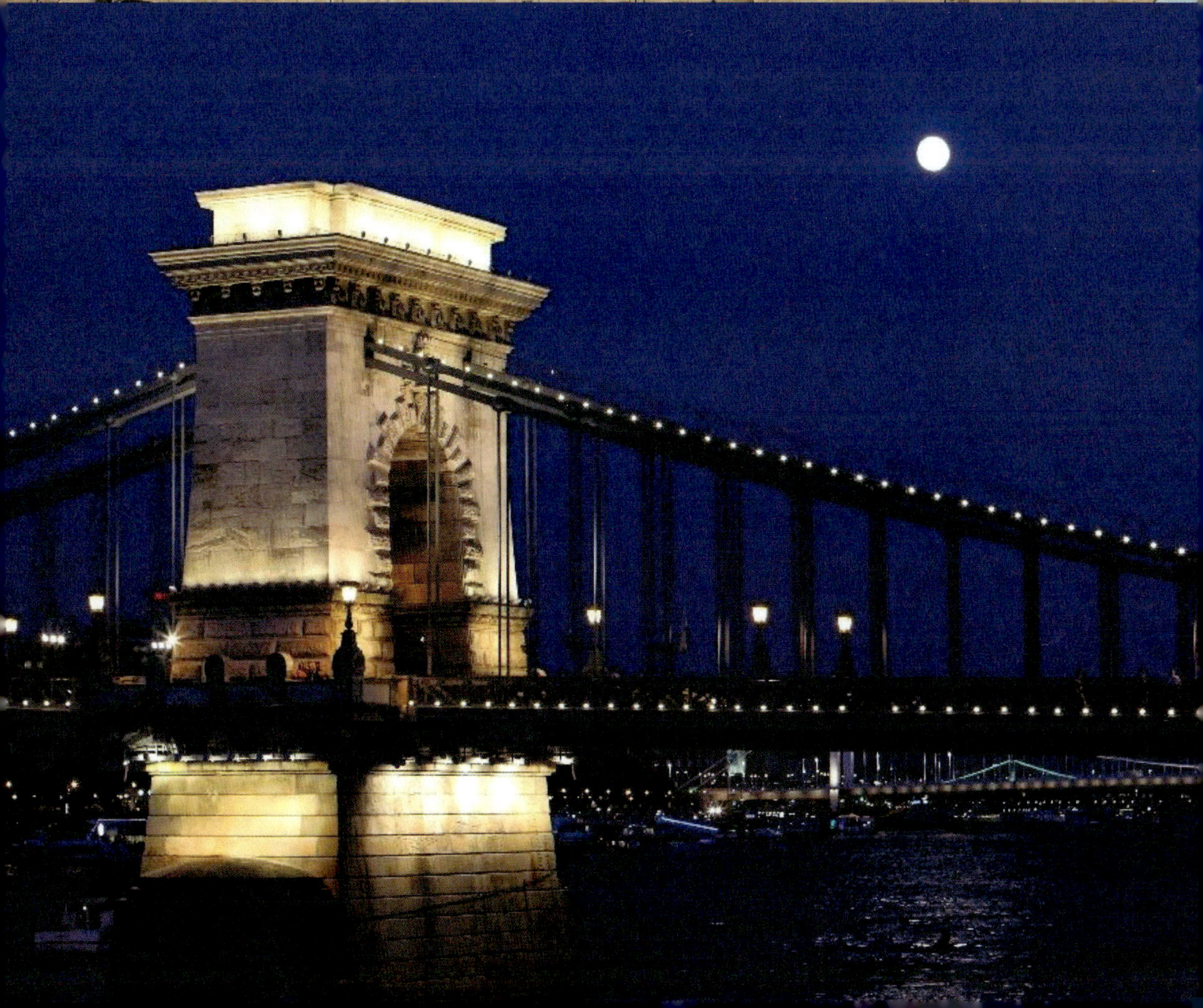

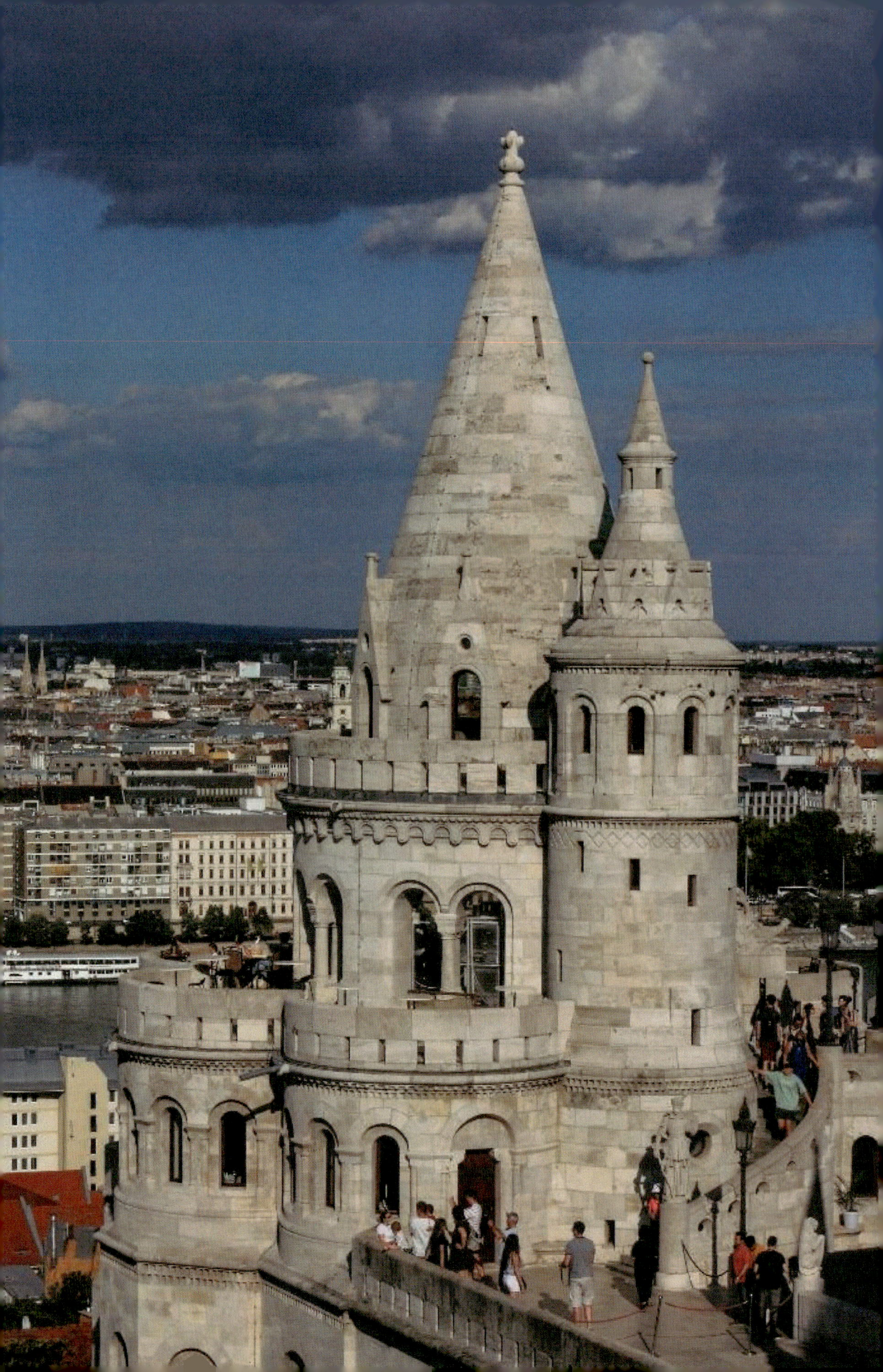

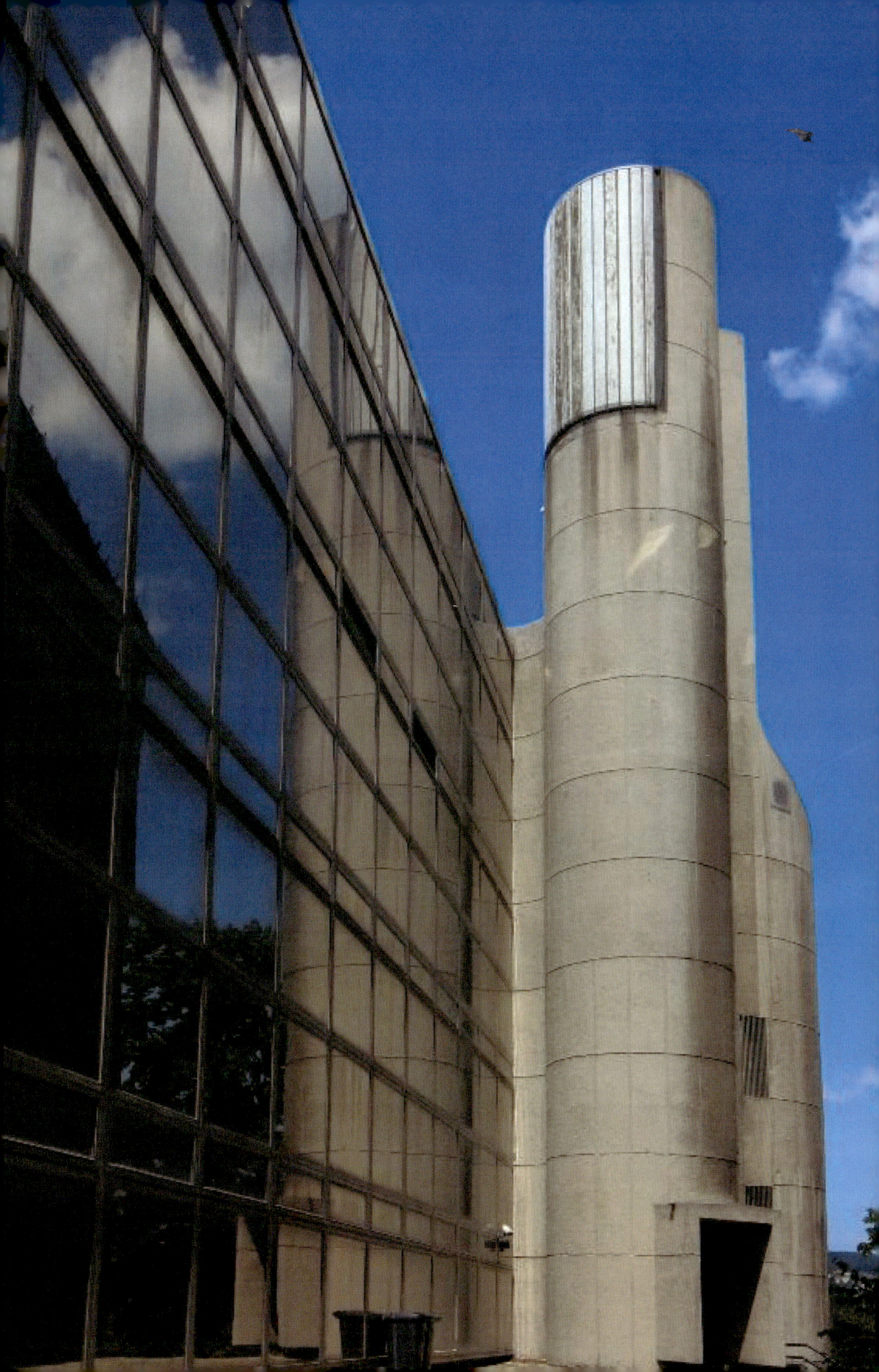

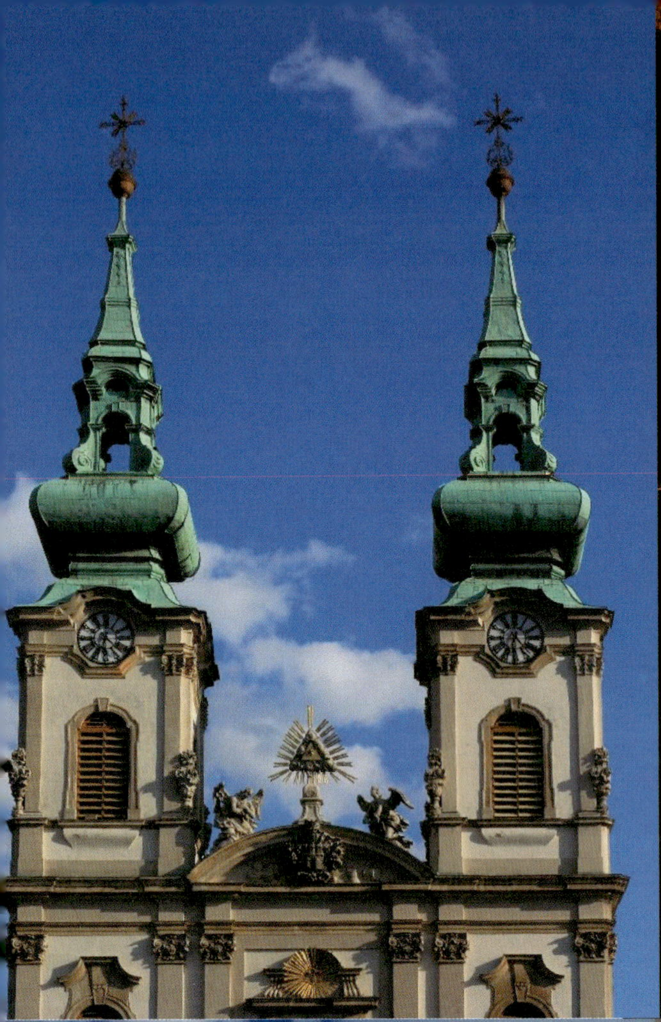
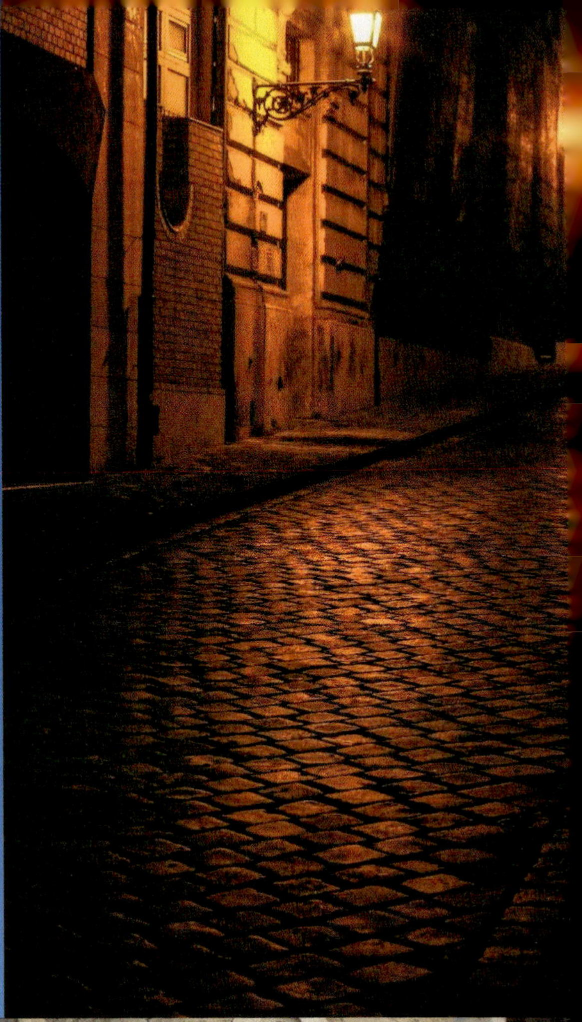
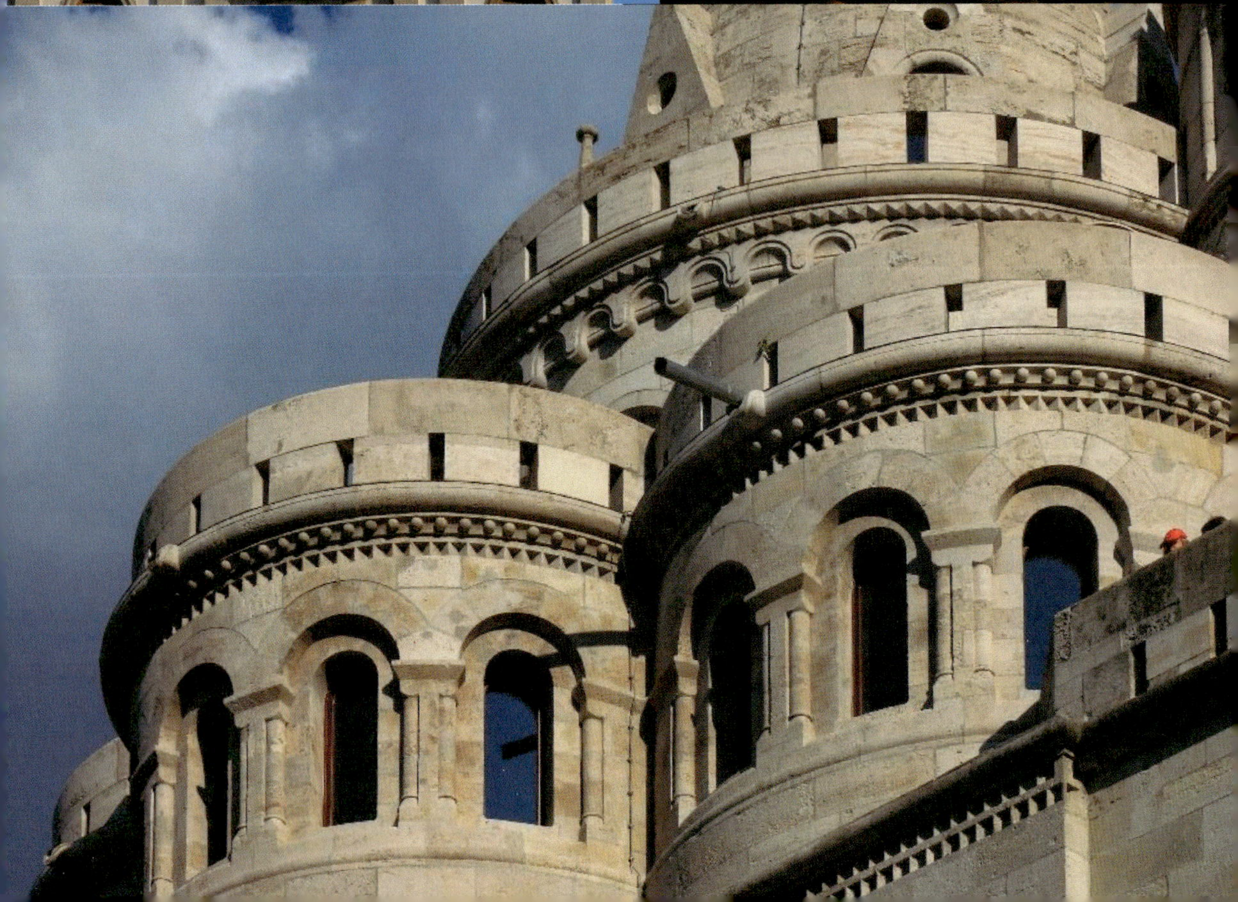

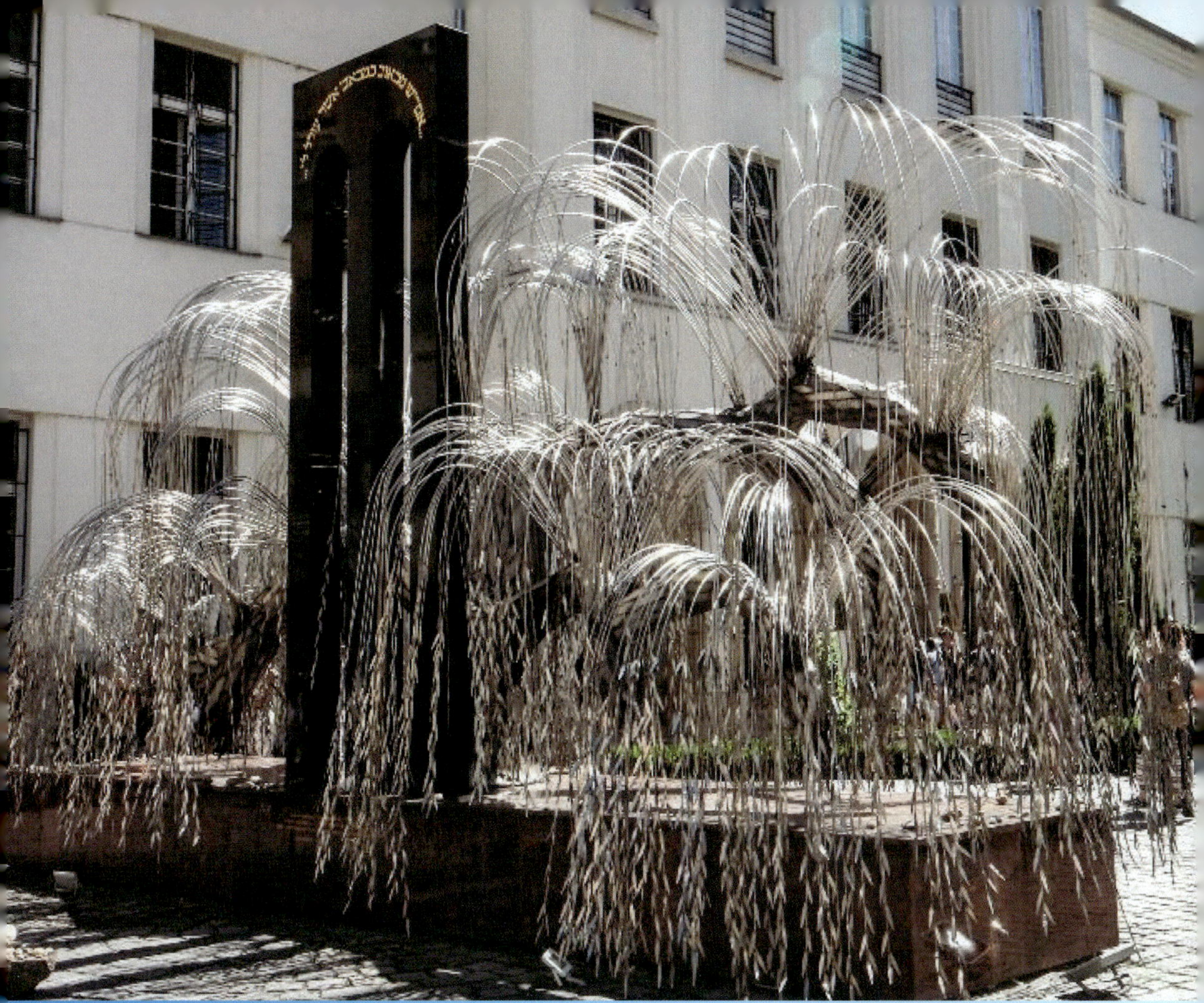

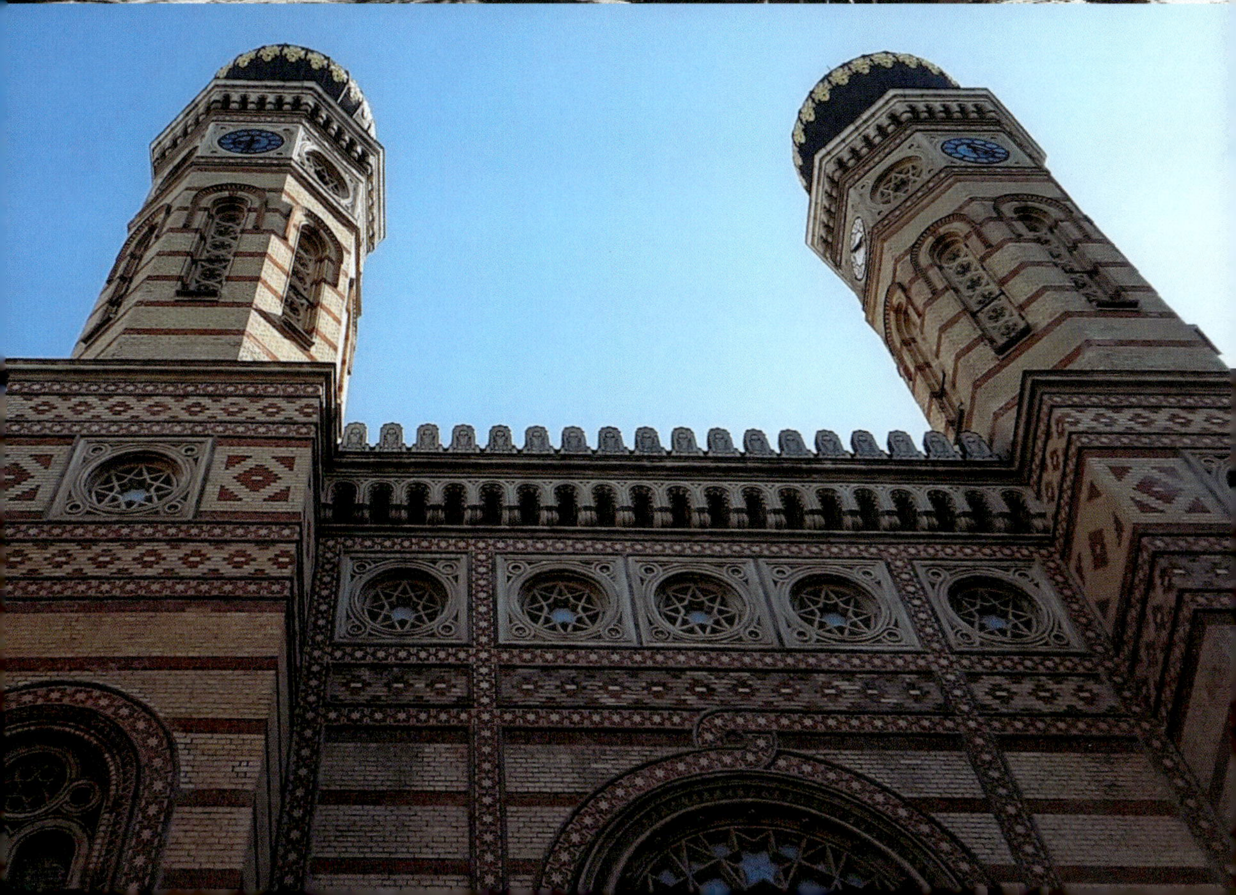

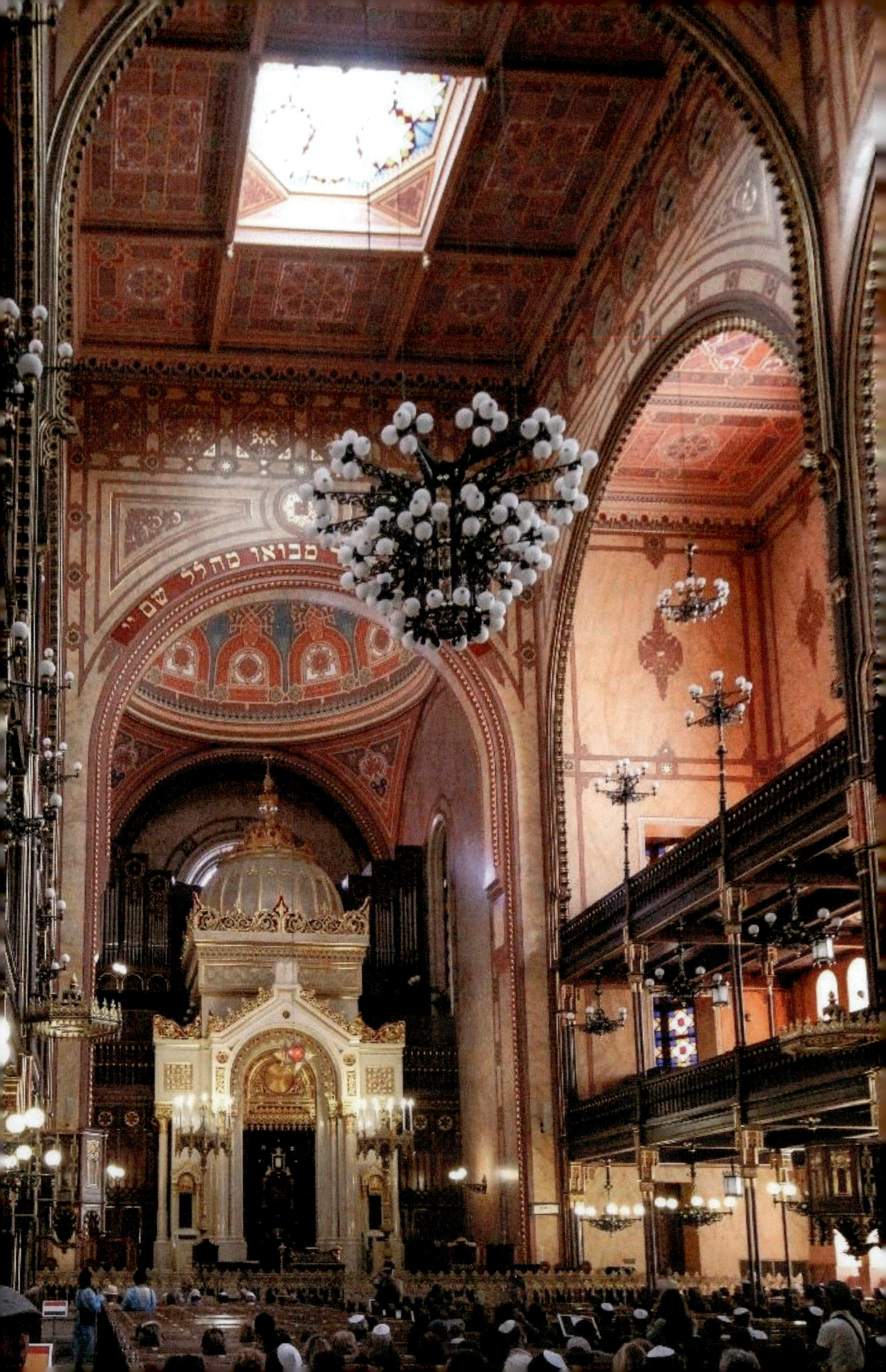
מבואו מהלל שם יי

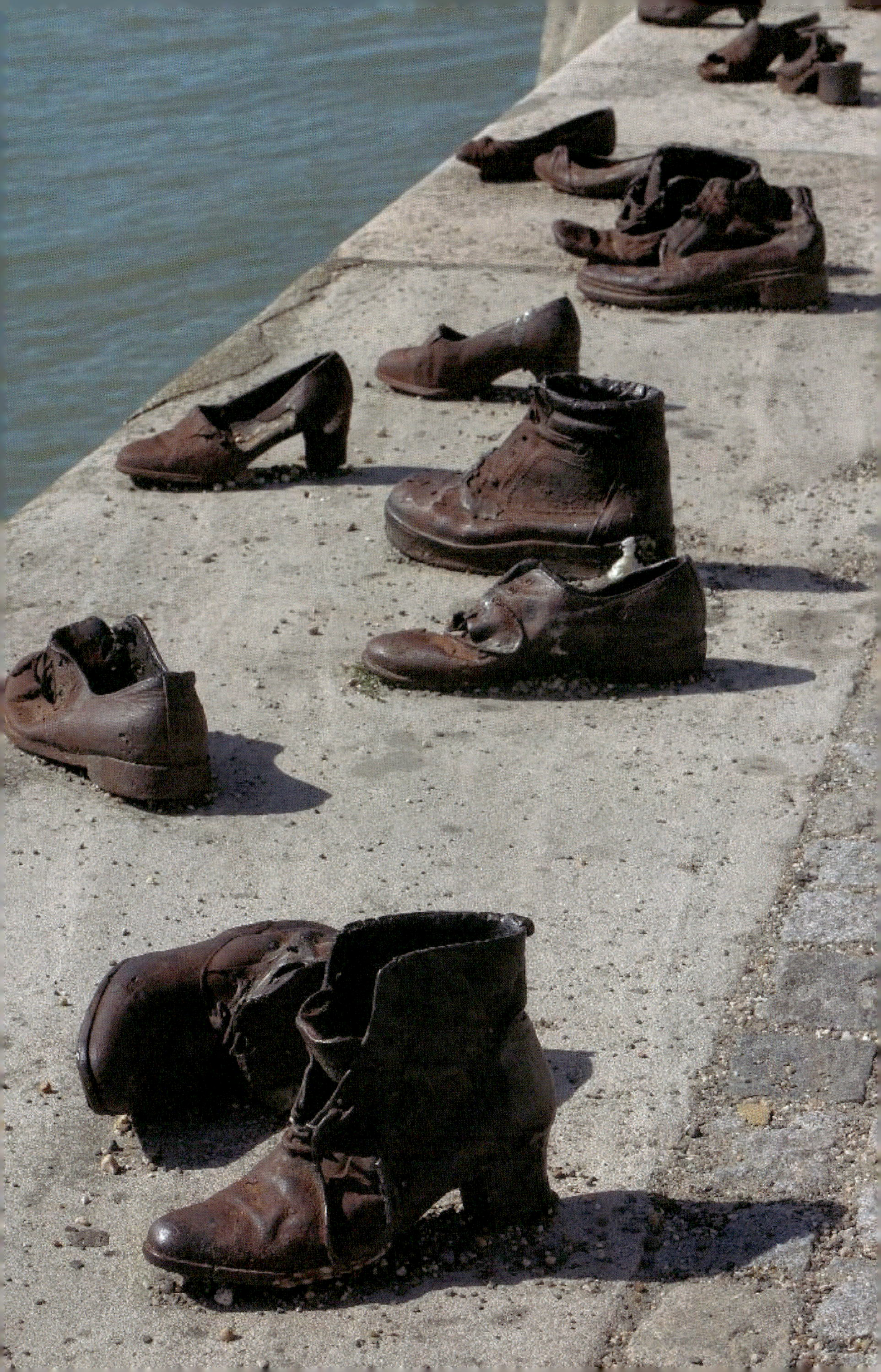

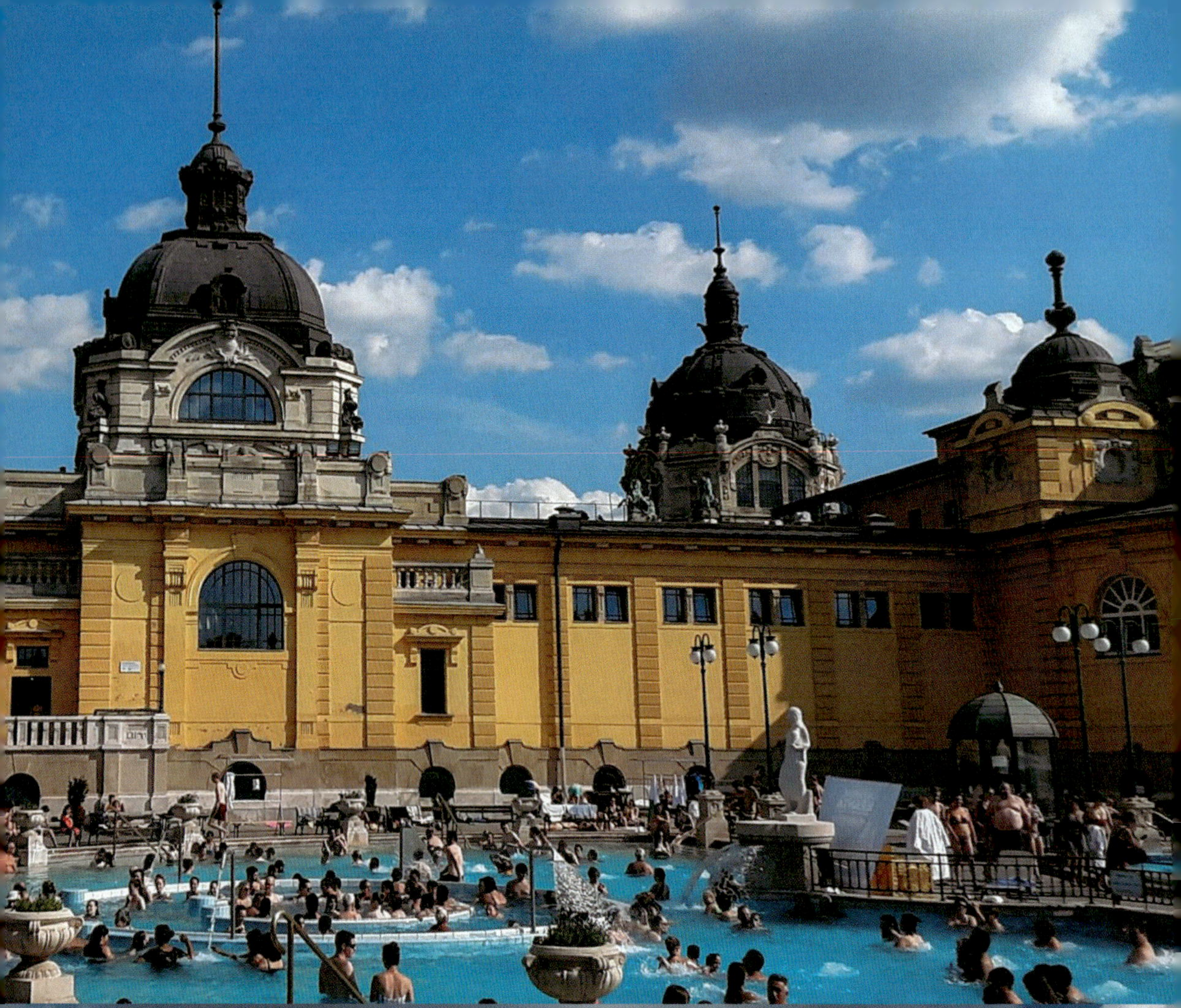

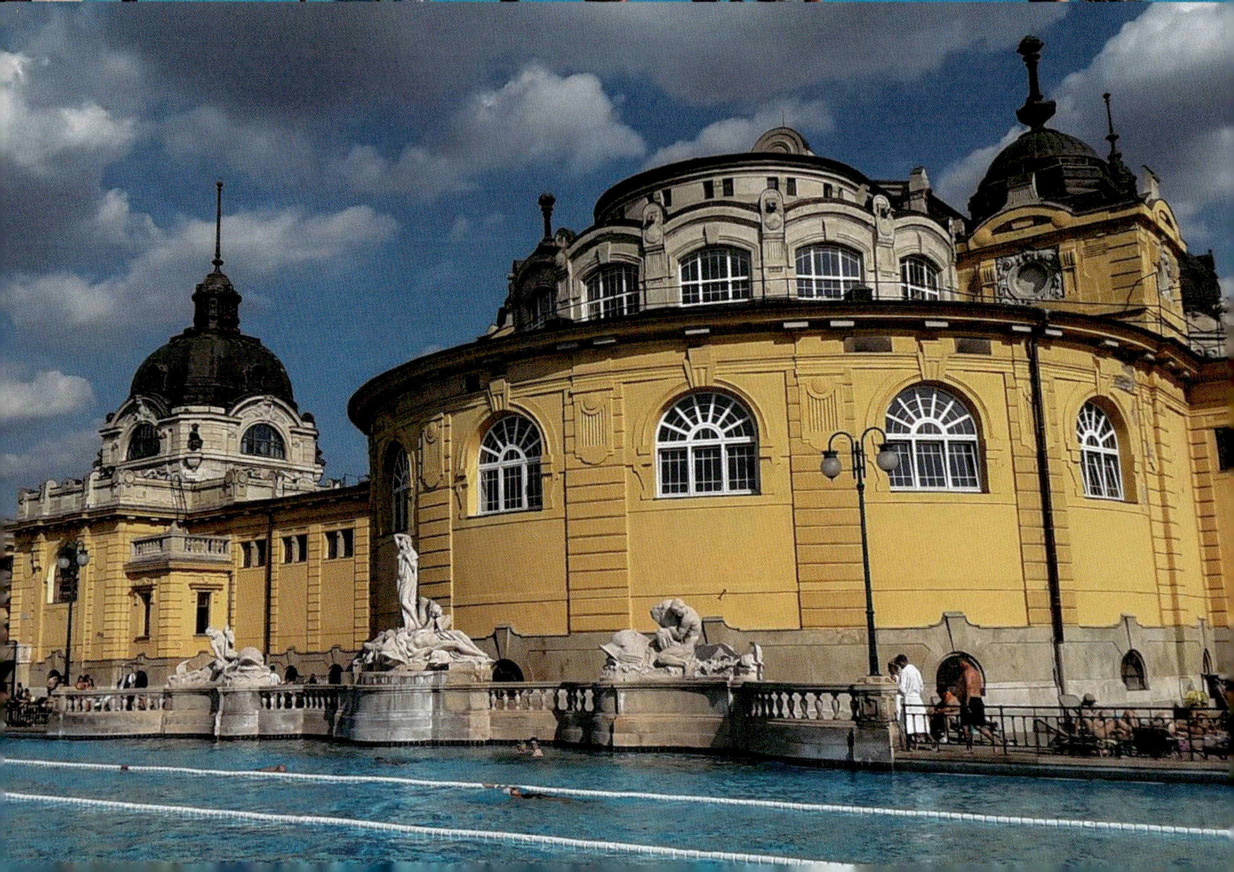

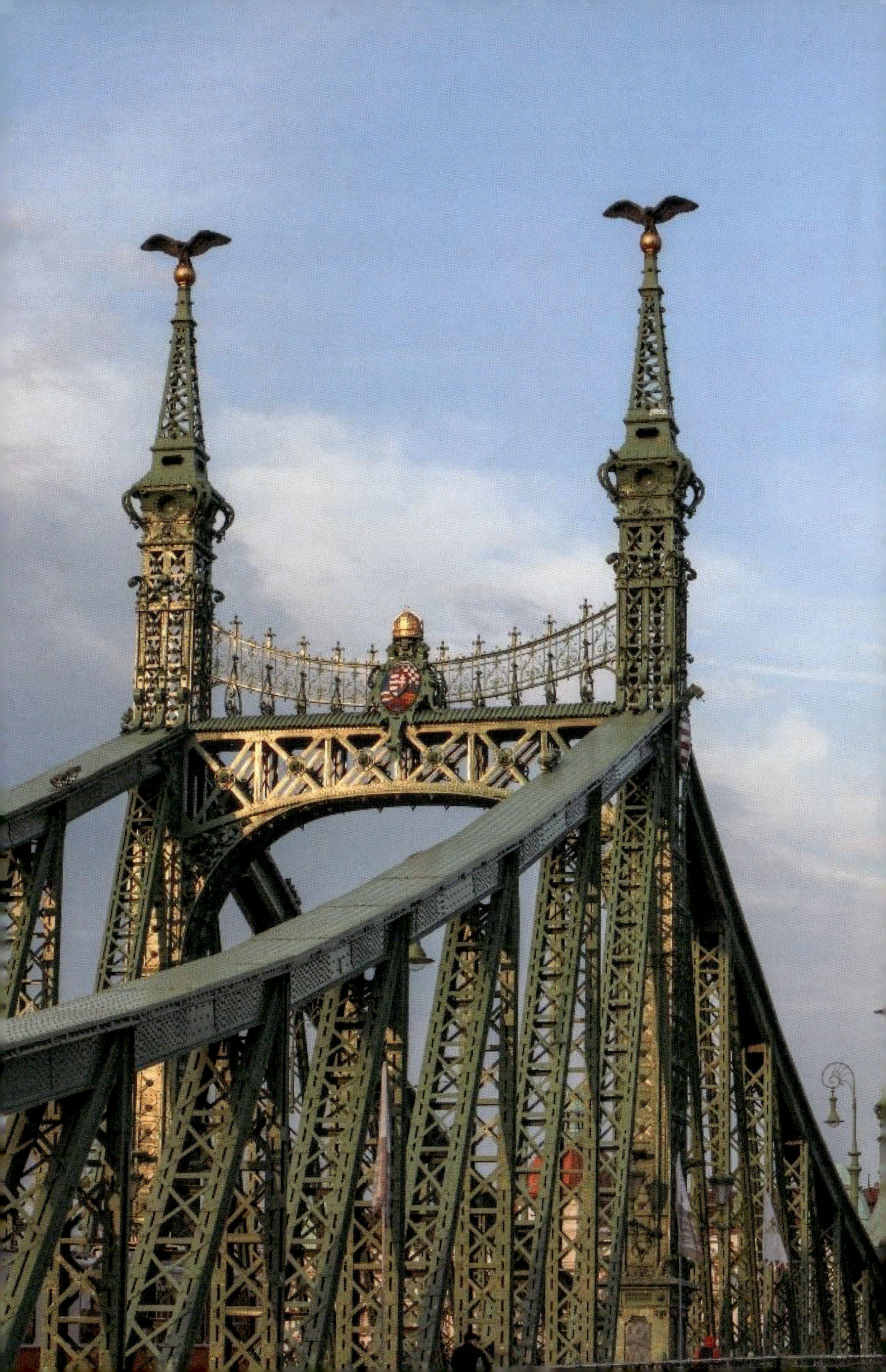

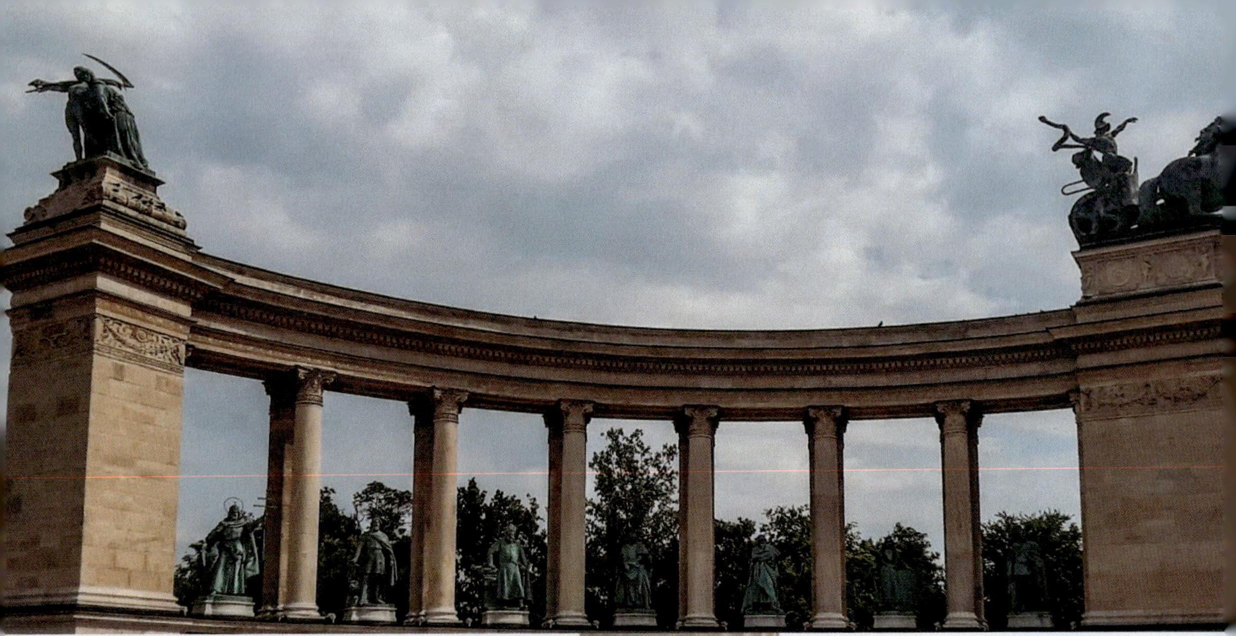
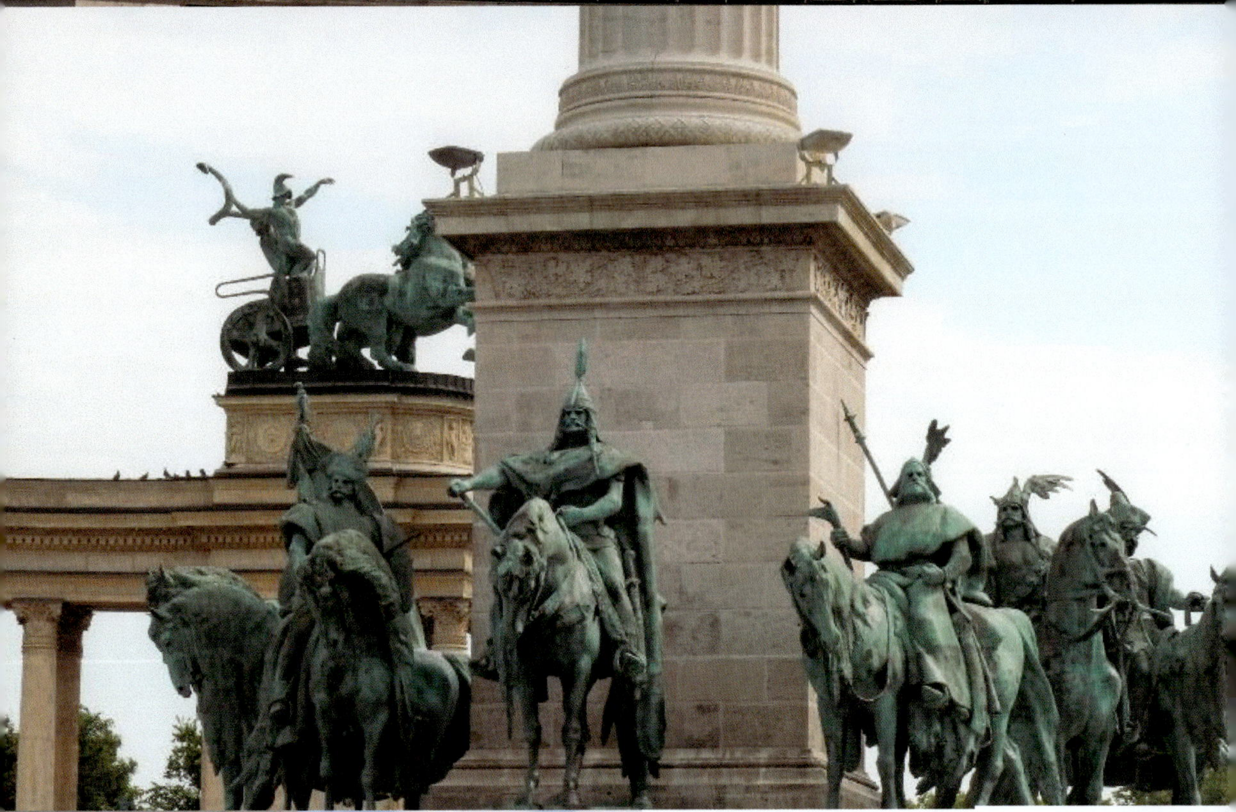
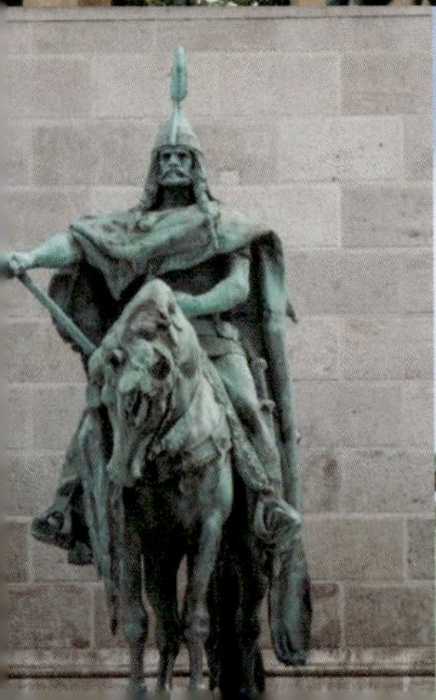
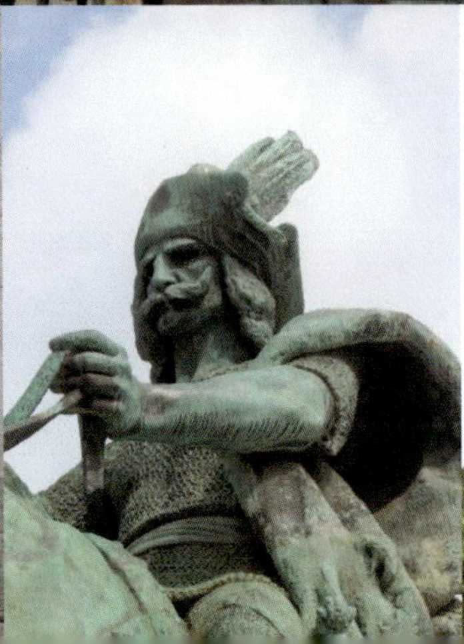
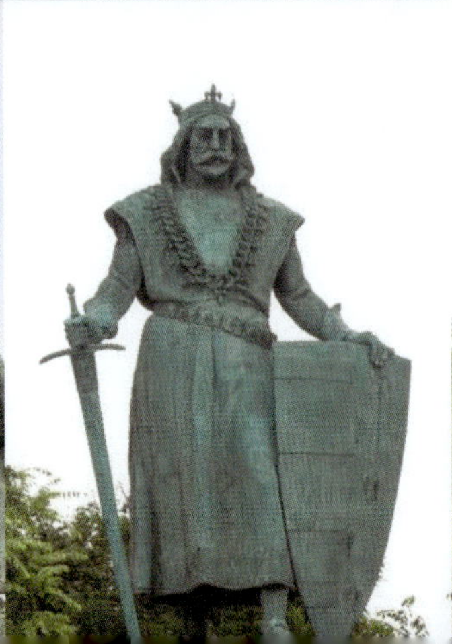
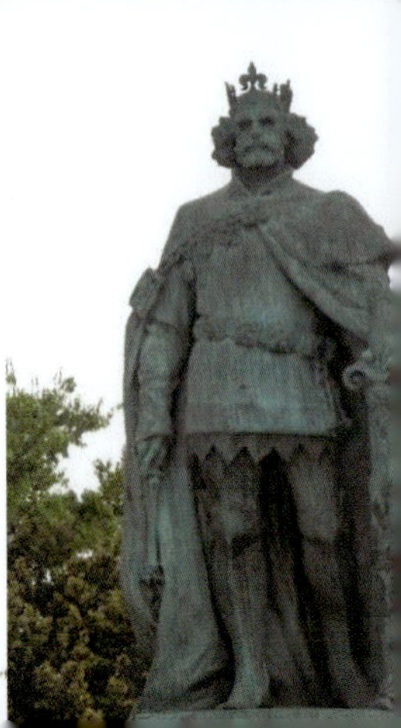

DARÁNYI IGNÁC

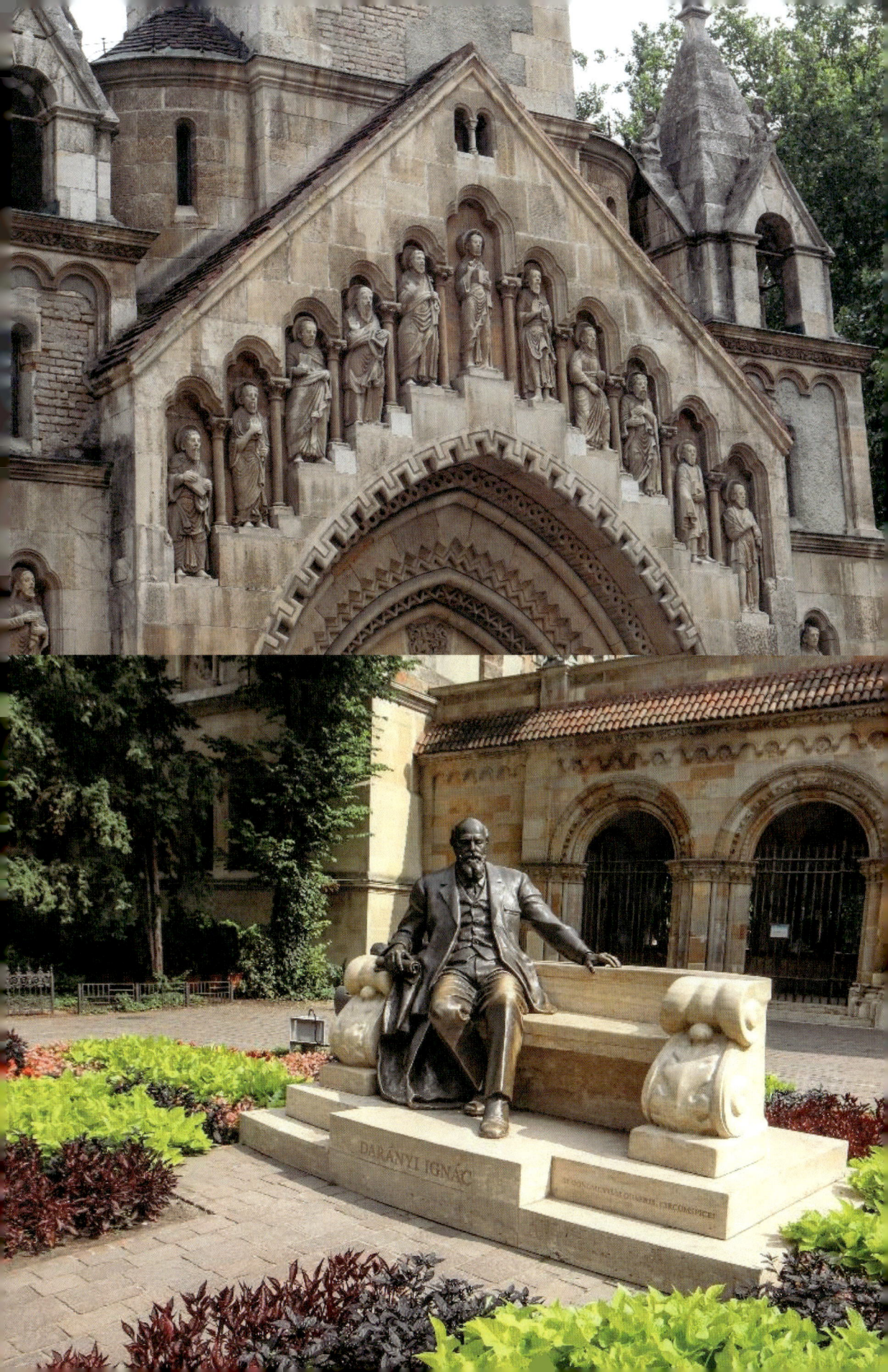

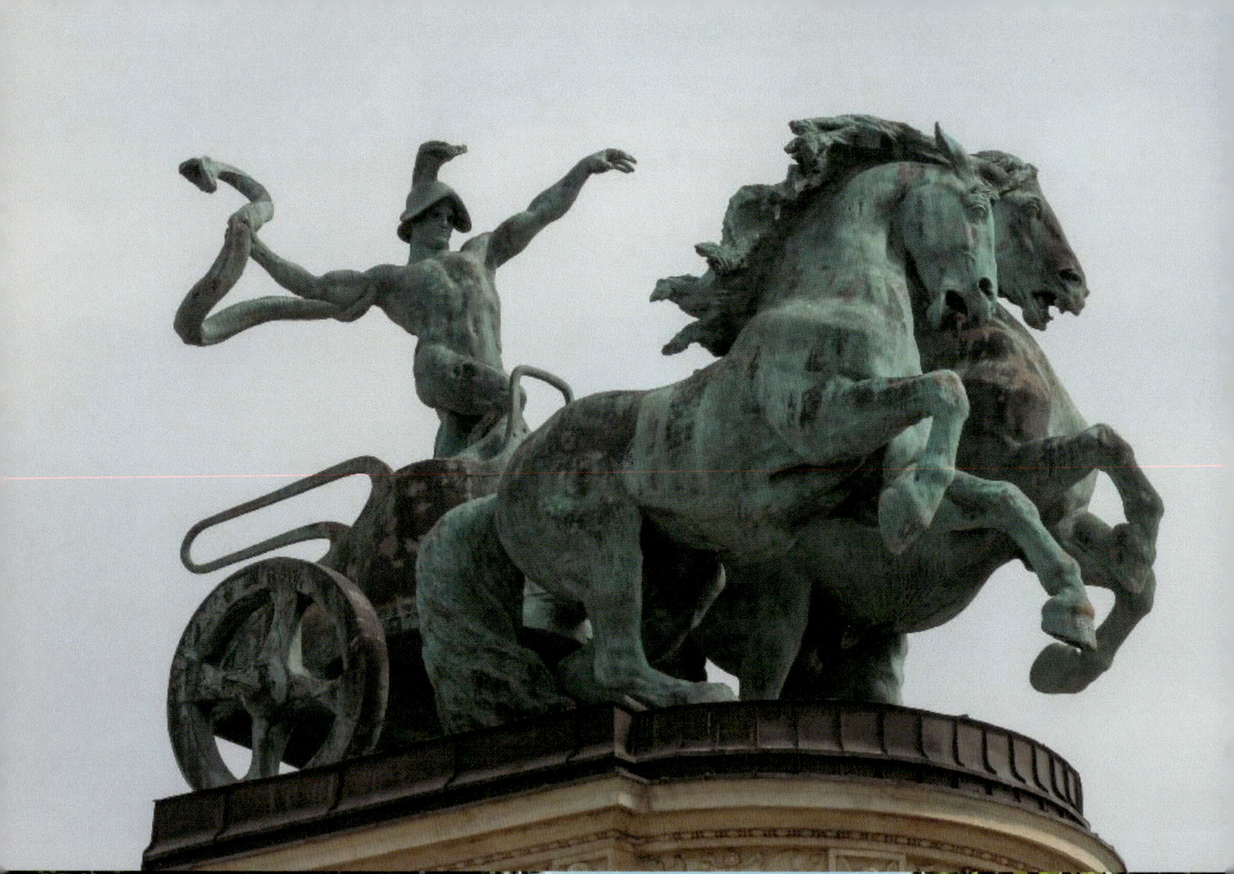

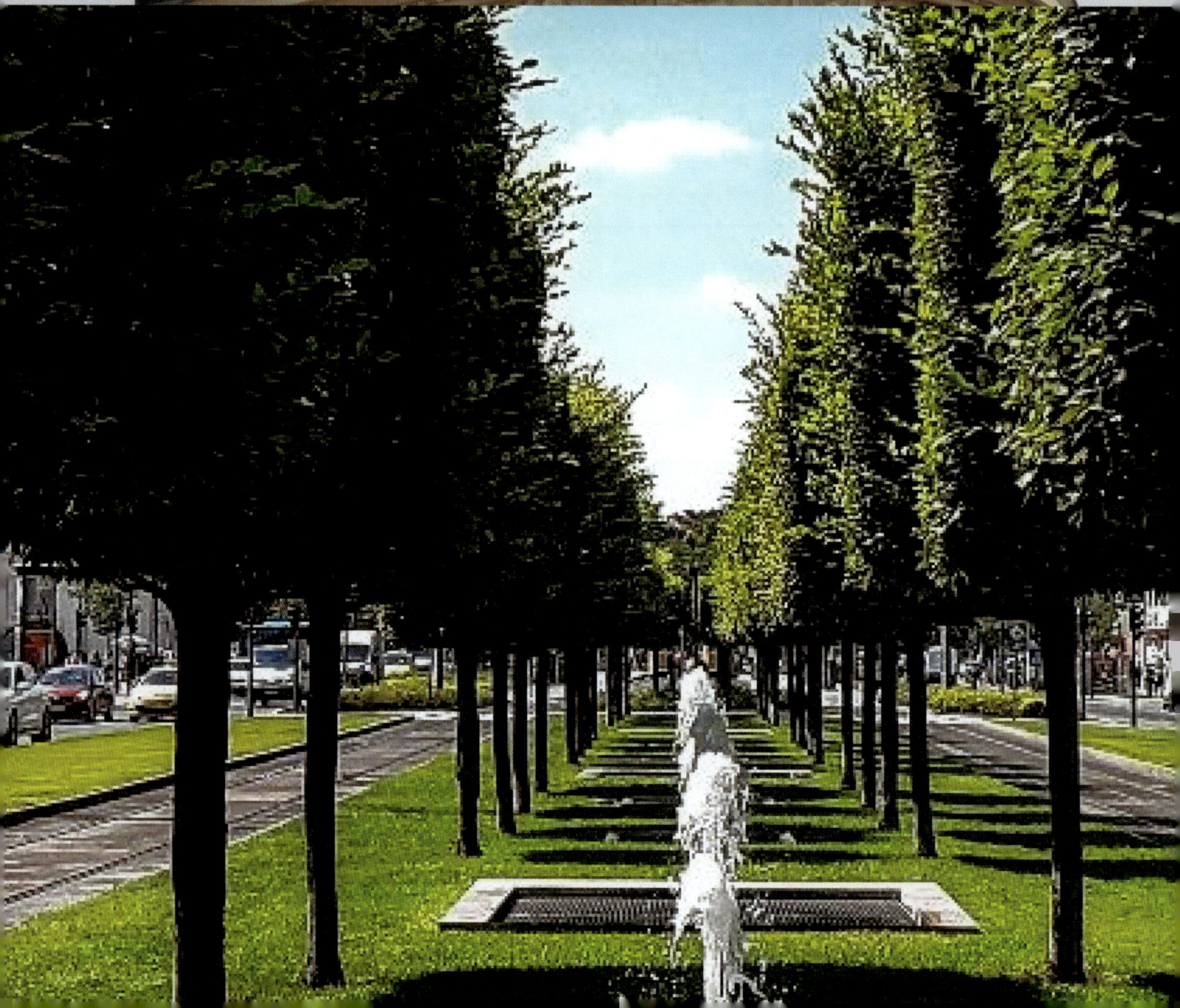

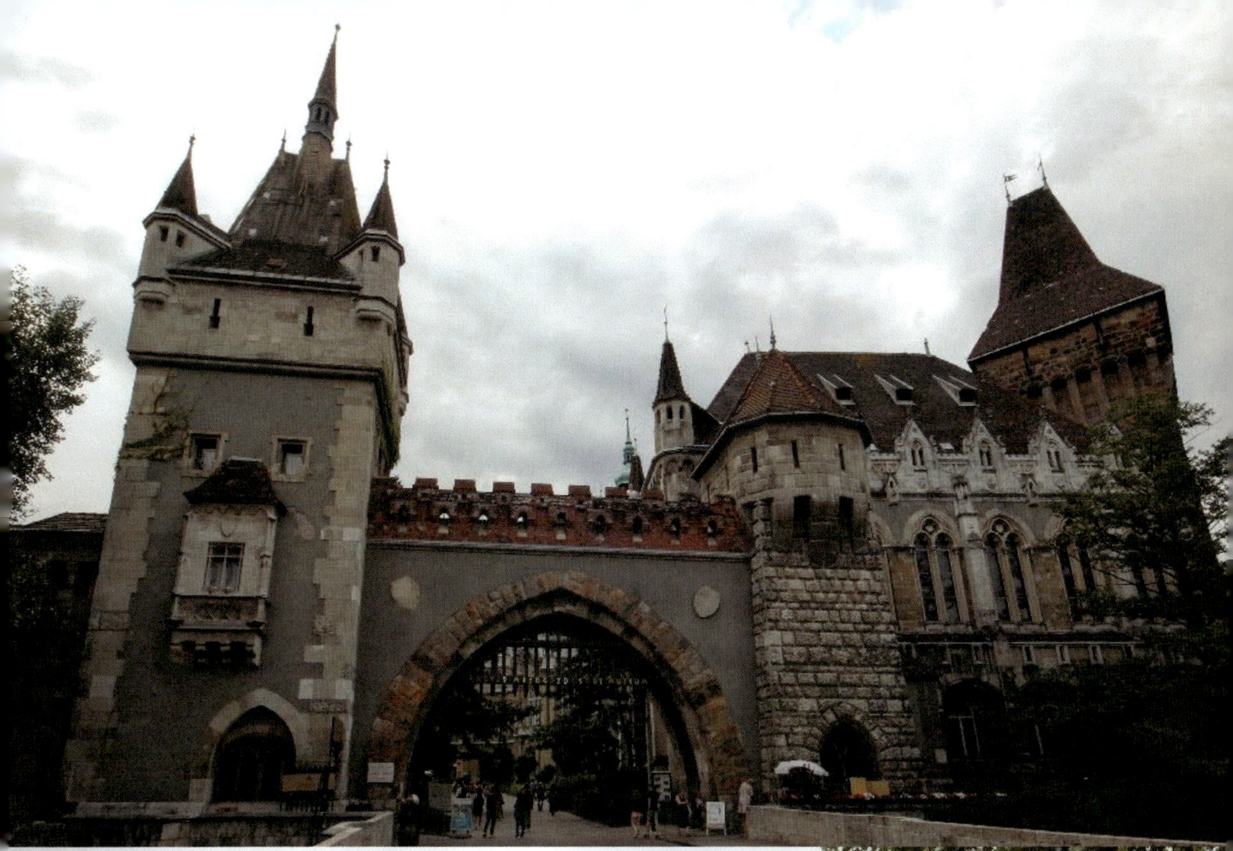
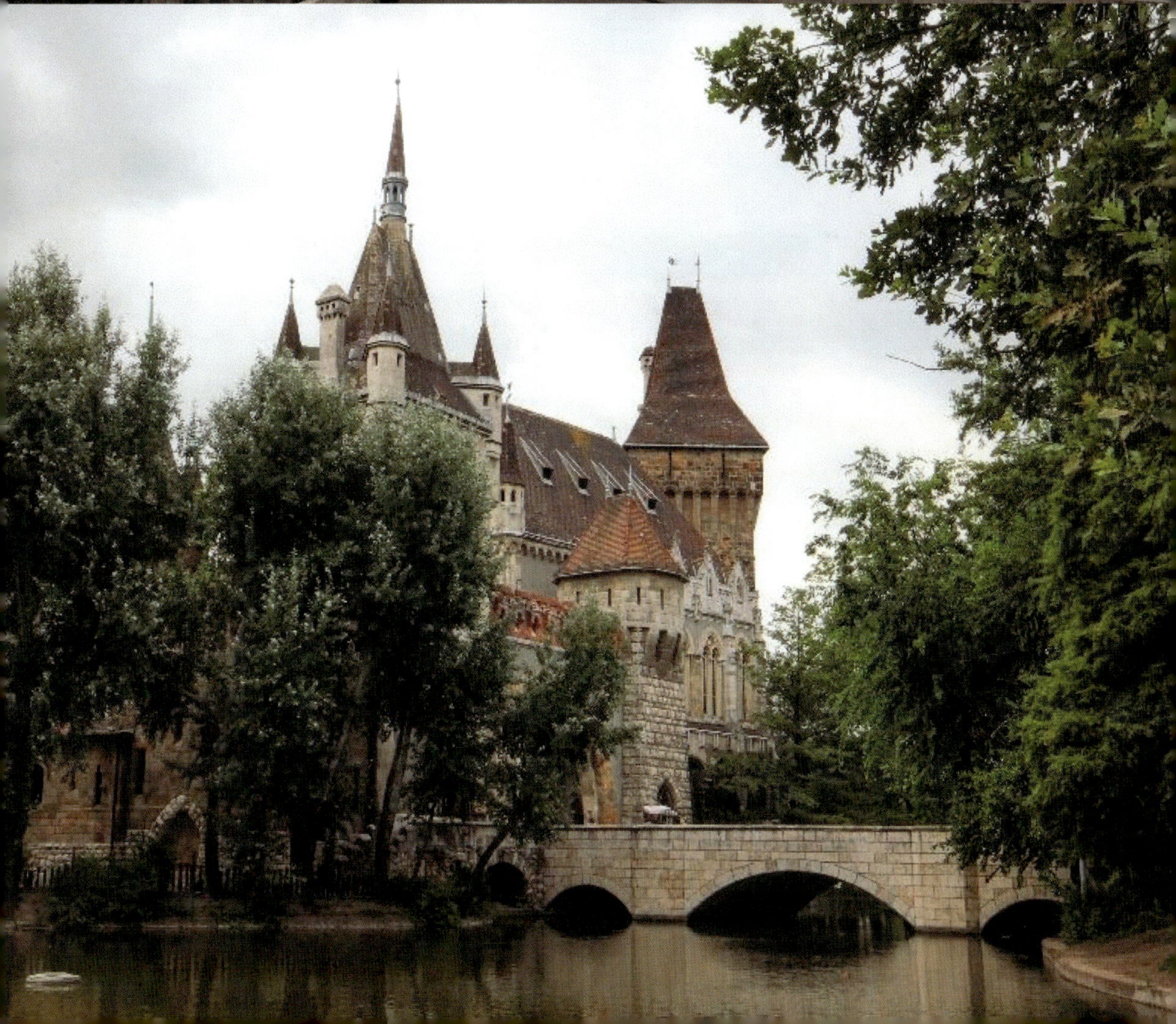

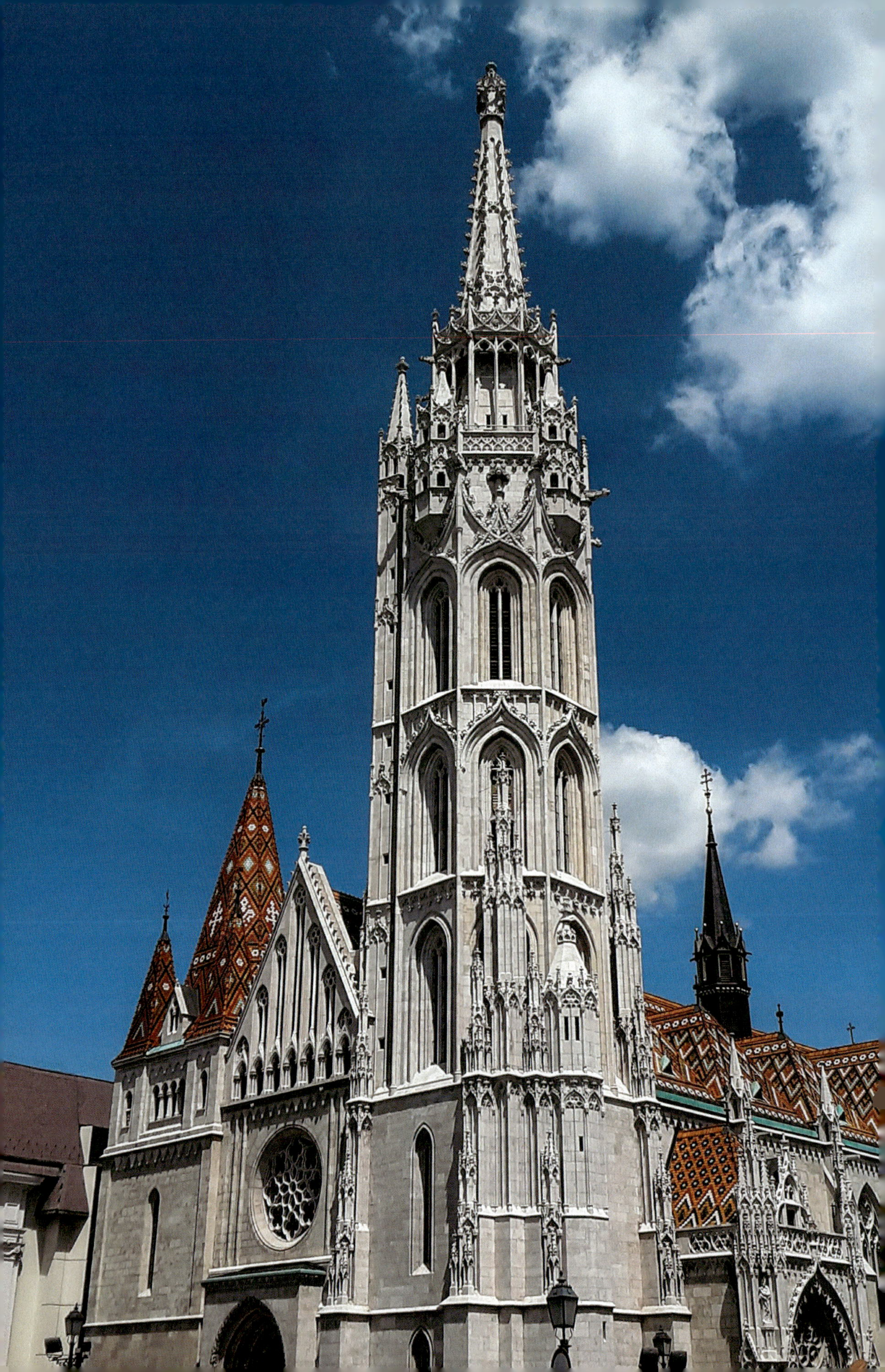

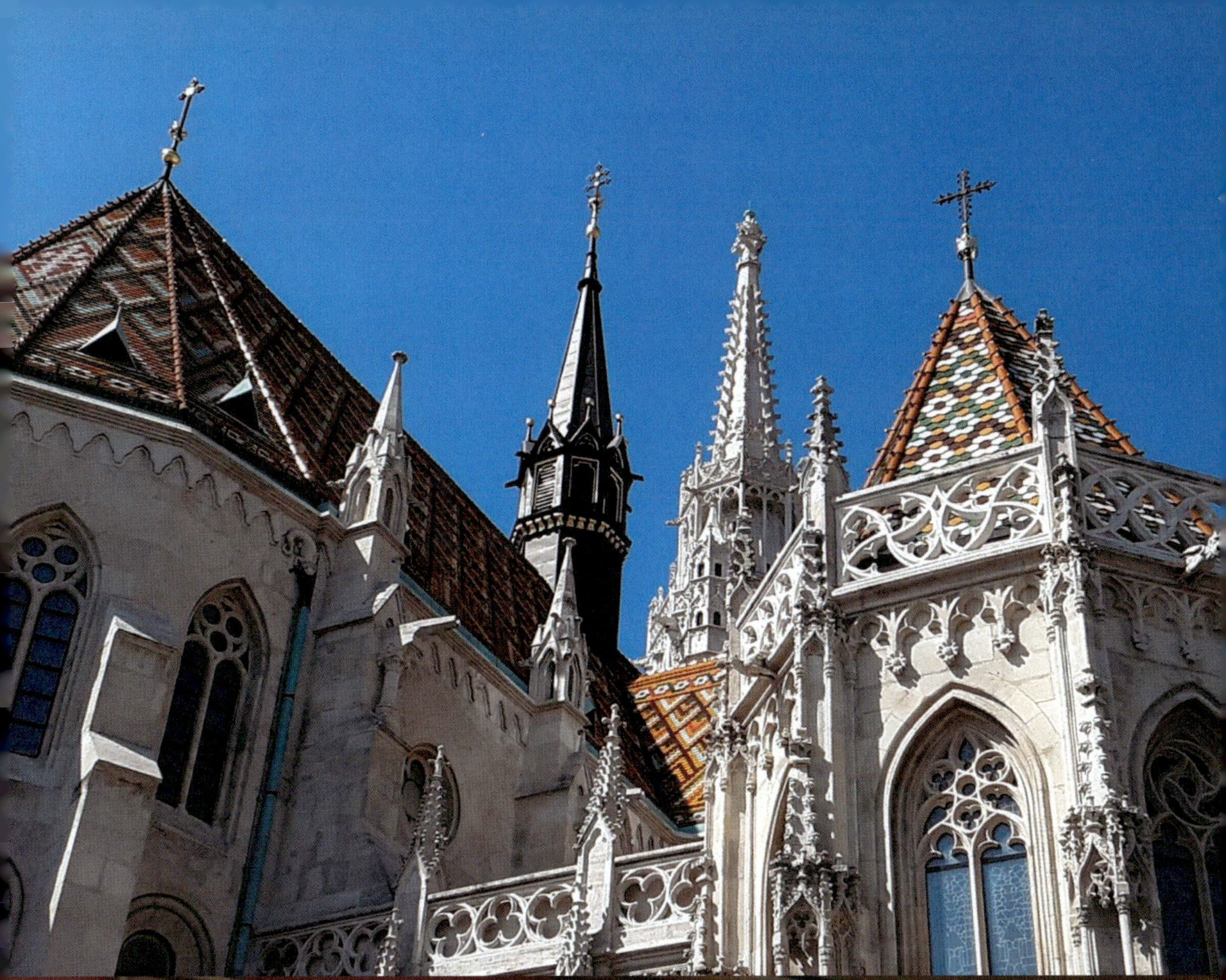

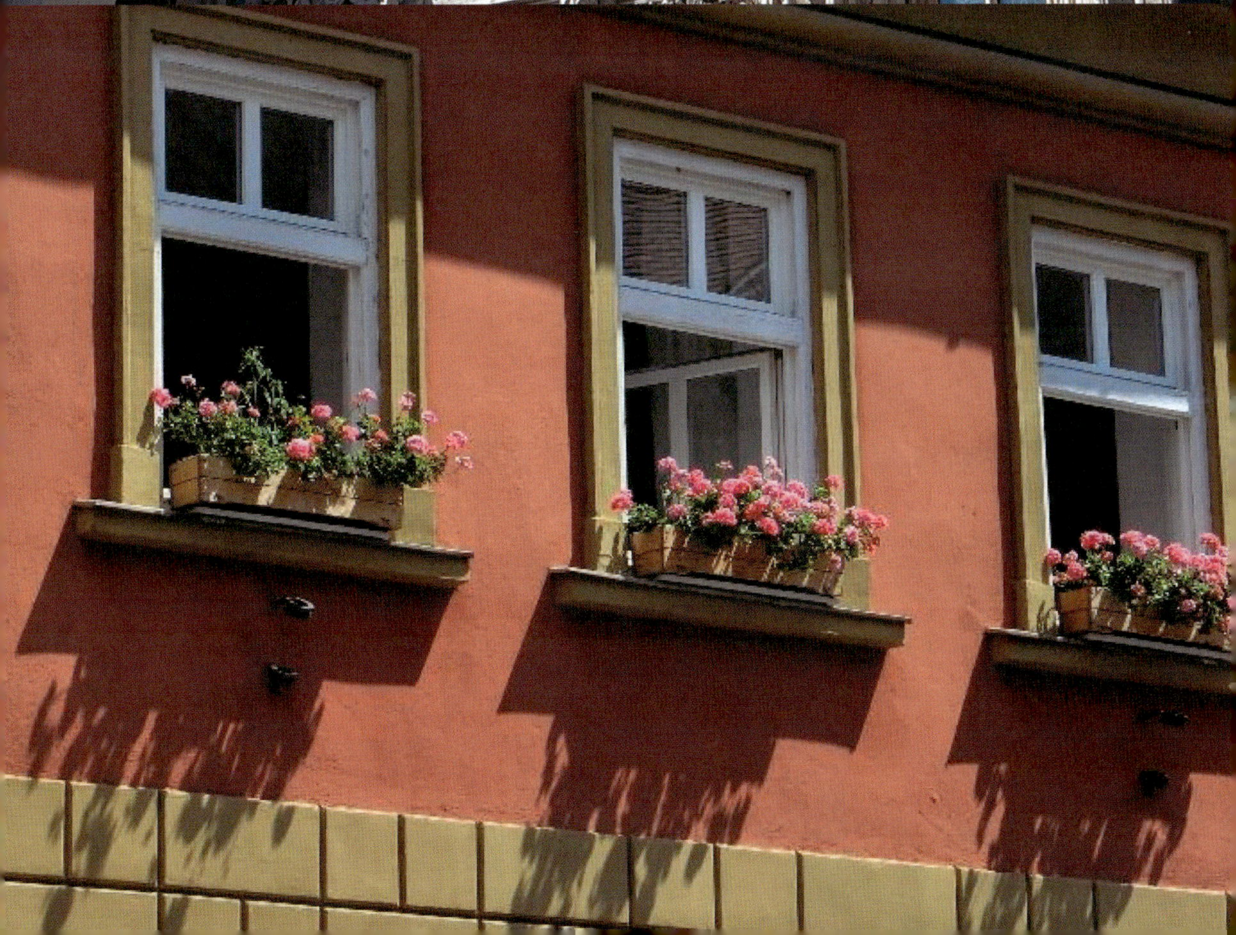

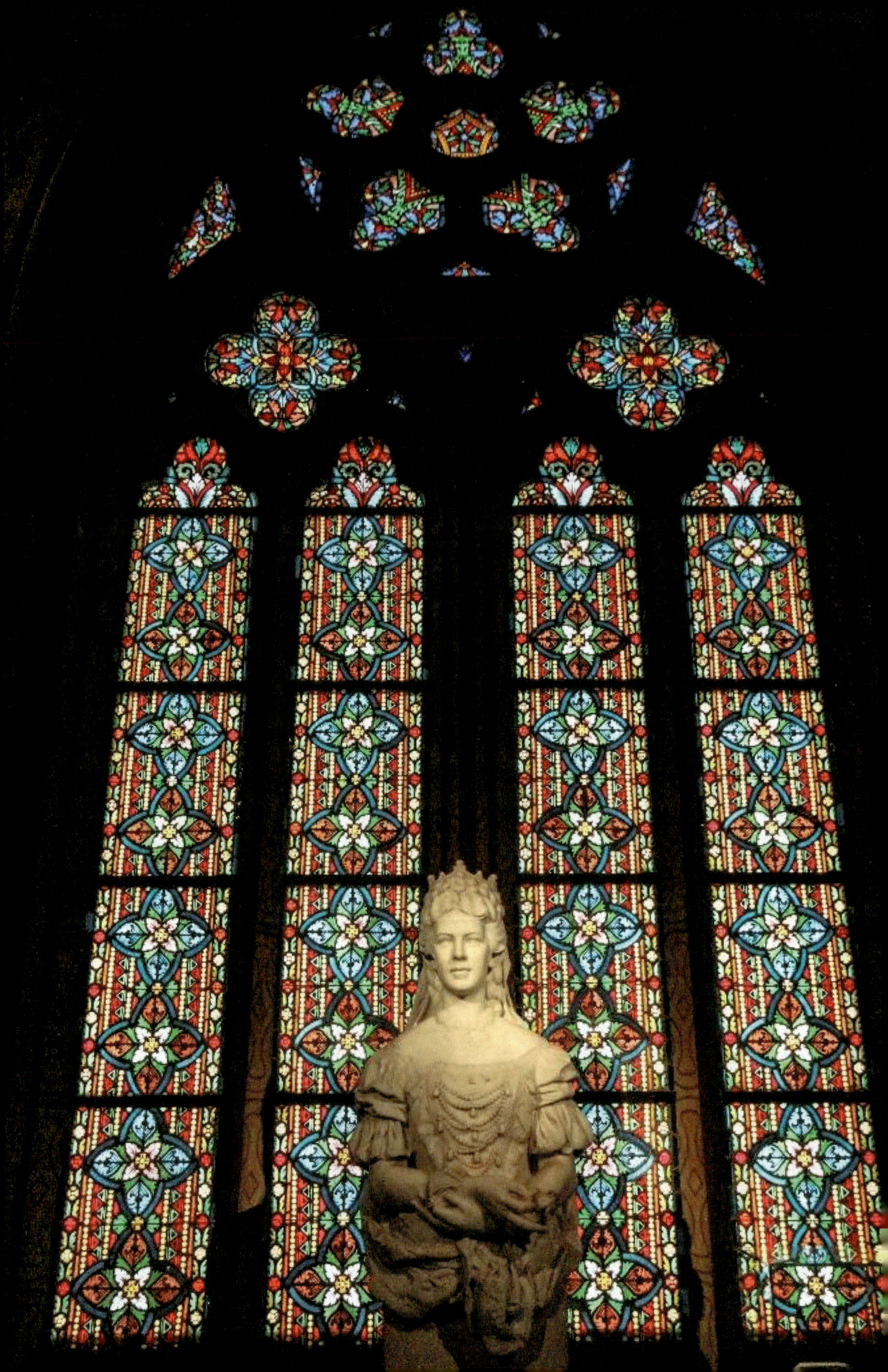

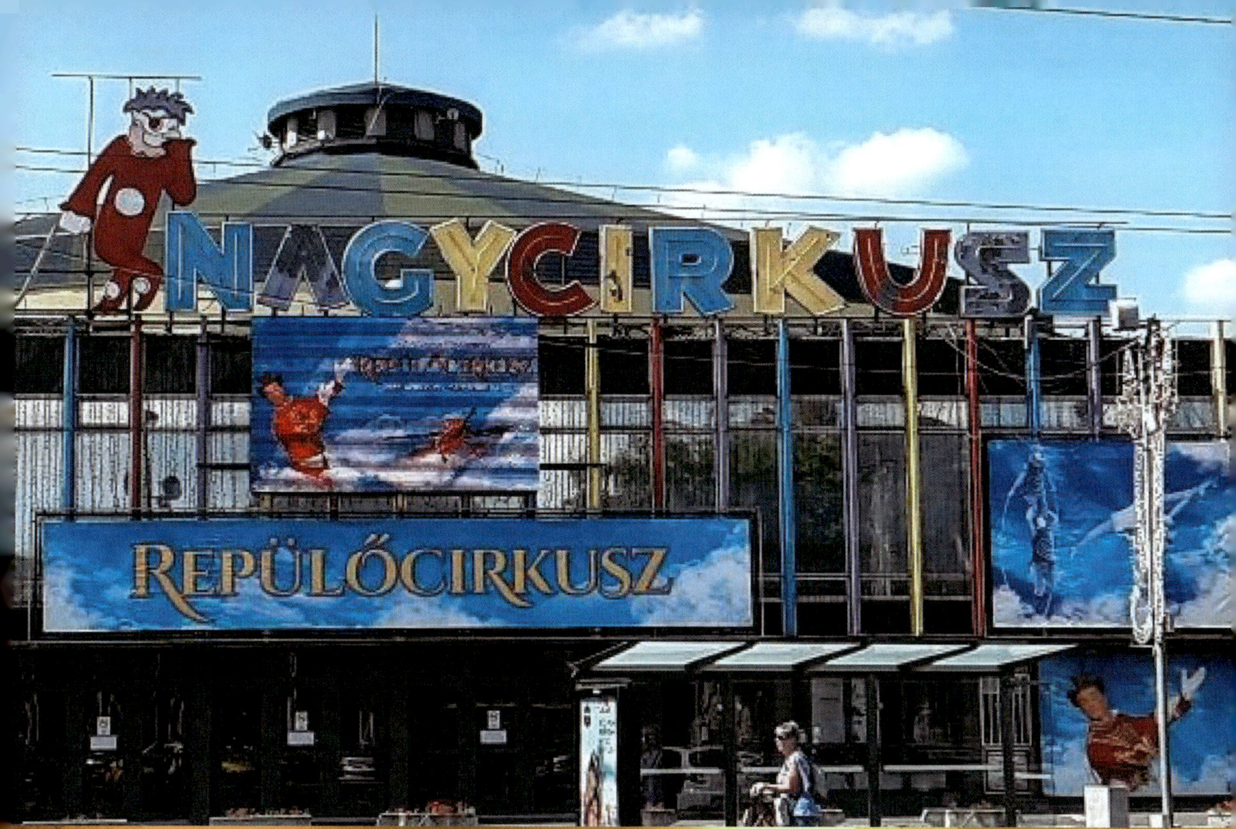
NAGYCIRKUSZ
REPÜLŐCIRKUSZ

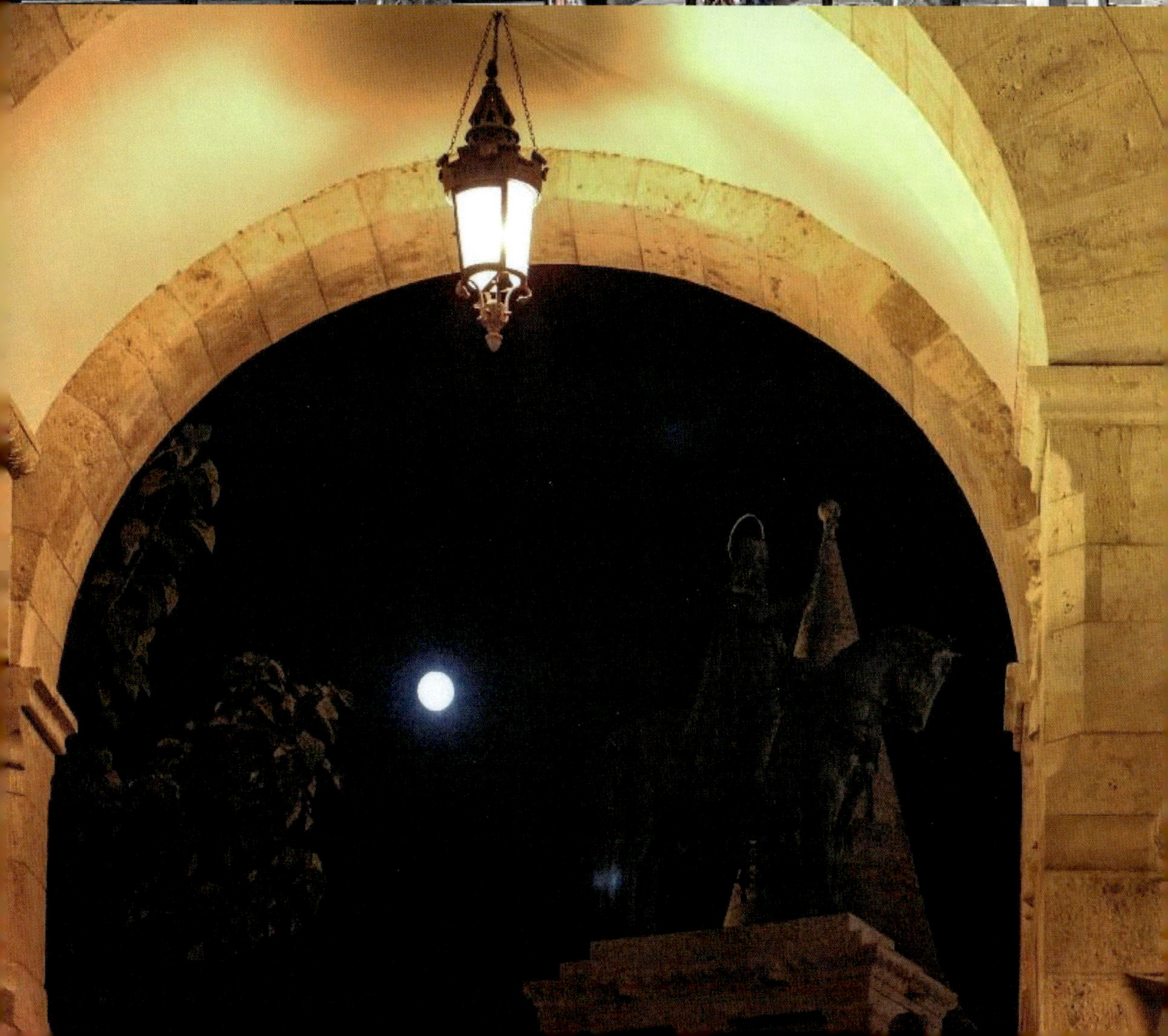

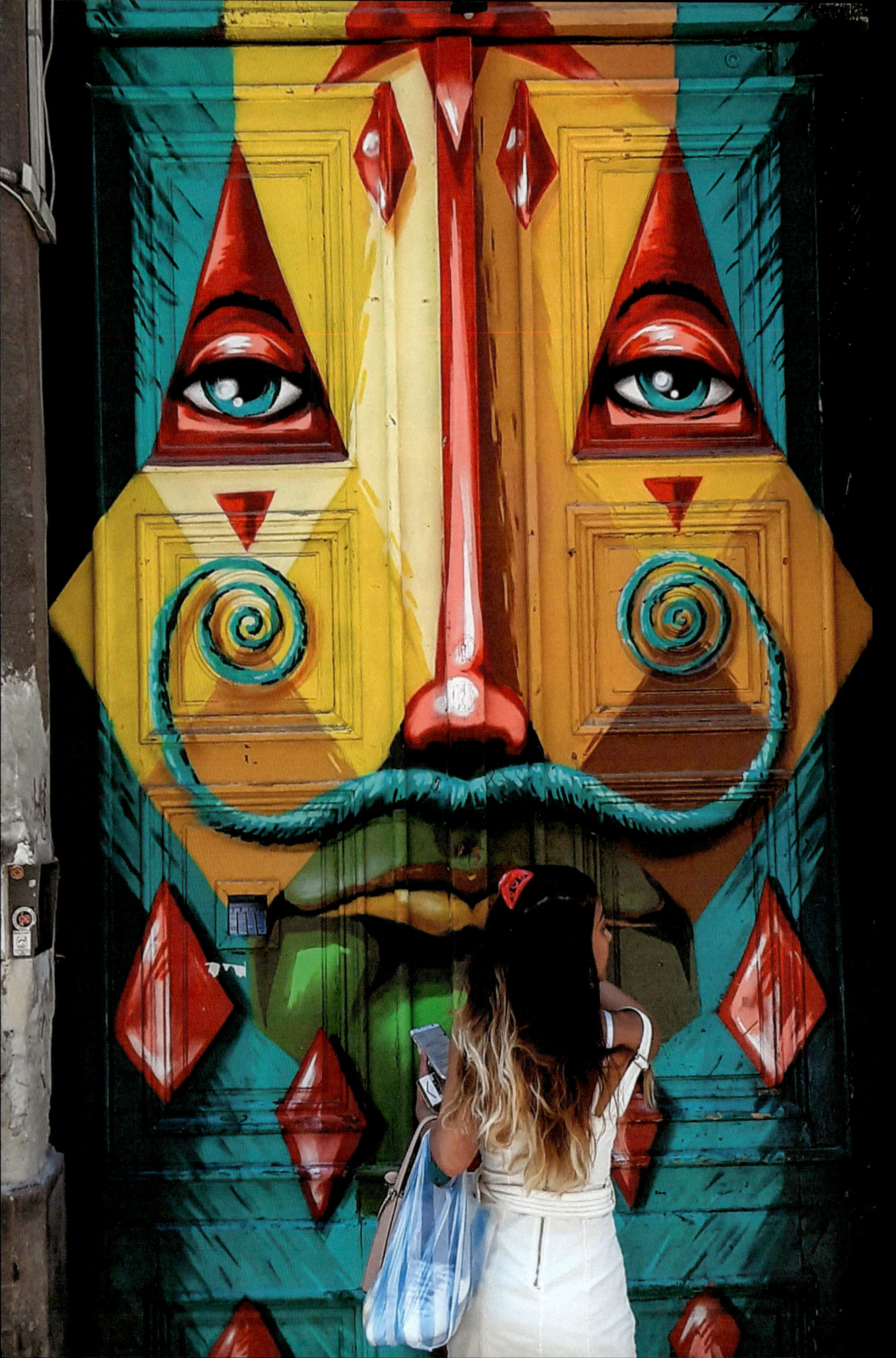

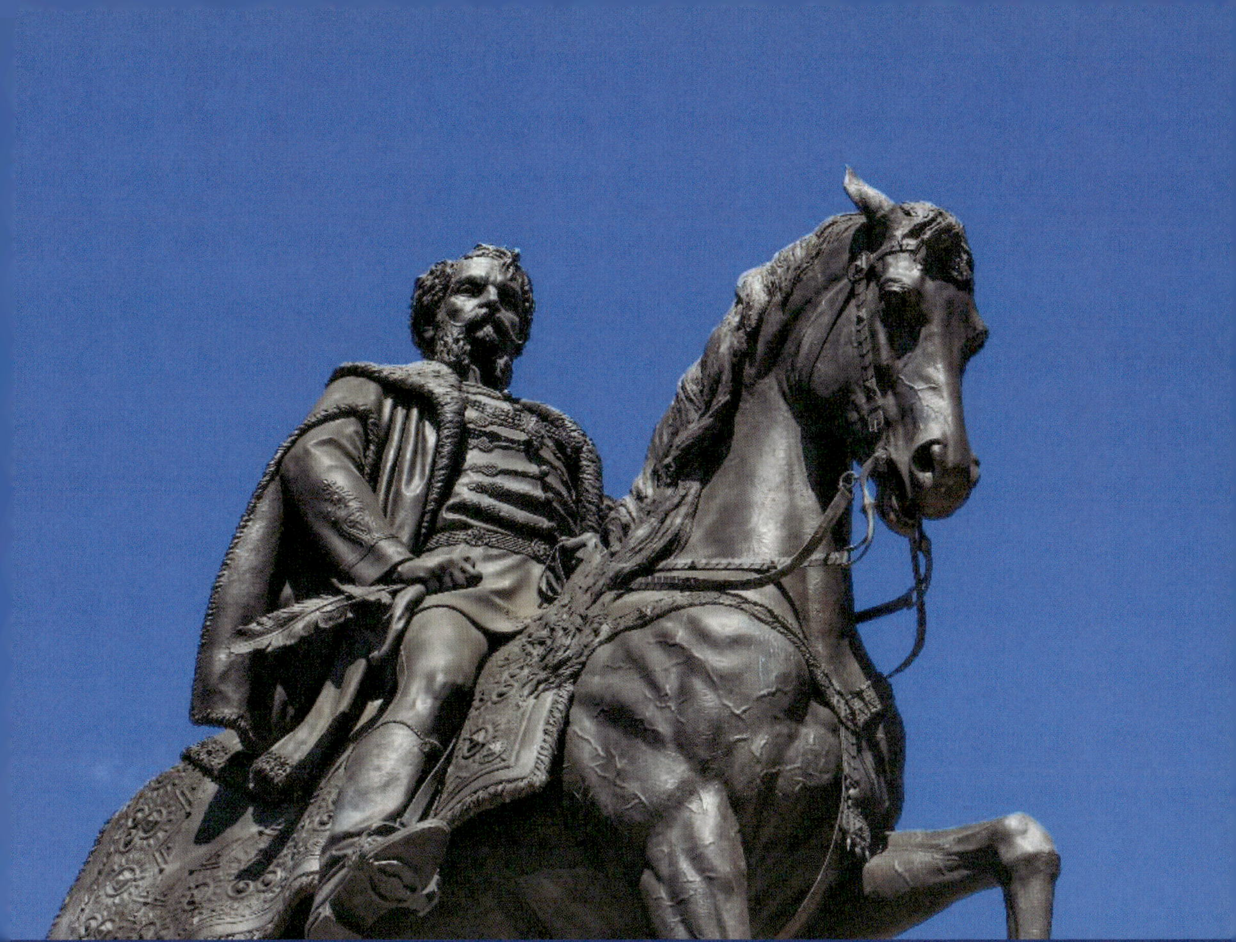

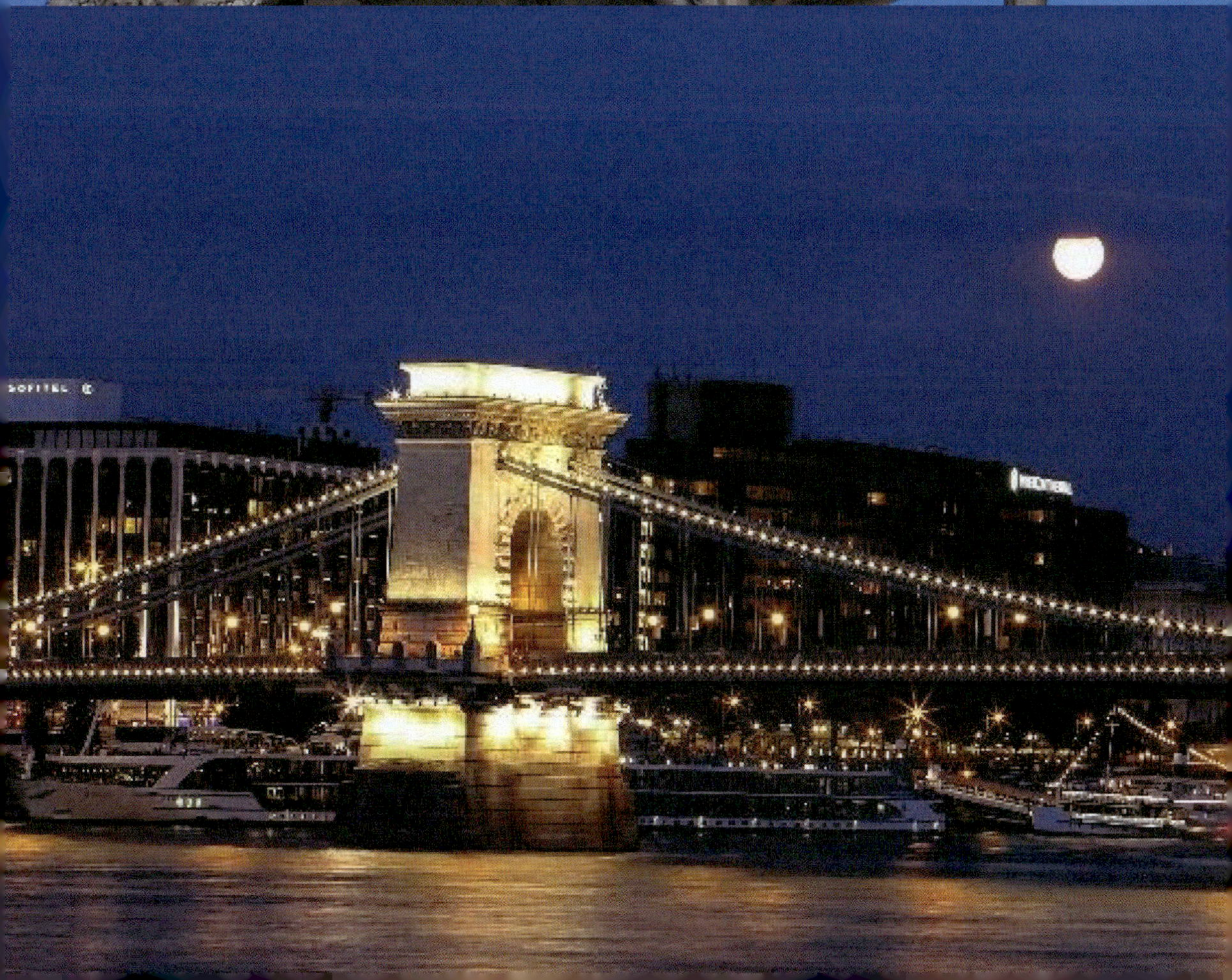
SOFITEL

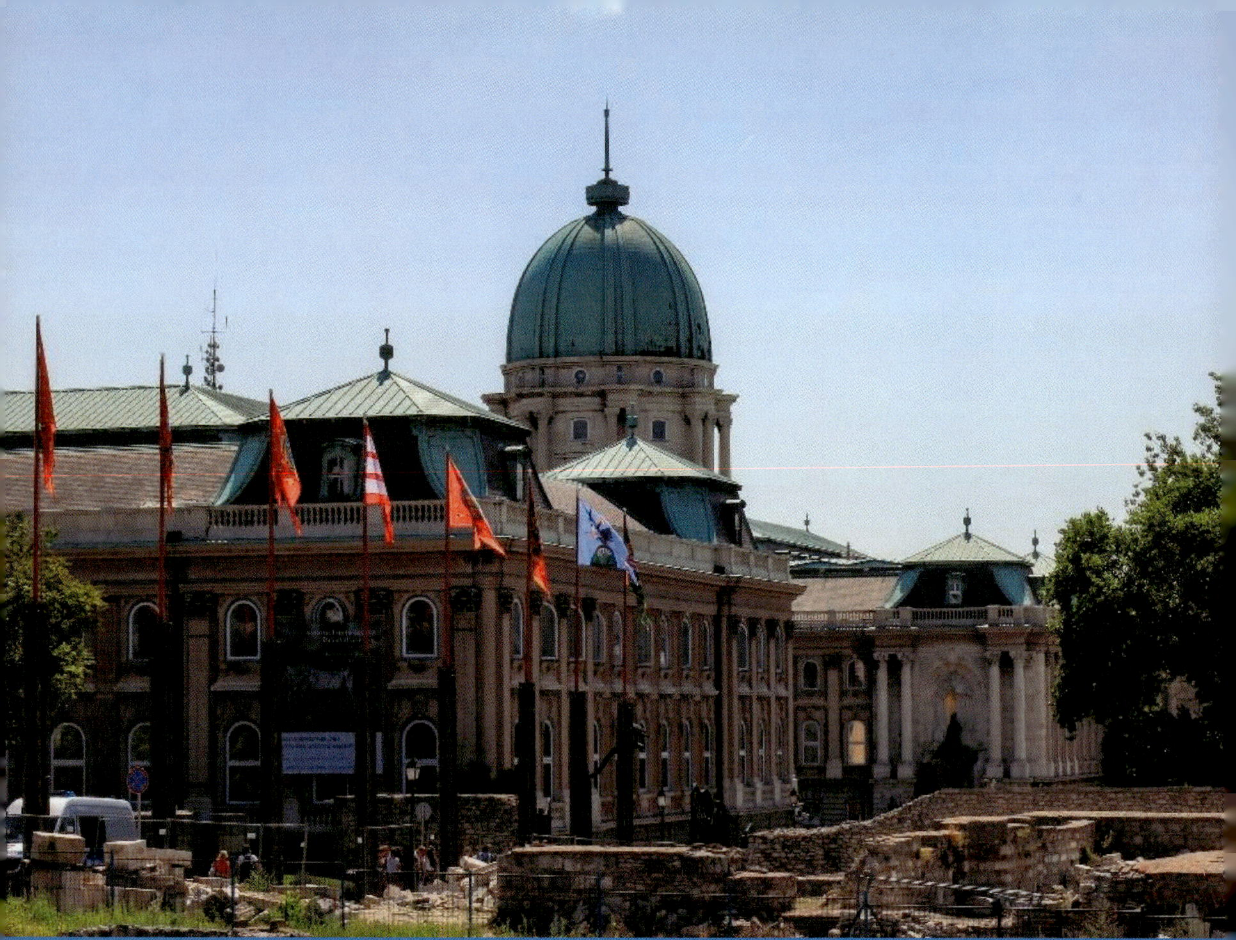

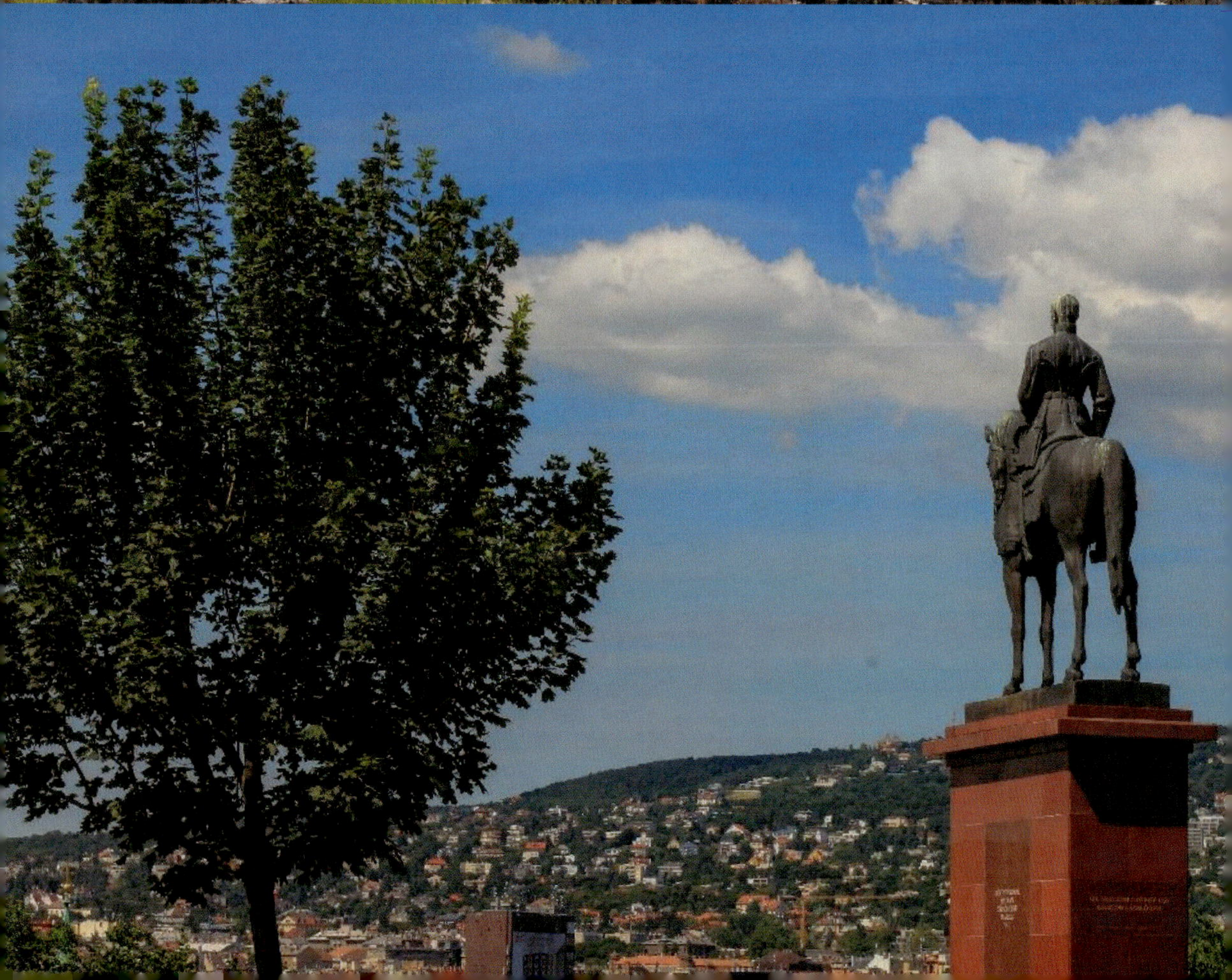

KOSSUTH

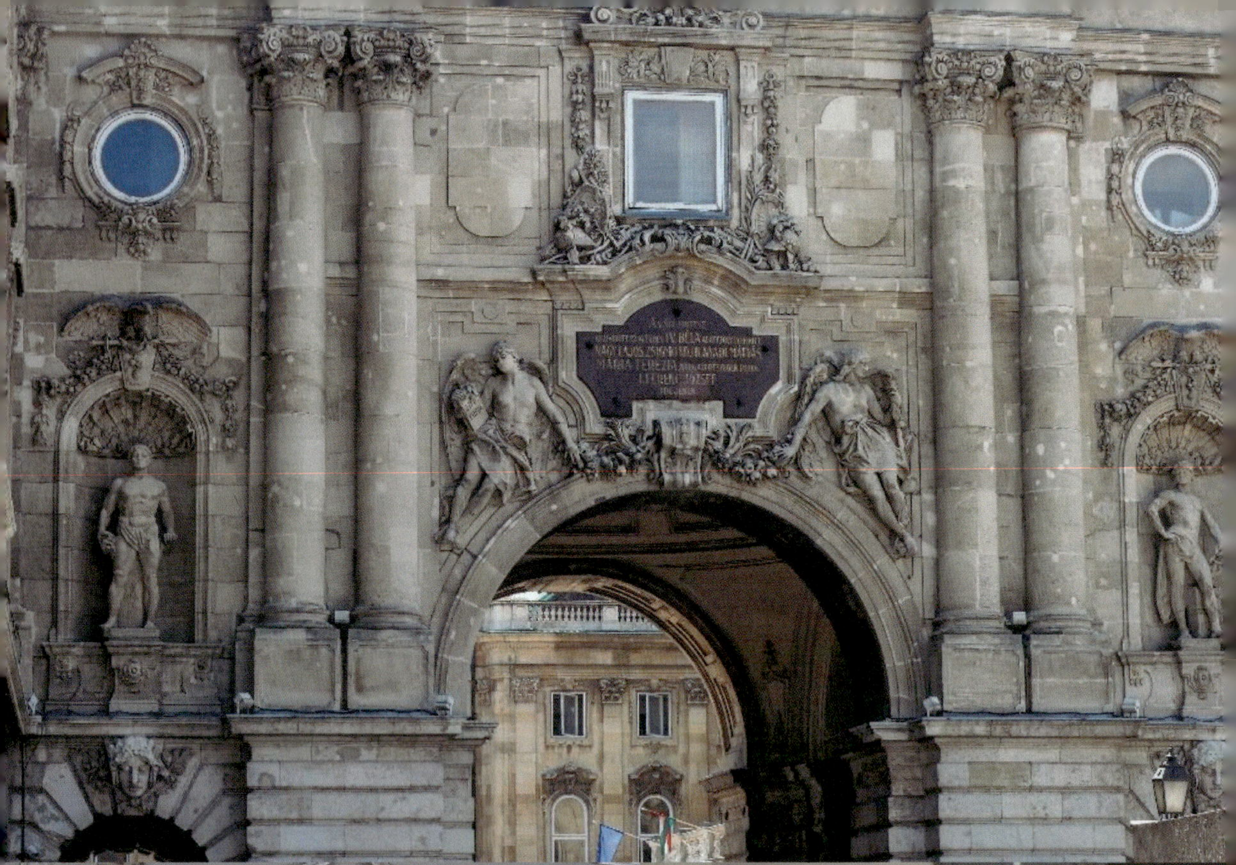

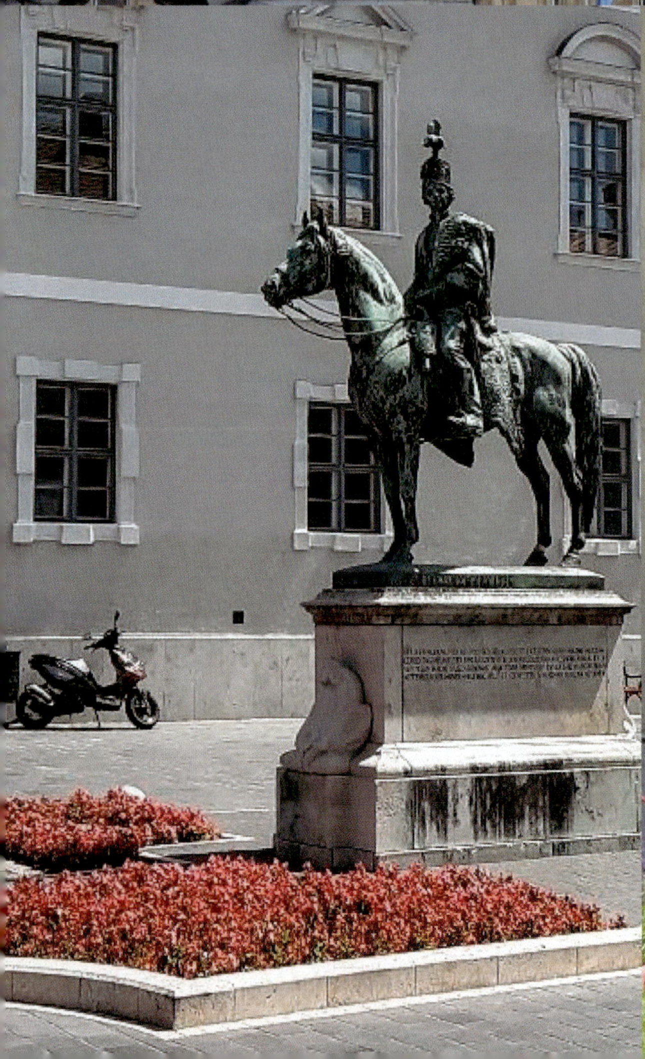

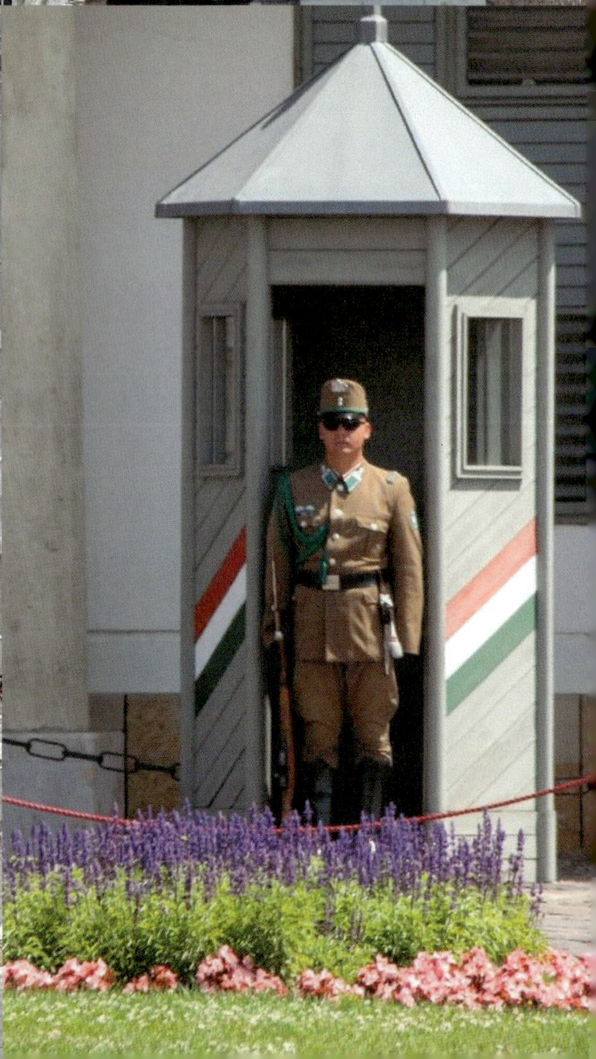

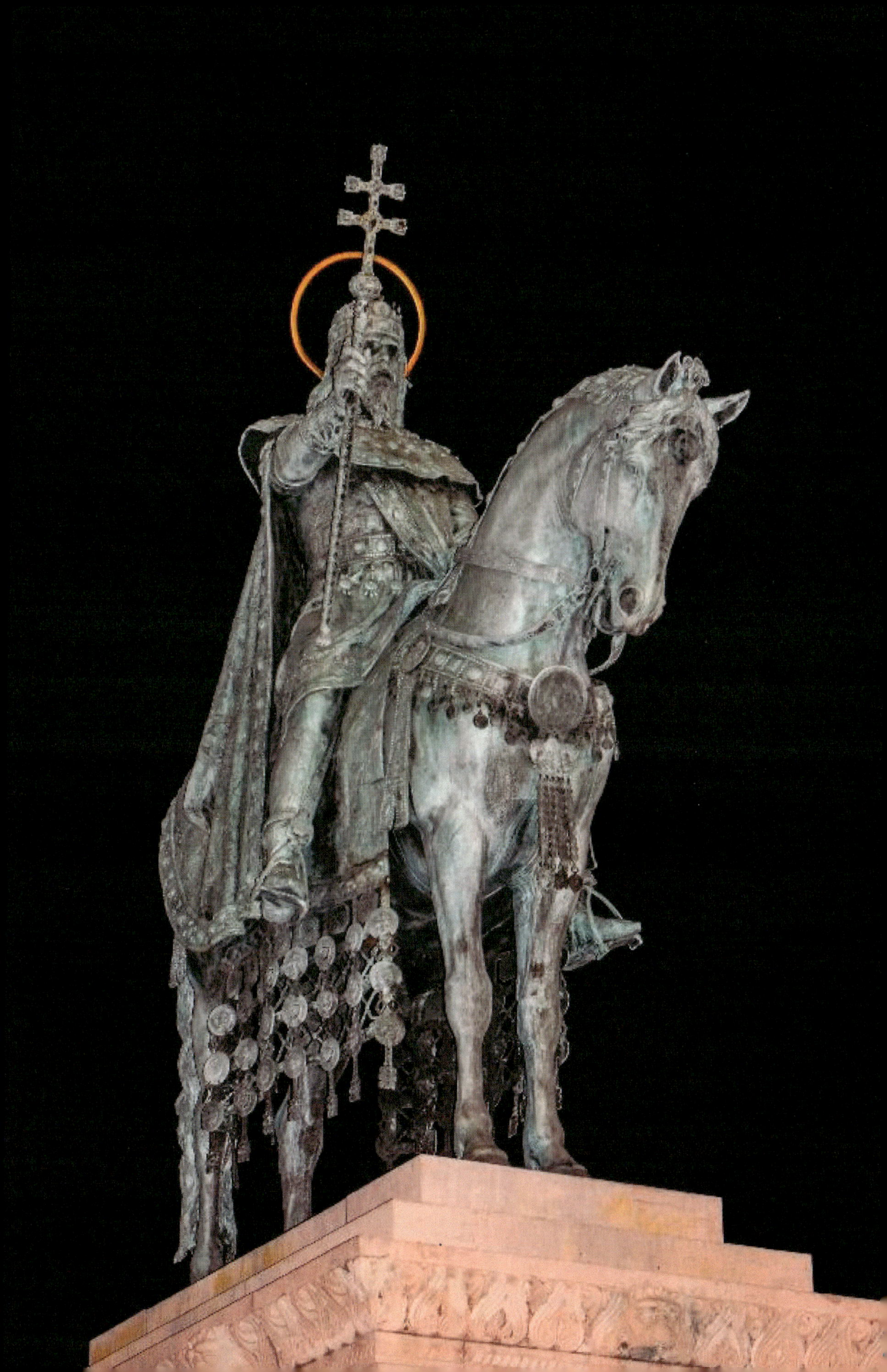

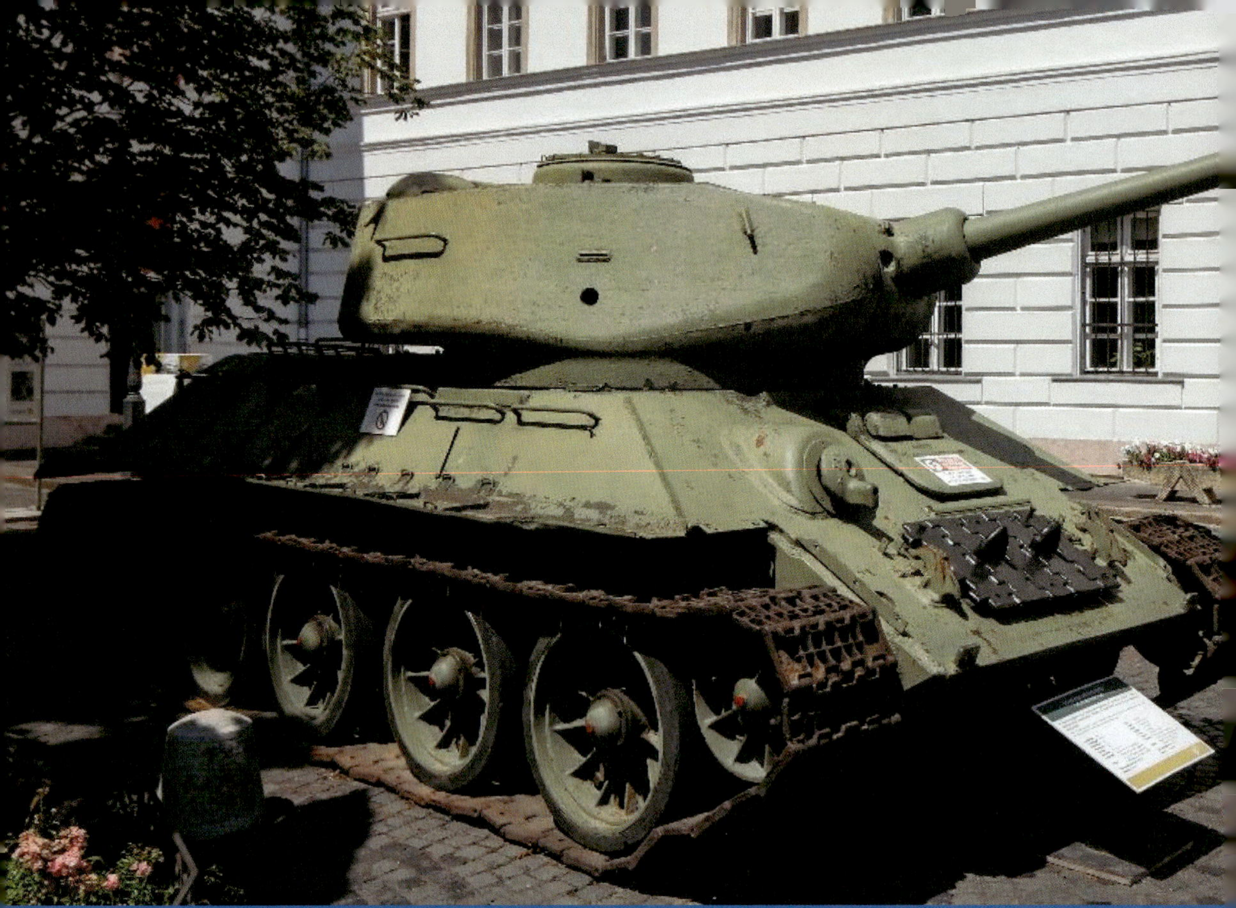

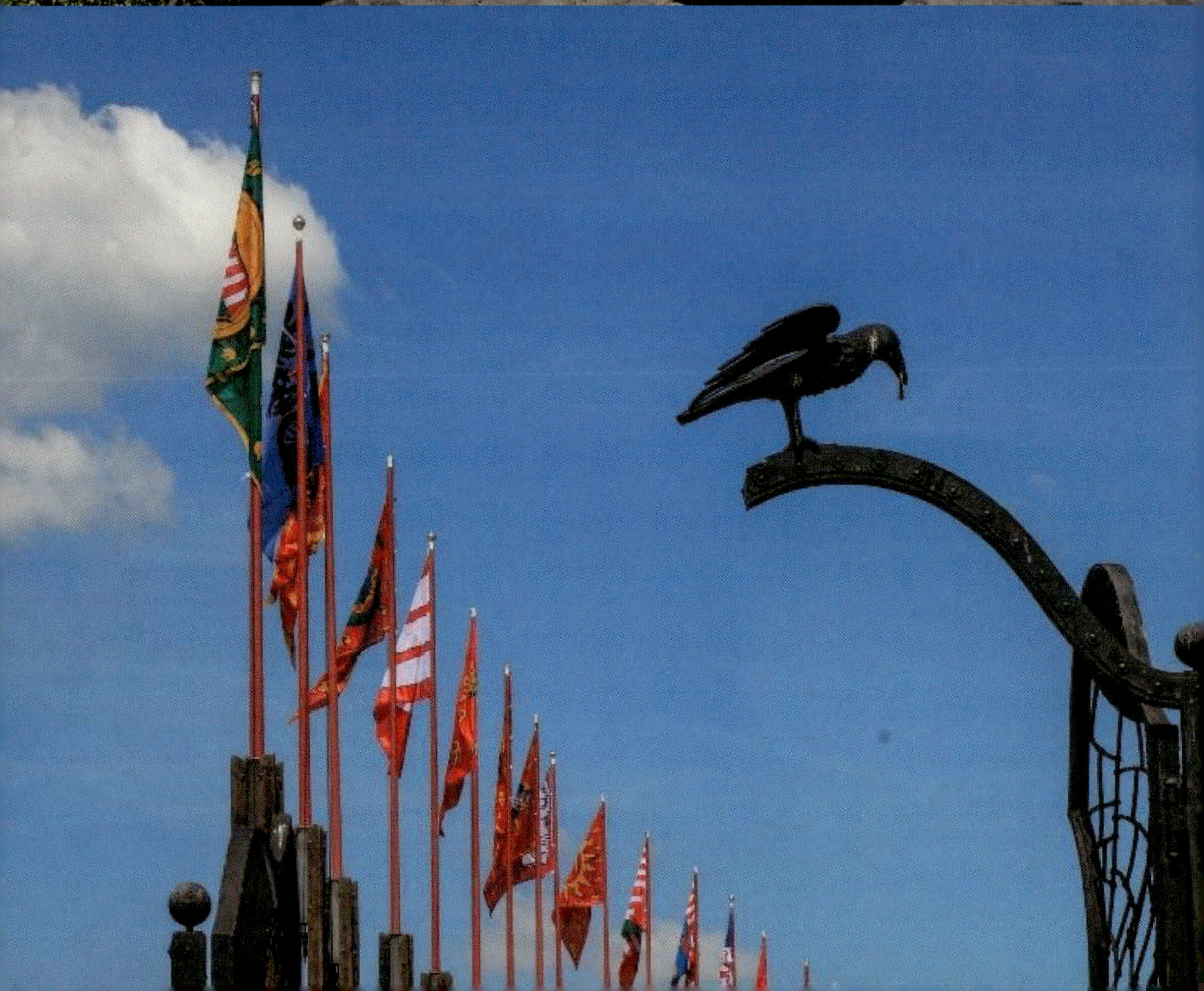

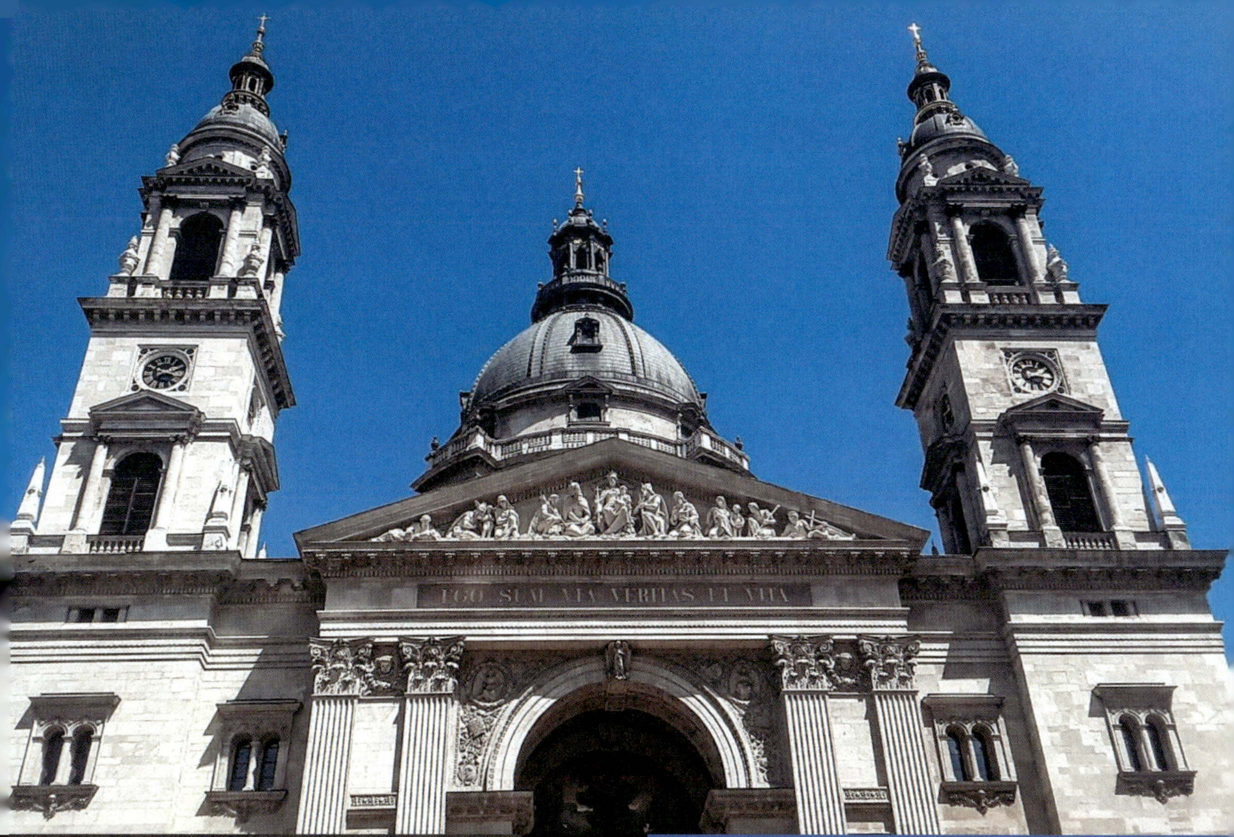

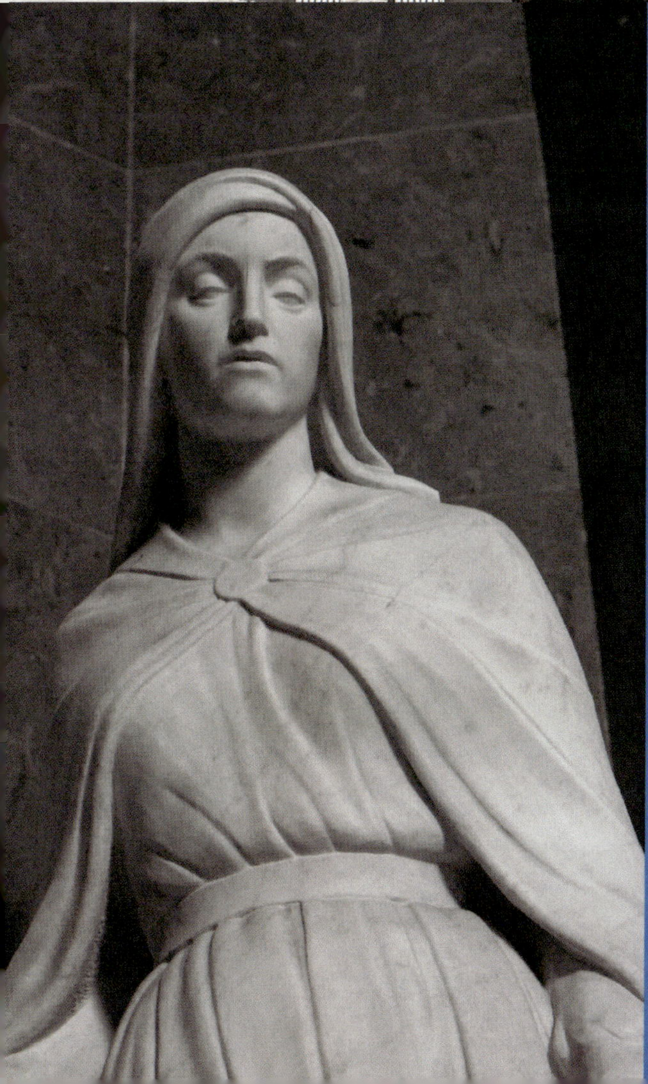

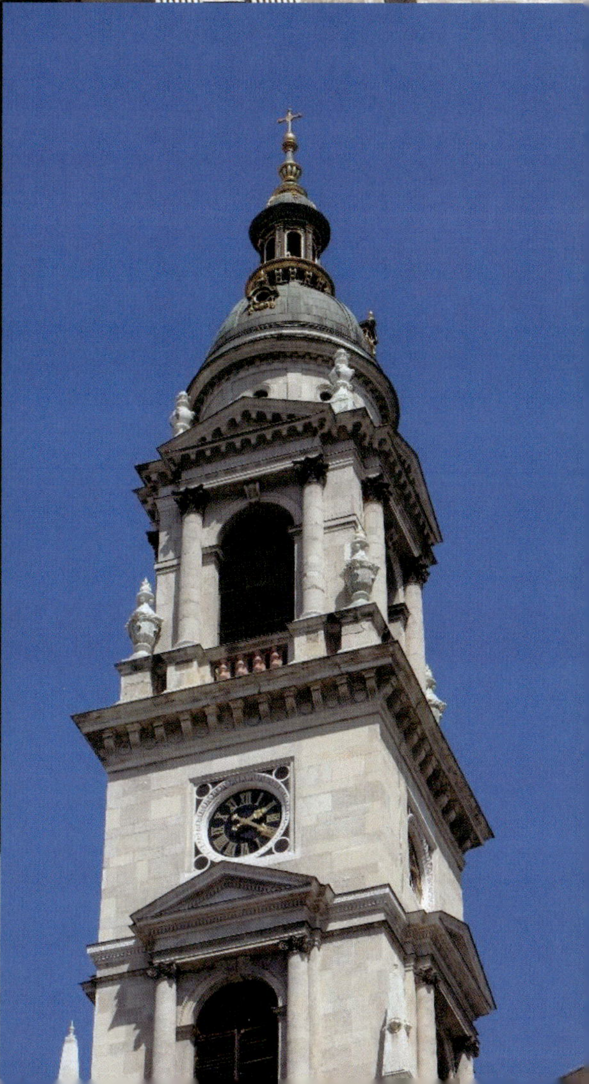

MAGYAR TUDOMÁNYOS AKADÉMIA

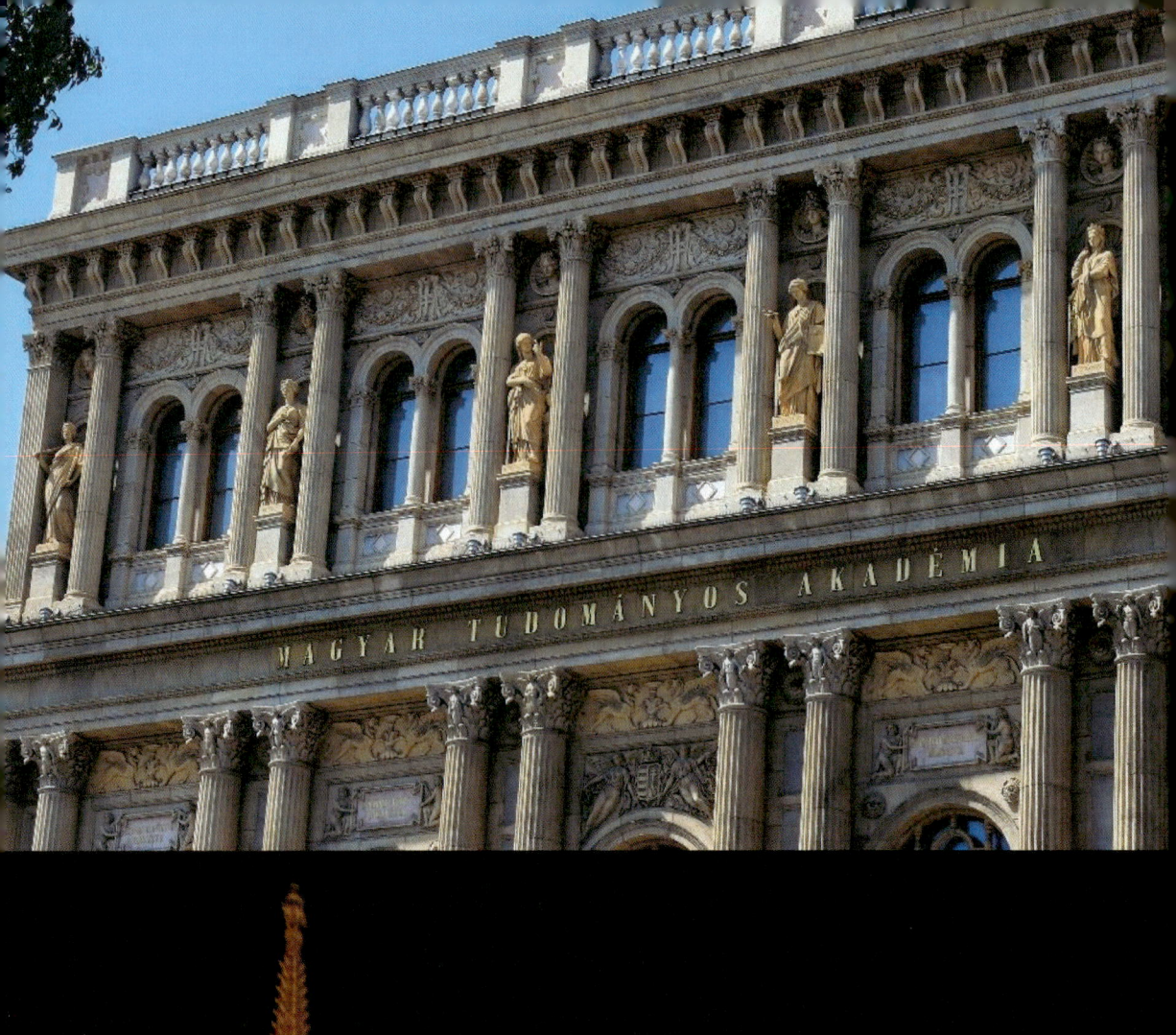

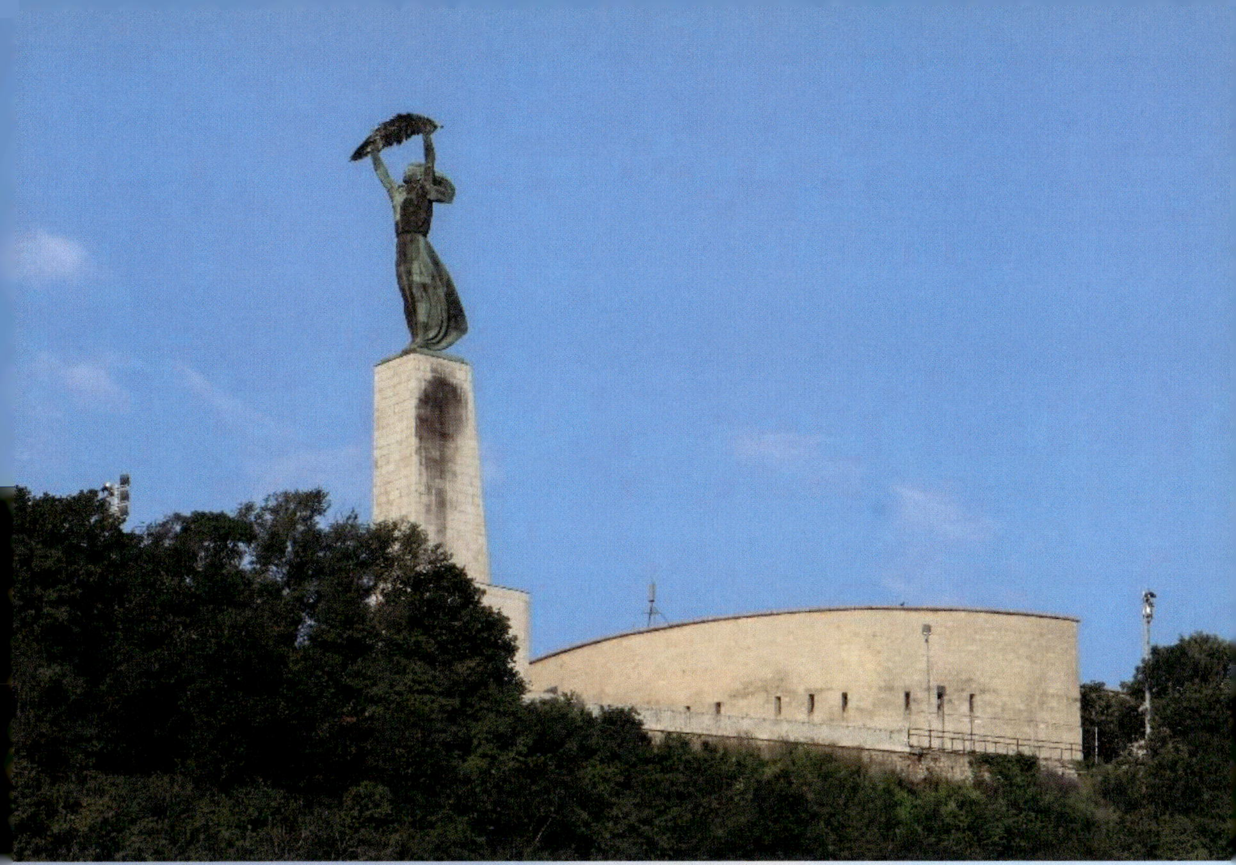

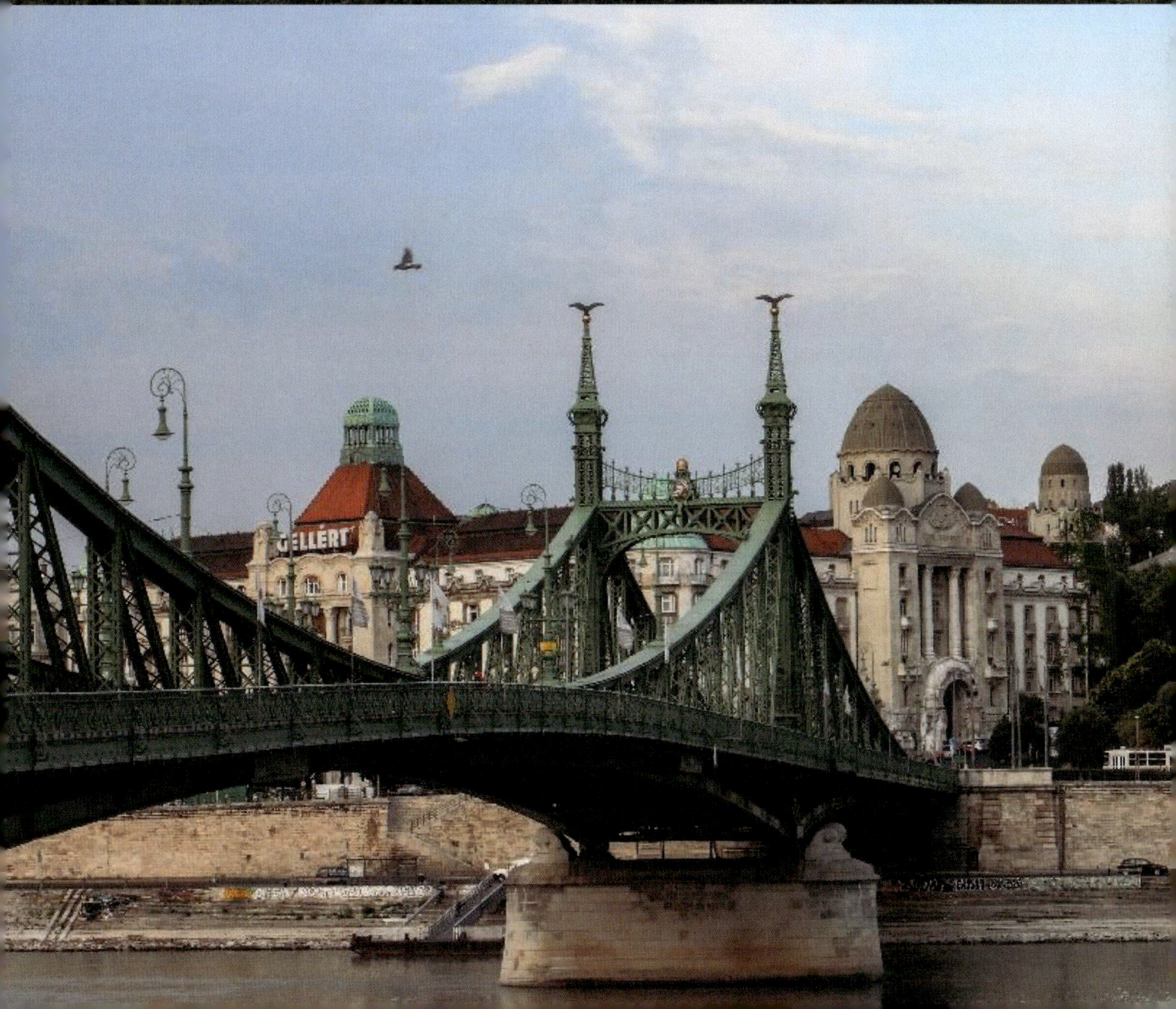
GELLÉRT

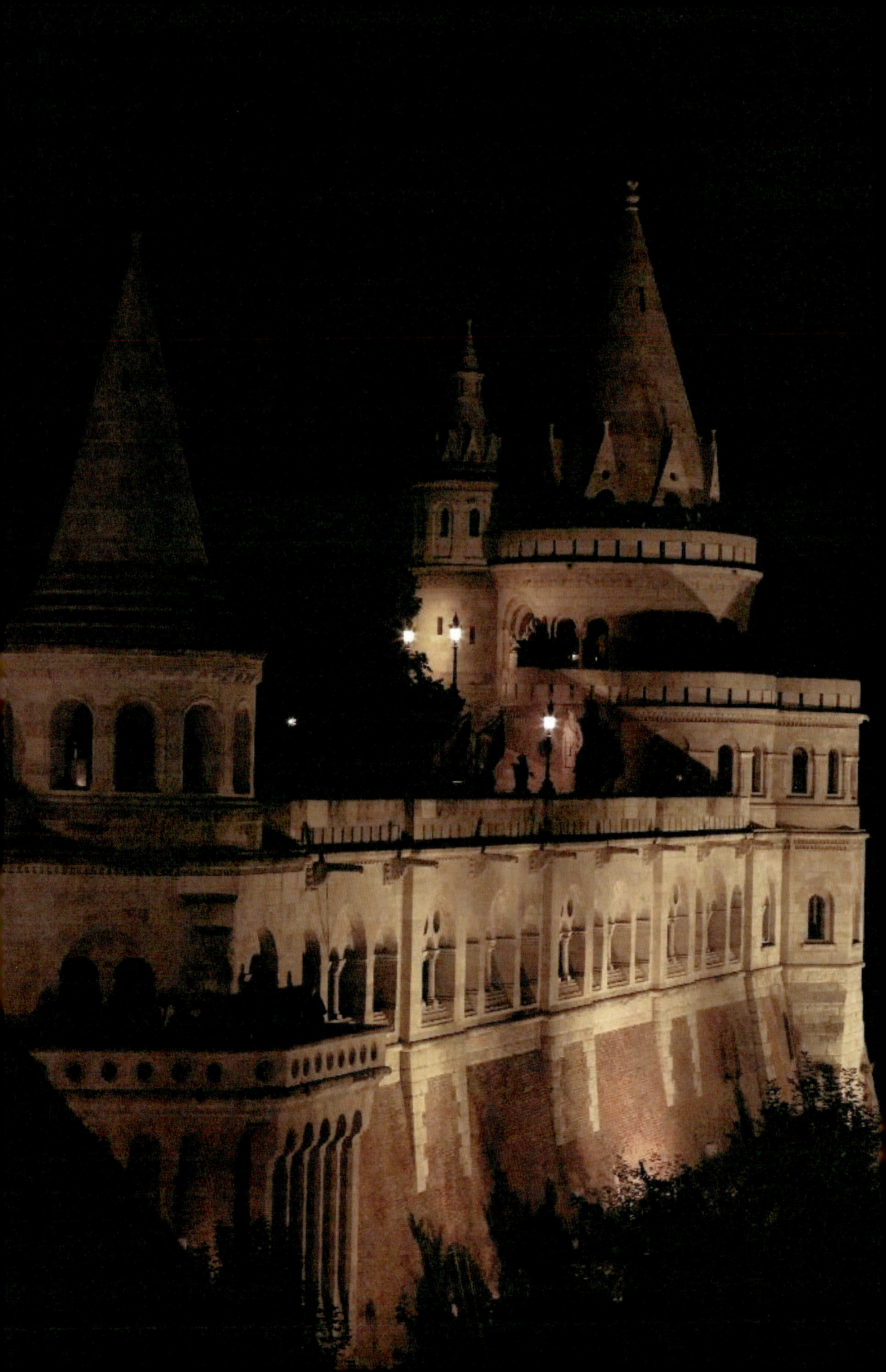

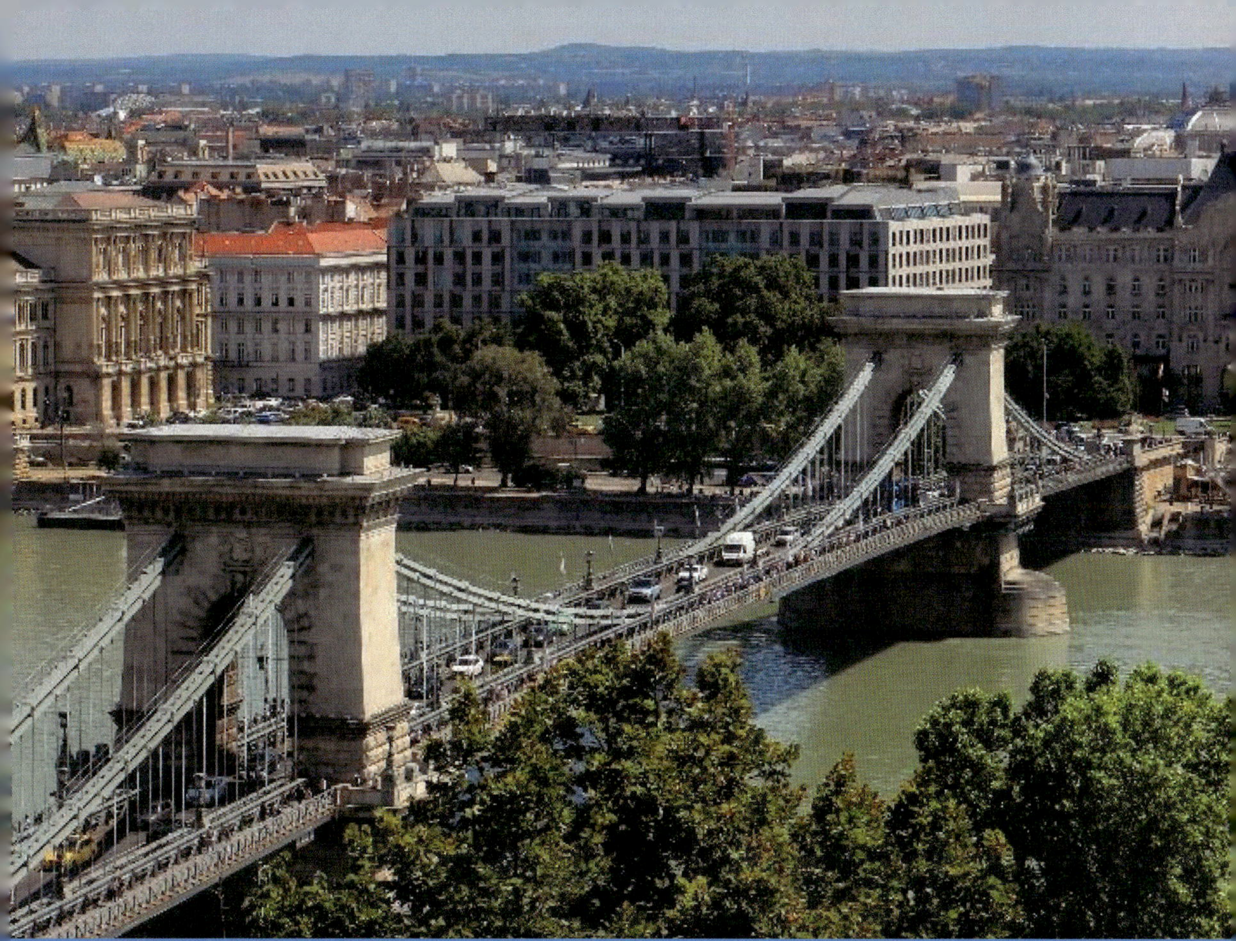

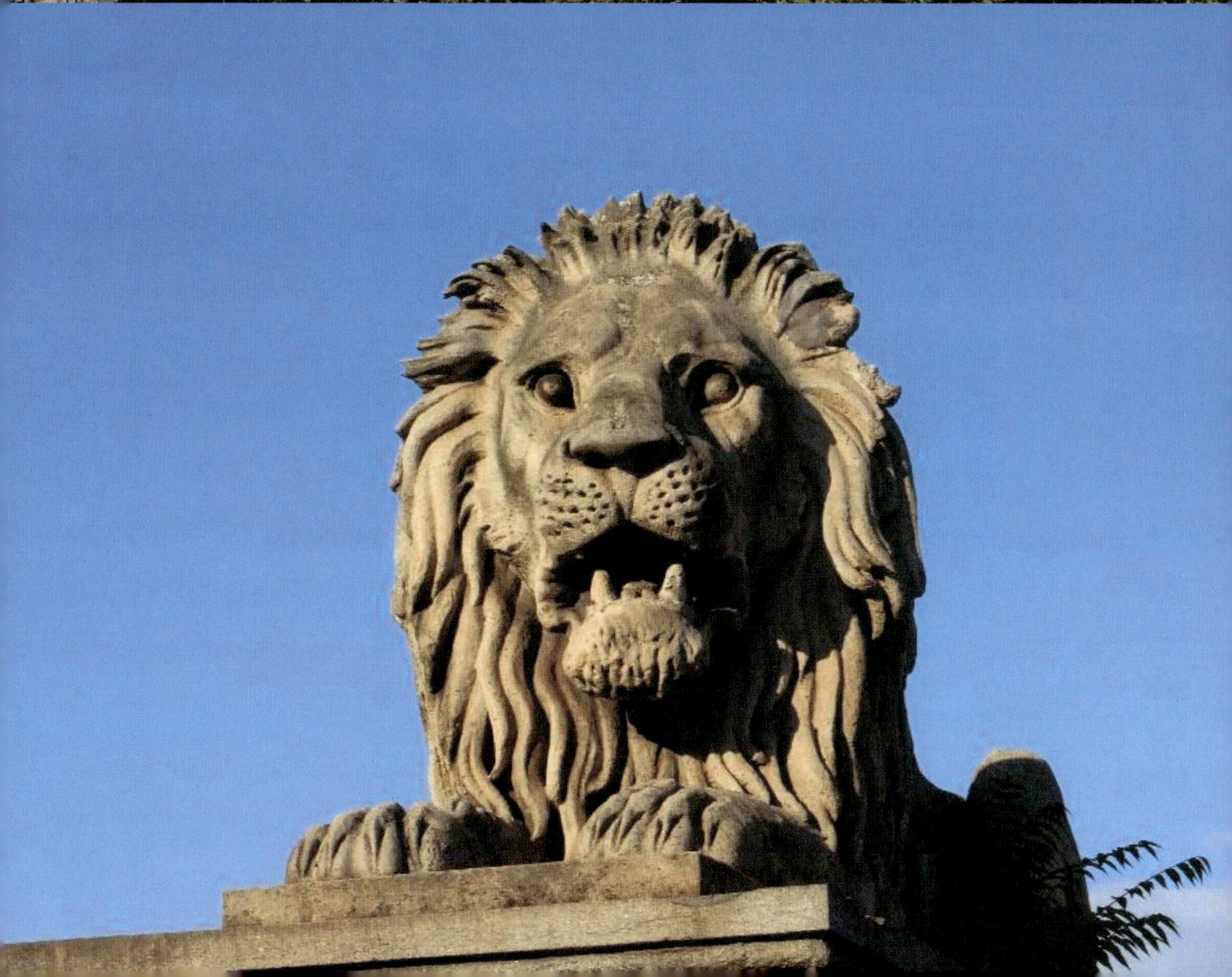

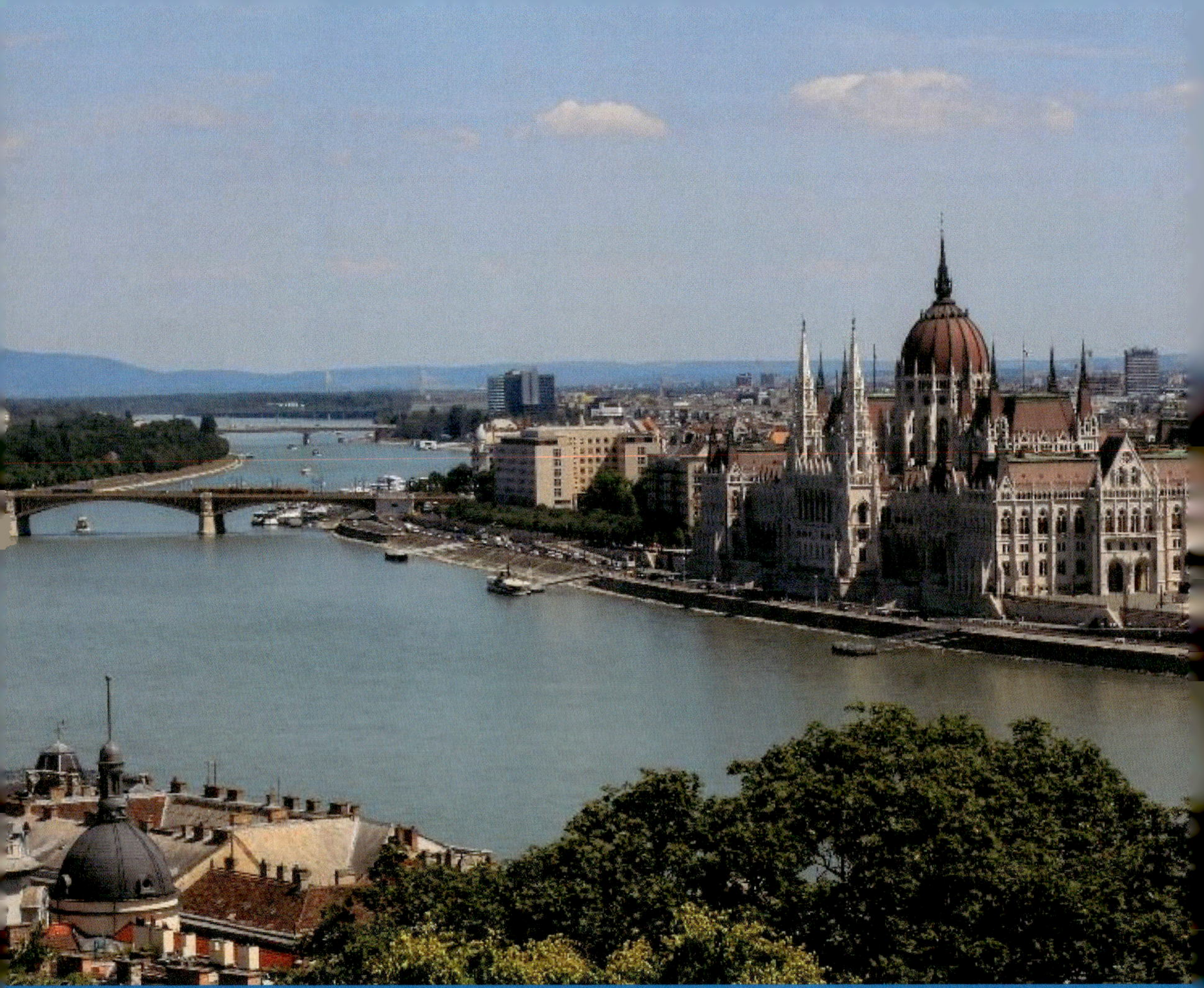

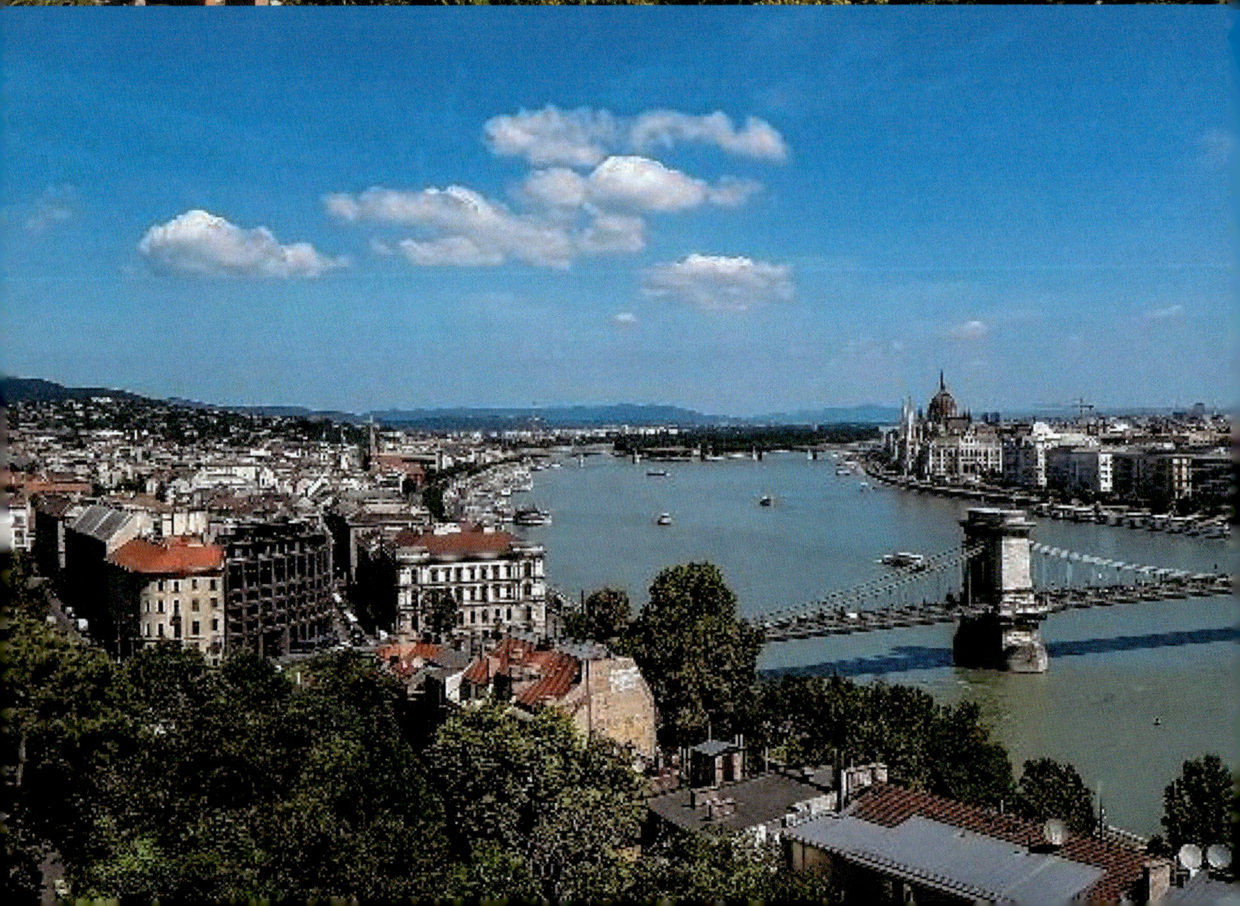

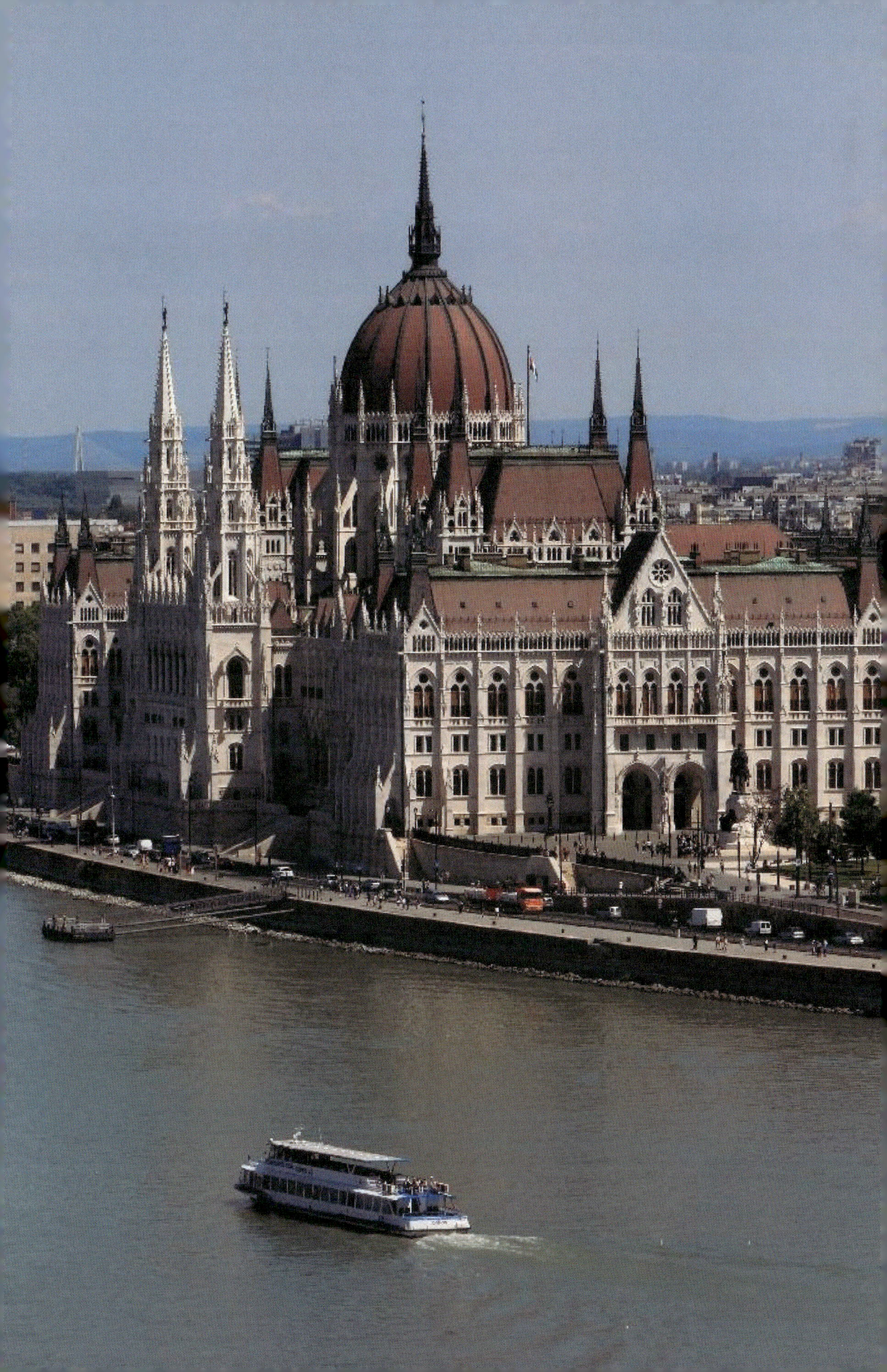

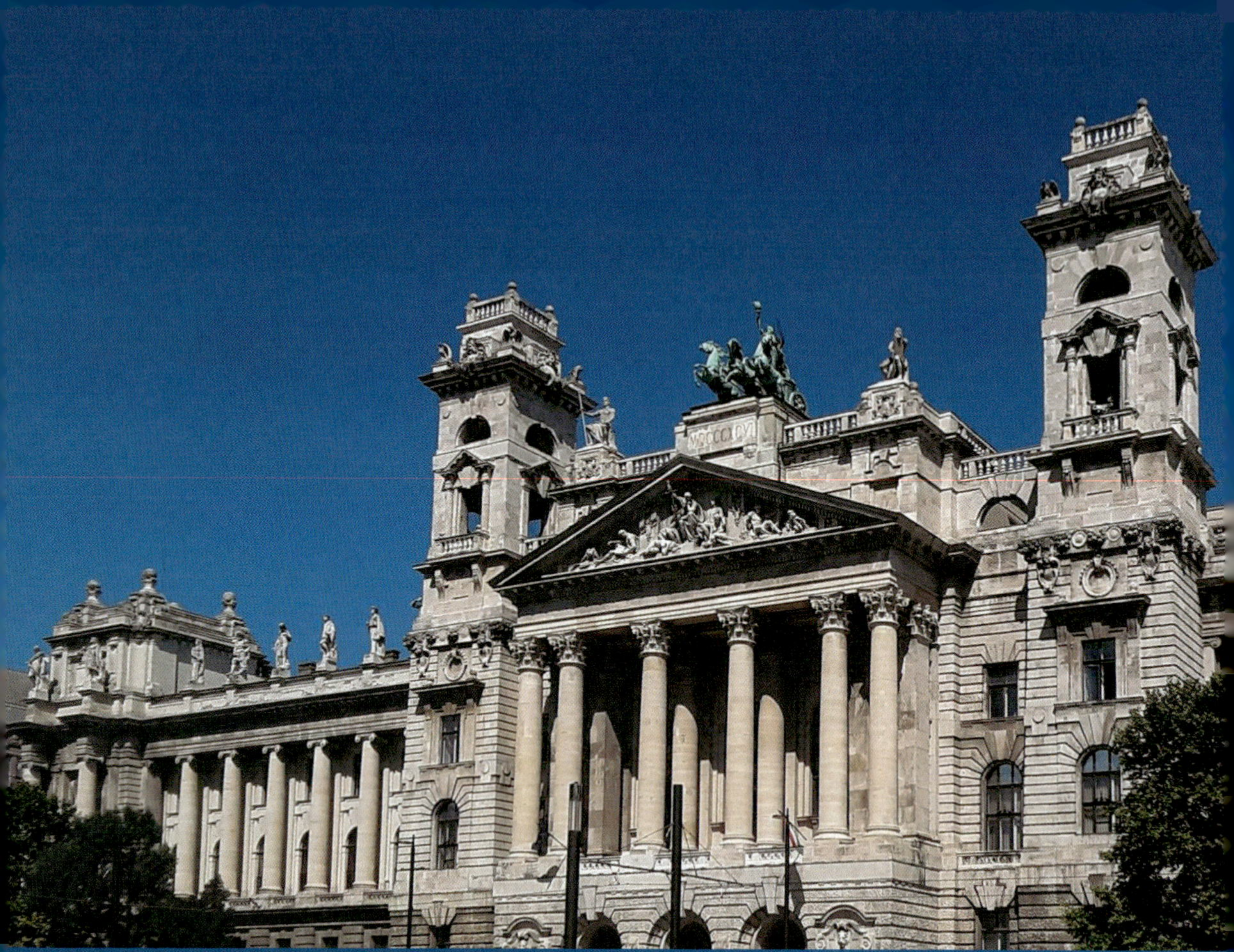

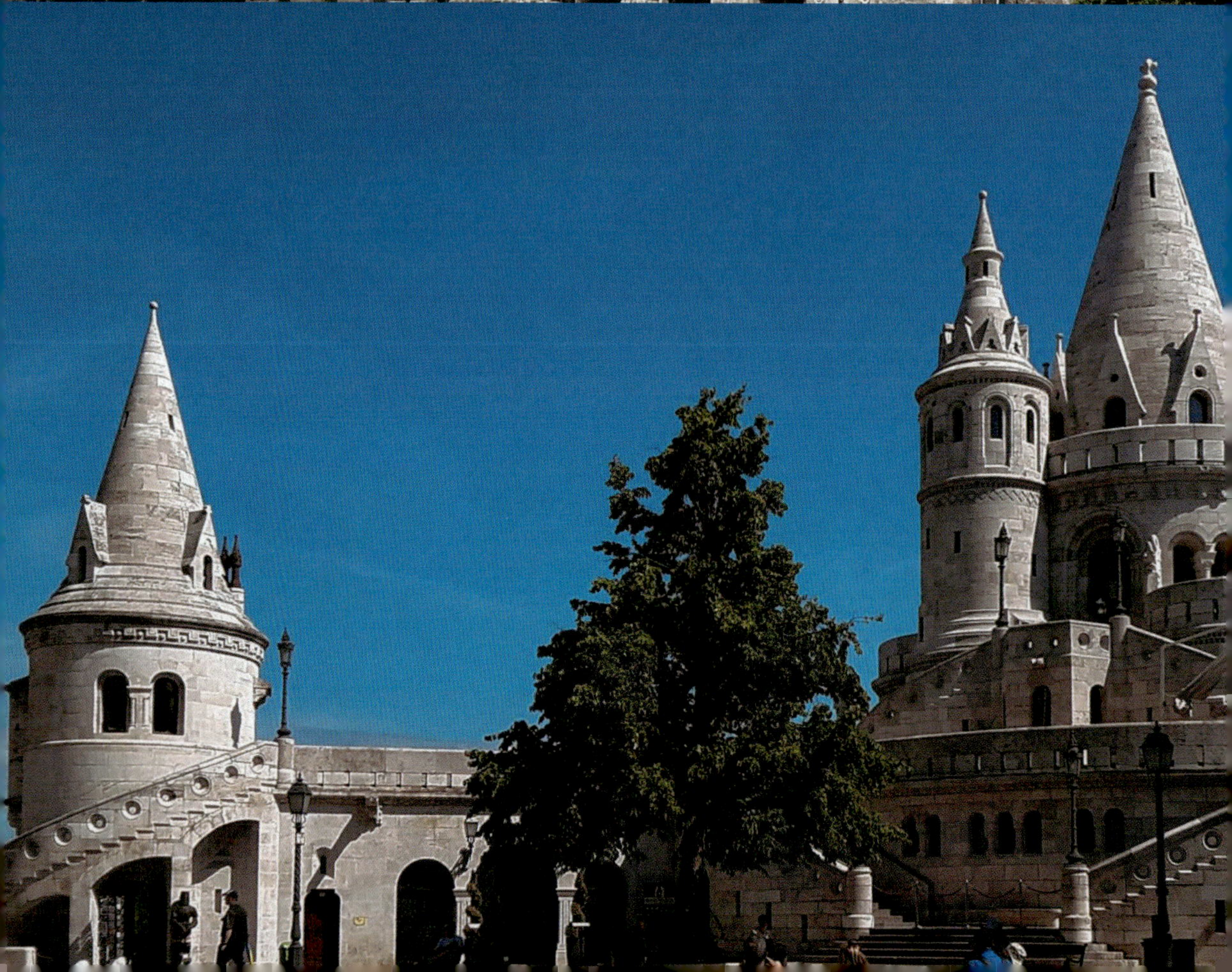

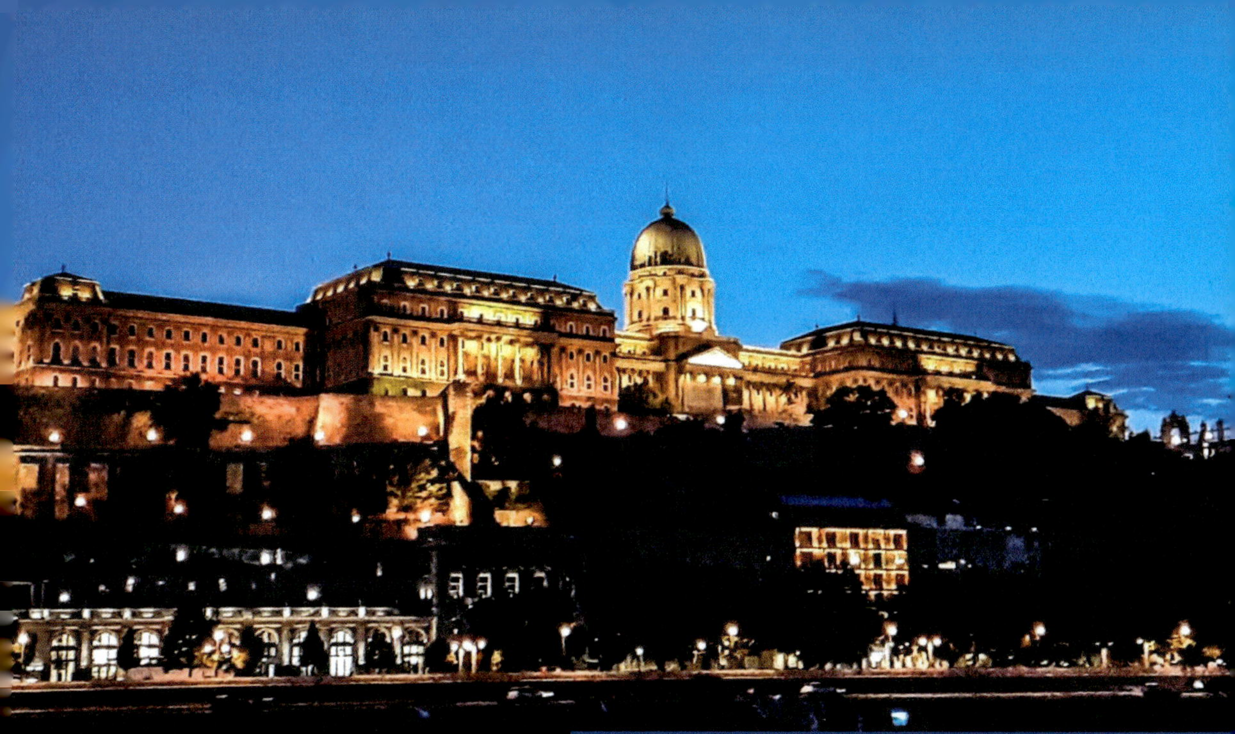
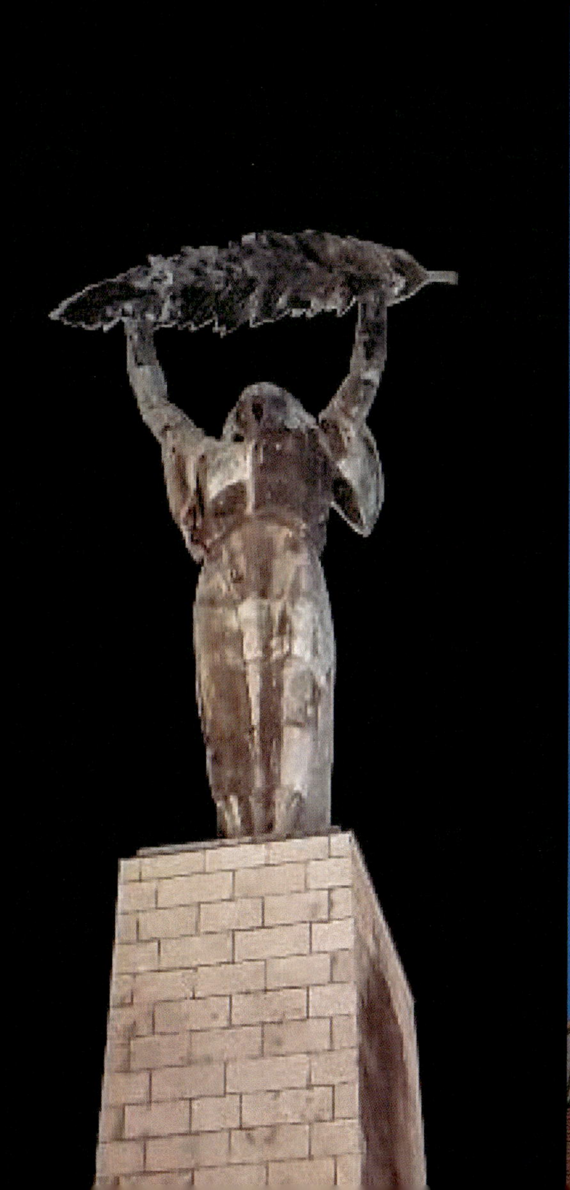
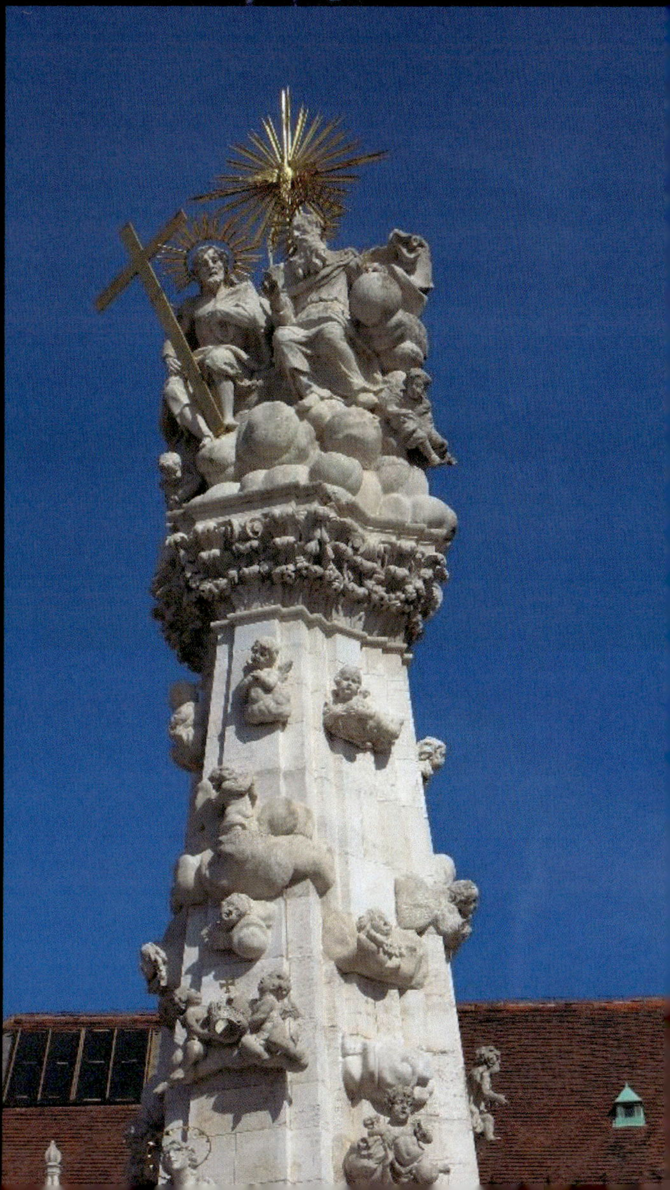

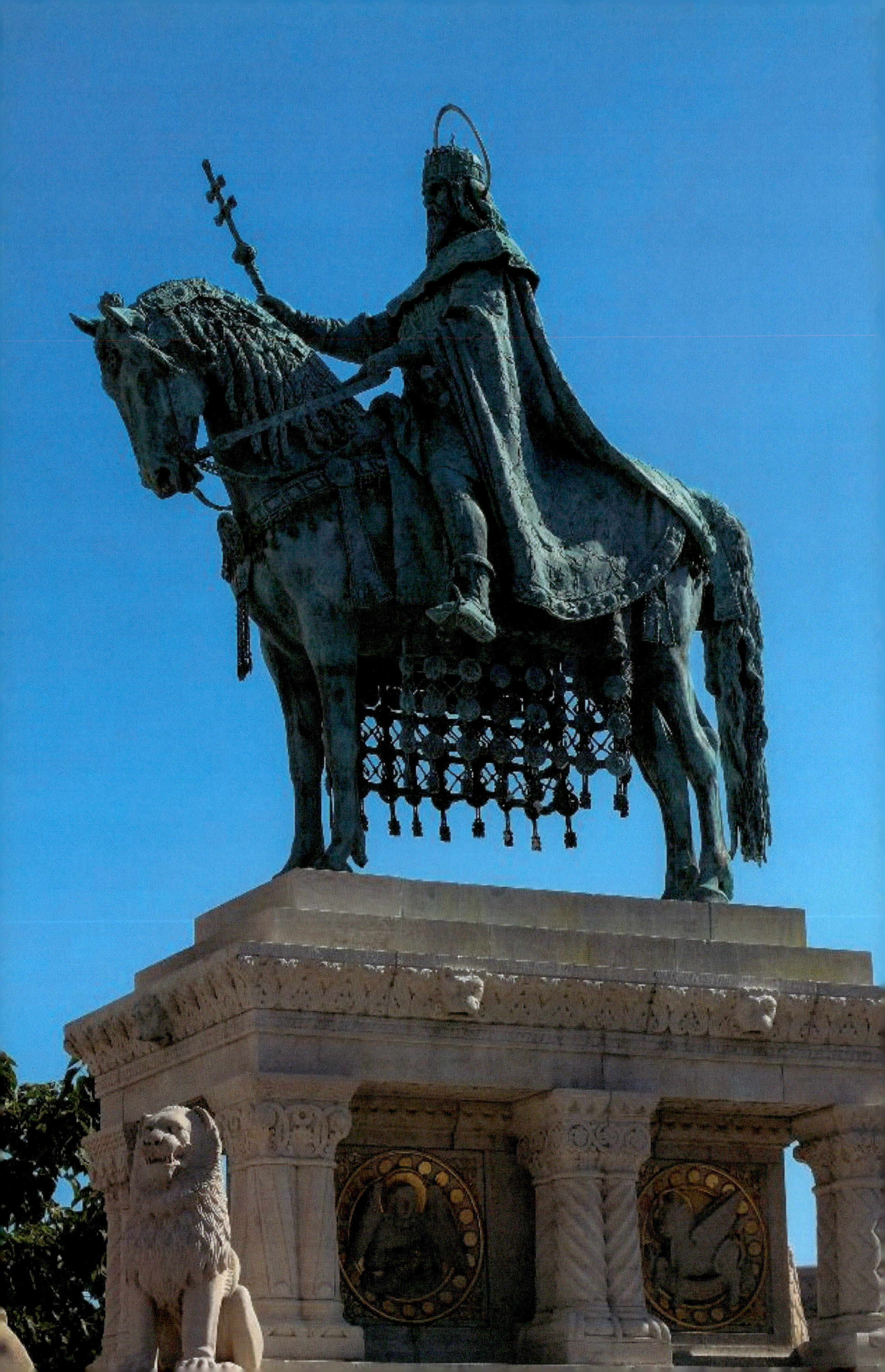

WINE BAR

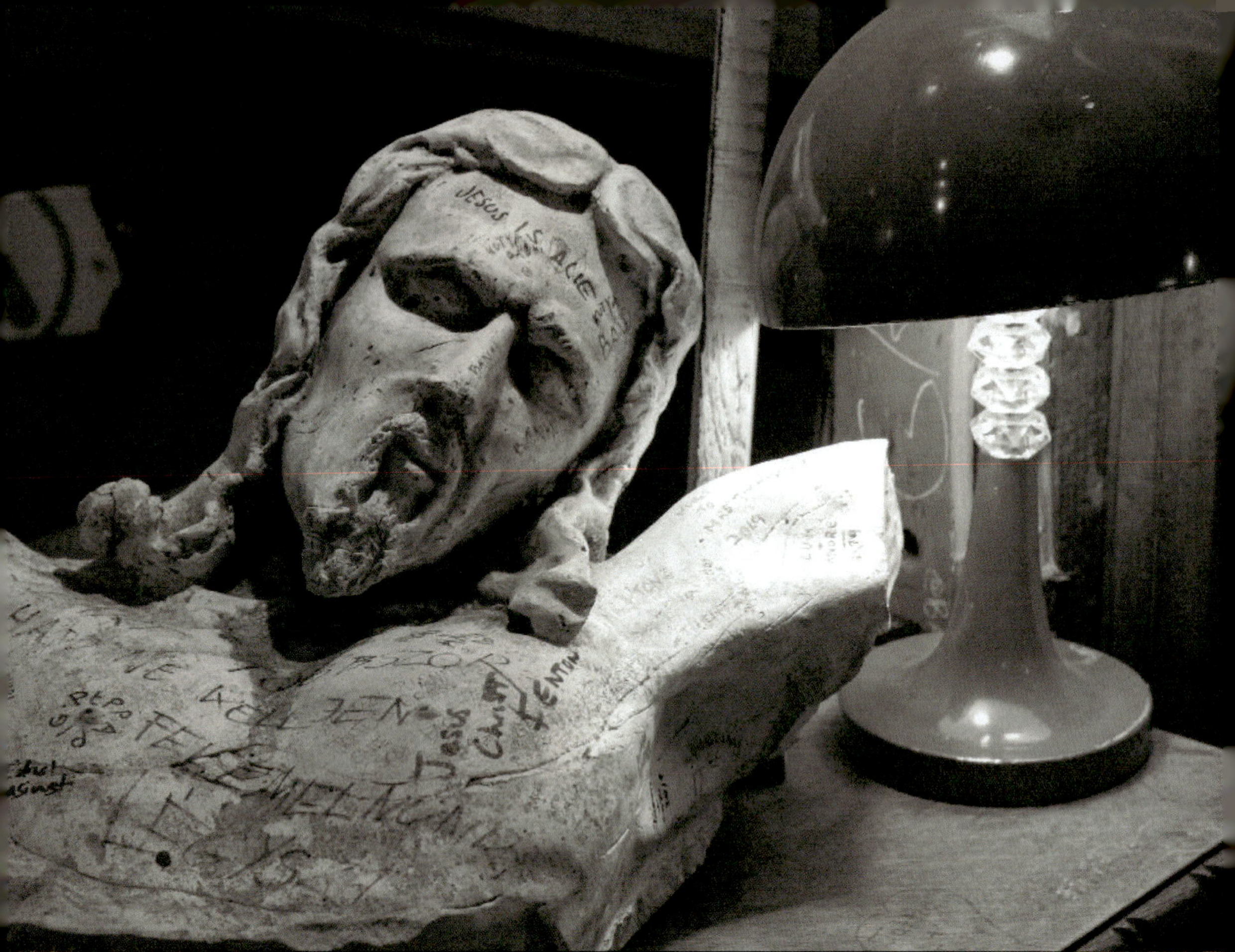

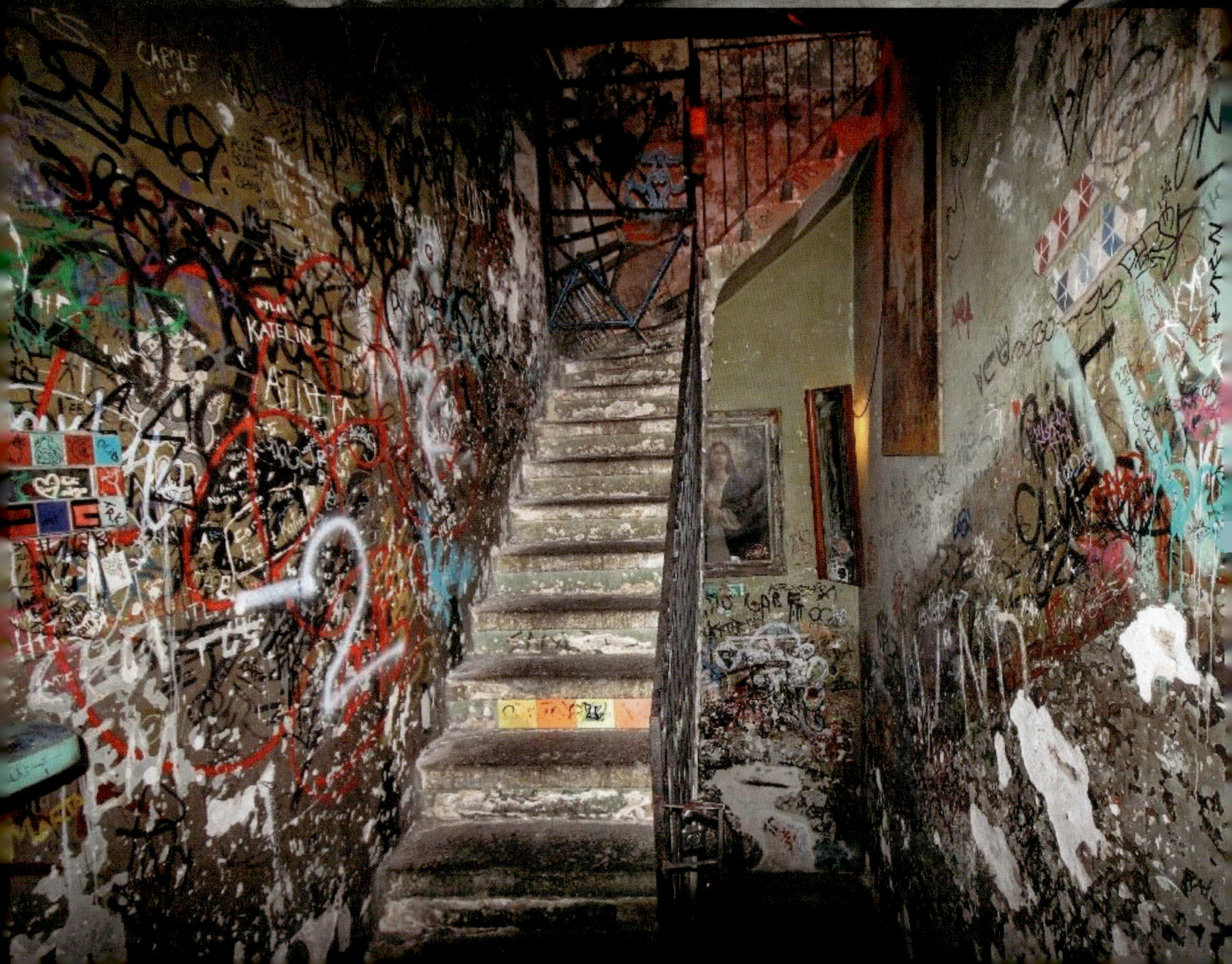

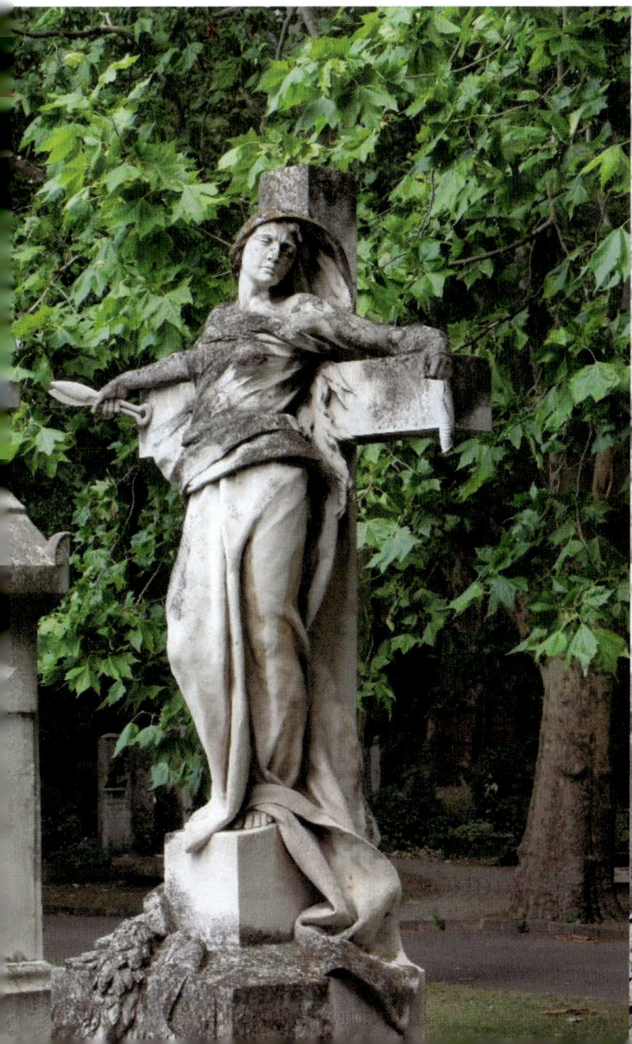
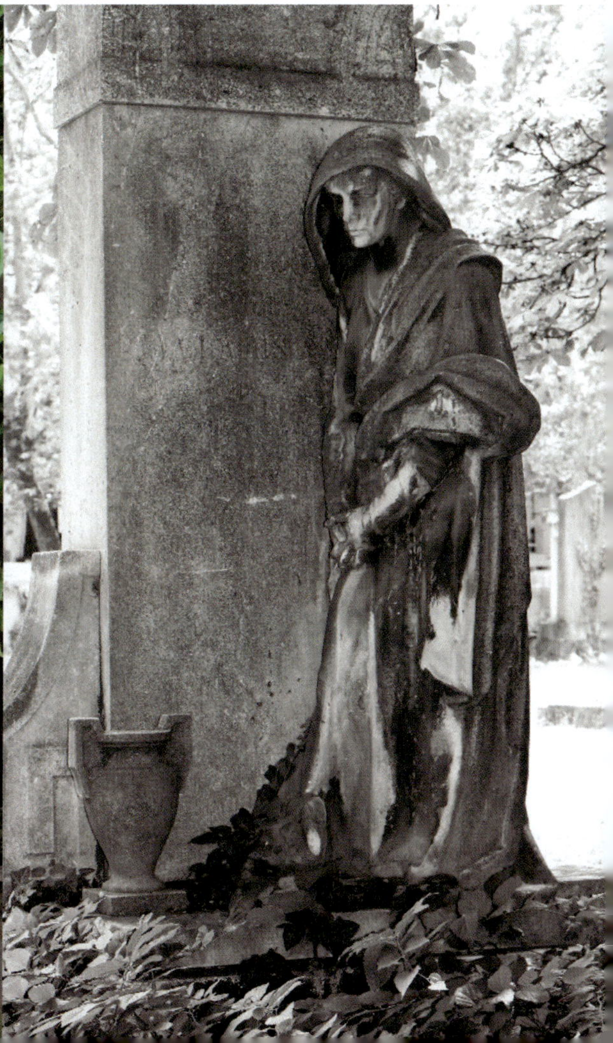

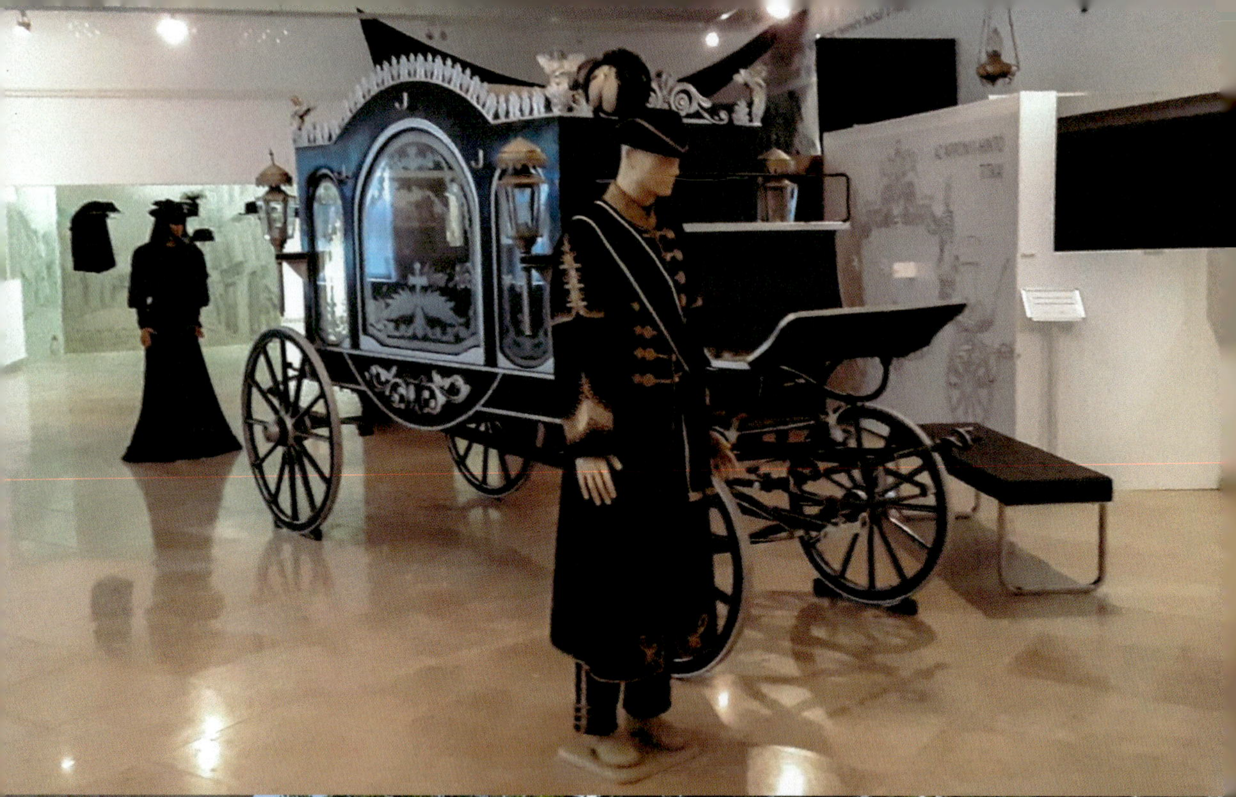

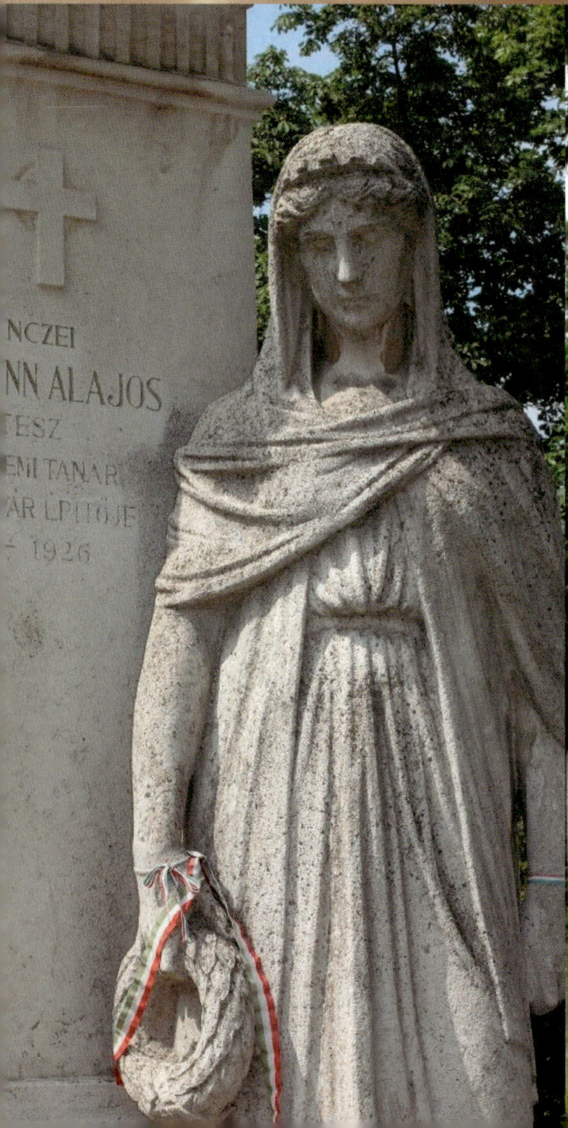
NCZEI
NN ALAJOS
1926

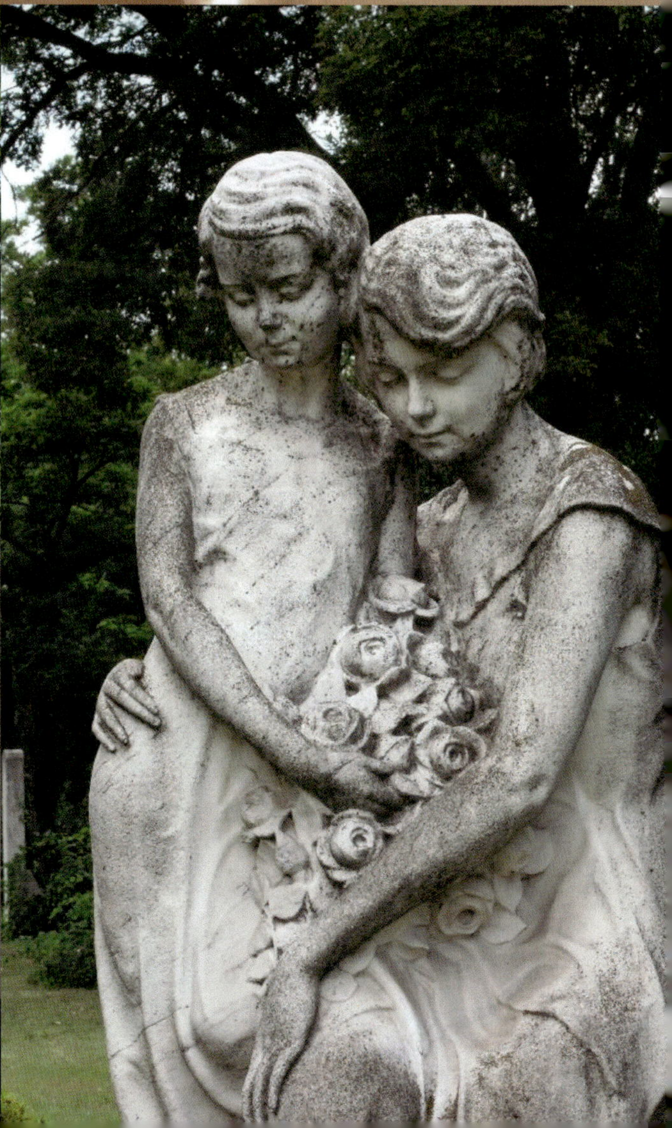

BRATISLAVA, SLOVAK REPUBLIC

One of my camera lenses broke and I walked from the ship into town. No one smiled as I passed and the few locals I stopped to ask for directions spoke no English. When I finally found the well-equipped camera store the clerk, who spoke English well, said that the person who could help me was away until the next day. We would be gone by then.

Bratislava is the capital of Slovakia. The first stop for our visit was to take an excursion bus up the hill to Bratislava Castle. There is a great view of the city from the castle. The castle is interesting on the outside and there is a nice garden in the back of the building. We didn't tour the inside.

When we reached the bottom of the hill, we were left with our guide in the old town area. Within 10 minutes it started to rain so hard that we took shelter wherever we could find respite from the torrential rain. It seemed appropriate to me that it rained because the town seemed dreary. By the end of the 20-minute tour the rain cleared, and we were left to explore on our own.

We went inside some small churches and we stumbled upon a very small park that had some interesting modern sculpture. We saw artwork around town that helped to liven up the otherwise drab atmosphere of the town. There was a doorway with a painting of a cat and a garden scene. Ivy crawled up the walls of the building and surrounded the doorway. There was a store that had a painting of a horse drawn on each side of its doorway.

One of the architectural highlights was the Opera of the Slovak National Theater building; designed by Viennese architects.

St. Martin's church was unique because part of the old city fortress is built into the side of the building. Right near there is a building with many pictures drawn on the side. I'm not sure why they are there, but it adds color to an otherwise drab area.

The Old Town Hall used to serve as a prison and is one of the oldest buildings in Bratislava.

We were able to see the well-known "Man at Work" statue that was made as a joke but has grown a life of its own. You may have seen it before. (The man peering out of a manhole with a sign behind/next to him.)

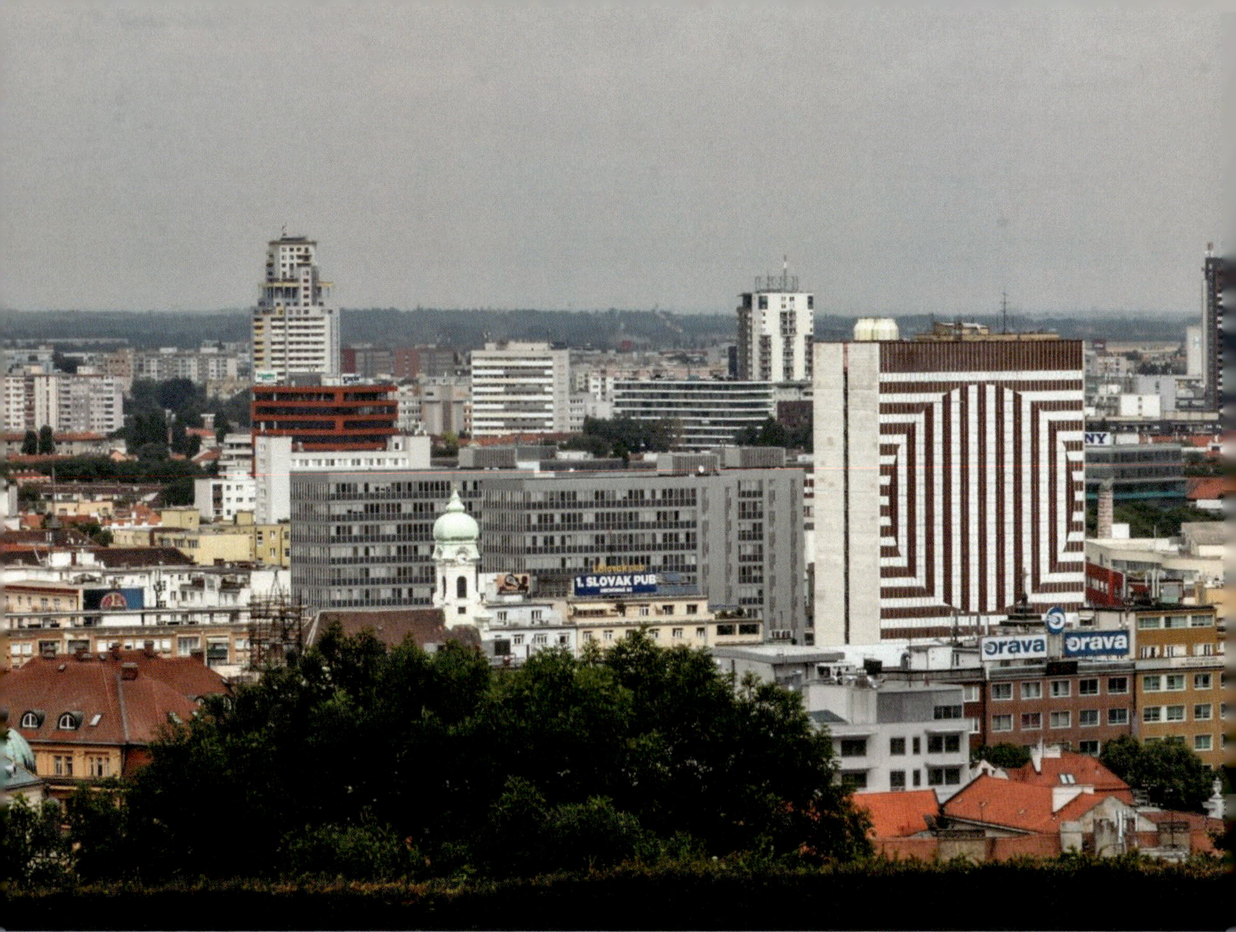
1. SLOVAK PUB
orava
orava

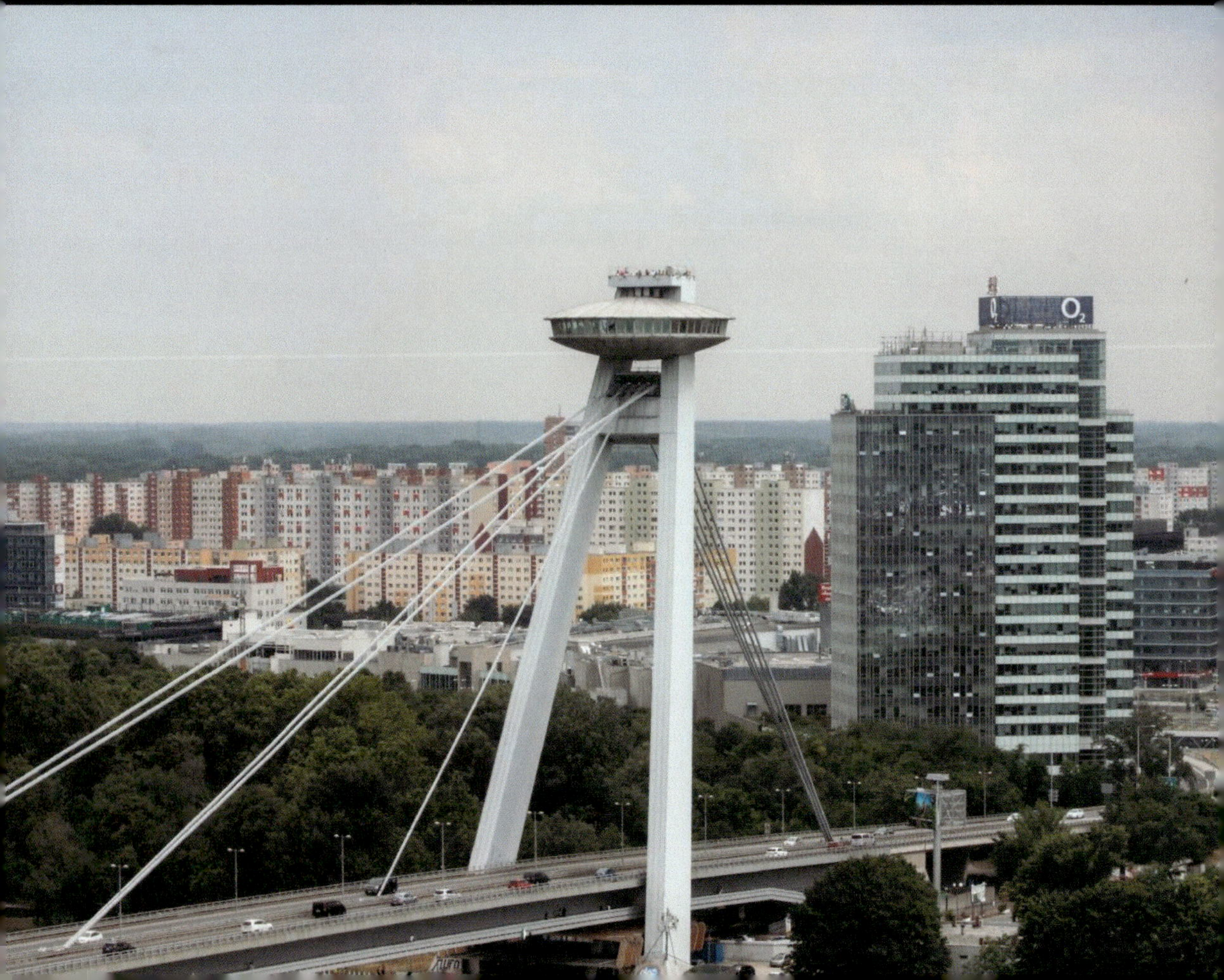
O2

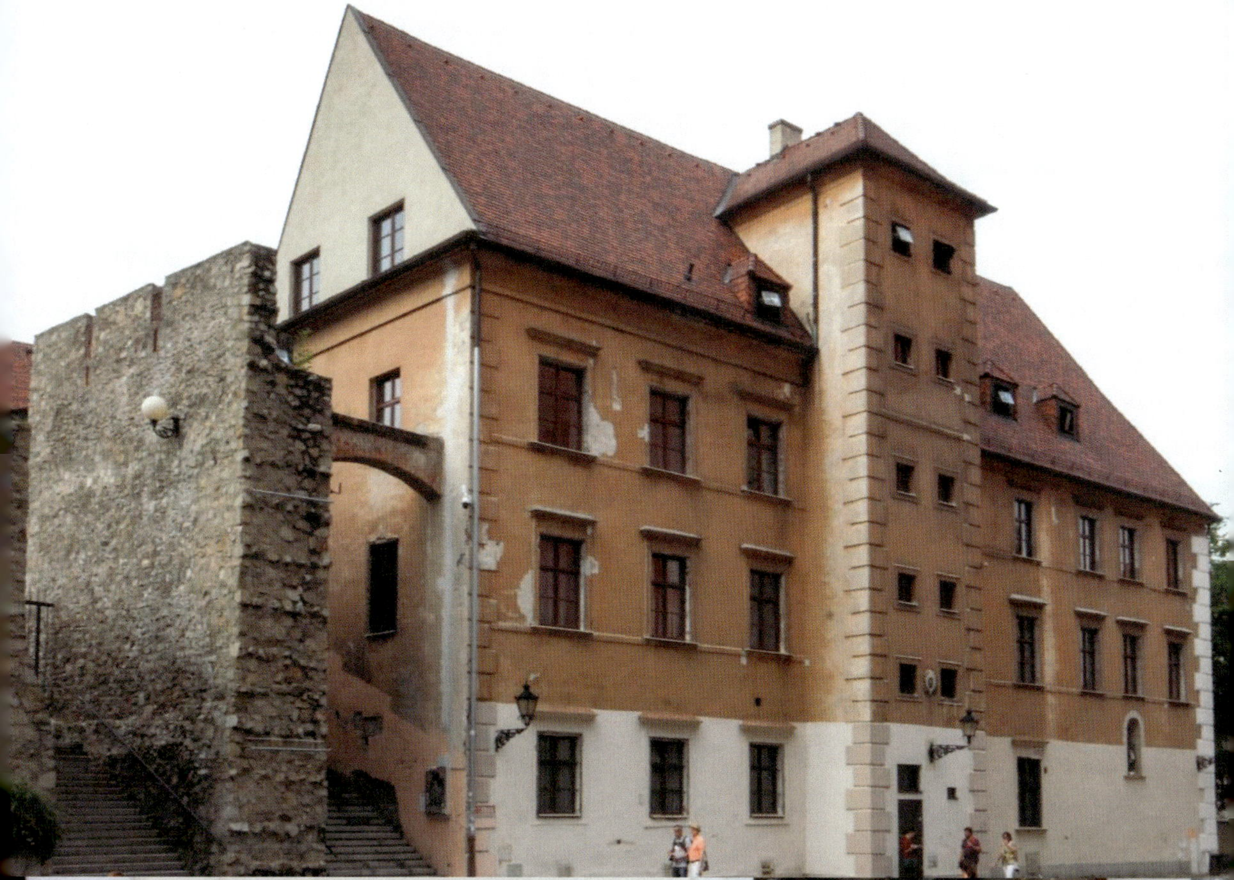

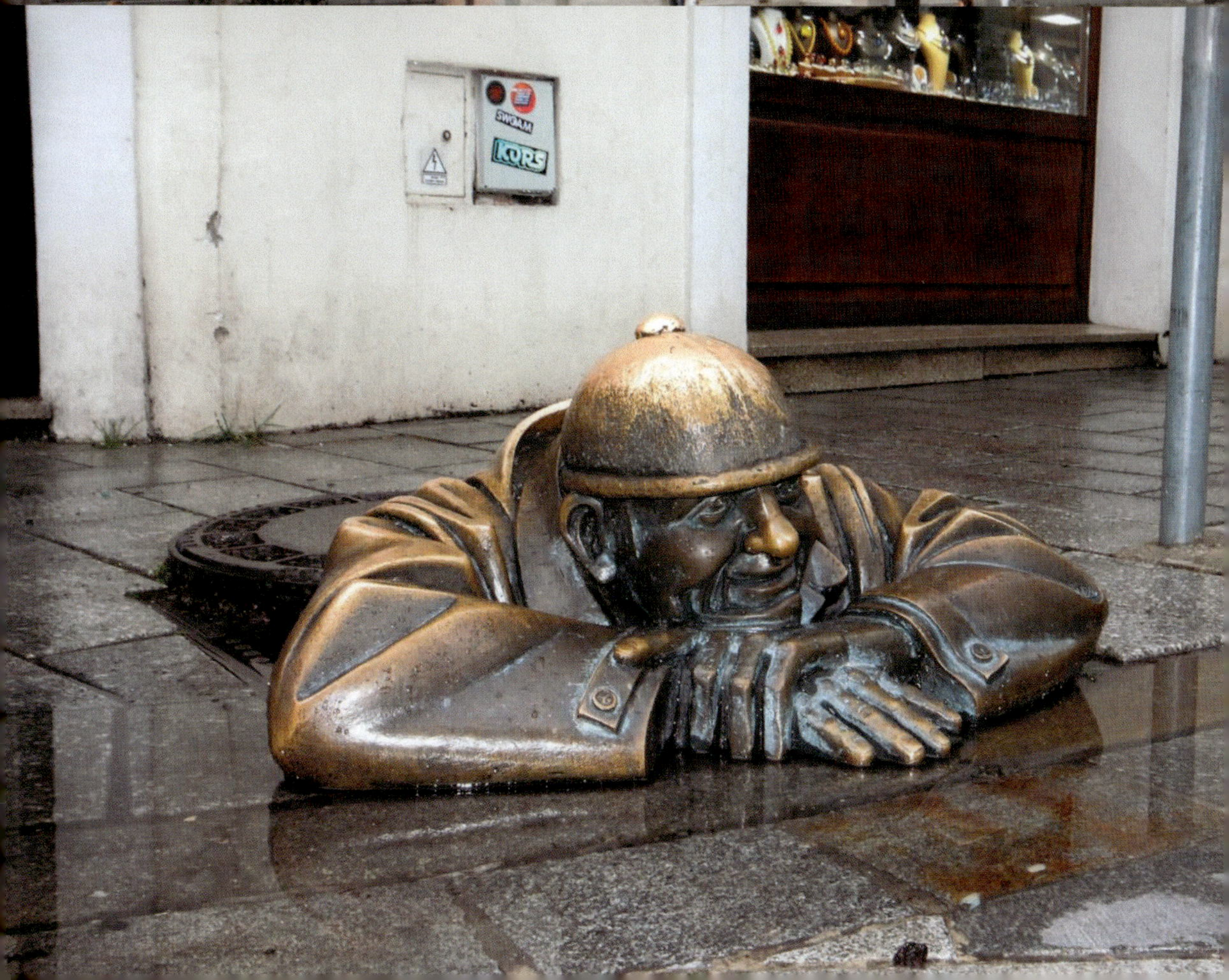
KURS

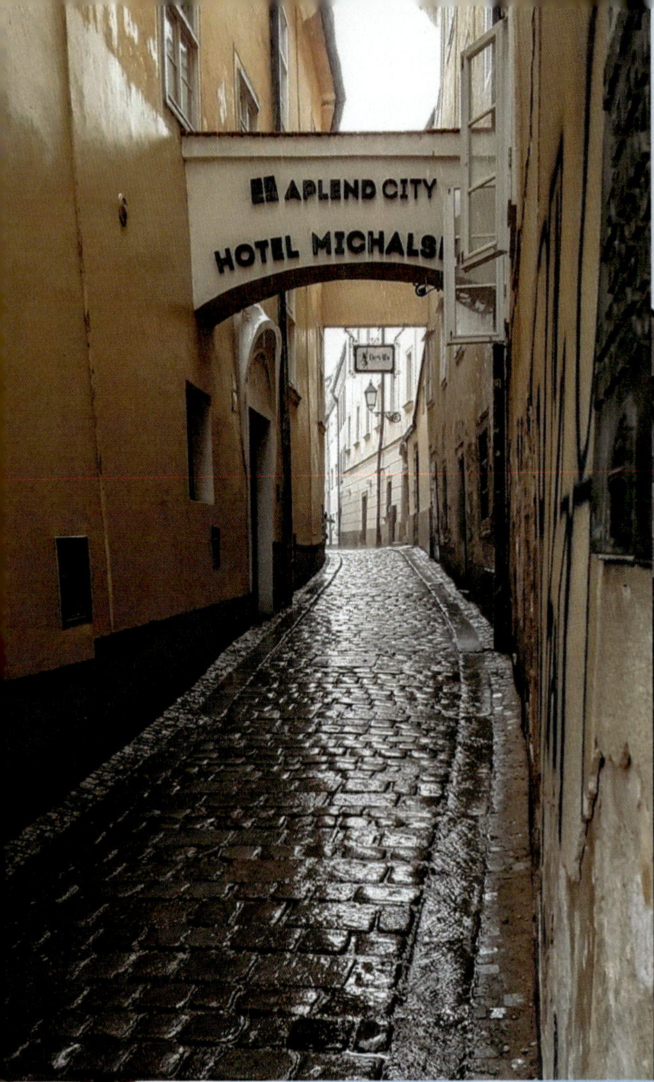
APLEND CITY
HOTEL MICHALS

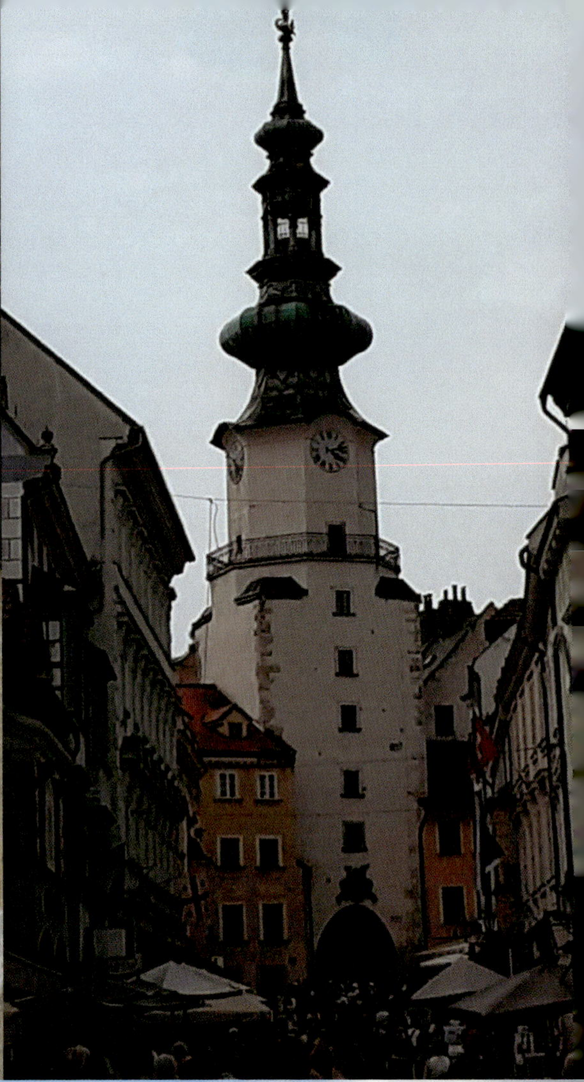

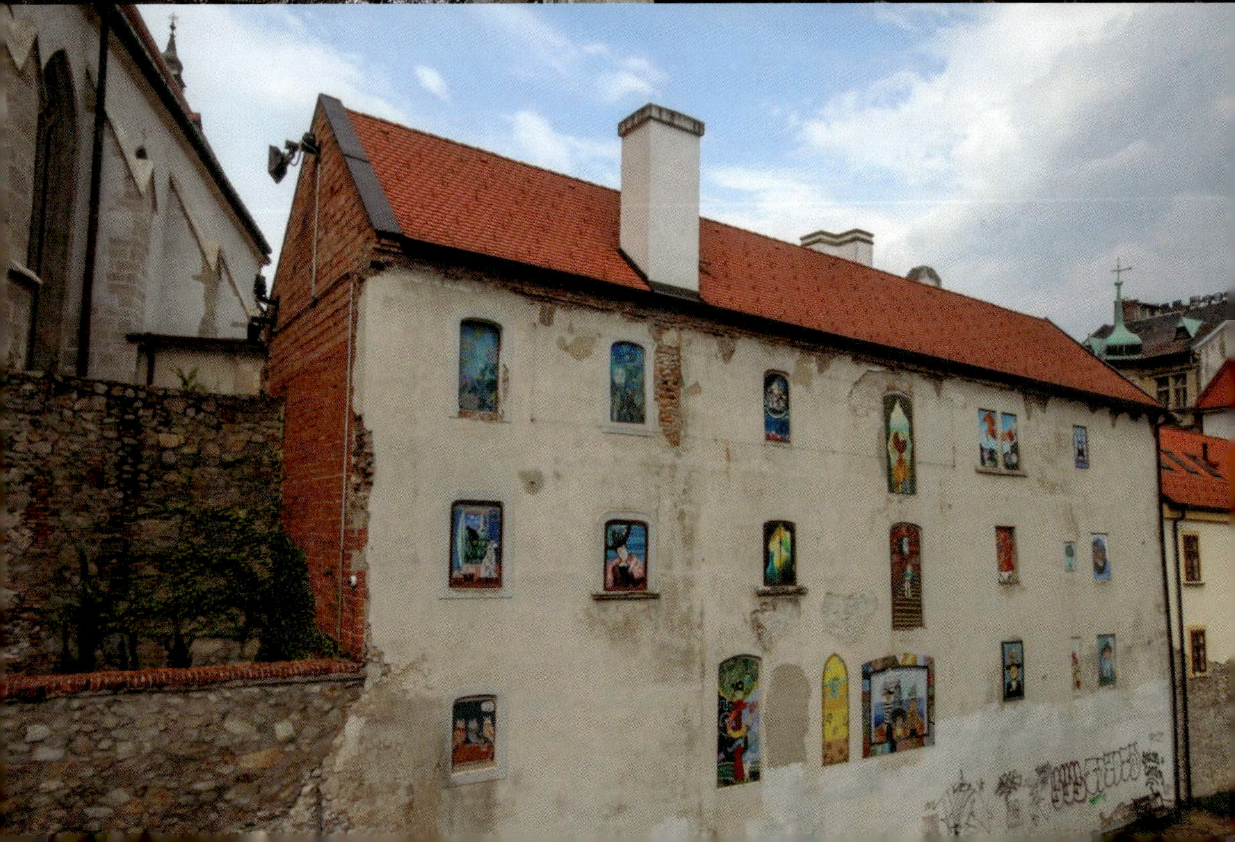

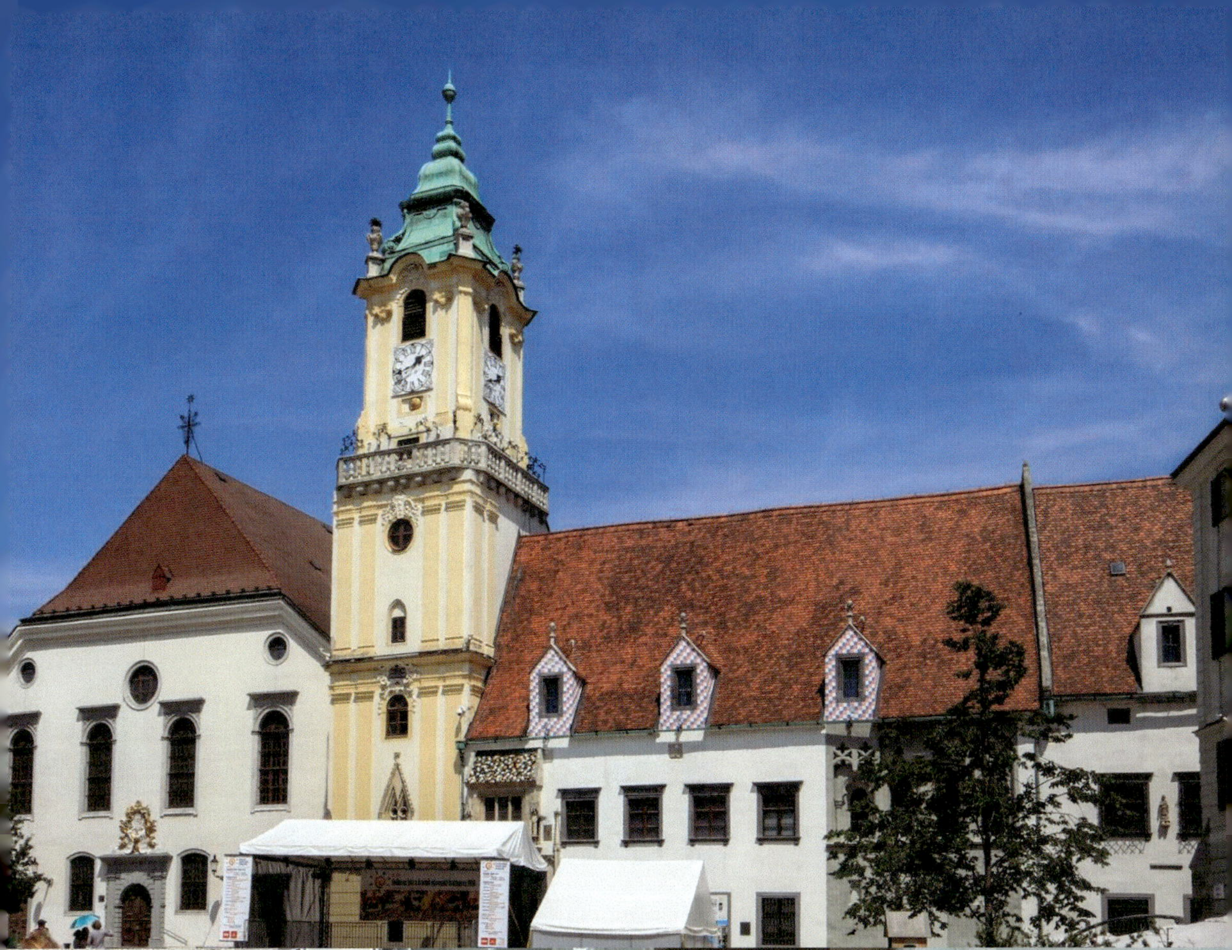

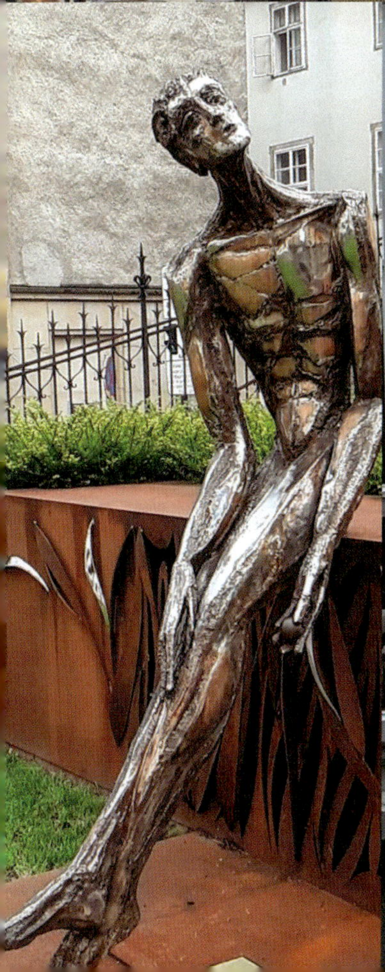

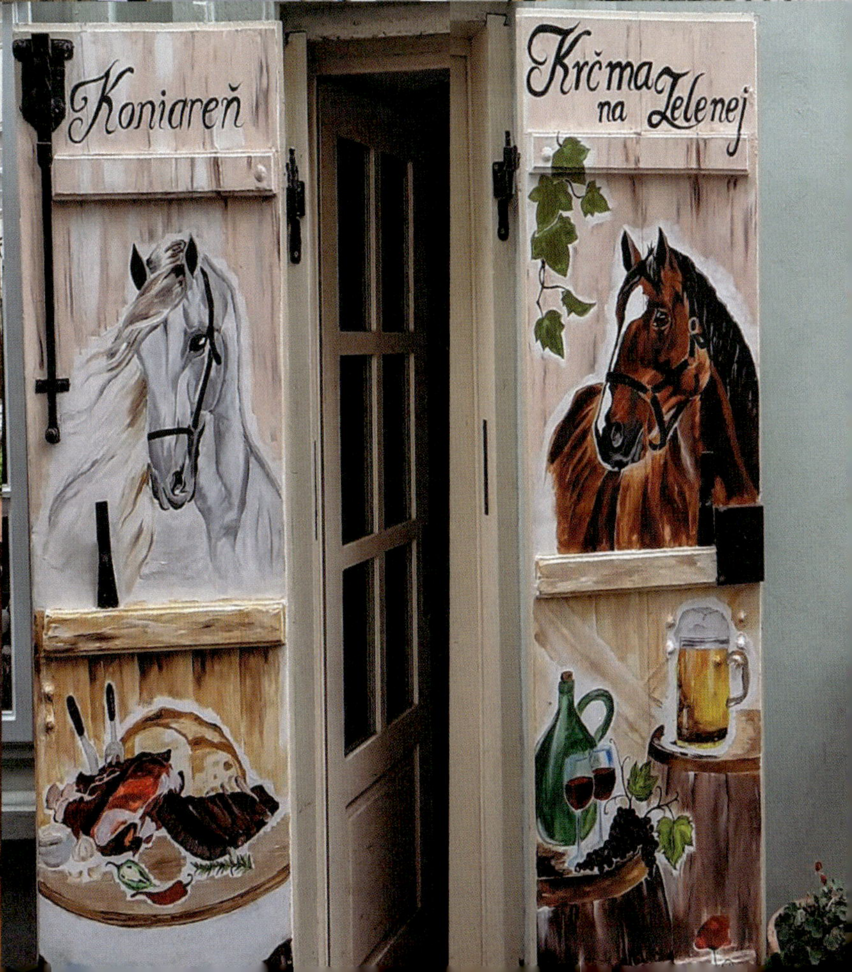
Koniareň
Krčma na Zelenej

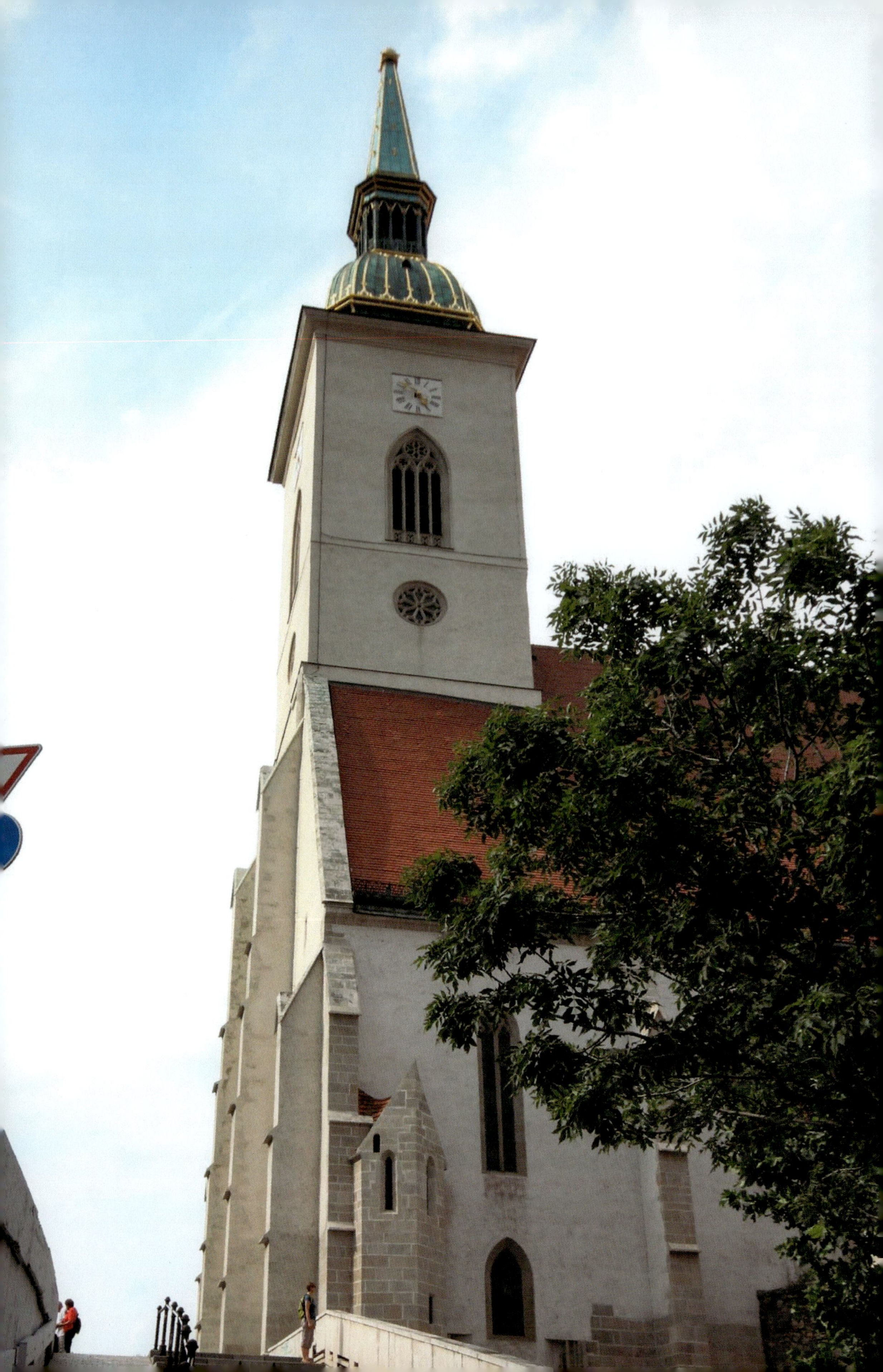

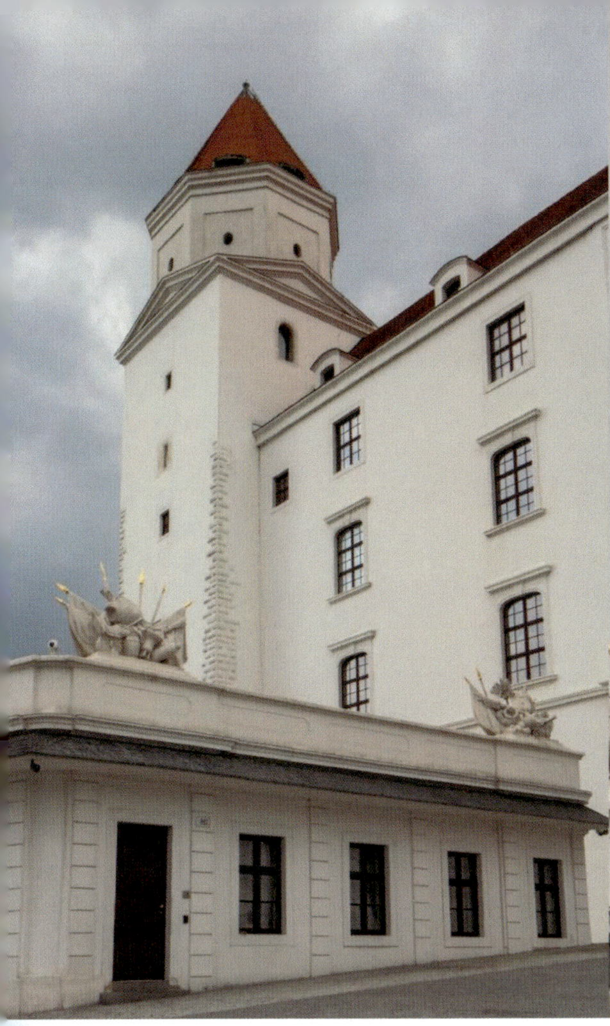
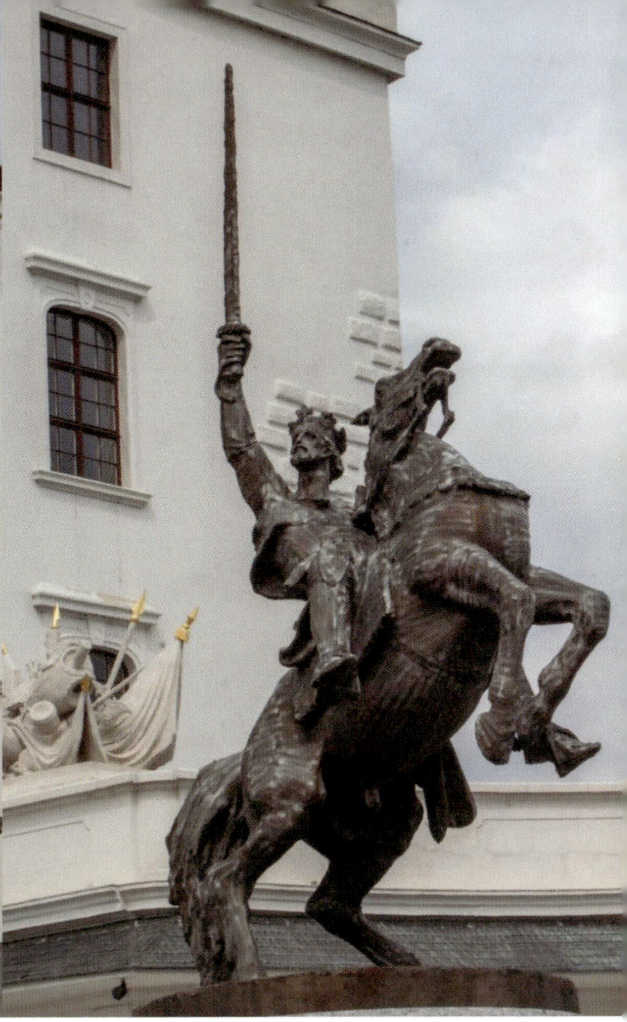
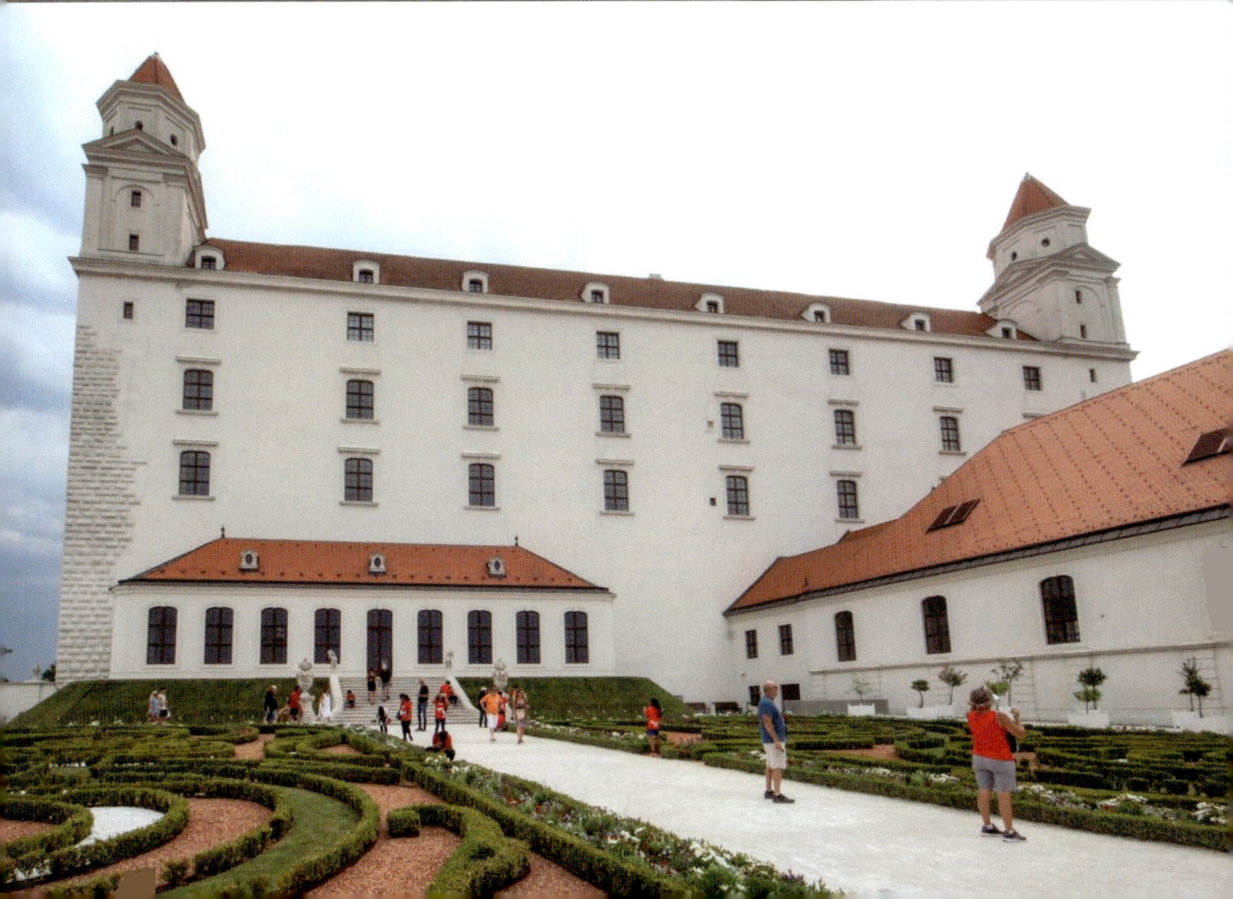

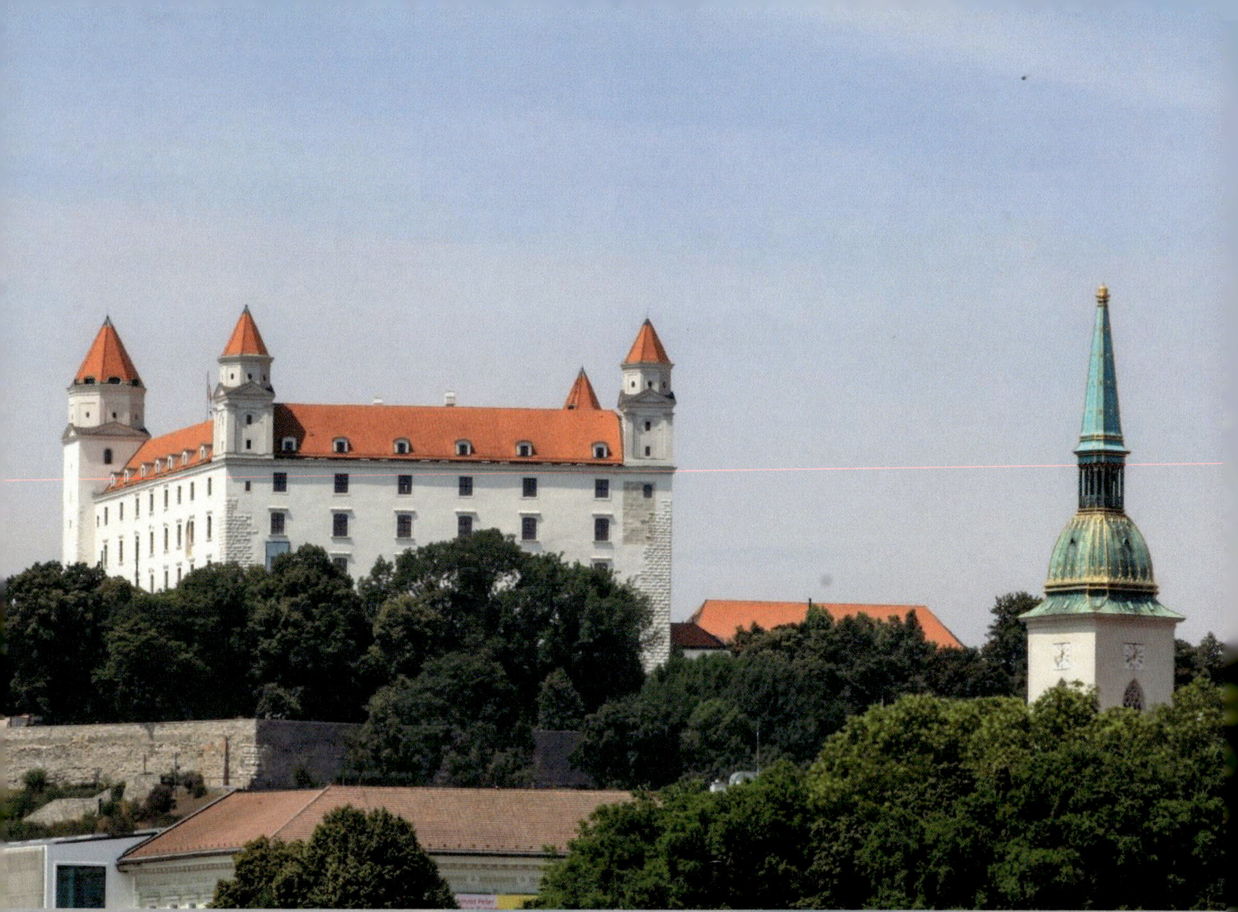

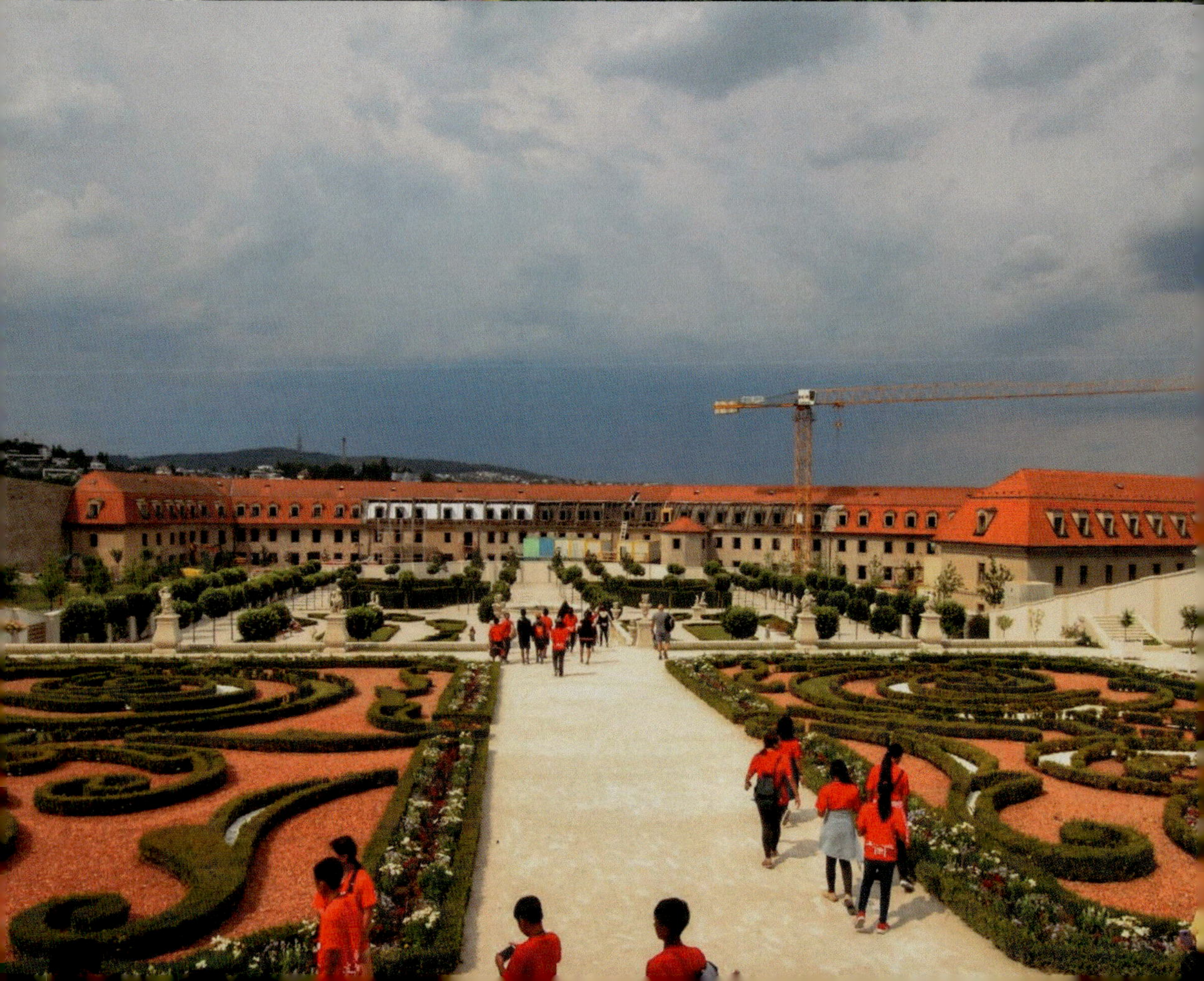

HVIEZDOSLAV

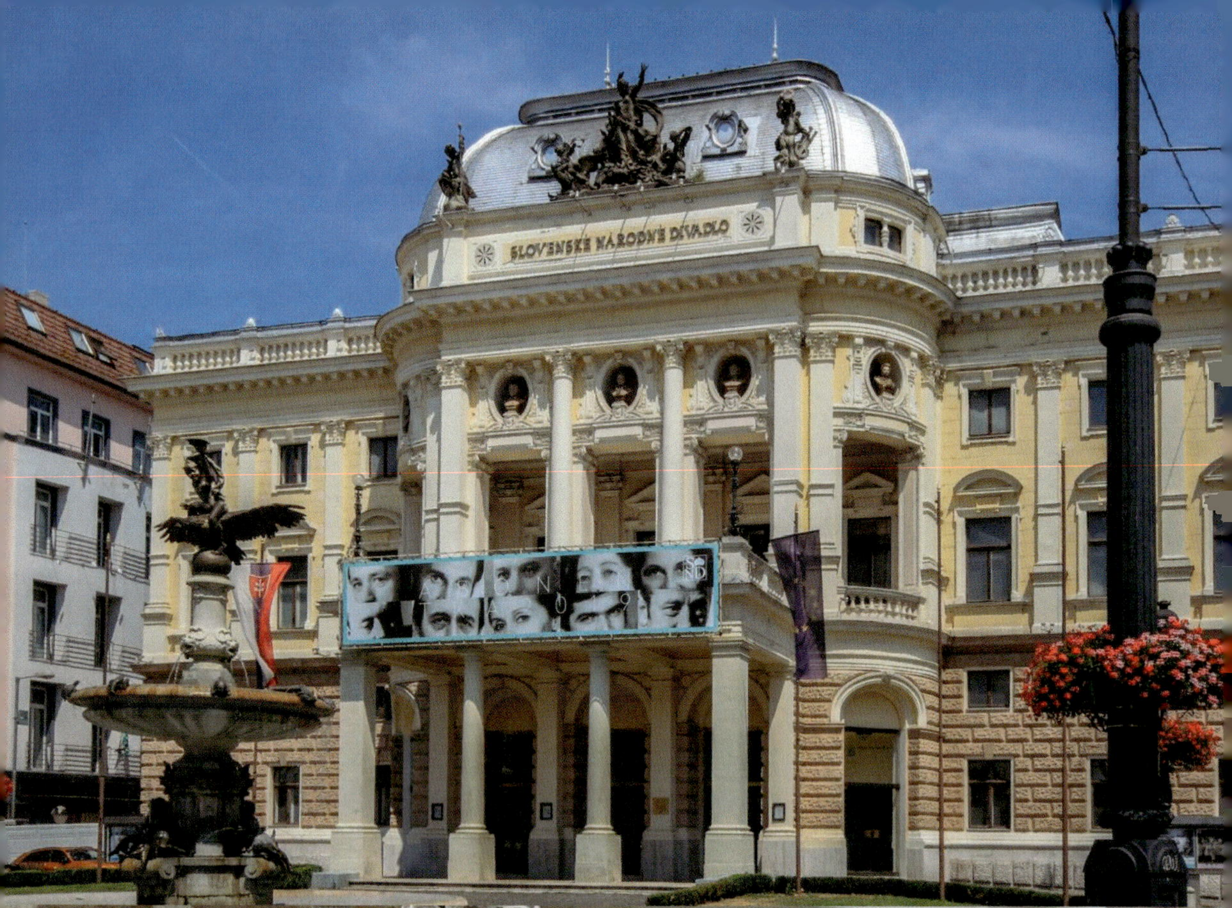
SLOVENSKÉ NÁRODNÉ DIVADLO

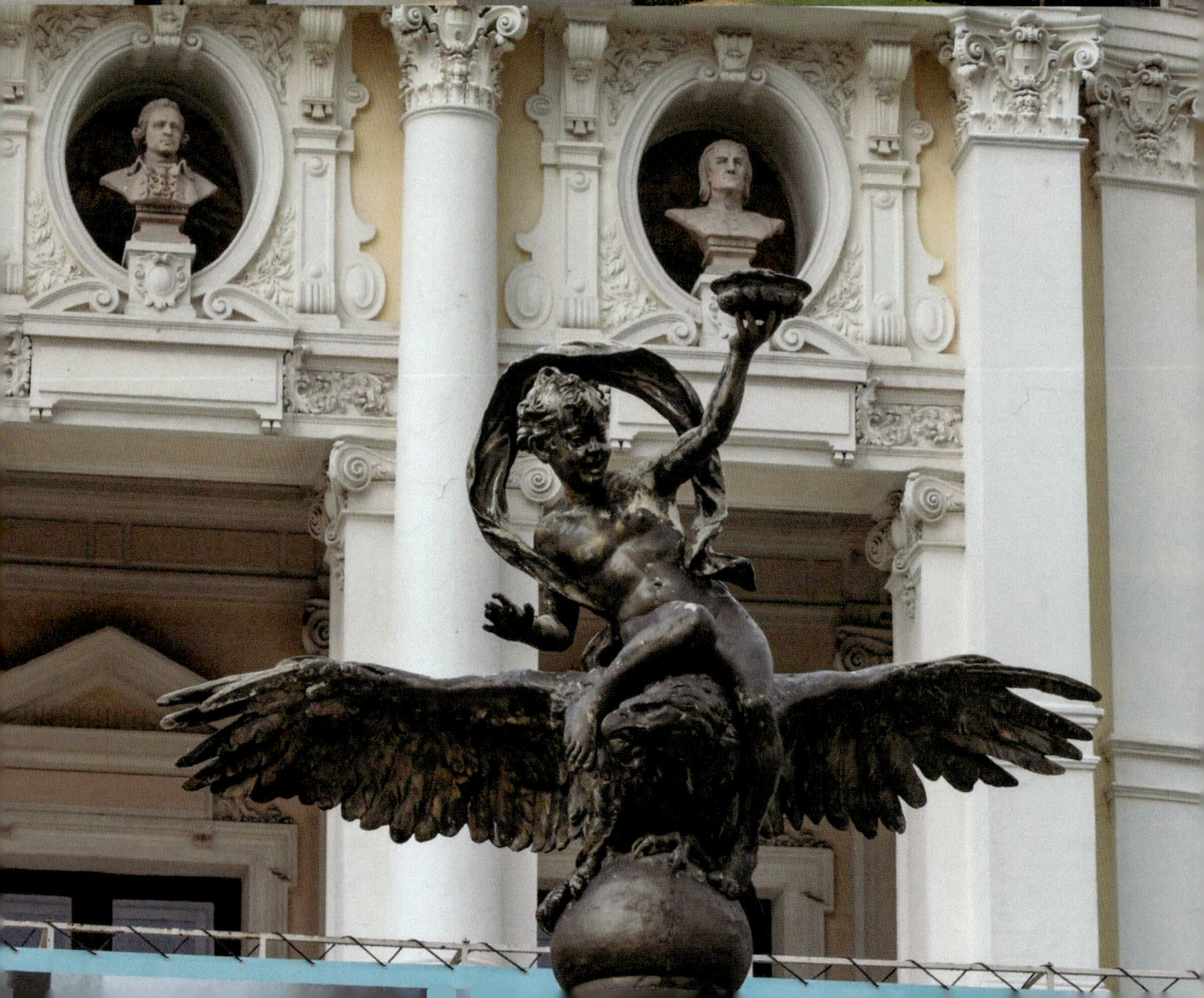

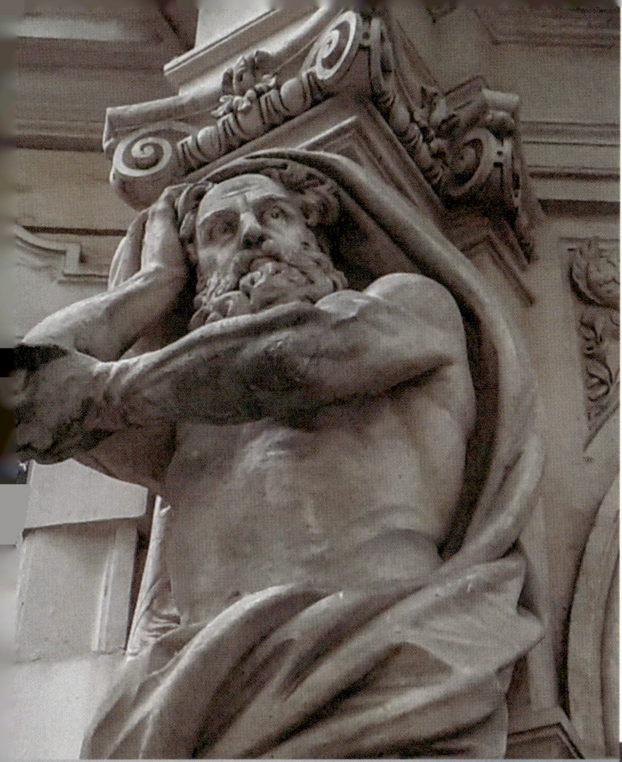

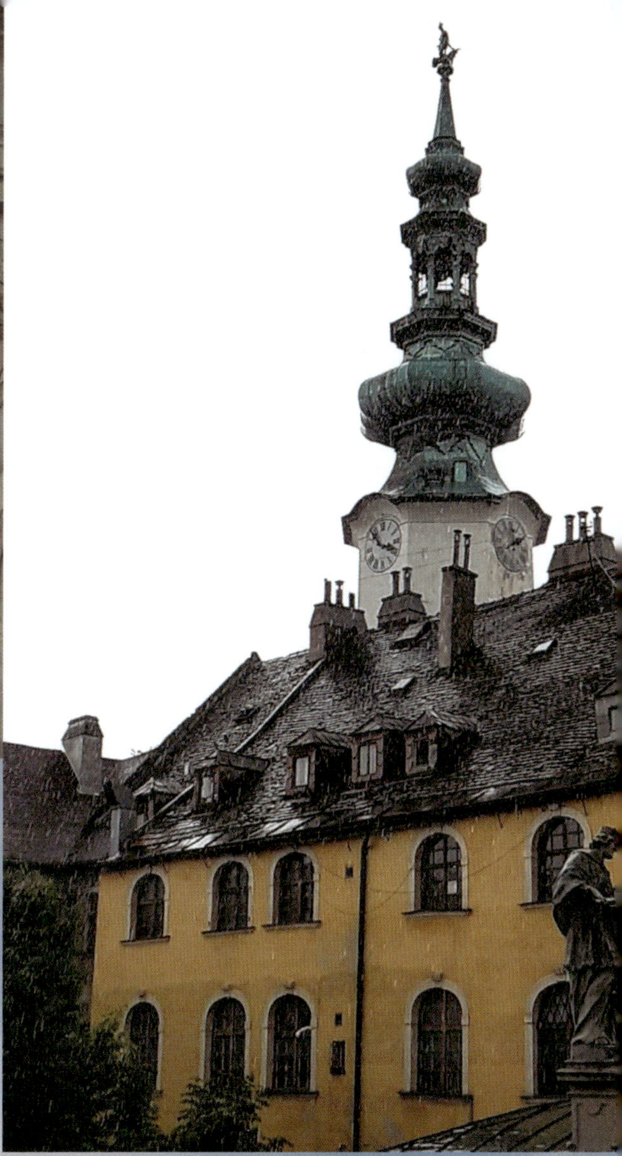

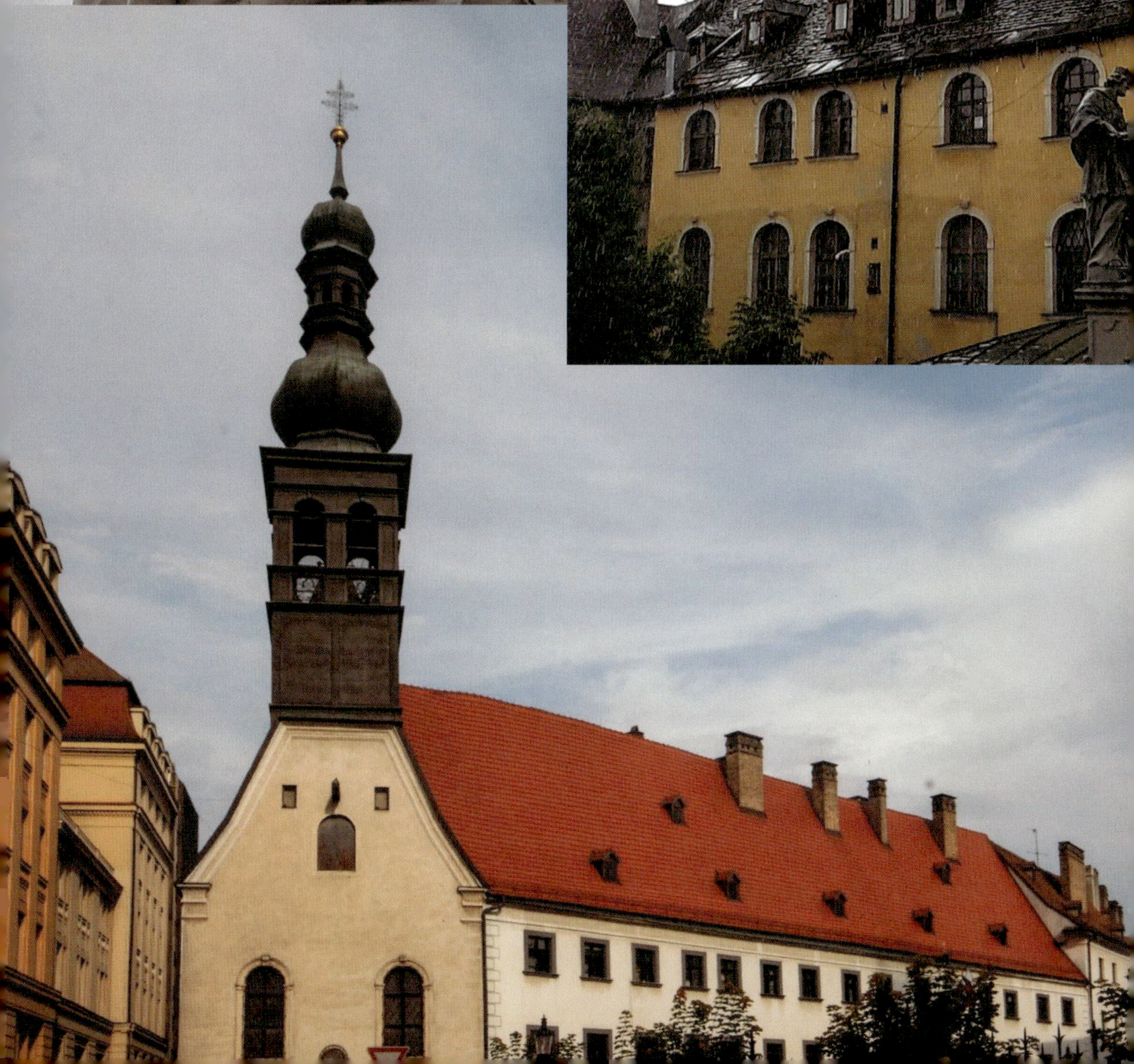

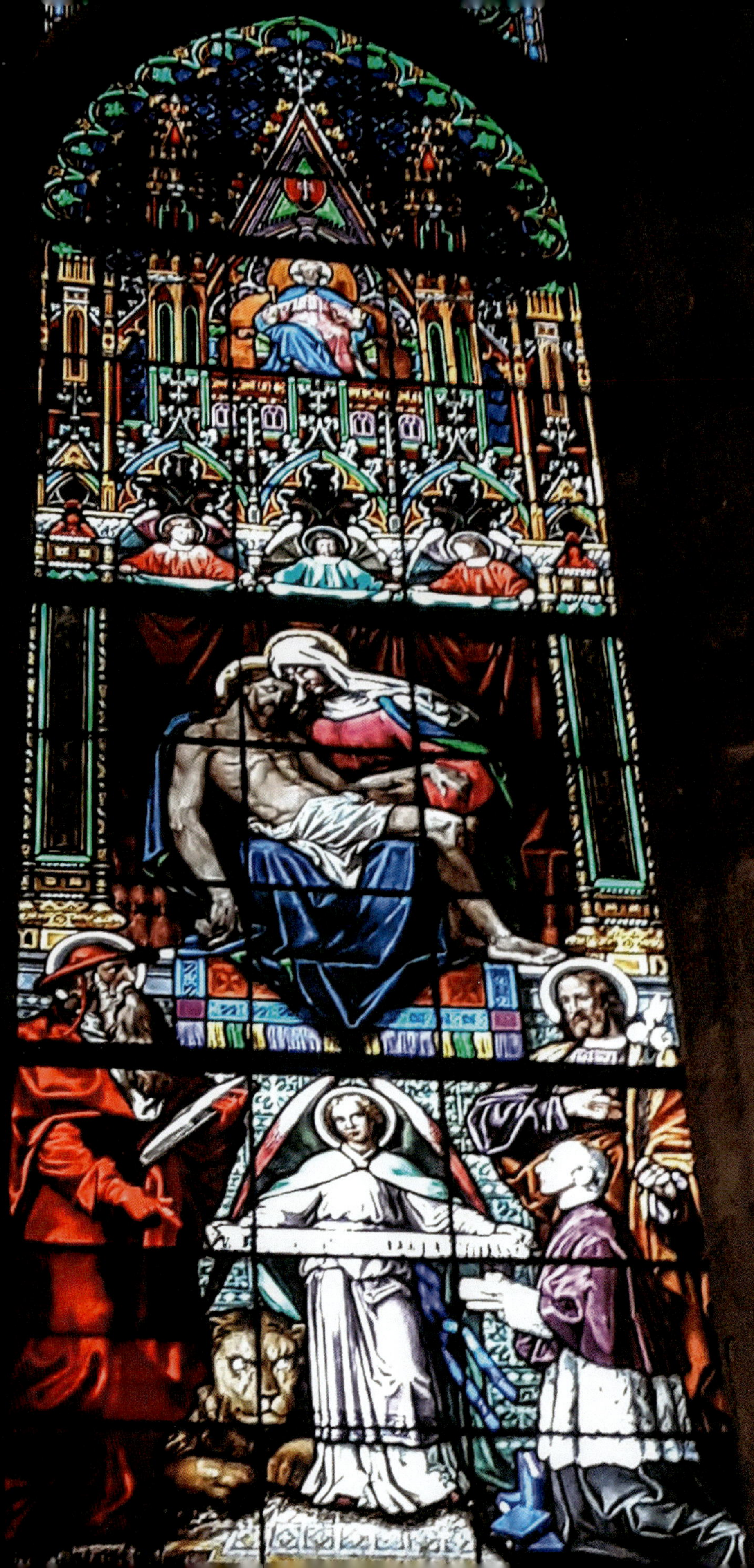

VIENNA, AUSTRIA

The town was a 10-minute bus ride from our ship. We did the usual drive-by sightseeing which included several buildings that were challenging to see from the bus, but which sounded impressive.

When we were dropped off in town our guide took us on a walking tour. We tried to stay in the shade as much as possible since it was an extremely hot day. The tour started near the Museum of Fine Arts and the large statue that sits between that museum and the Museum of Natural History. Then we passed Hofberg Palace. The Palace and nearby building were large and imposing but didn't have an abundance of character. This contrasted with St. Stephen's Cathedral which was both large and unique in its design. The tour ended without a visit inside the cathedral, but we went inside right after the tour.

The two couples from the ship tagged along. We weren't sure what to see next, so we asked the guide. She made some recommendations, however we were hungry then, so we walked to the restaurant where I had made a reservation. Originally the reservation was for 2, then the couple from western Pennsylvania wanted to come, and then the couple from California also wanted to join us.

We ate at Brezl Gwölb. The dining for lunch was outside at picnic tables with umbrellas. A cool breeze drifted through the area. At the table near us was a woman with a small dog. I'm not sure what kind of dog it was, however, it looked like a miniature greyhound.

There were large soft pretzels hanging on a stand on the table. We later found out that if you eat them you are charged on the bill. We were hungry, and they were tasty, so we didn't mind (much.) The food there was a mixed bag, but the atmosphere of the outdoor garden was relaxing and best of all, it was far away from the hordes of tourists near St. Stephen's Cathedral.

There is too much to see in Vienna in one day, with no easy way to get around to see all of it. I had found what I thought would be an interesting sight, so our group walked to the nearby Imperial Crypt, also known as Capuchins' Crypt (Kapuzinergruft in German.) This is where 150 Imperial Habsburg family members (including 12 emperors and 18 empresses) are buried. It sits below the church and monastery of the Order of the Capuchin Friars. Visitors can see 107 metal sarcophagi. I found it to be a fascinating, if not quirky, attraction. We heard that there is also some type of crypt under St Stephen's Cathedral.

At this point the group split up because three people were going to attend a concert that evening, so they wanted to rest. I ended up on my own to explore the town. Since it was so hot, I decided to go to the Museum of Fine Arts. The building was beautiful inside and out and the artwork and artefacts were superb.

I walked around the gardens and then went to see the Museum Quarter. I noticed many young people dressed in costumes. Some were superheroes. I found two young women and asked them about the event. They were friendly and explained that it was like Comic Con.

I left the area and walked around side streets and enjoyed the shopping area. There was a large pedestrian zone with a lot of people and shops. I wanted to get back to the ship, so I stopped in a store that sold soap and such to ask for directions. The clerk, an older woman, took a long time to help me find my way. I got on the Metro and headed toward the ship.

I decided to get off the Metro at the Prater stop so I could see the Wiener Riesenrad Ferris wheel that was used in the 1949 British film noir movie The Third Man. The Ferris wheel was to be demolished; however, the city didn't have the funds to remove it, so it remained until it eventually became an attraction. When I arrived at the underground Metro station, I heard a woman singing and dancing. She had a pull-up banner with her name and photo. She sang well so I recorded a few seconds of video. When we returned to the States, I looked her up
online and it turns out that she is well known for her singing in the Metro stations.

The Ferris wheel sits inside the Wurstelprater (called the "Prater") amusement park. I enjoyed walking around the park. To see the Ferris wheel was a highlight for me since I enjoy the movie. The seats are not like regular Ferris wheel seats. They are like a small long shed, or something like that.

Soon I returned to the ship to say goodbye to my wife who was leaving to attend a Mozart/Schubert concert. Later she told me that the concert was the highlight of Vienna for her.

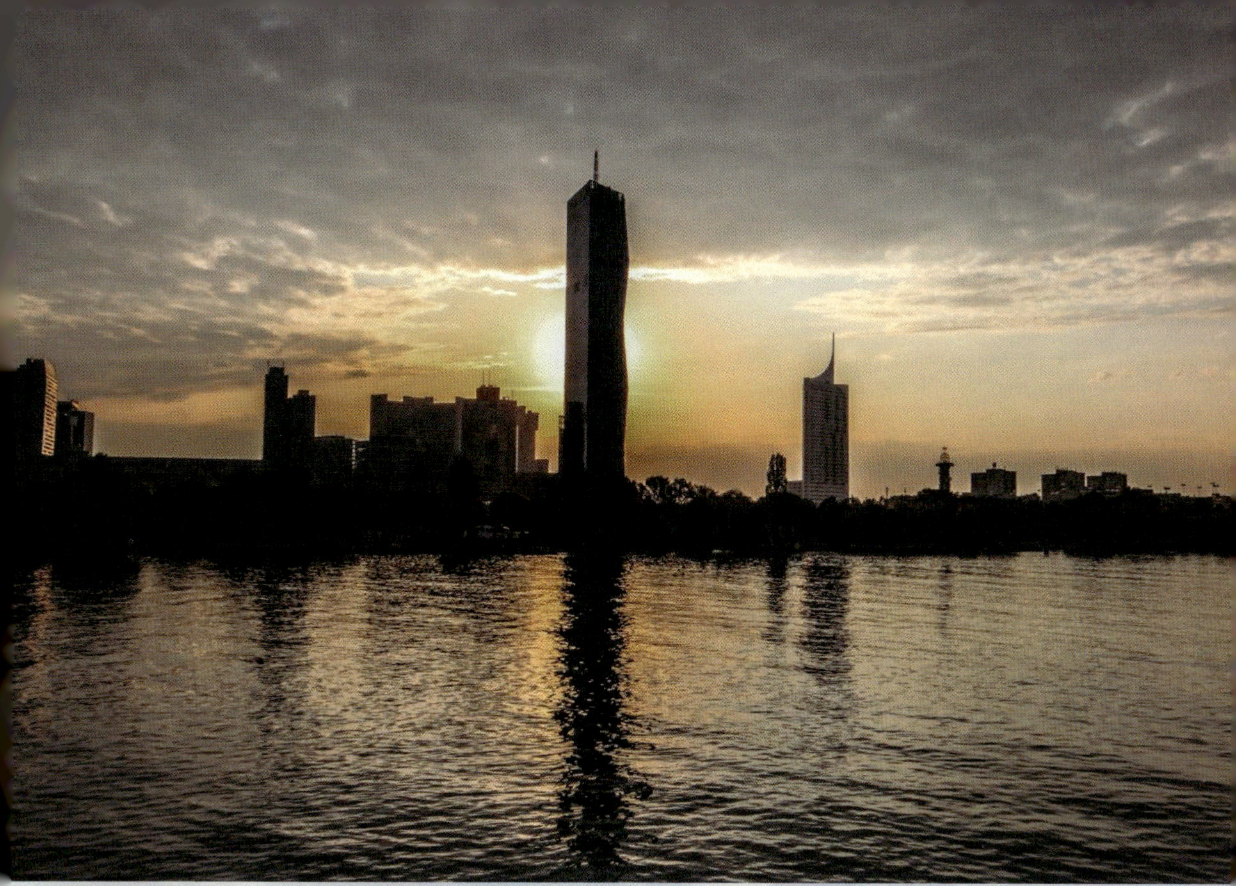

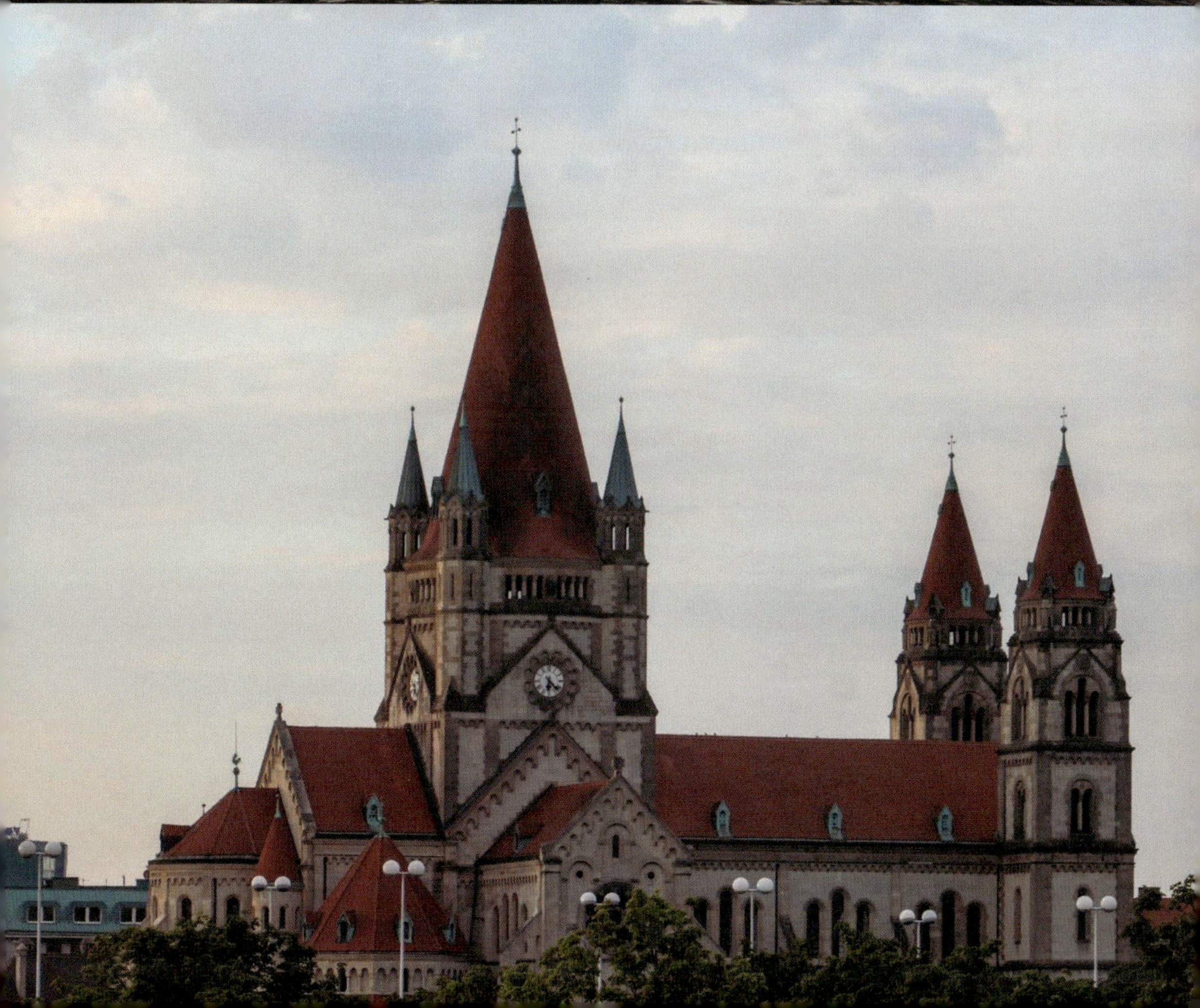

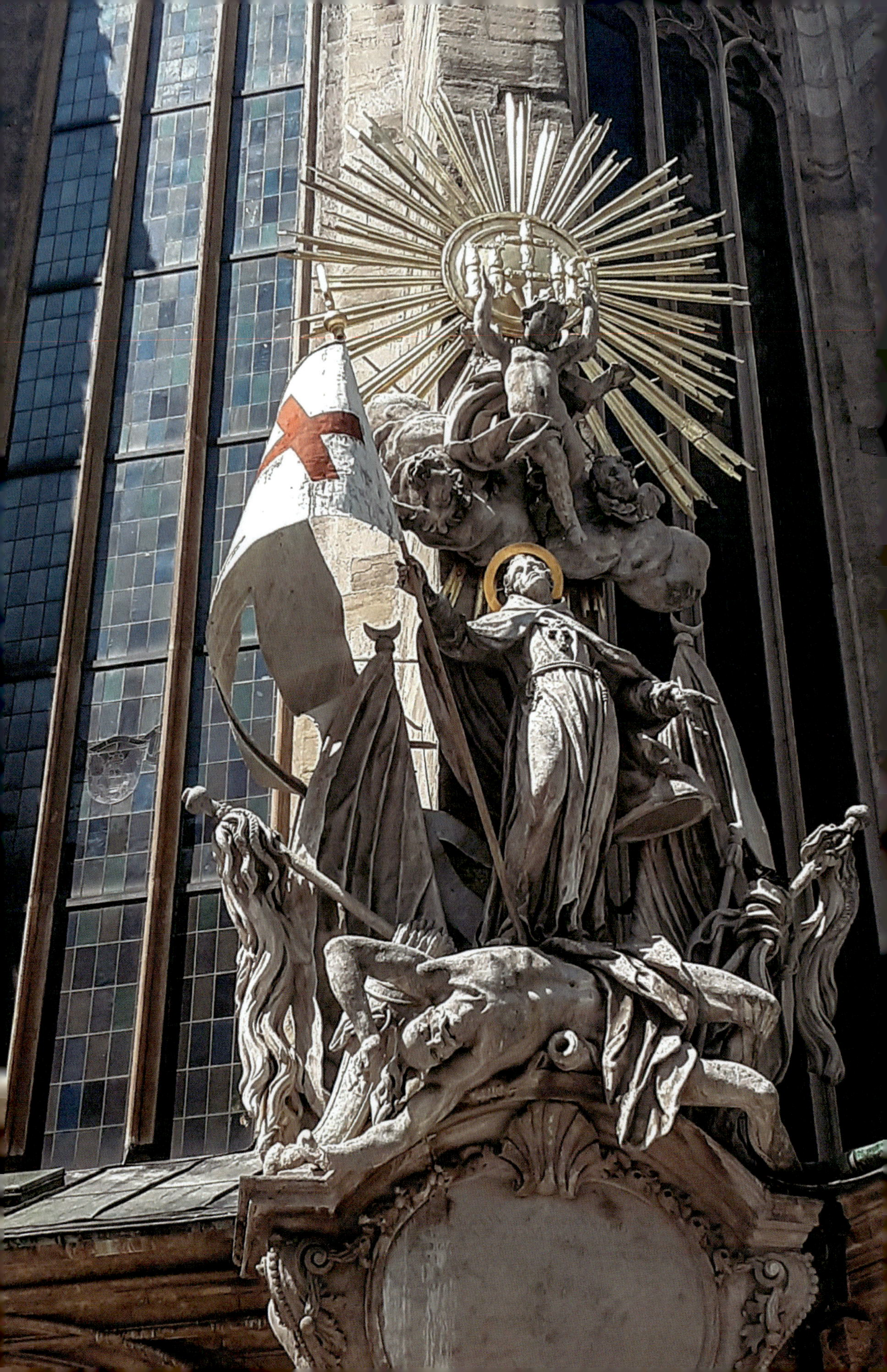

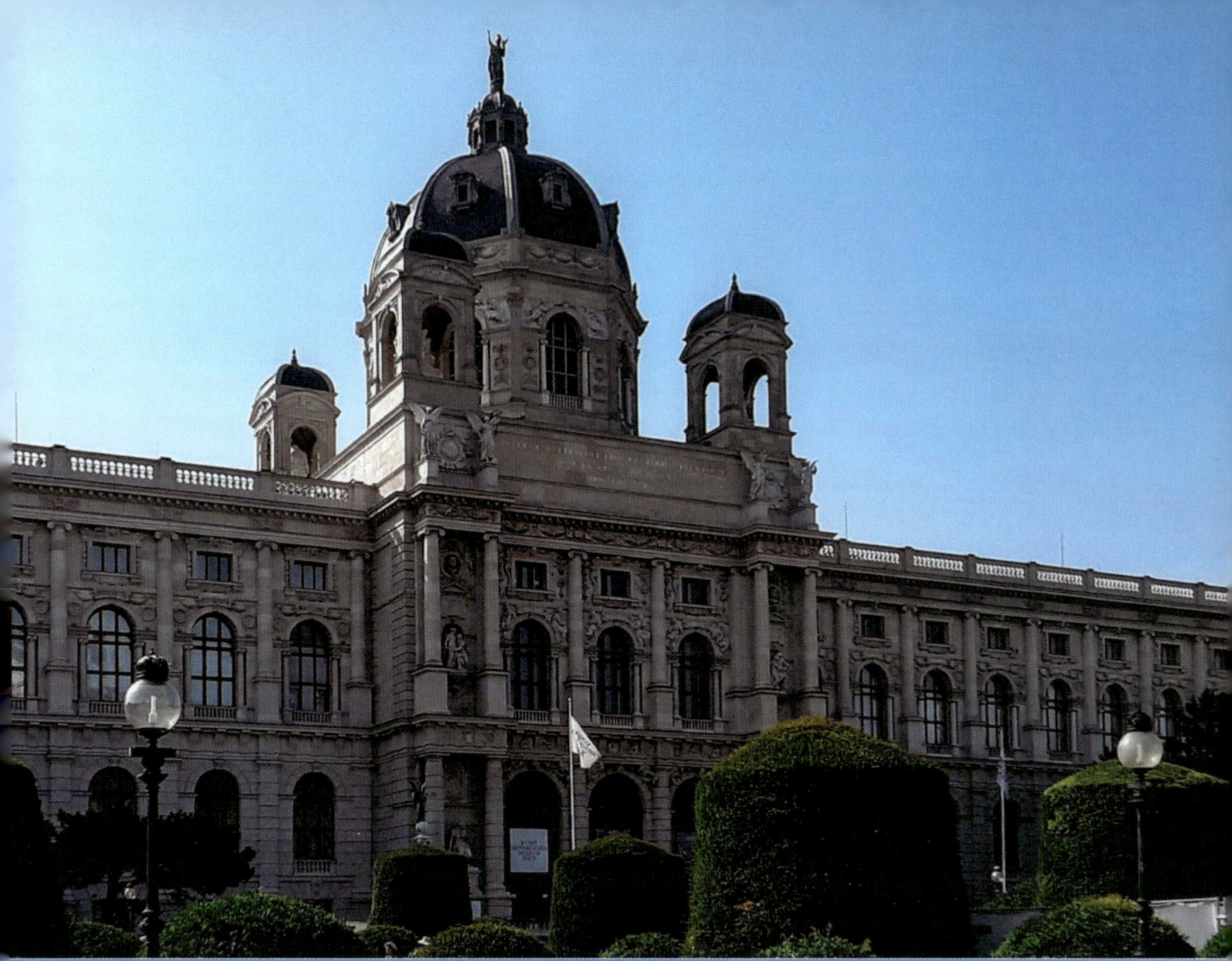

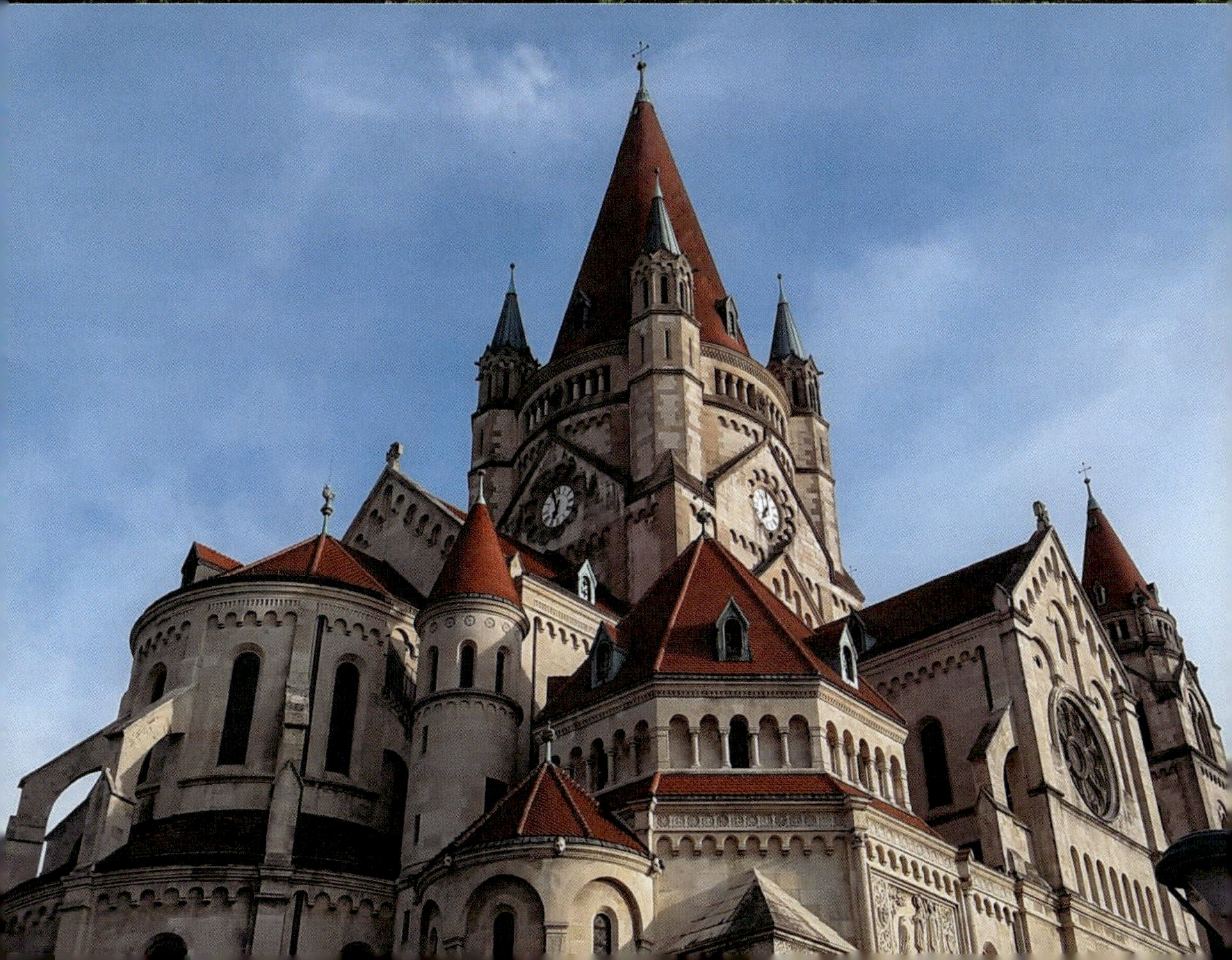

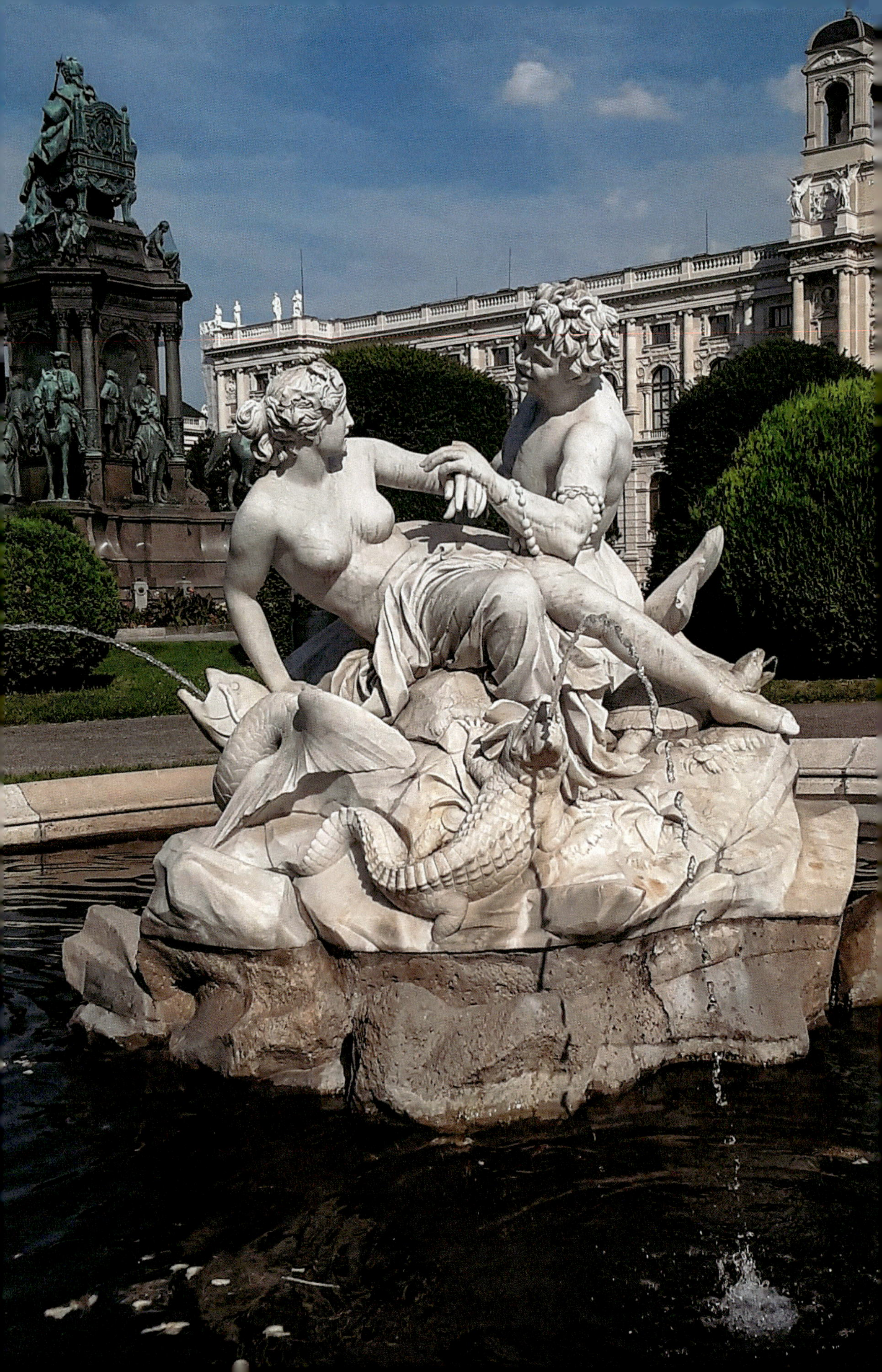

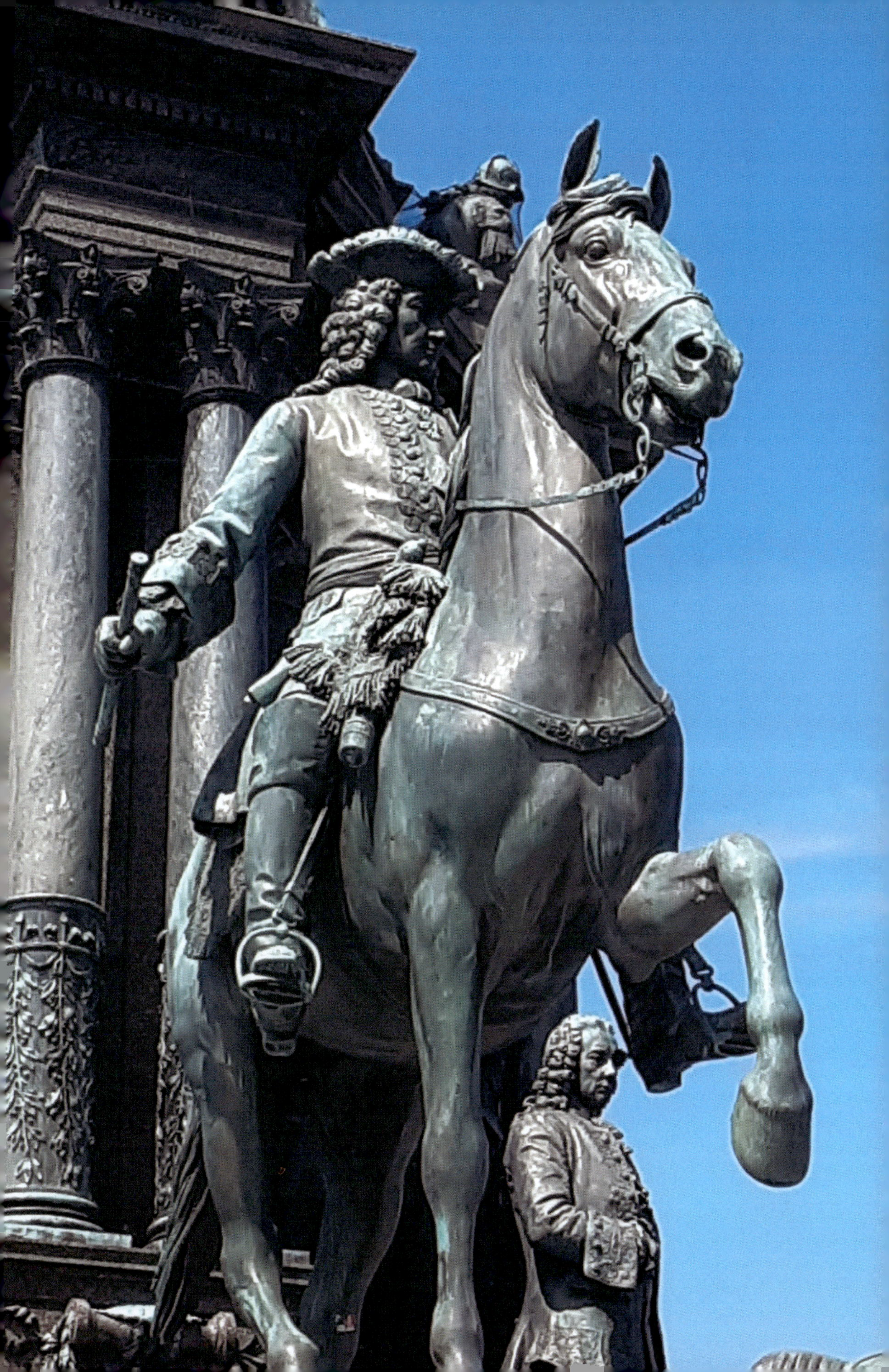

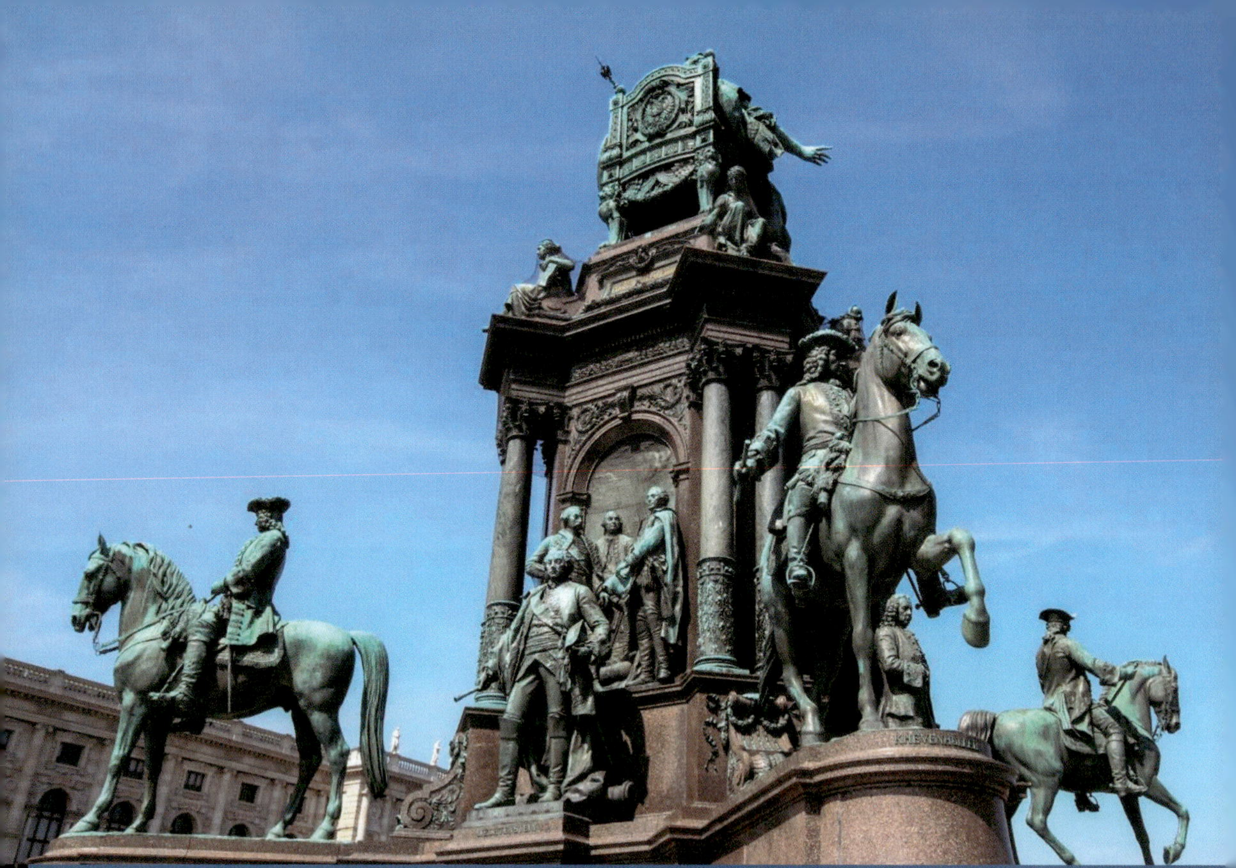

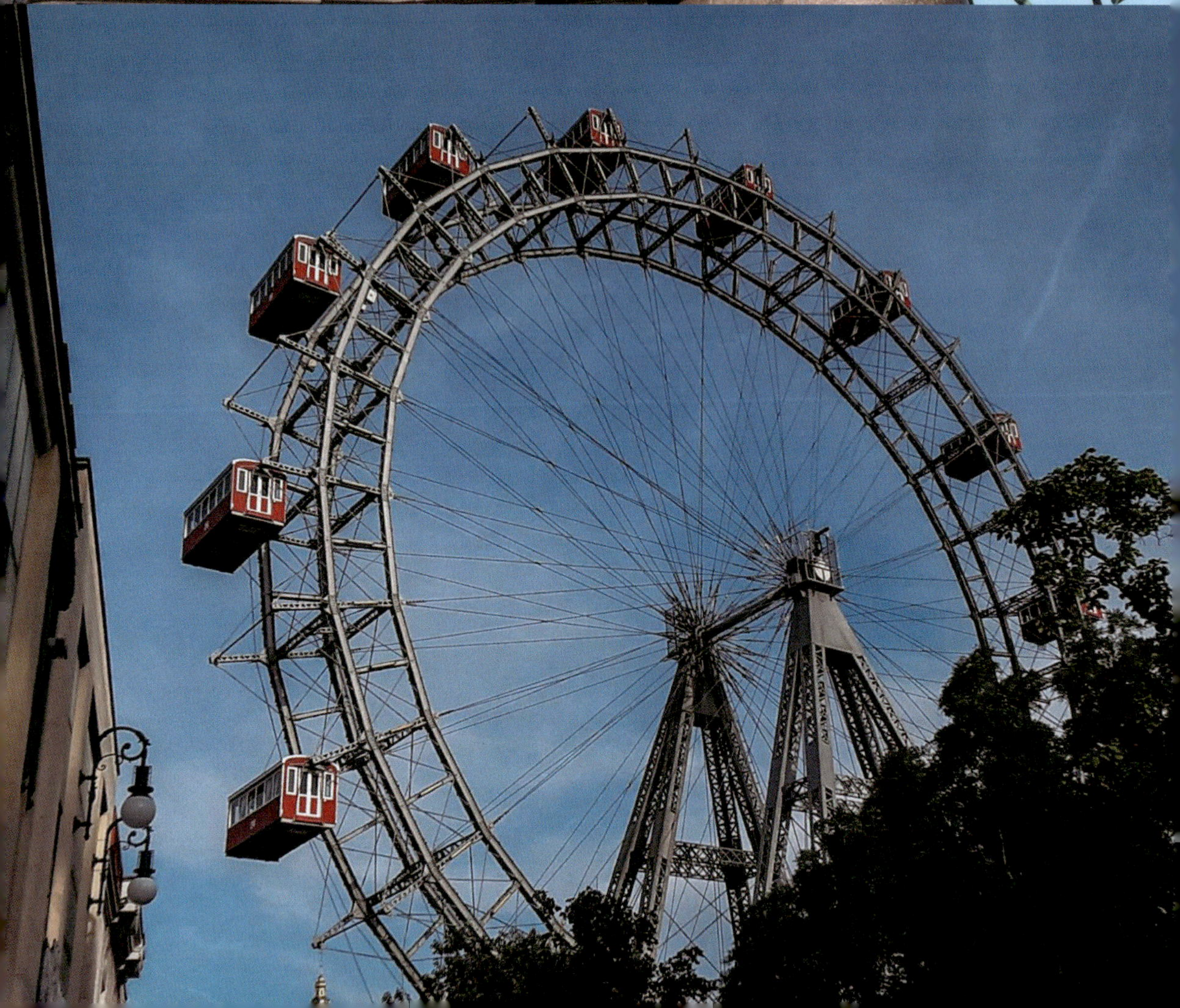

AMOREM · MEVM · POPVLIS · MEIS

Erbaut 1736
Restauriert 1879

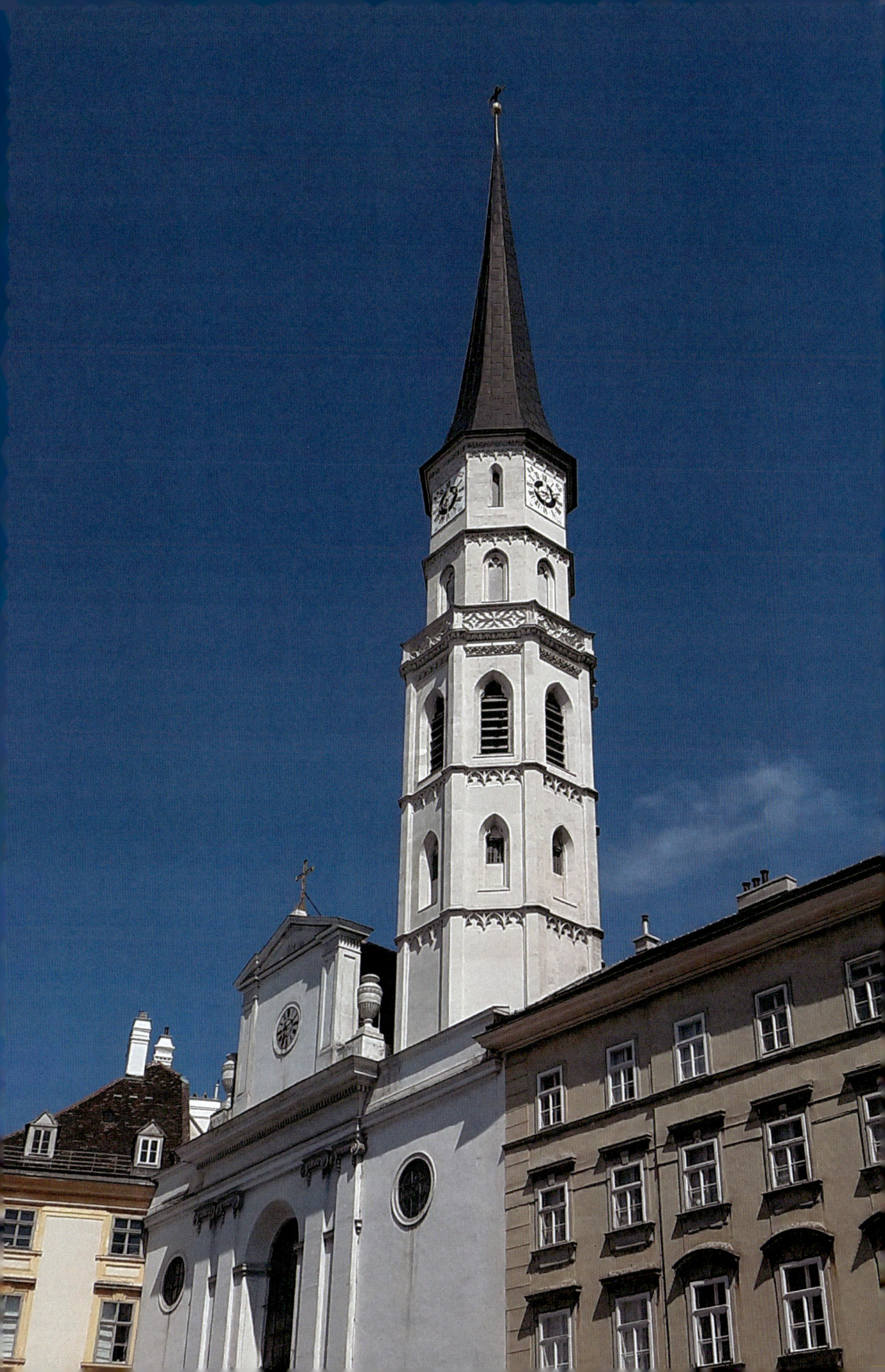

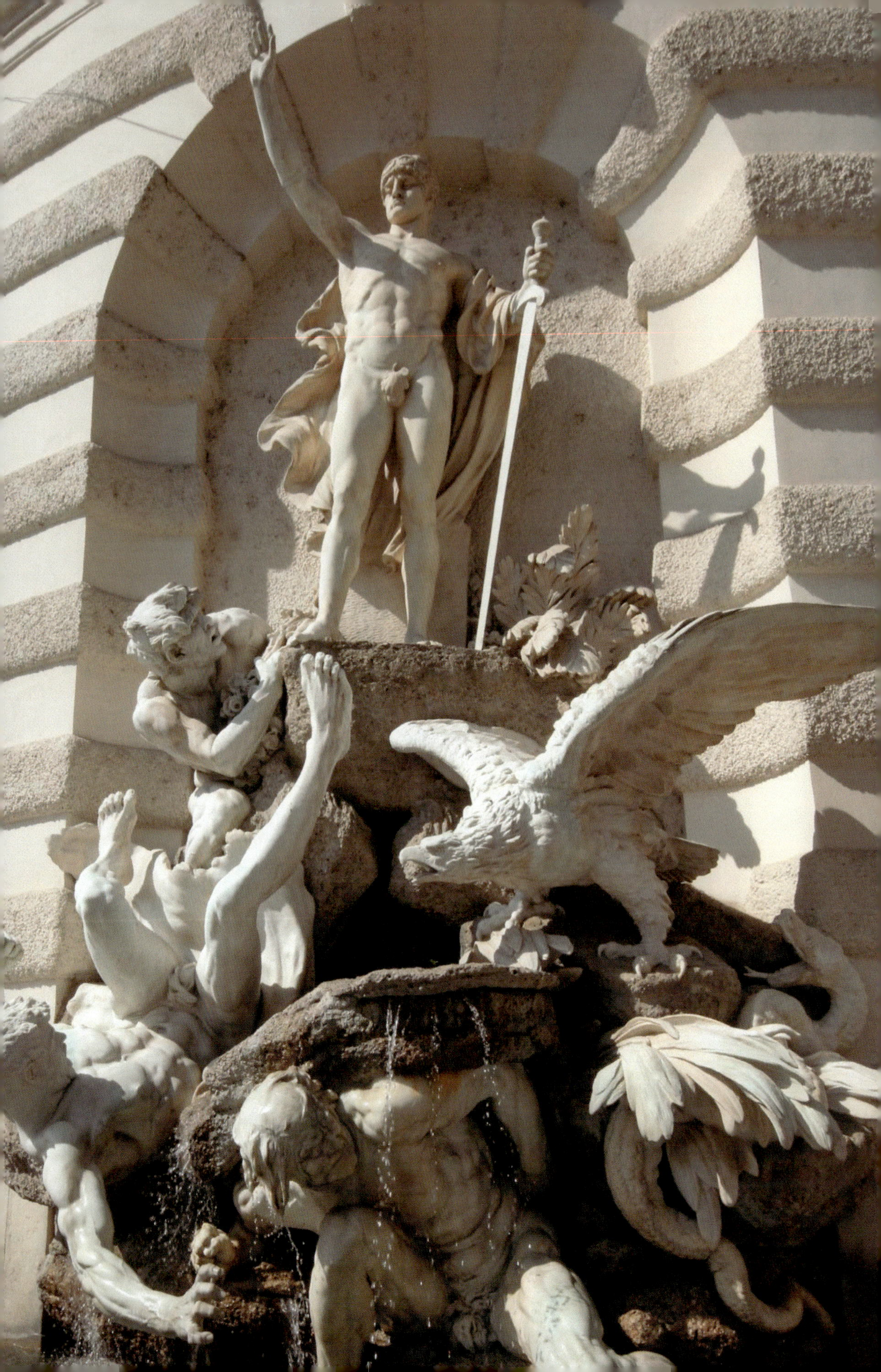

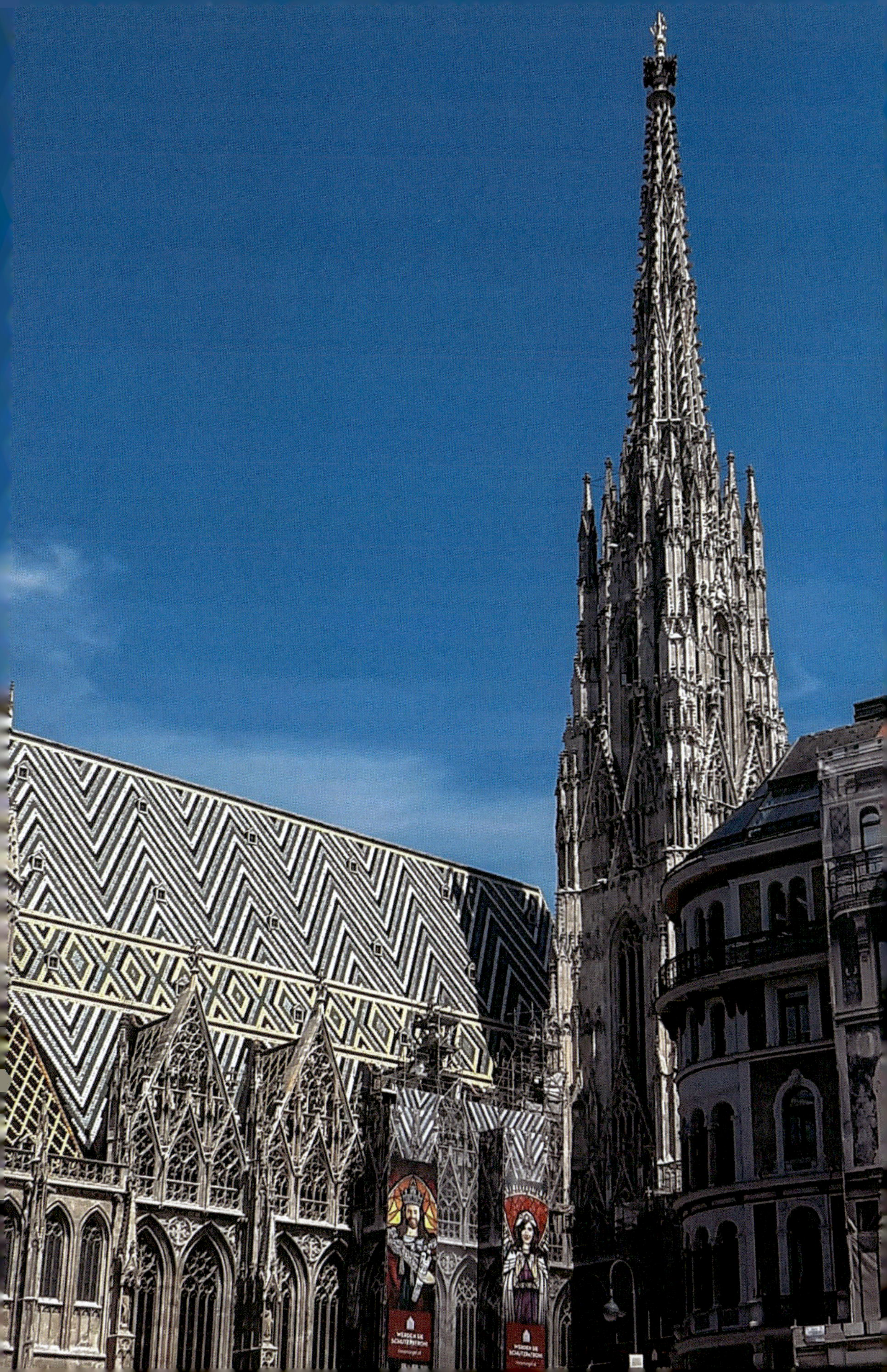

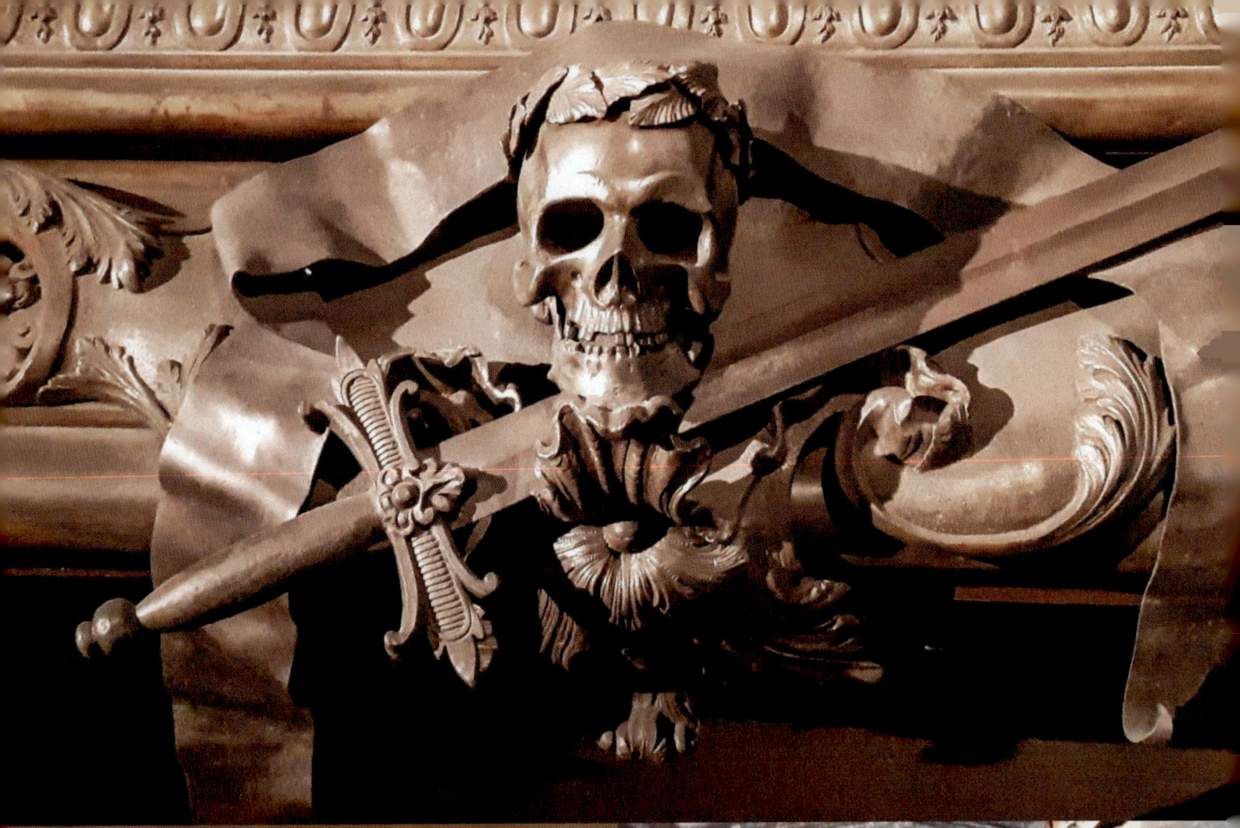
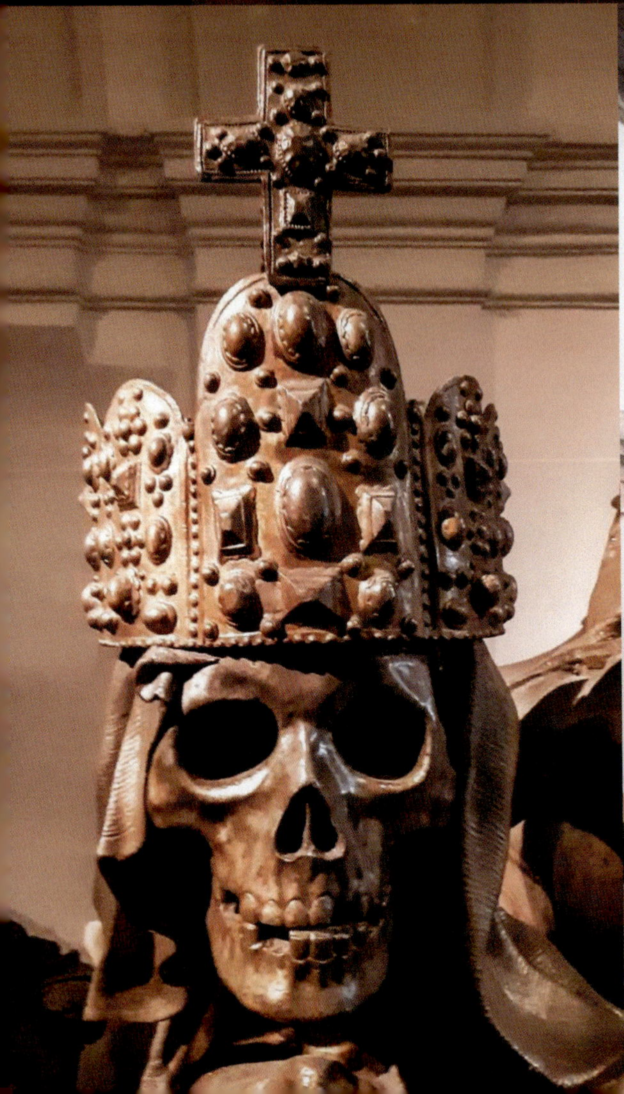
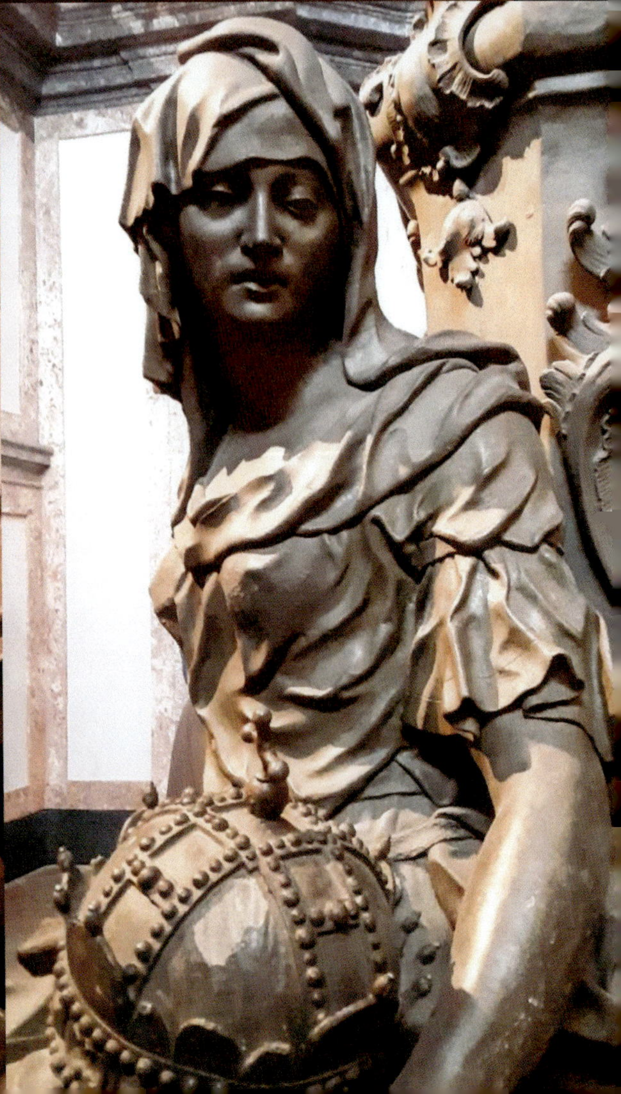

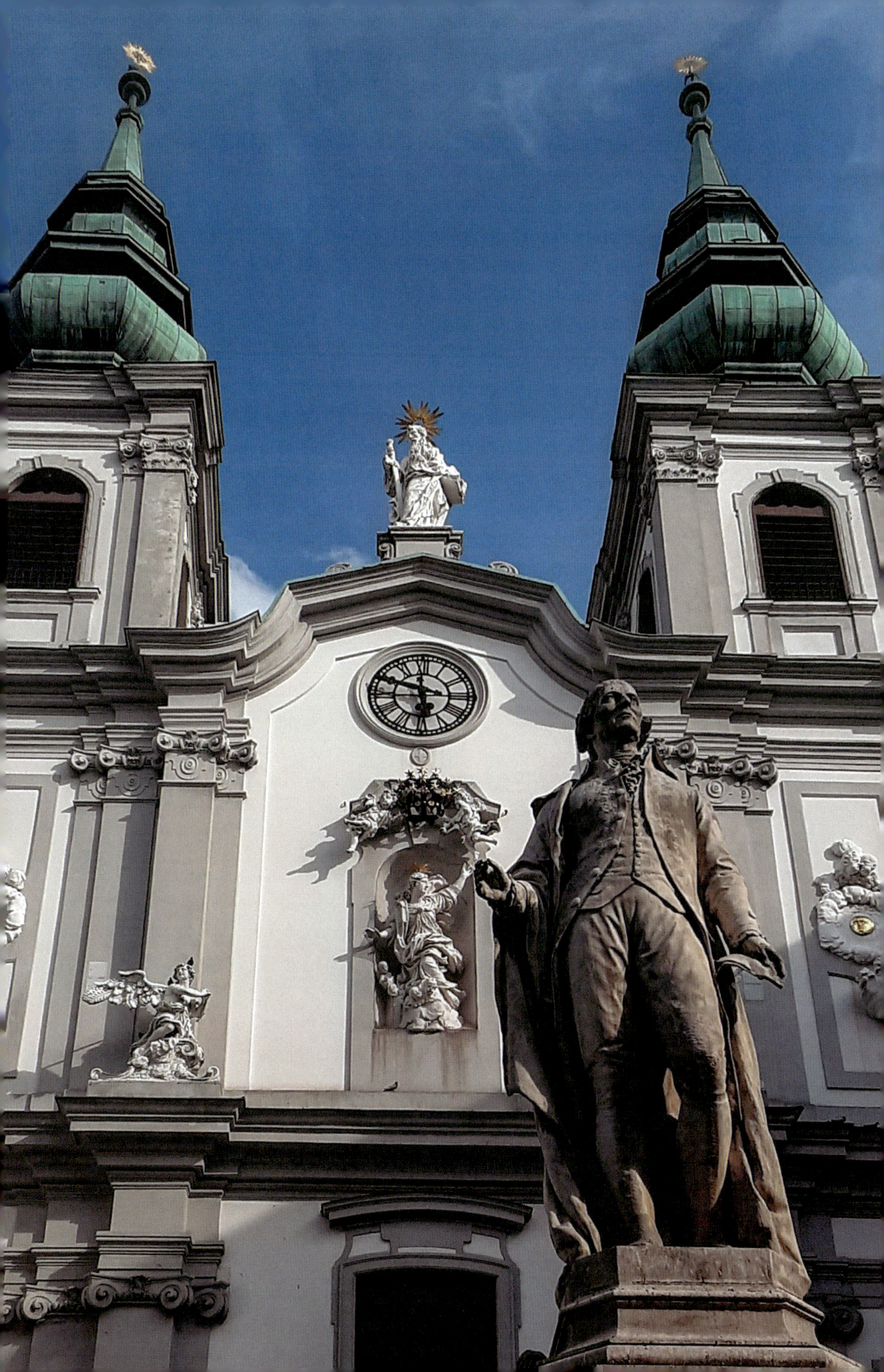

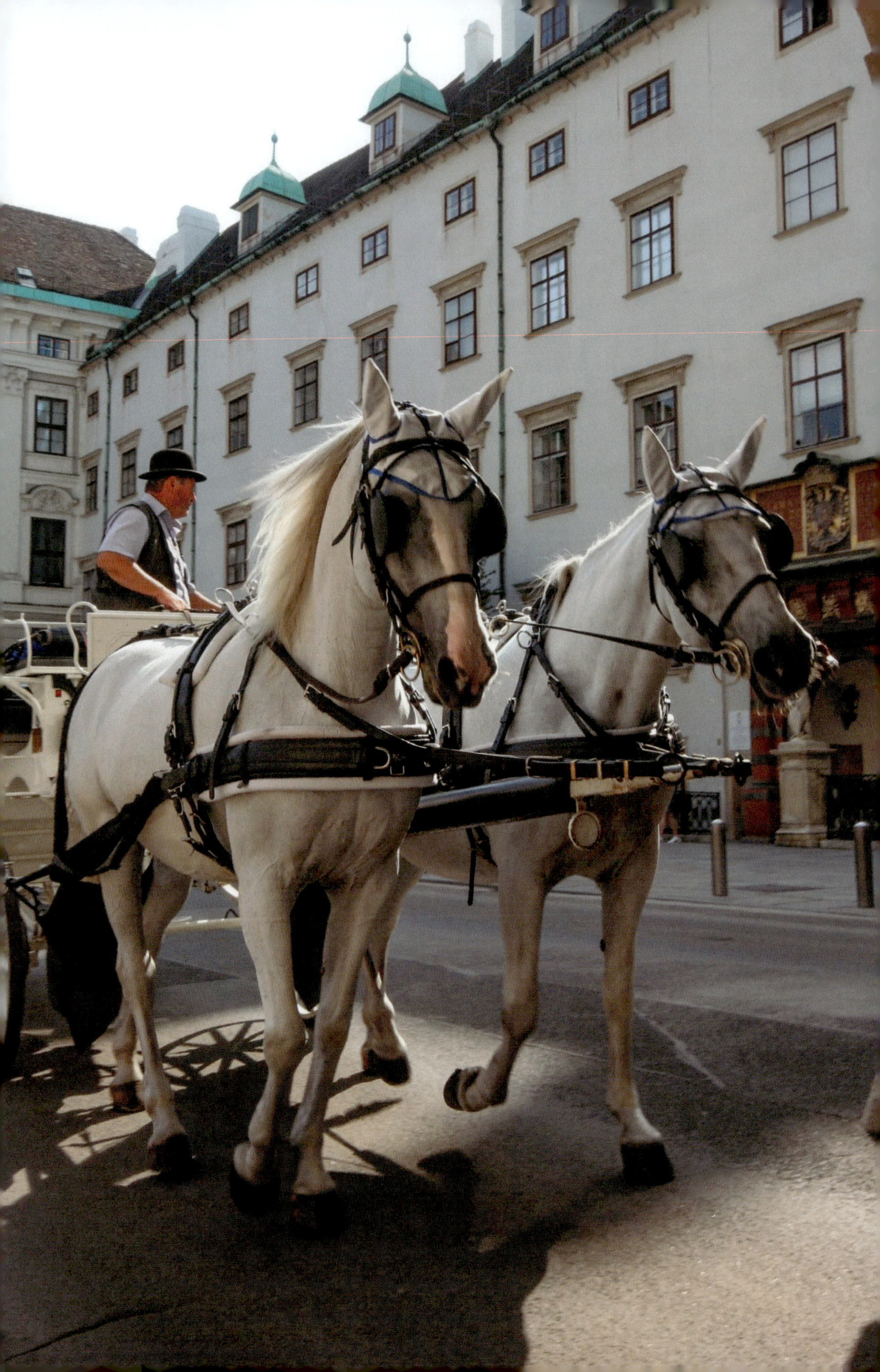

KREMS, AUSTRIA

The town of Krems is quaint with a pedestrian area with small shops. It takes about 15 minutes to walk through the town from one end to the other. We were there on a Sunday so most of the shops were closed and few people were there.

We took the excursion bus about 15 minutes away to the top of a large hill to visit Göttweig Abbey. About 48 monks live in the abbey today. The abbey is known for the apricots it grows and the apricot wine and brandy it produces.

When we arrived at the abbey there was apricot wine and apricot juice to taste. Then we were shown a 10-minute video about Göttweig Abbey. Then we broke out into our tour groups to explore. Our tour started in the apricot orchard and the view from there of the surrounding Wachau Valley was spectacular. The apricots were in season, so we saw them growing on the trees.

The inside of the abbey was large and interesting. The grand imperial staircase has a large fresco that was painted in 1739. The staircase under the fresco that leads to the second floor is one of the largest in Europe.

There was a worship service in progress when we arrived, however it let out near the end of our visit so we were able to see inside the beautiful church.

The path out of the abbey leads to a building that has a staircase that descends several floors. It goes past a small museum room that shows how life in the abbey may have been in the past. At the end of the hallway was a nice gift shop and a wine tasting counter. We brought a bottle of the apricot sparkling wine home and our family enjoyed tasting the unique and flavorful wine.

Krems

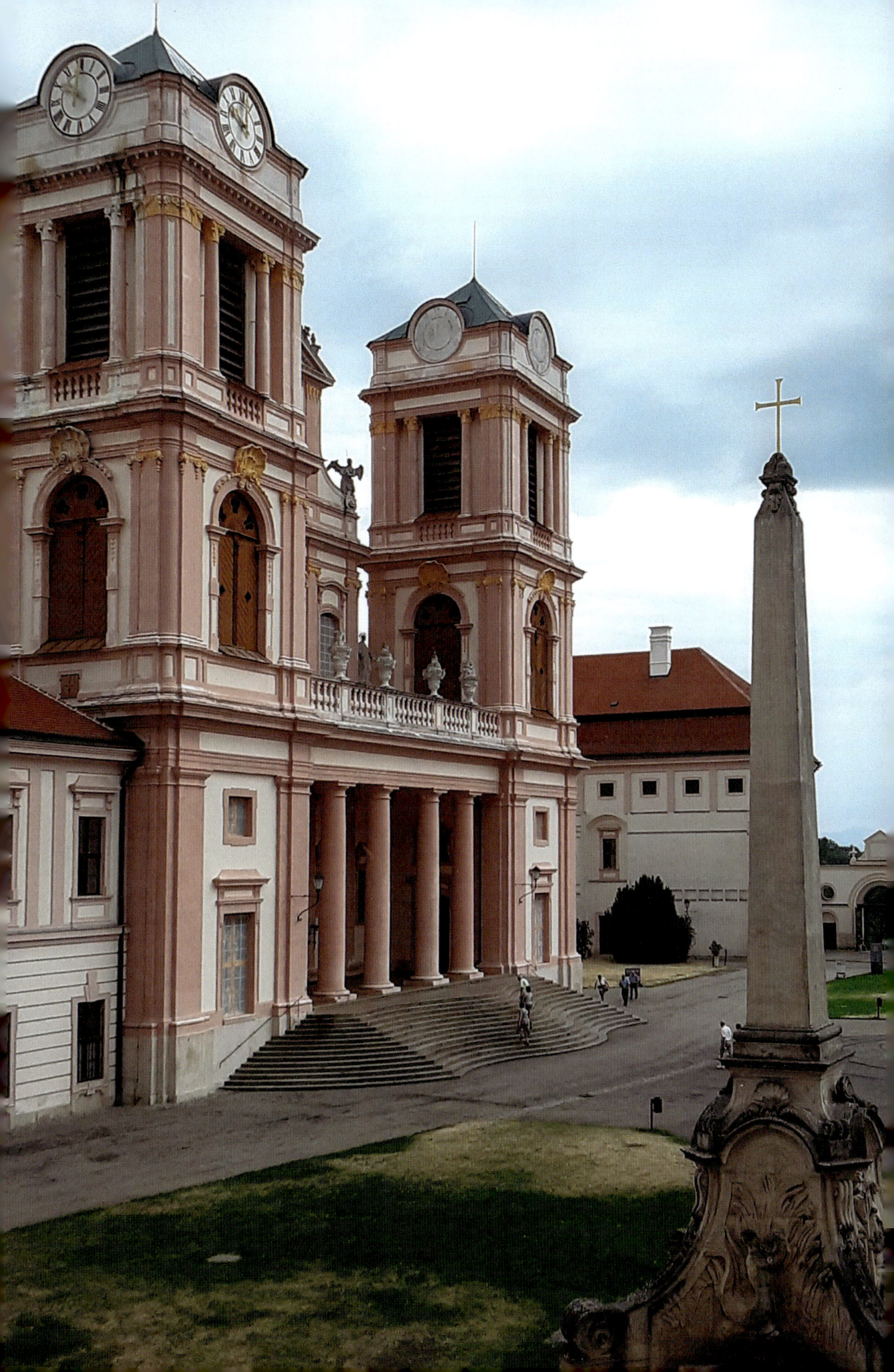

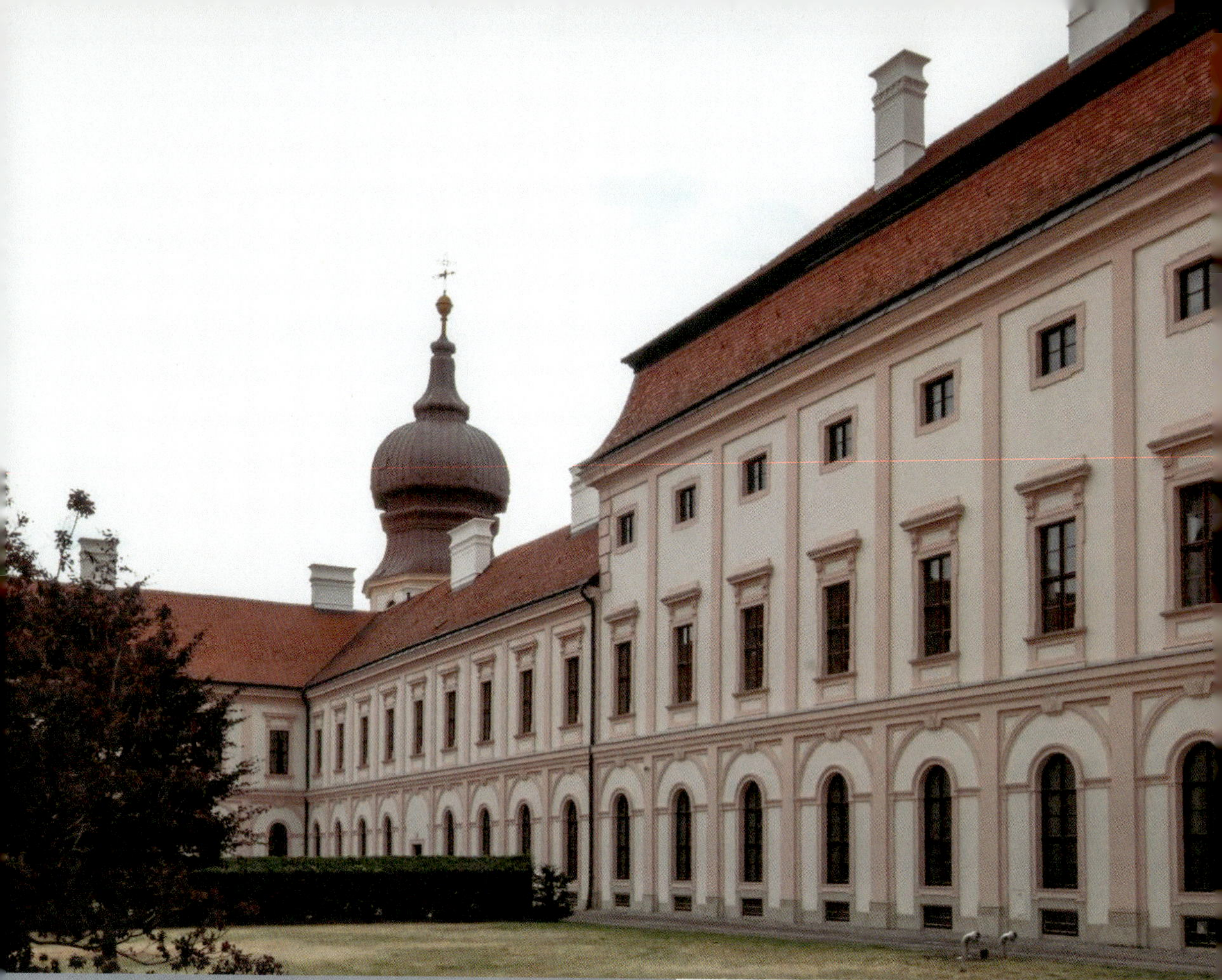

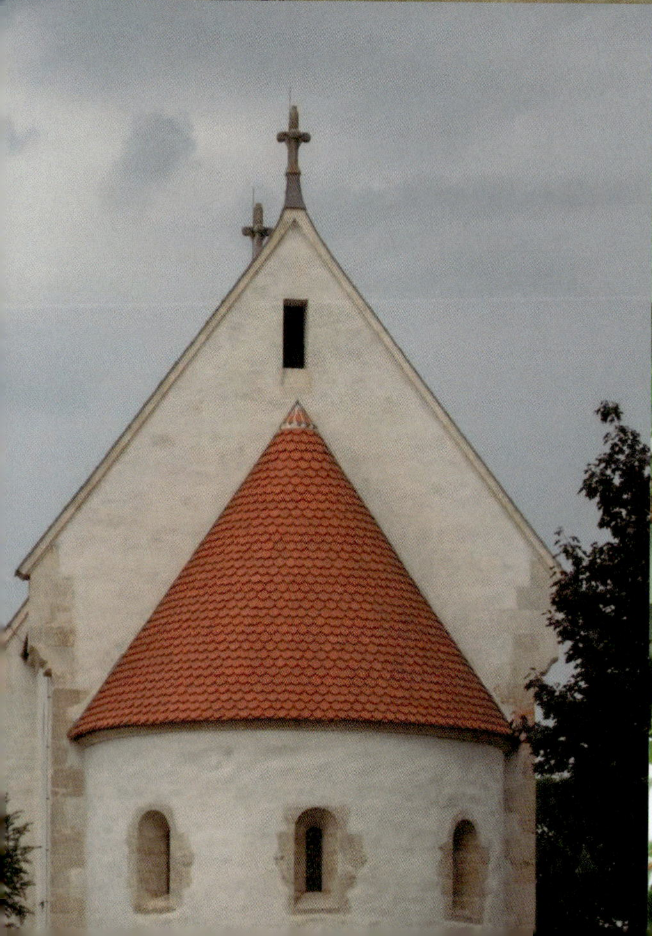

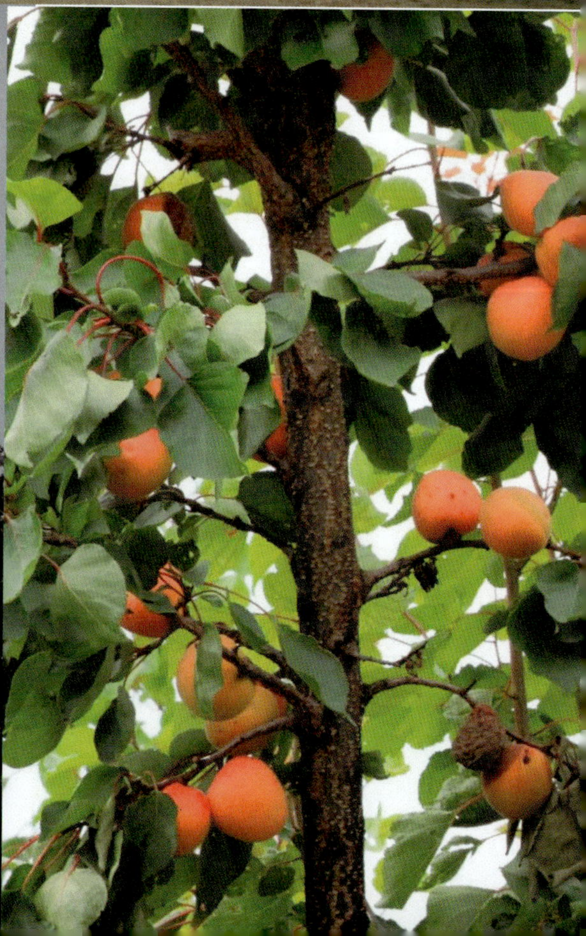

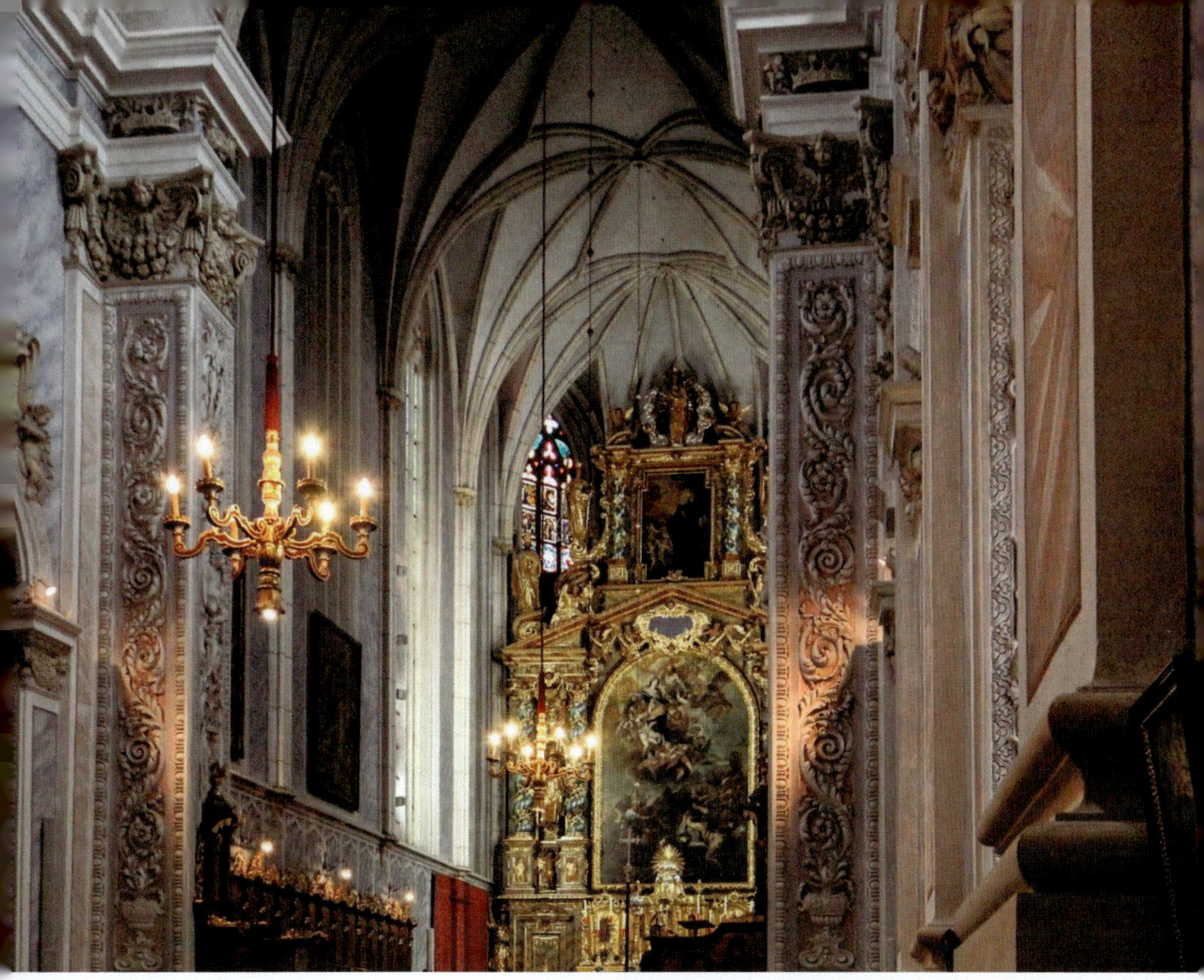
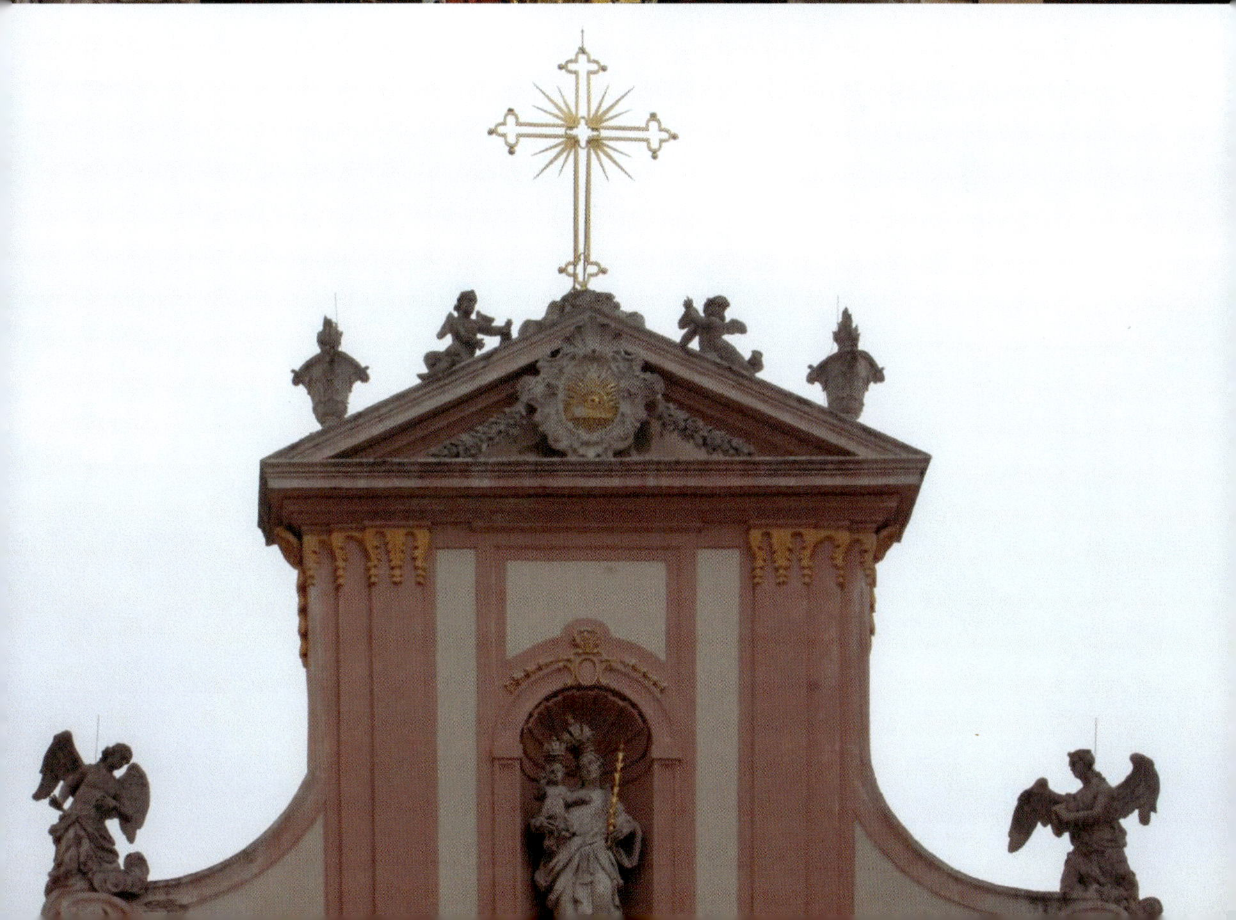

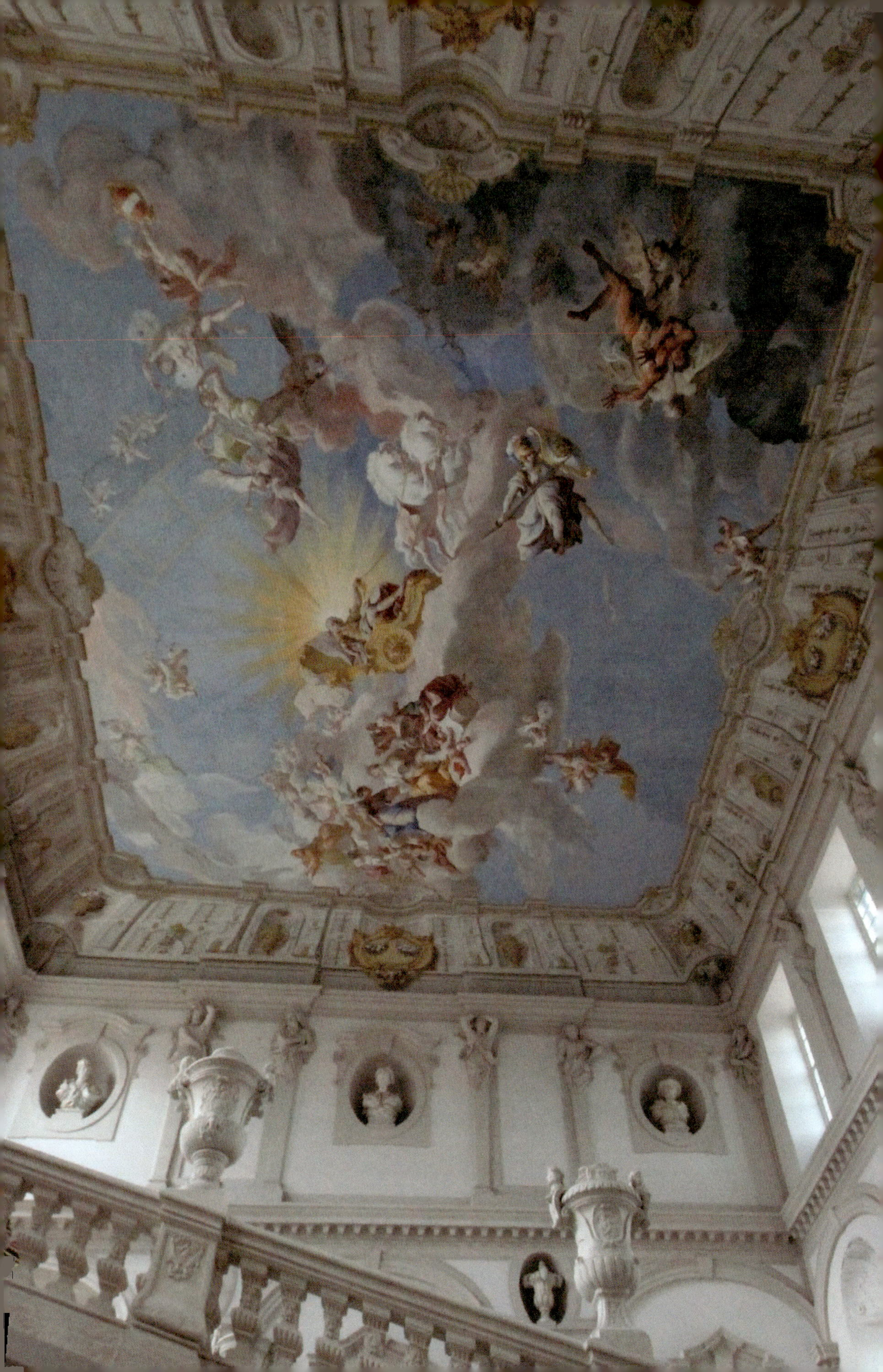

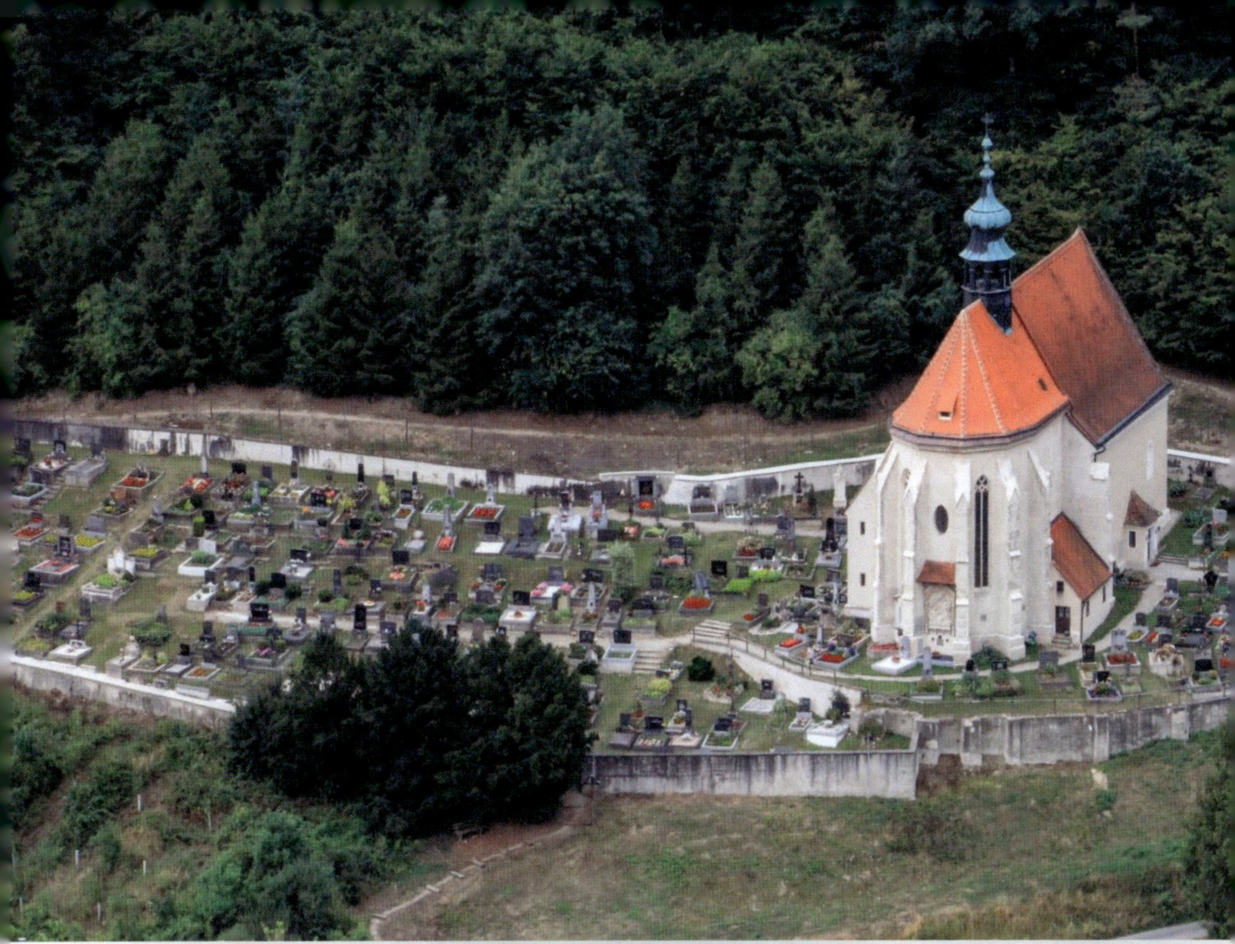

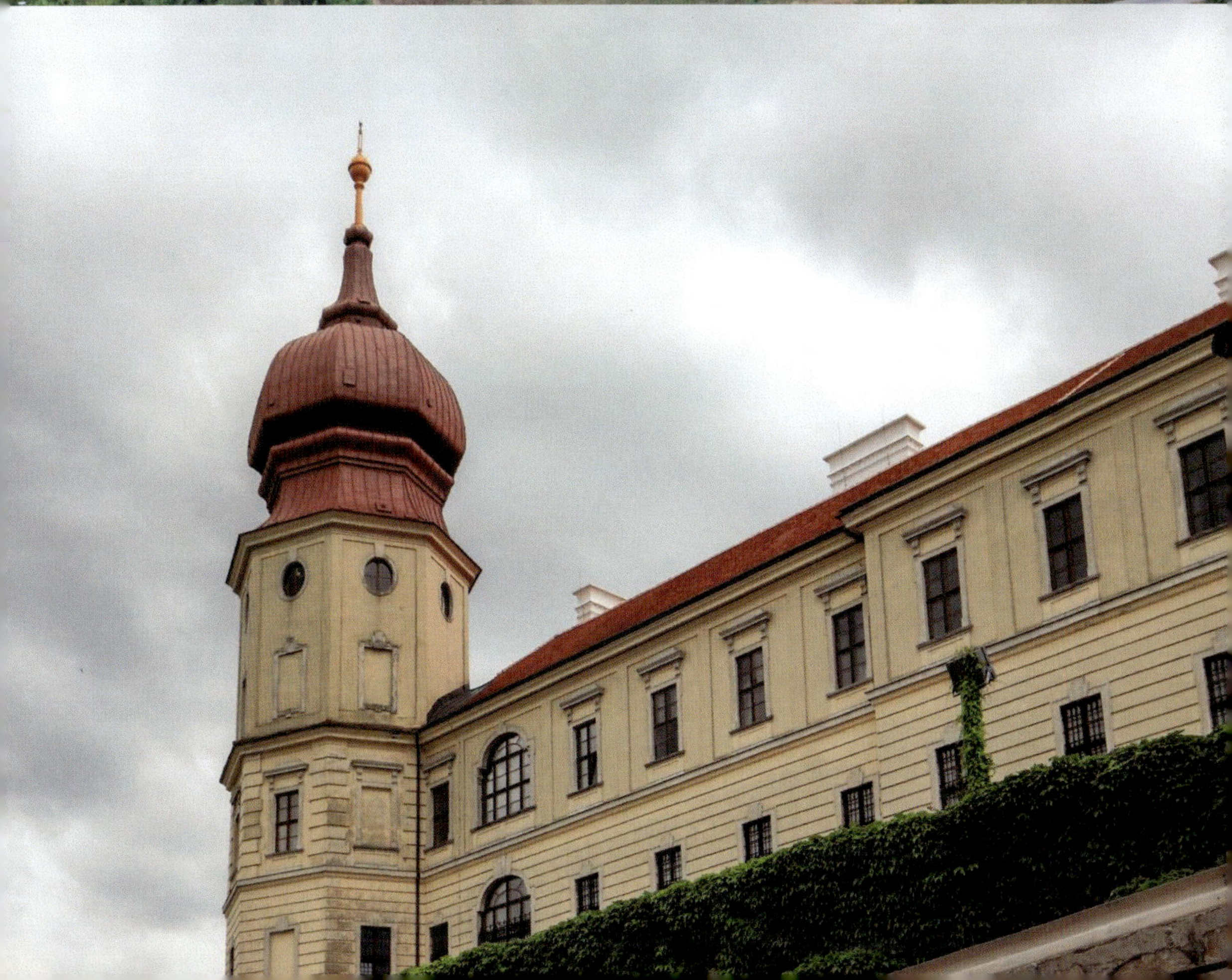

DEO
OPTIMO MAXIMO
RERVM OMNIVM CONDITORI
FRONTEM FABRICÆ MONRII AVSTRALEM
SVIS AVSPICIIS EDVCTAM
SVOQVE NOMINI SERVITVRAM
IN FIDELIS OBSEQVII PIGNVS
ET PERENNE GRATITVDINIS MONVMENTVM
CONSECRAT DICAT DEVOVET
MAGNVS ABBAS GOTTWICENSIS
ANNO SÆCVLARI SEPTIMO MDCCLXXXIII

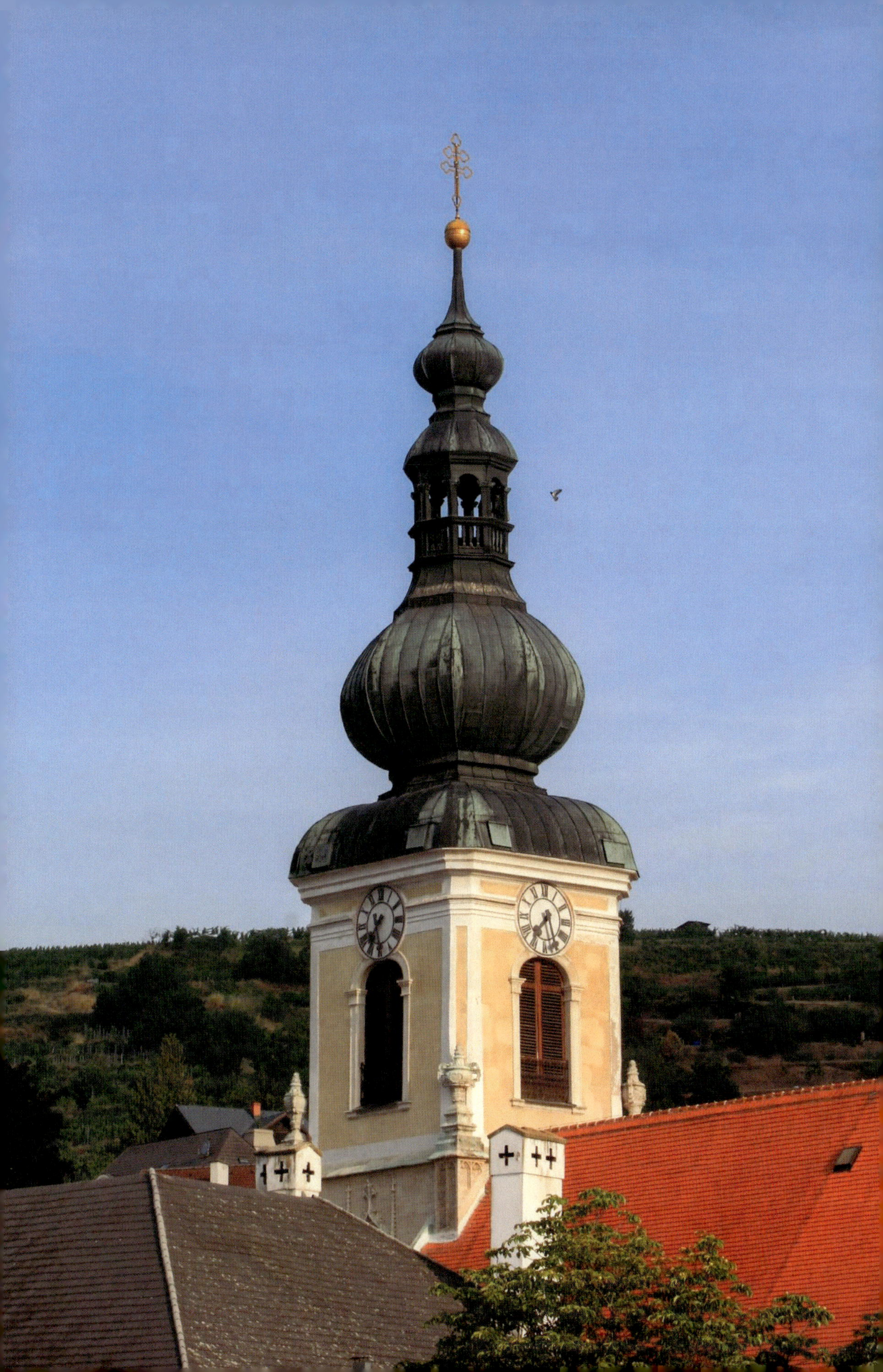

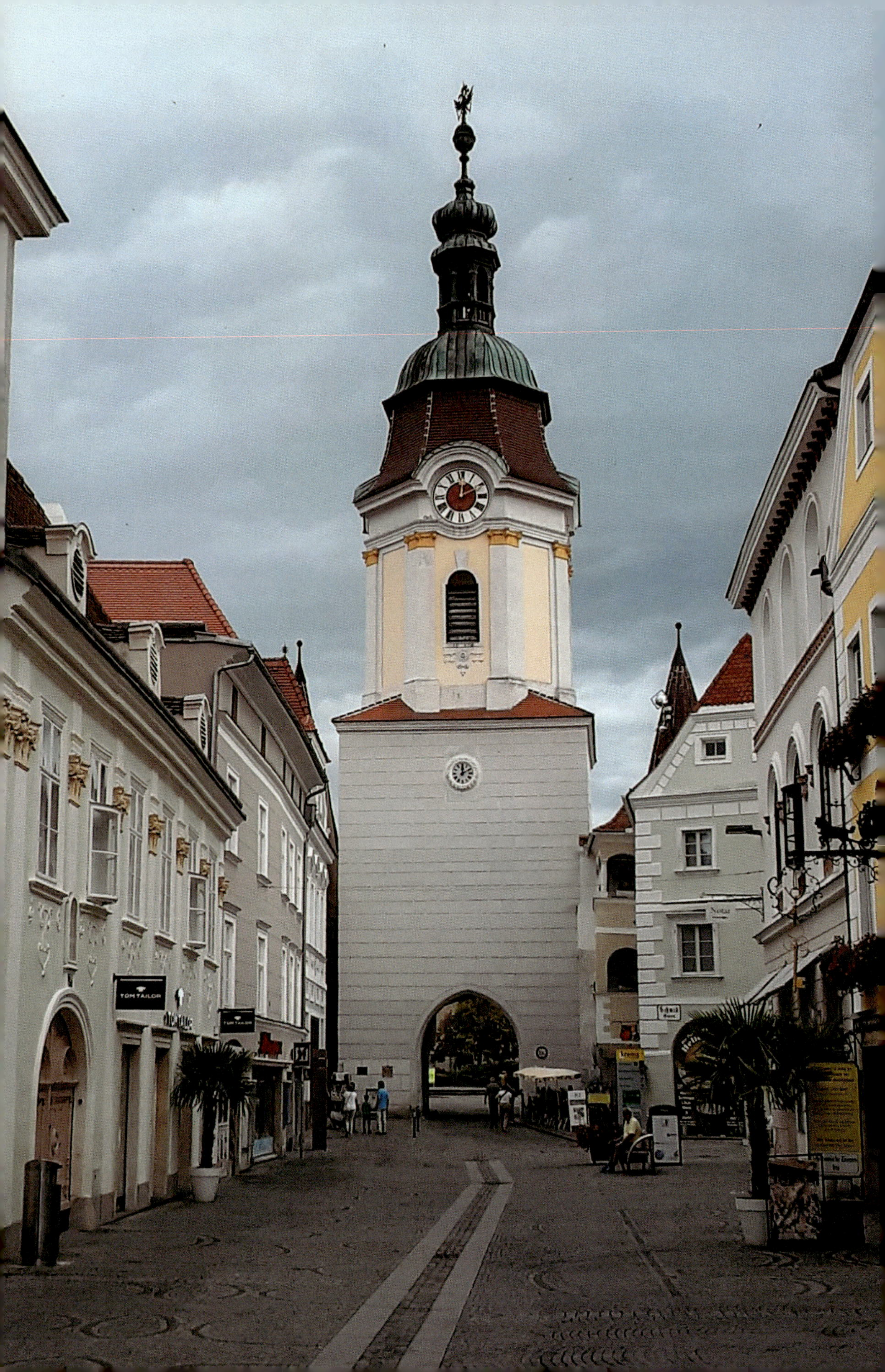
TOM TAILOR
TOM TAILOR

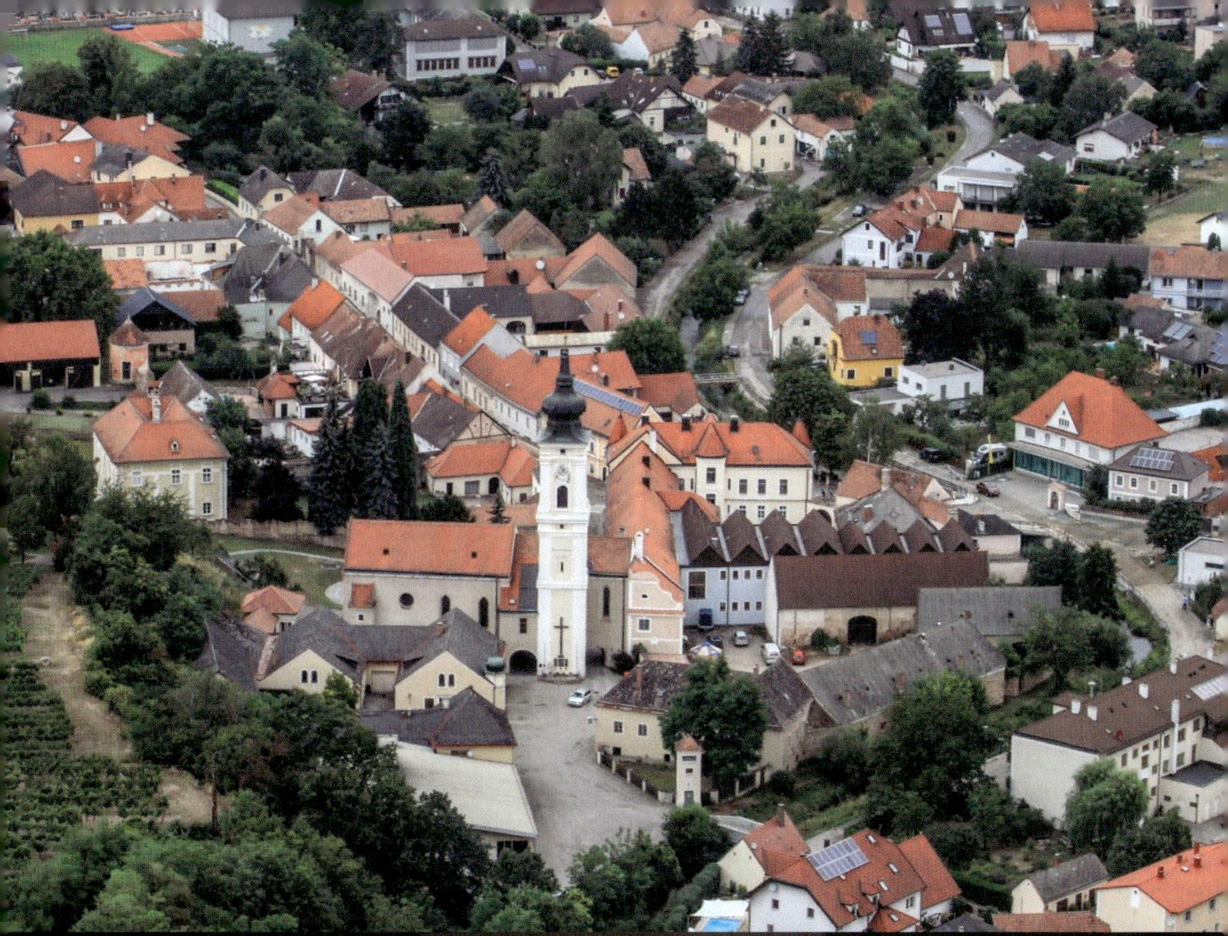

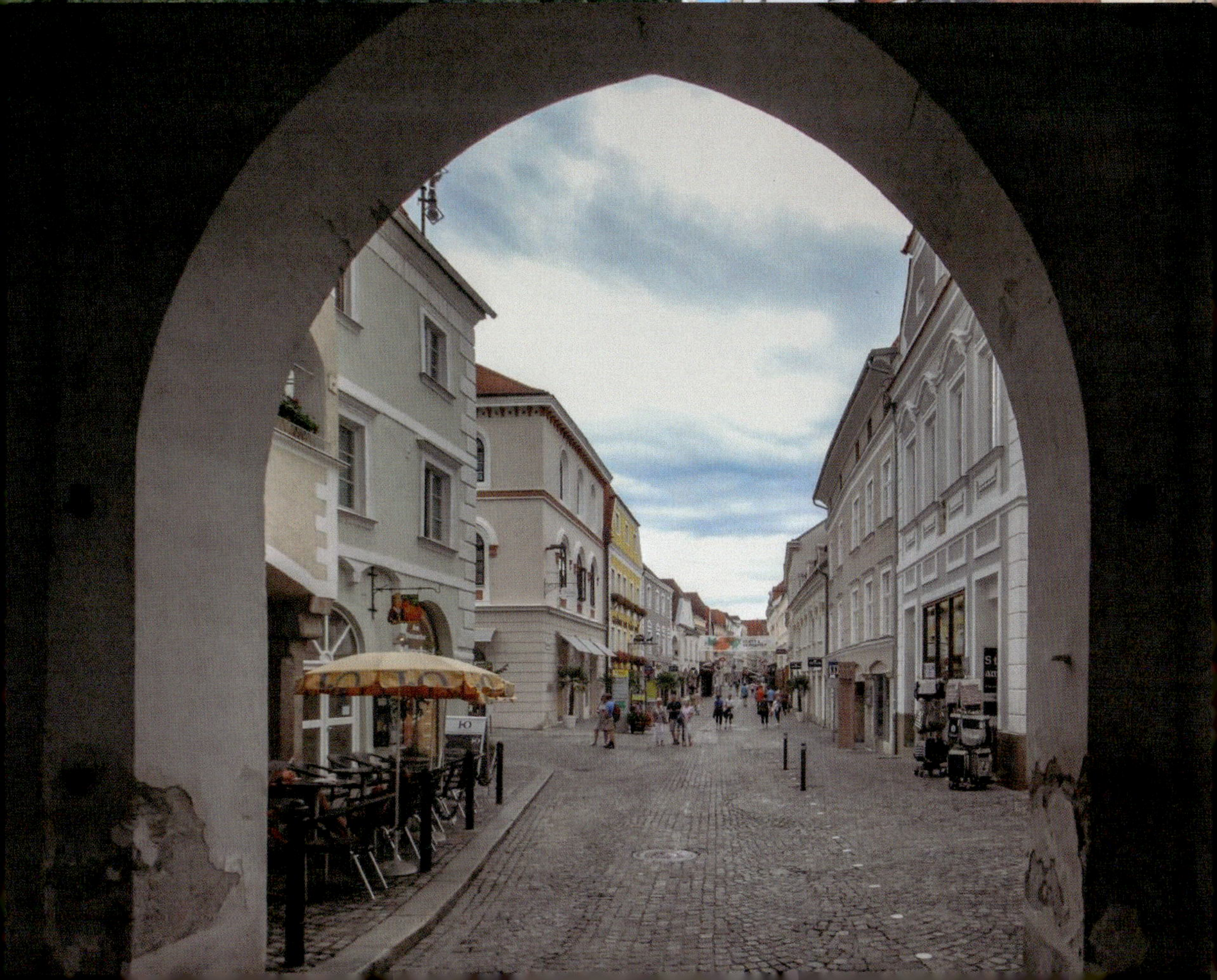

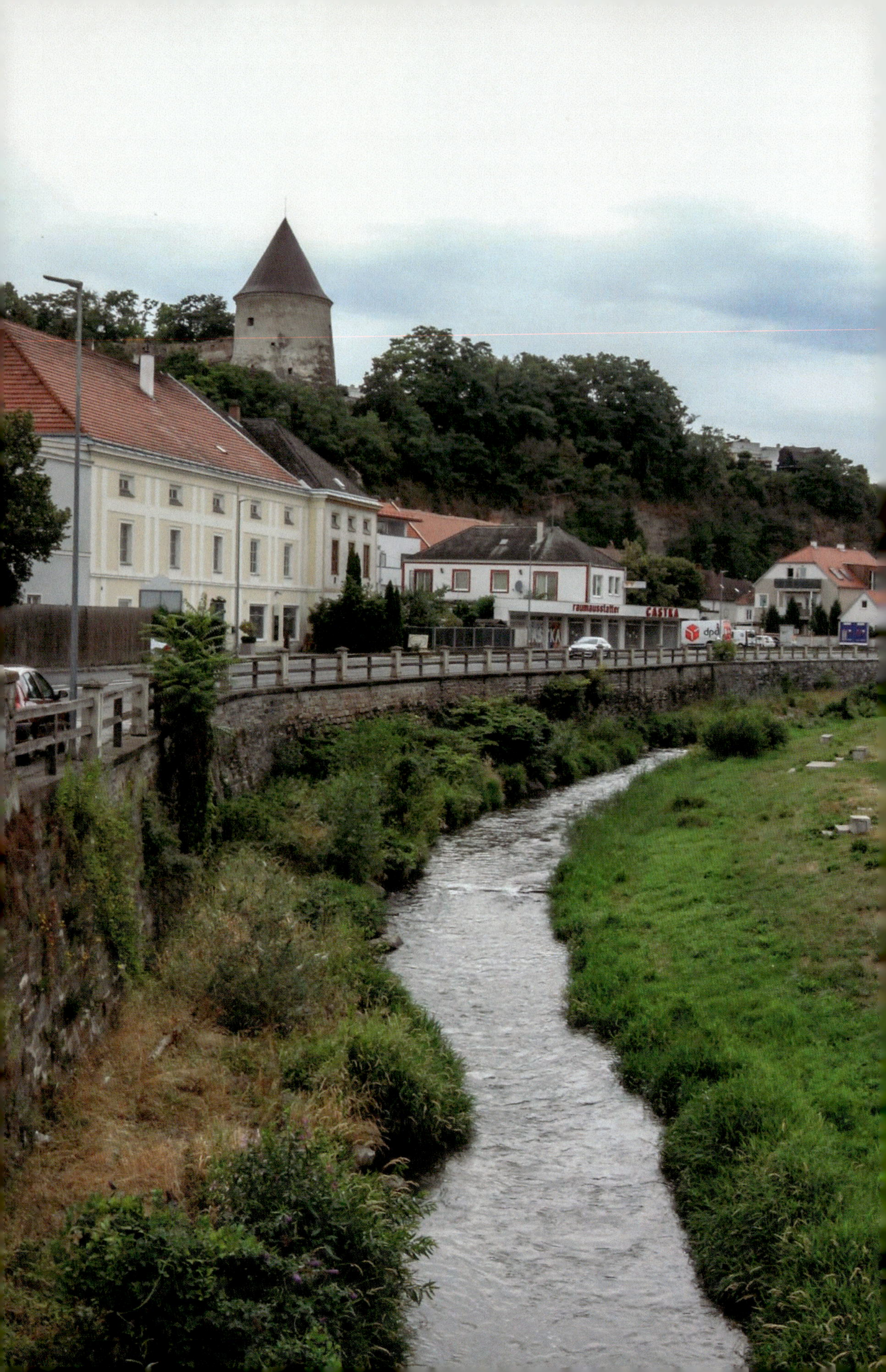
raumausstatter
CASTRA
dpd

WACHAU VALLEY, AUSTRIA

After we left Krems, Austria we sailed through the Wachau Valley. The views of the countryside were gorgeous. The ship sailed past grape orchards and small towns, each with the ubiquitous small church.

I spent 5 hours on the top deck and had a relaxing and wonderful time. I only left to use the restroom and to retrieve the Austrian themed desserts that were offered mid-afternoon.

Sometime mid-afternoon an apricot brandy toast was made as well as a wide variety of Austrian desserts.

We heard that the Rhine River cruise provided views like that every day, but with more castles. We passed one castle near the town of Dürnstein where Richard the Lionheart was held captive. The means of his escape are clouded in mystery and myths. It's likely that he paid a ransom and was released.

As the sun set on the Danube and we sailed past small towns with the lights from the houses reflecting in the water, I was at peace. It was a great day.

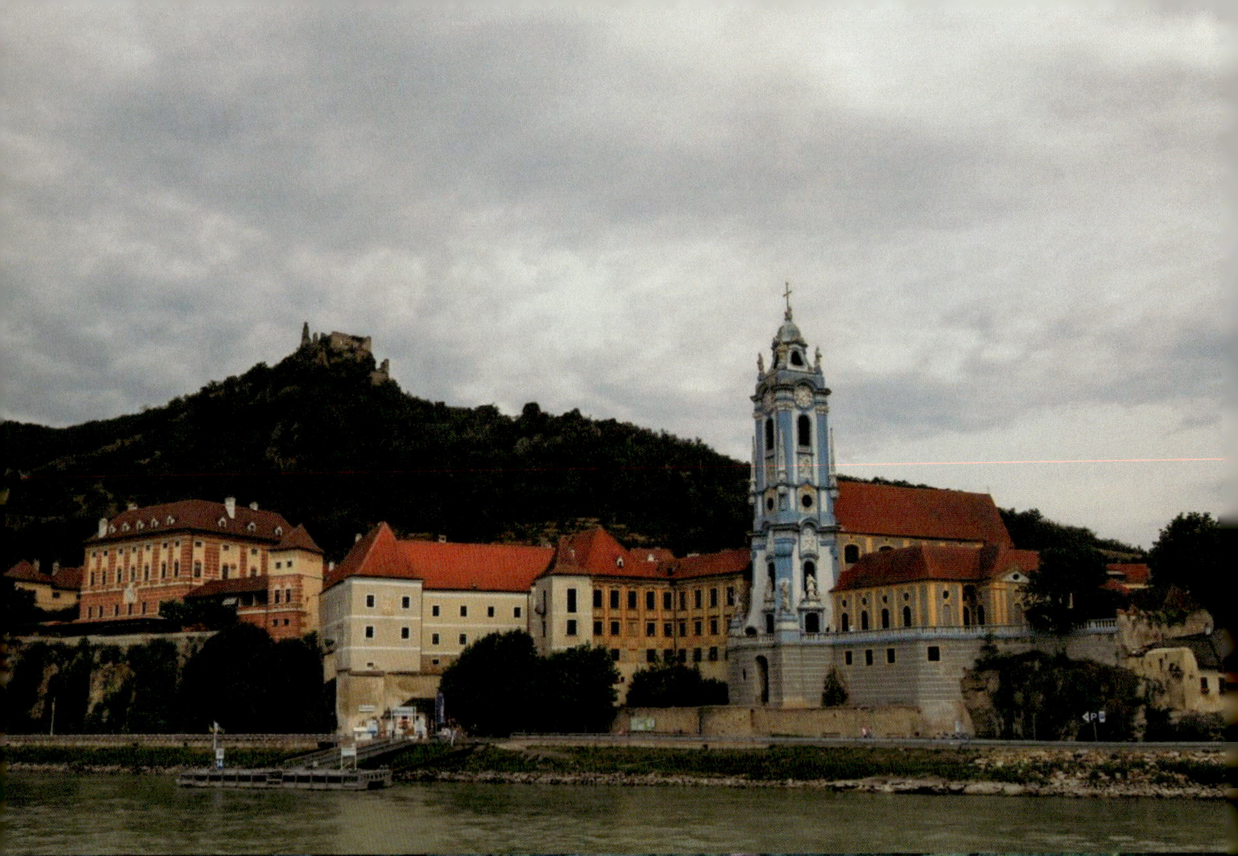

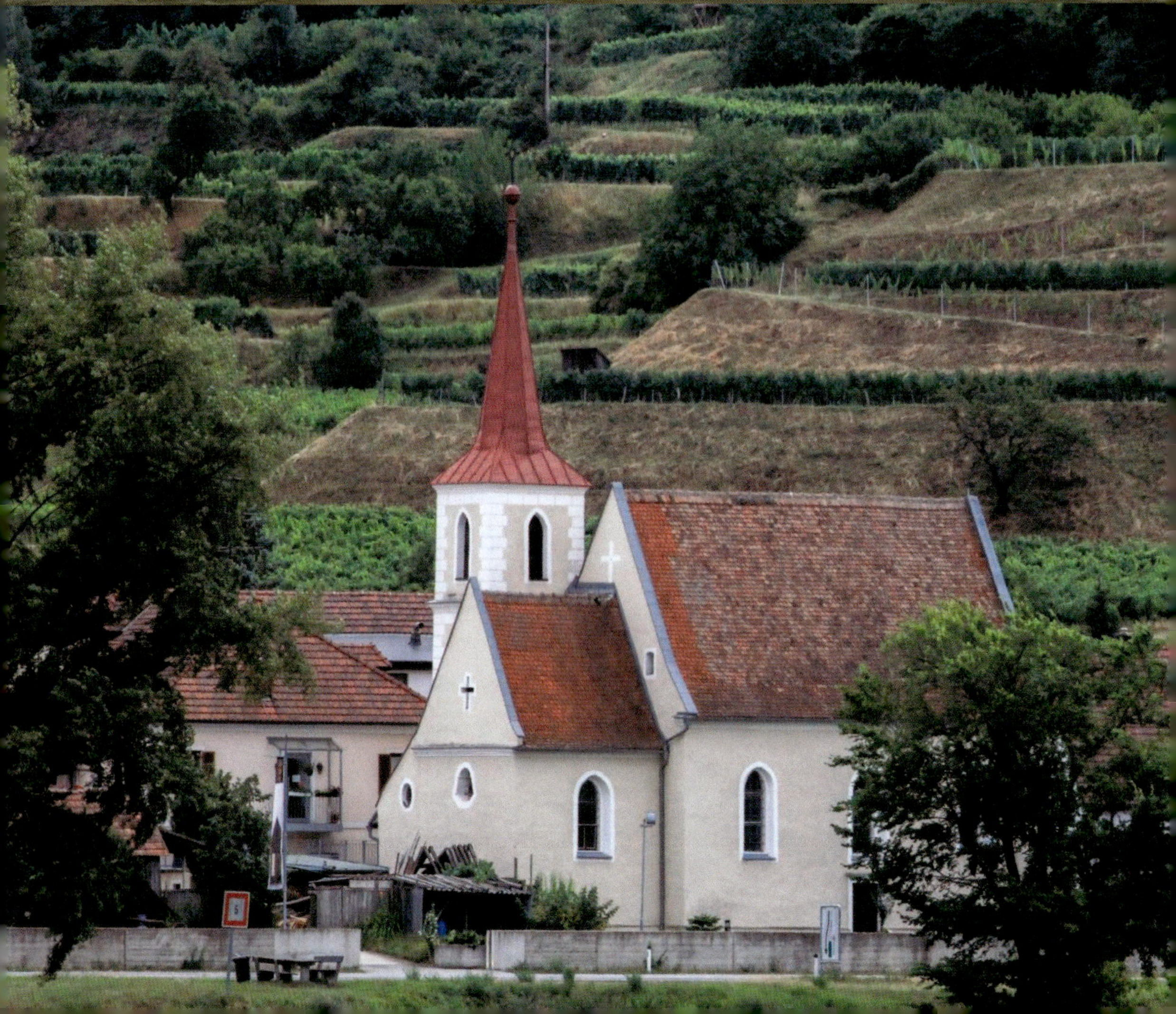

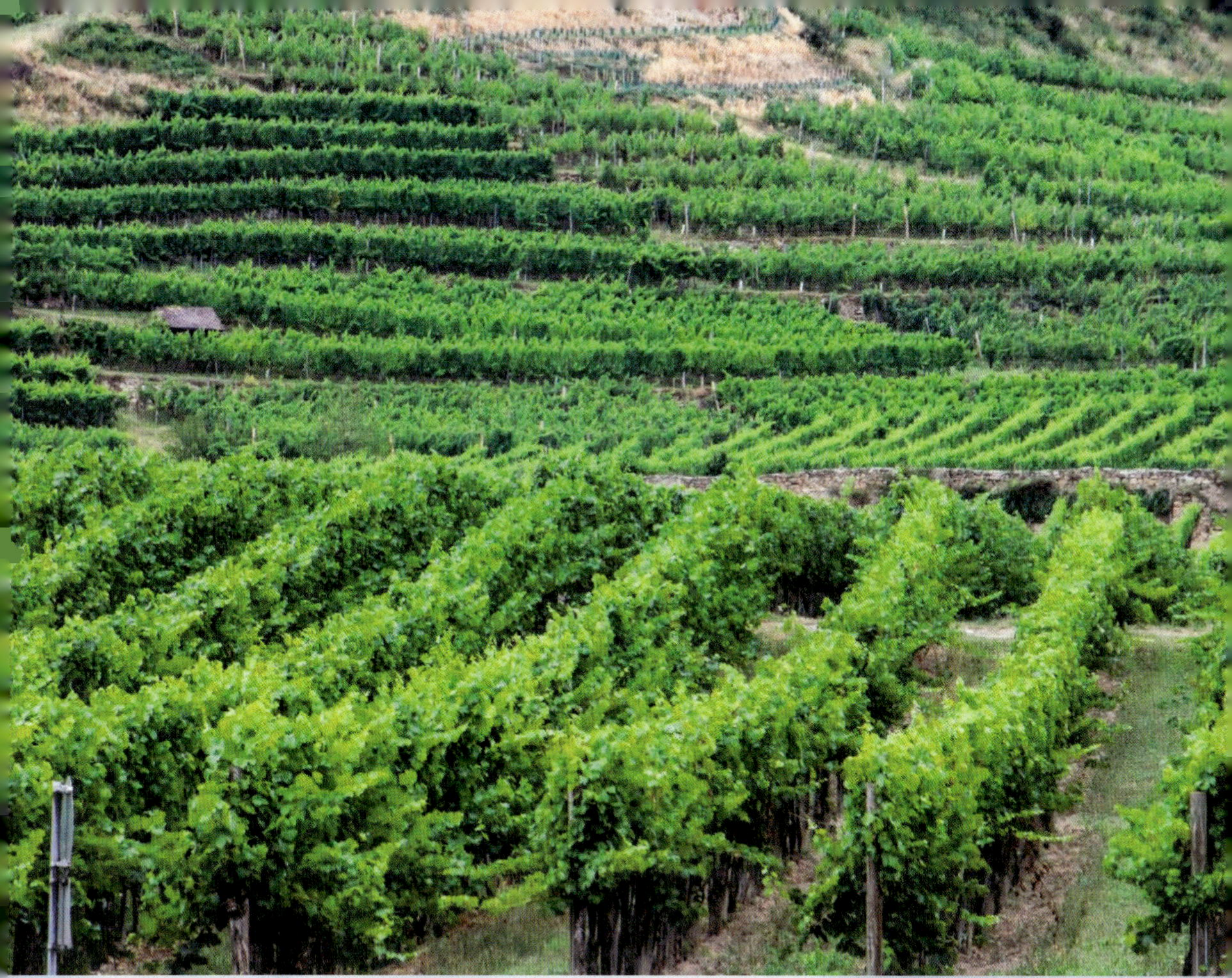

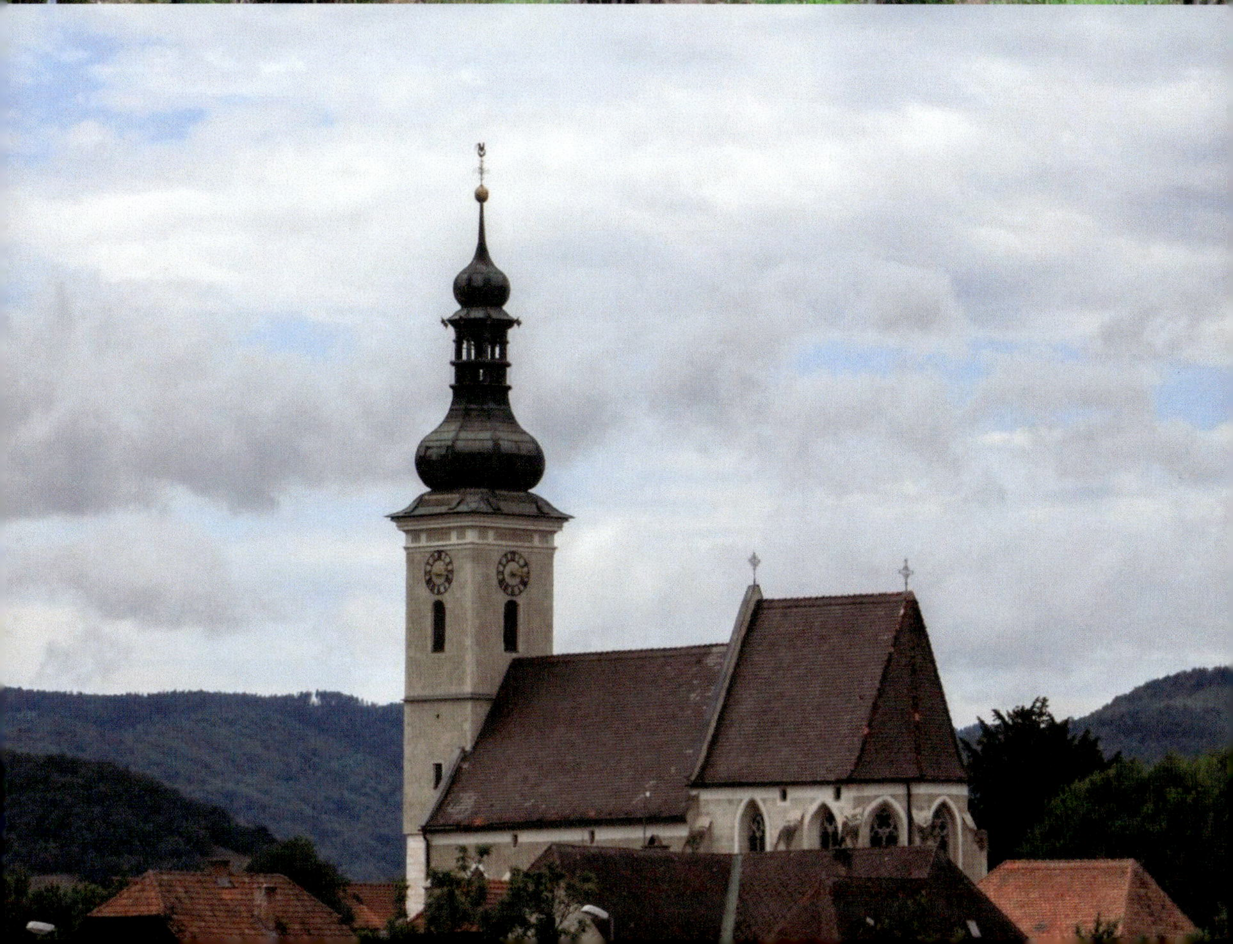

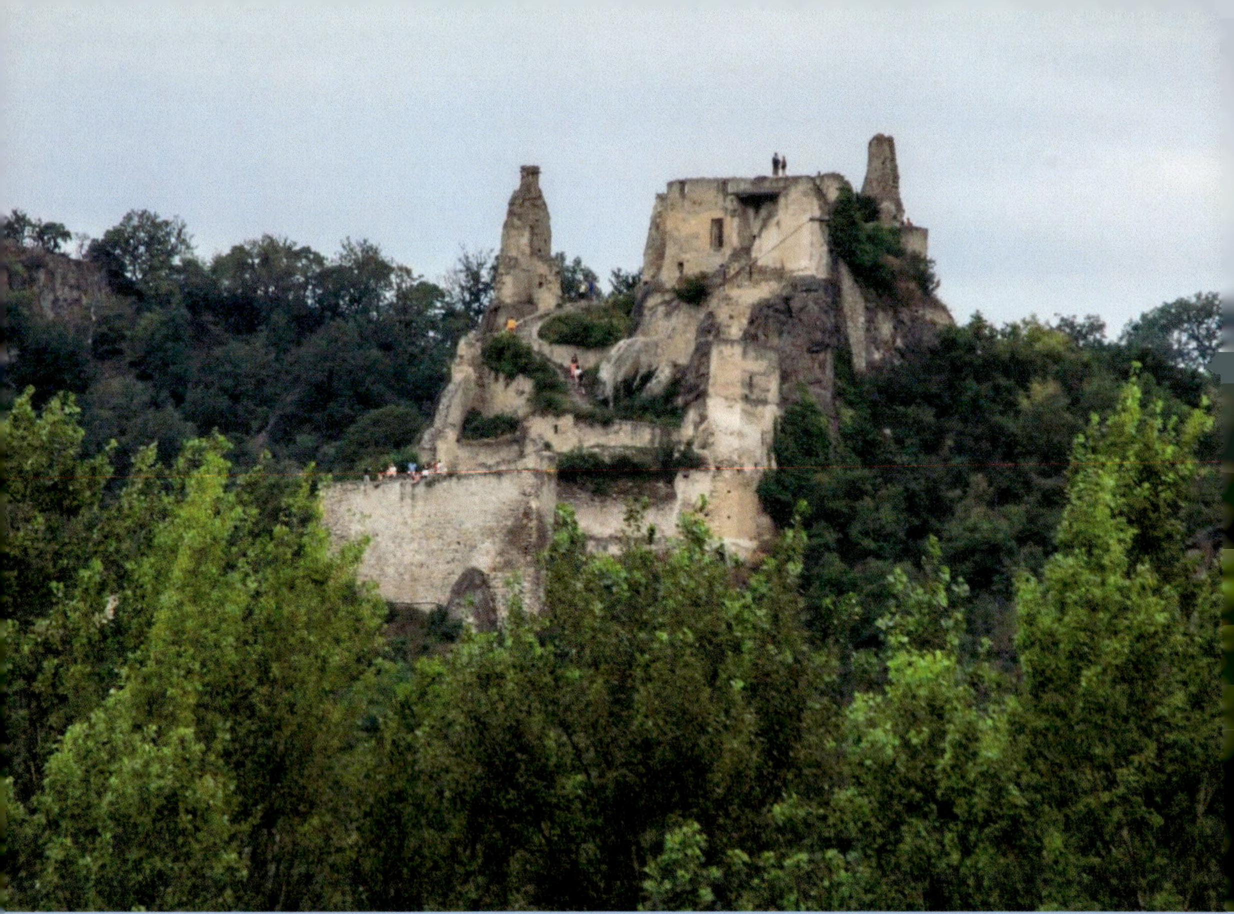

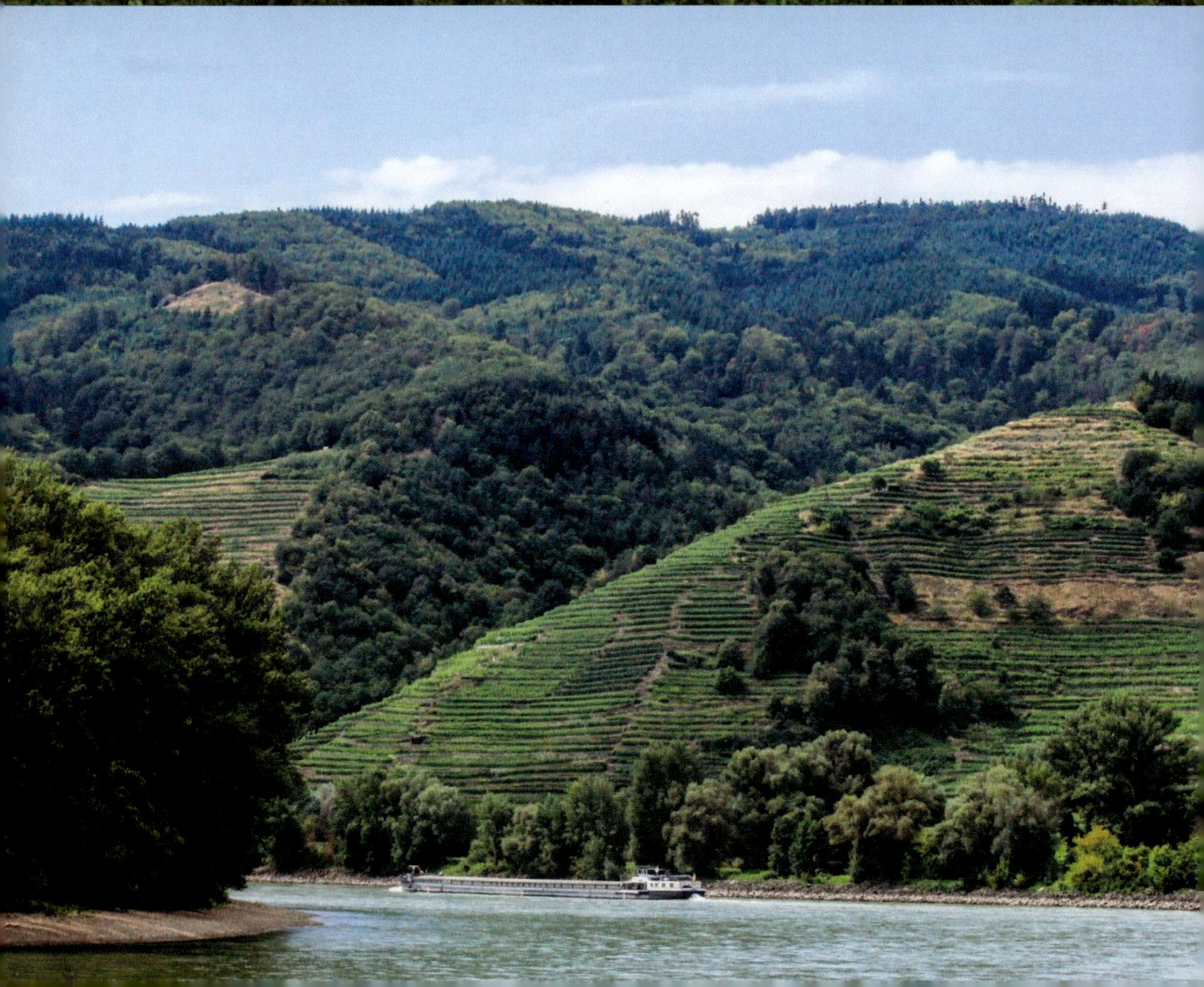

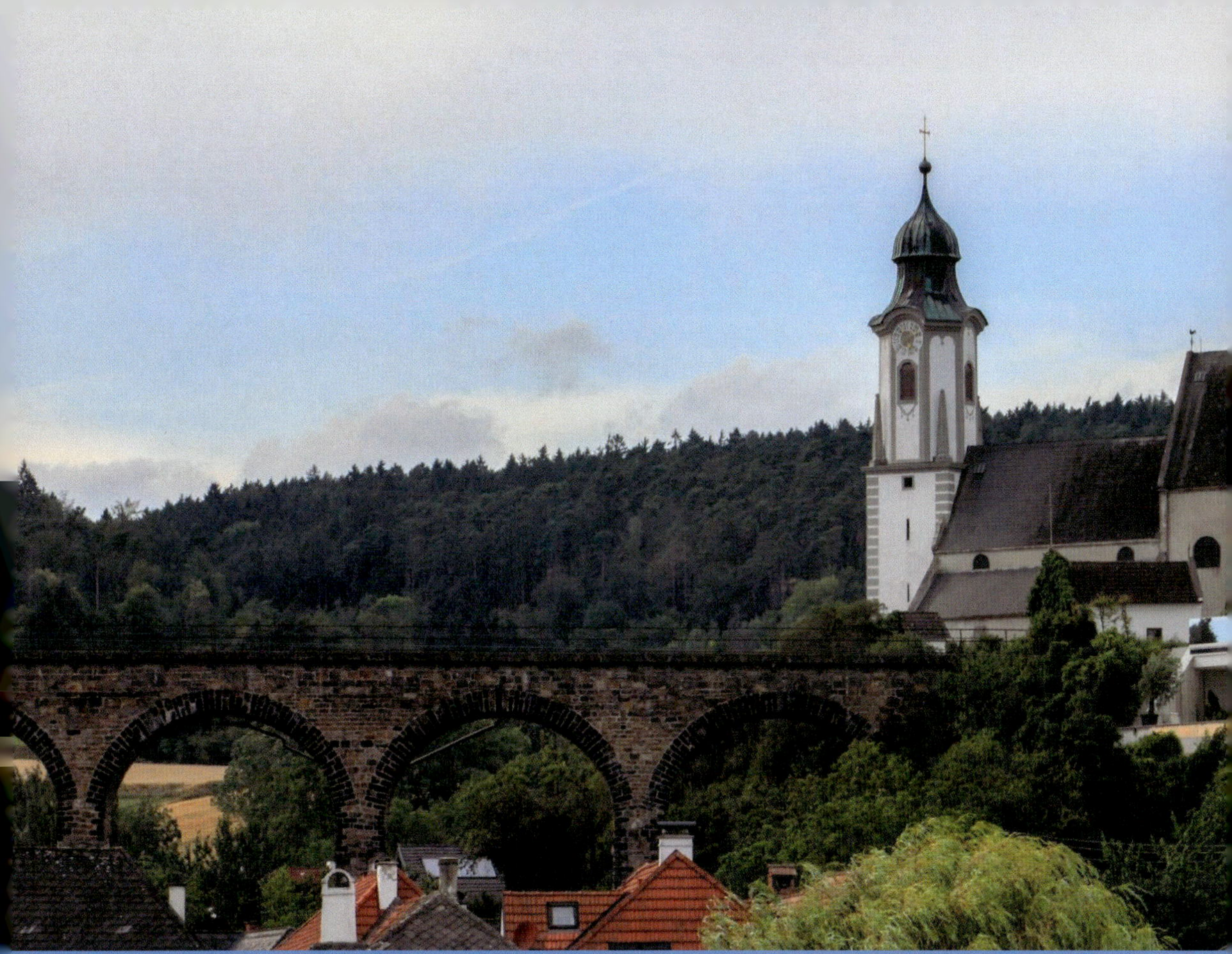

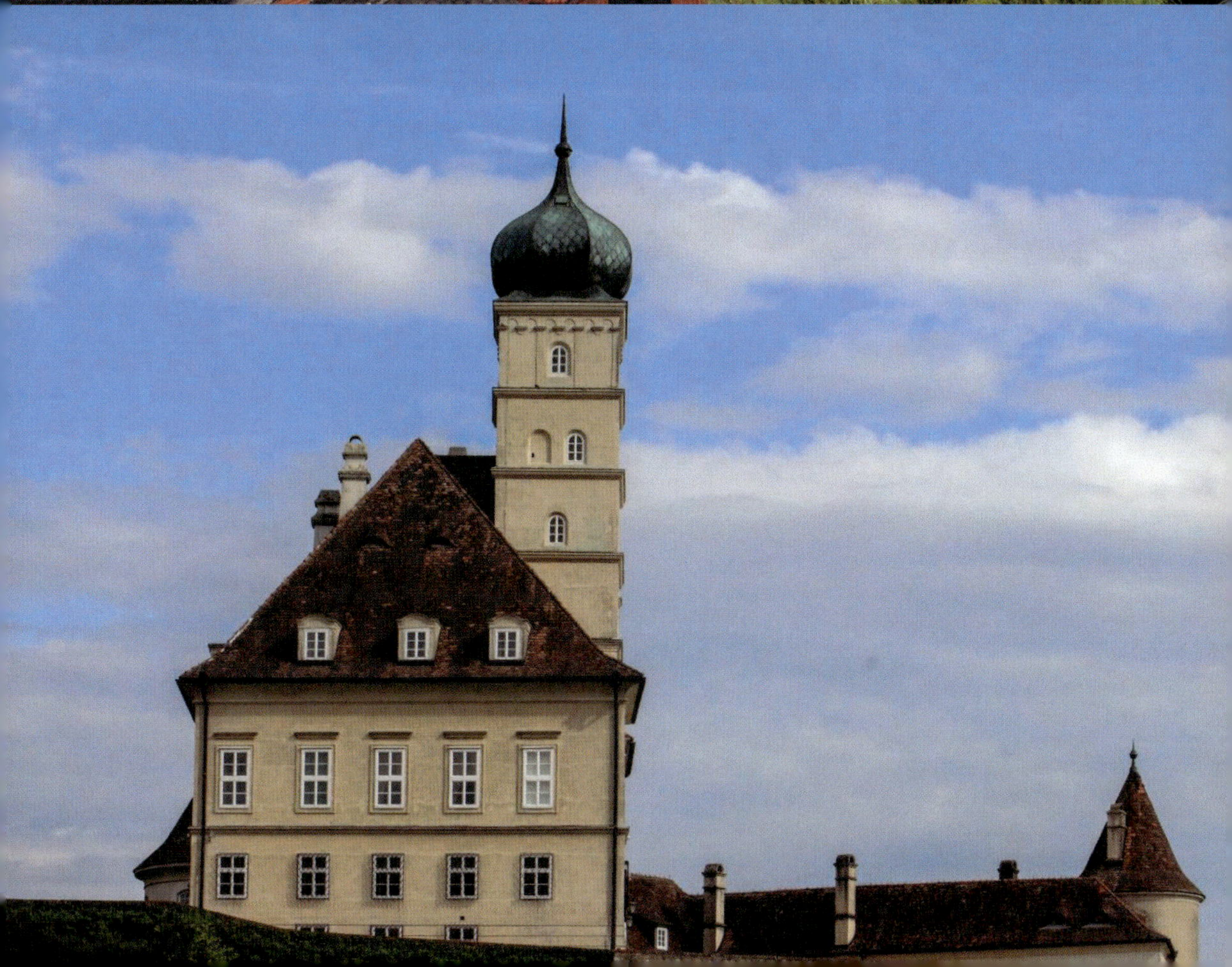

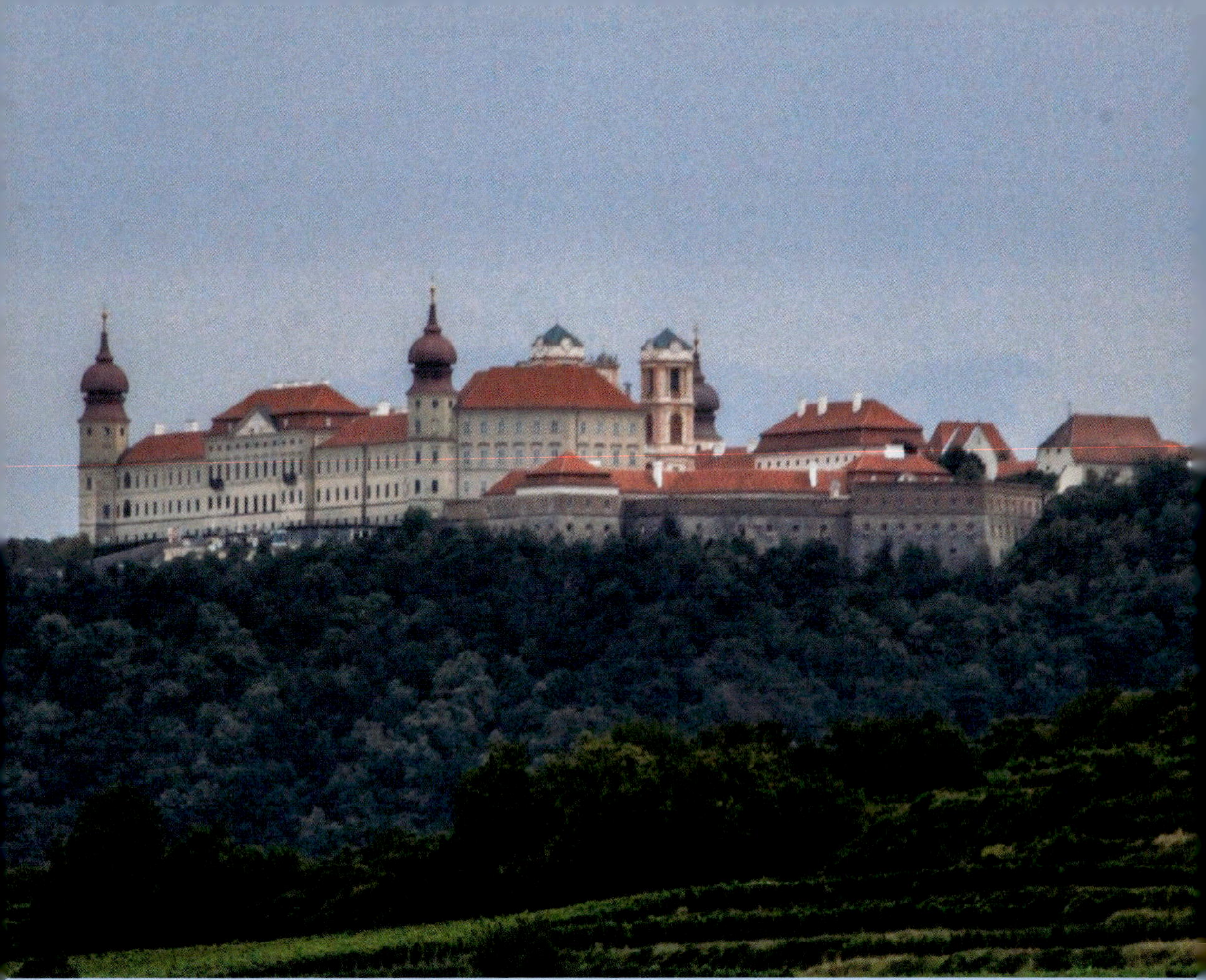

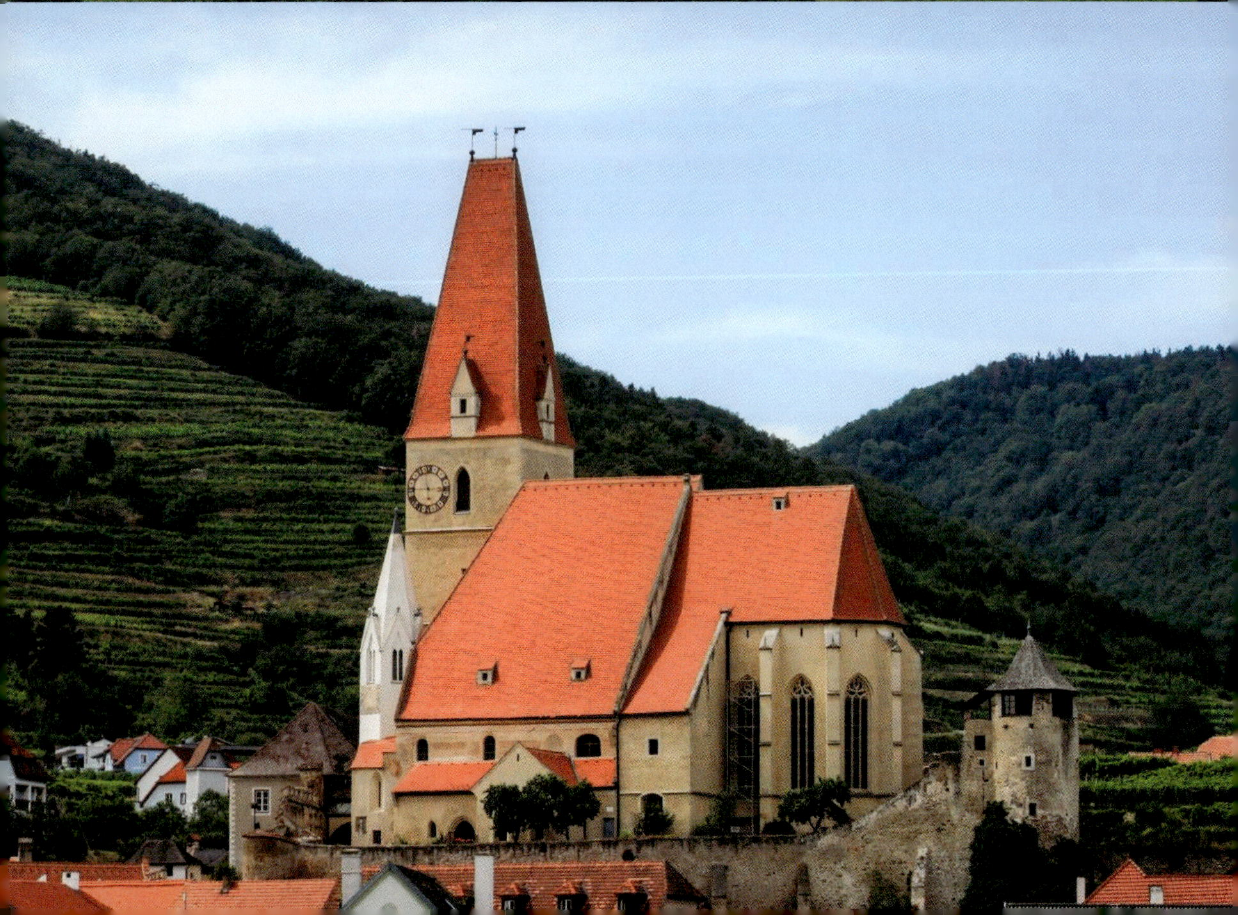

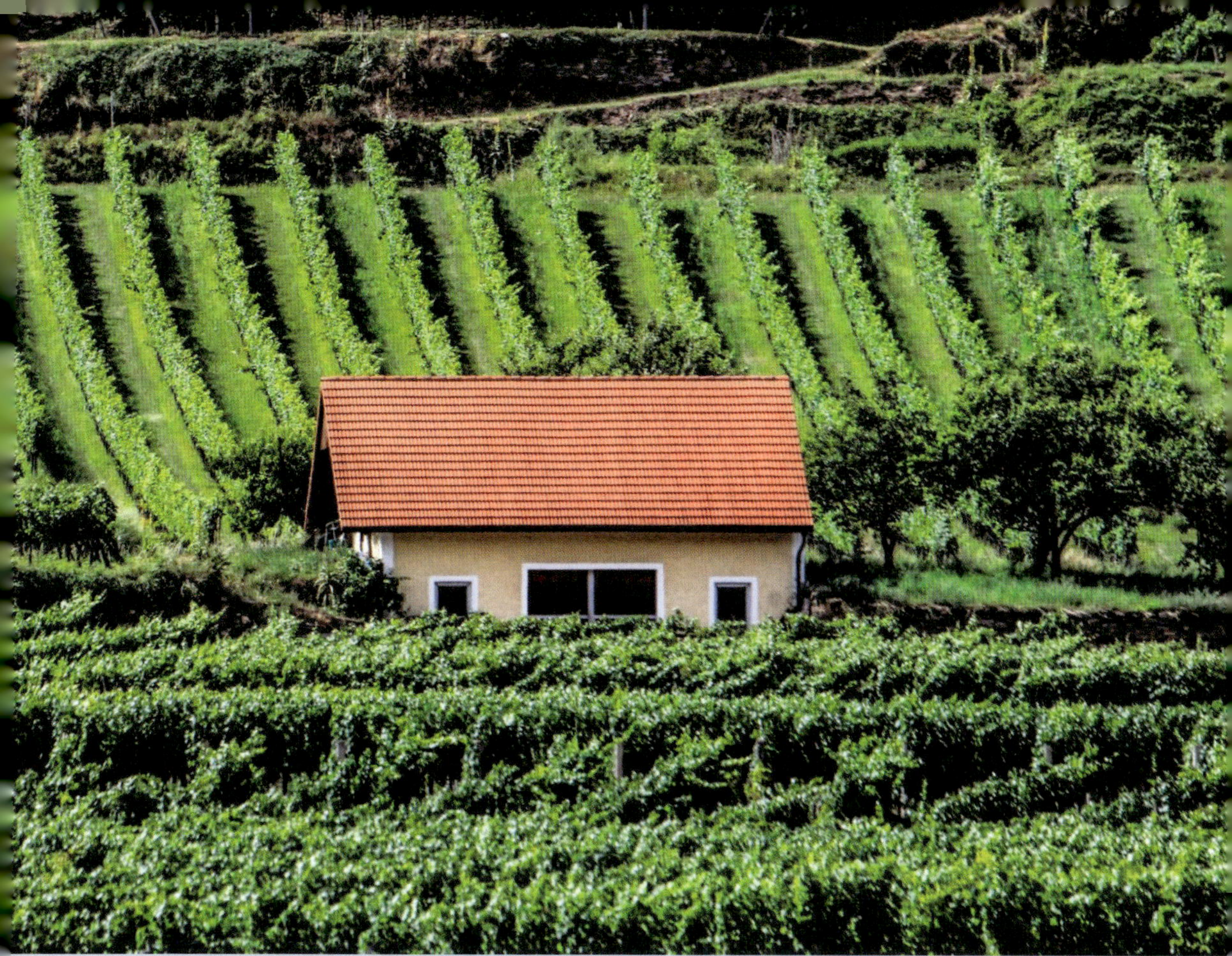

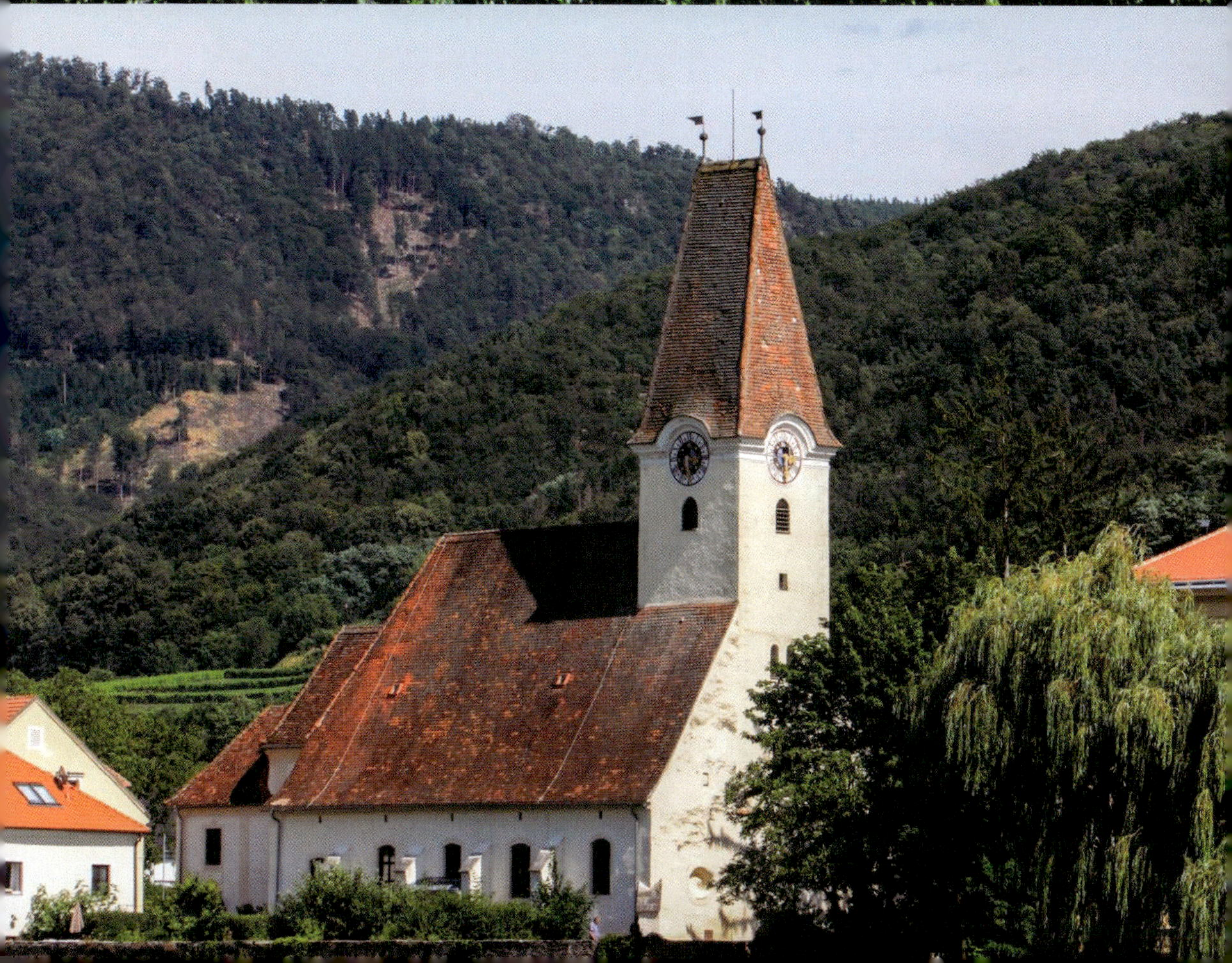

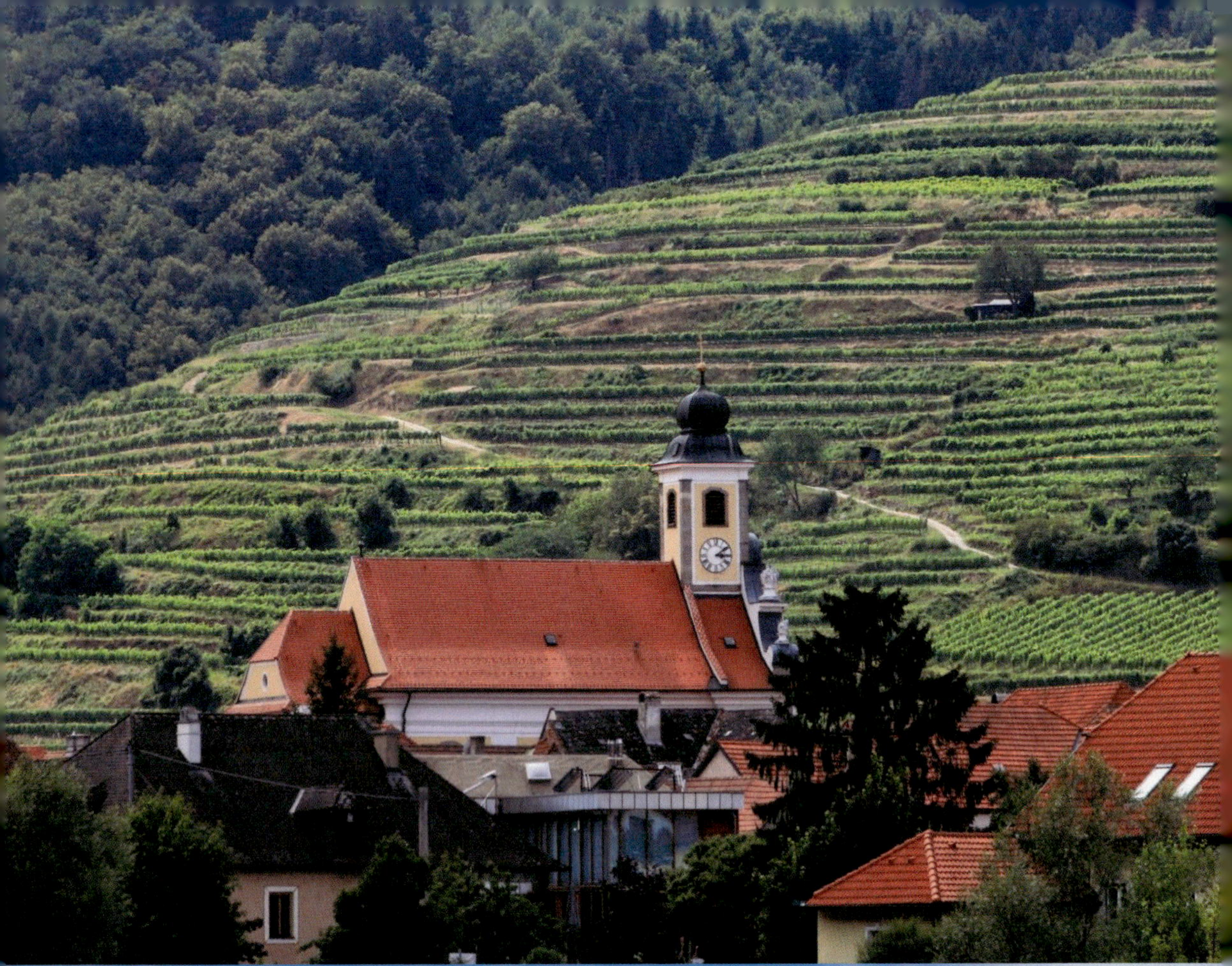

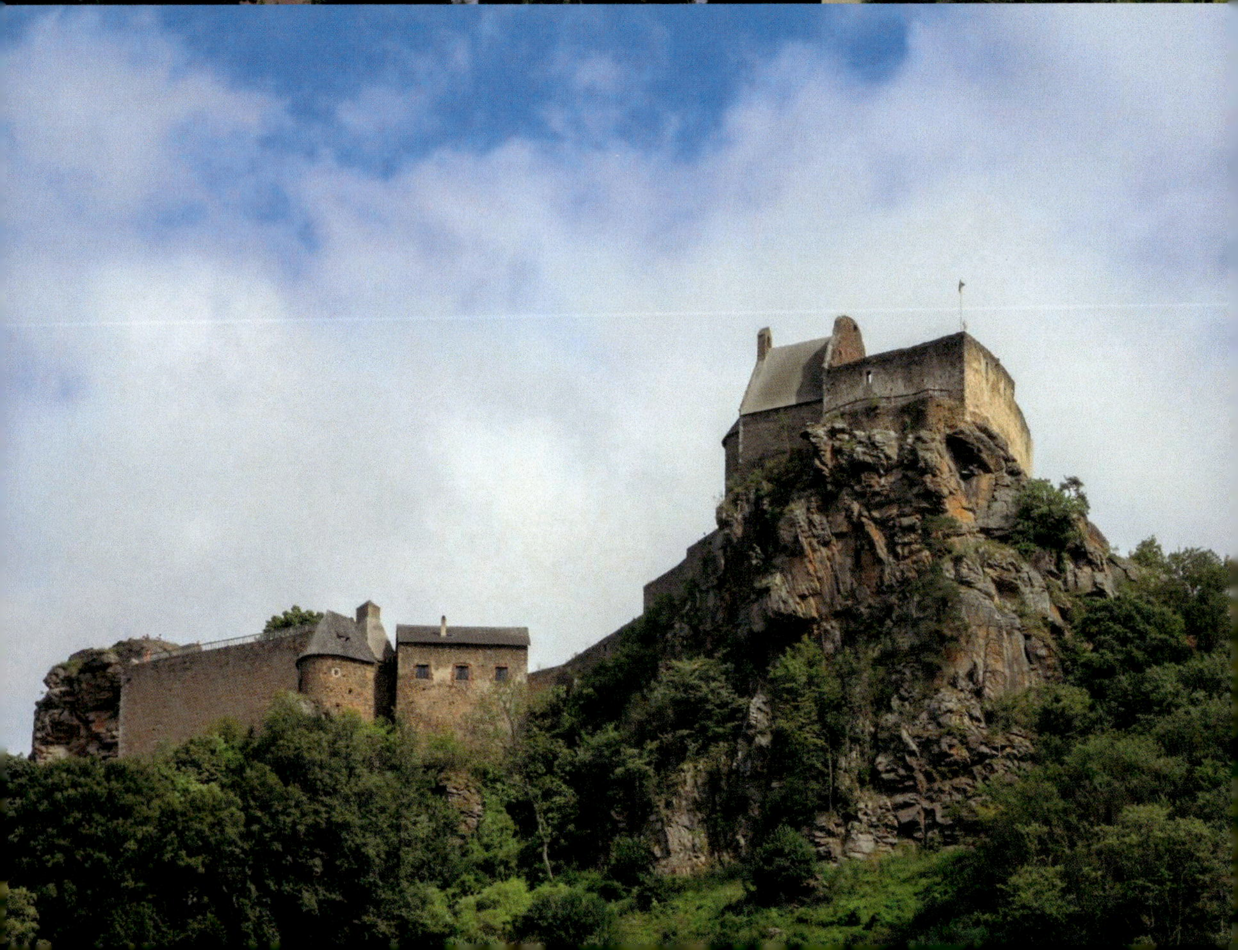

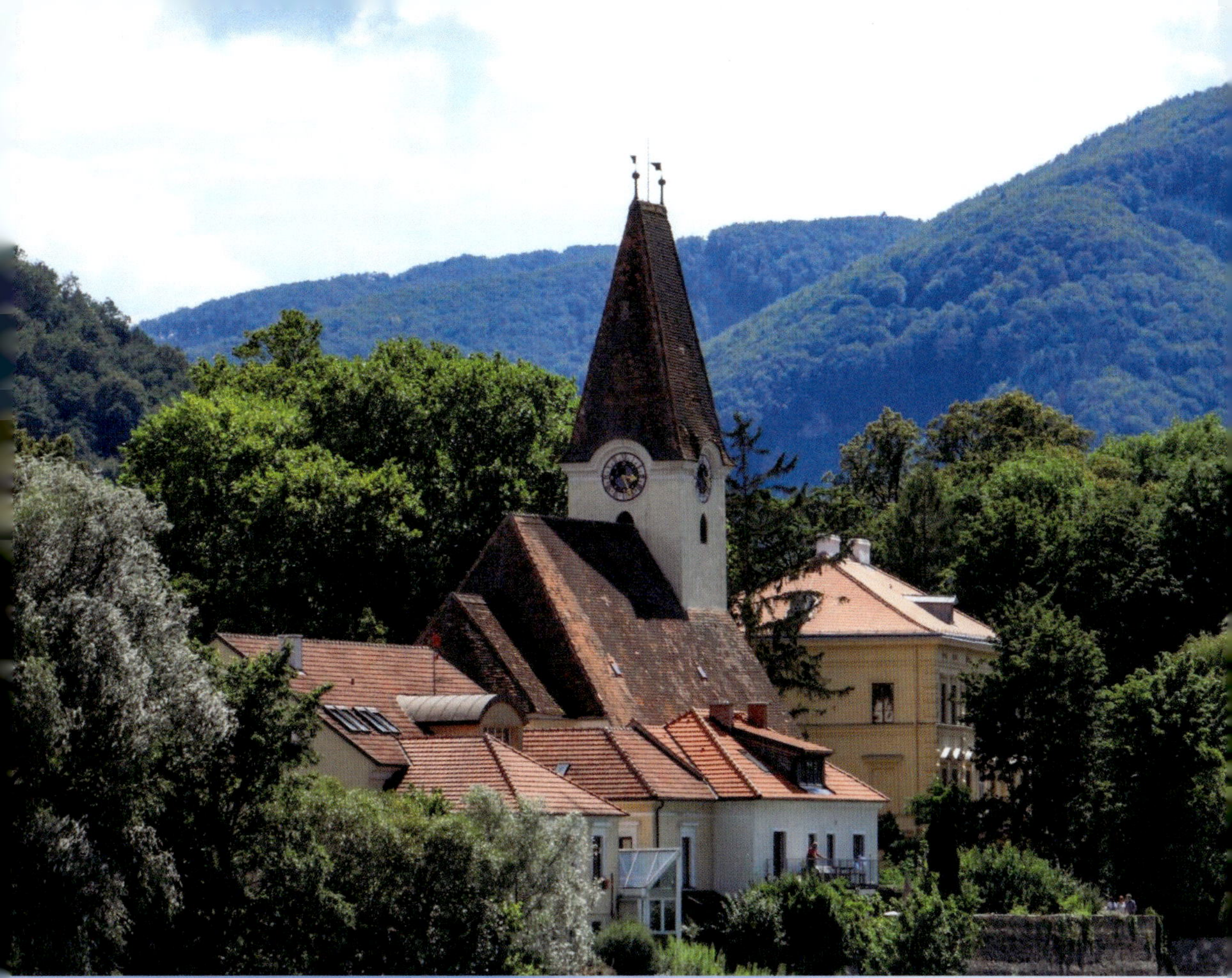

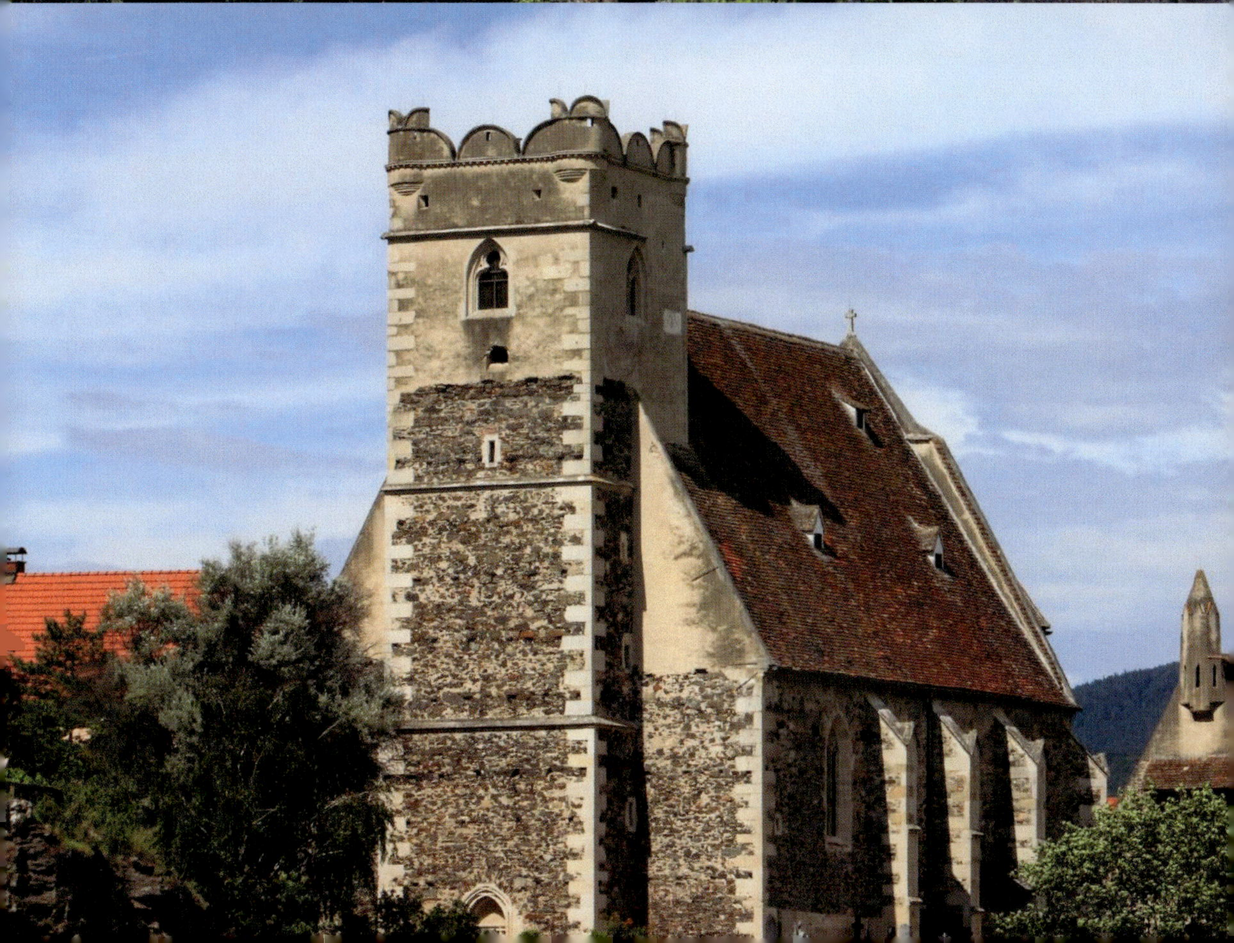

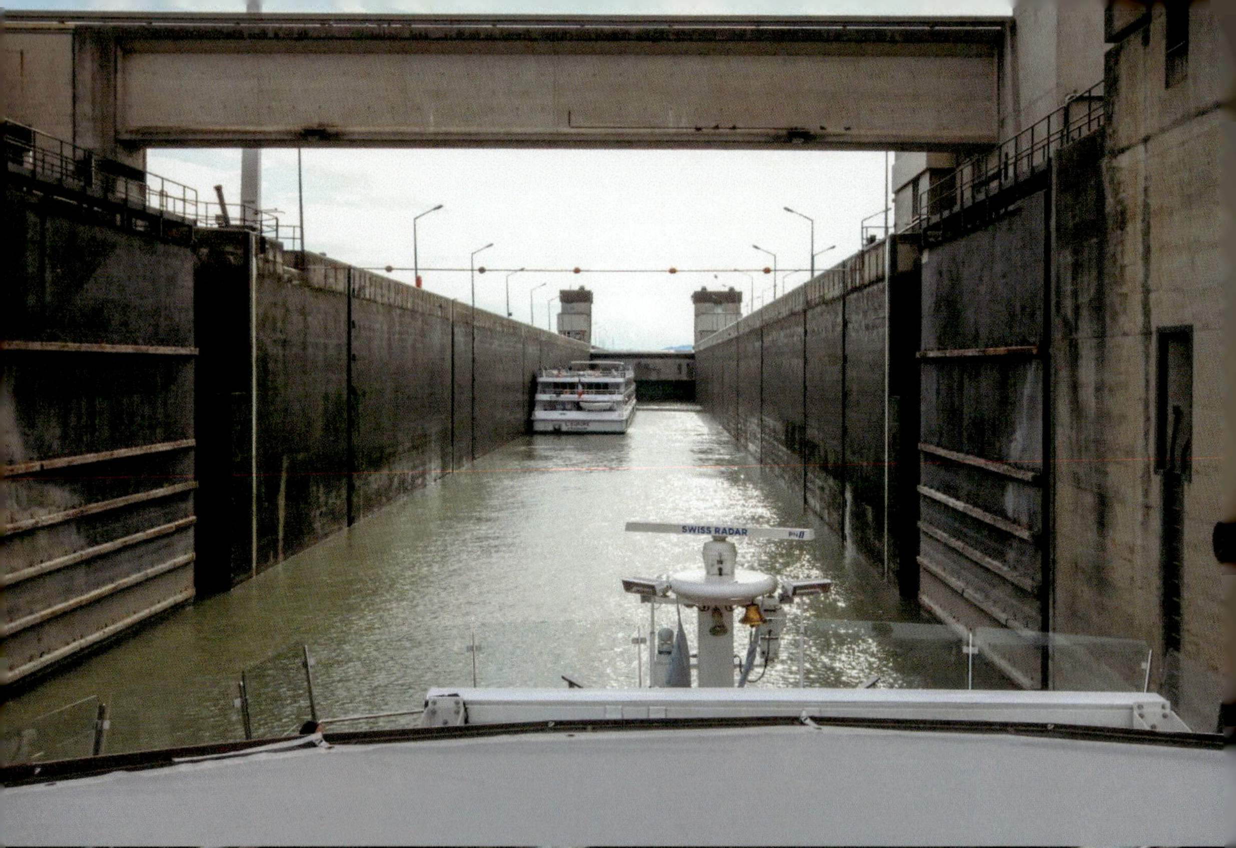
SWISS RADAR

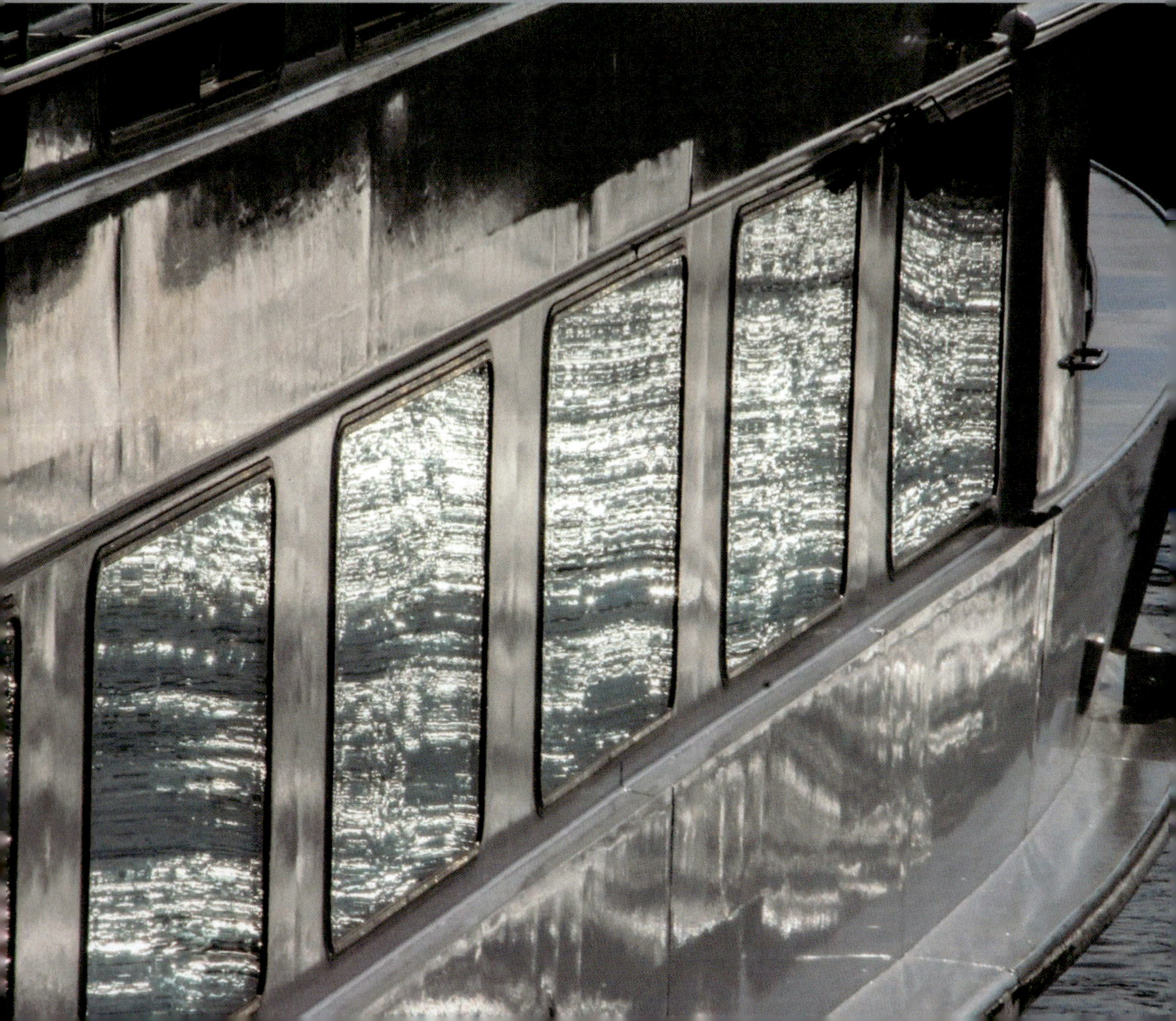

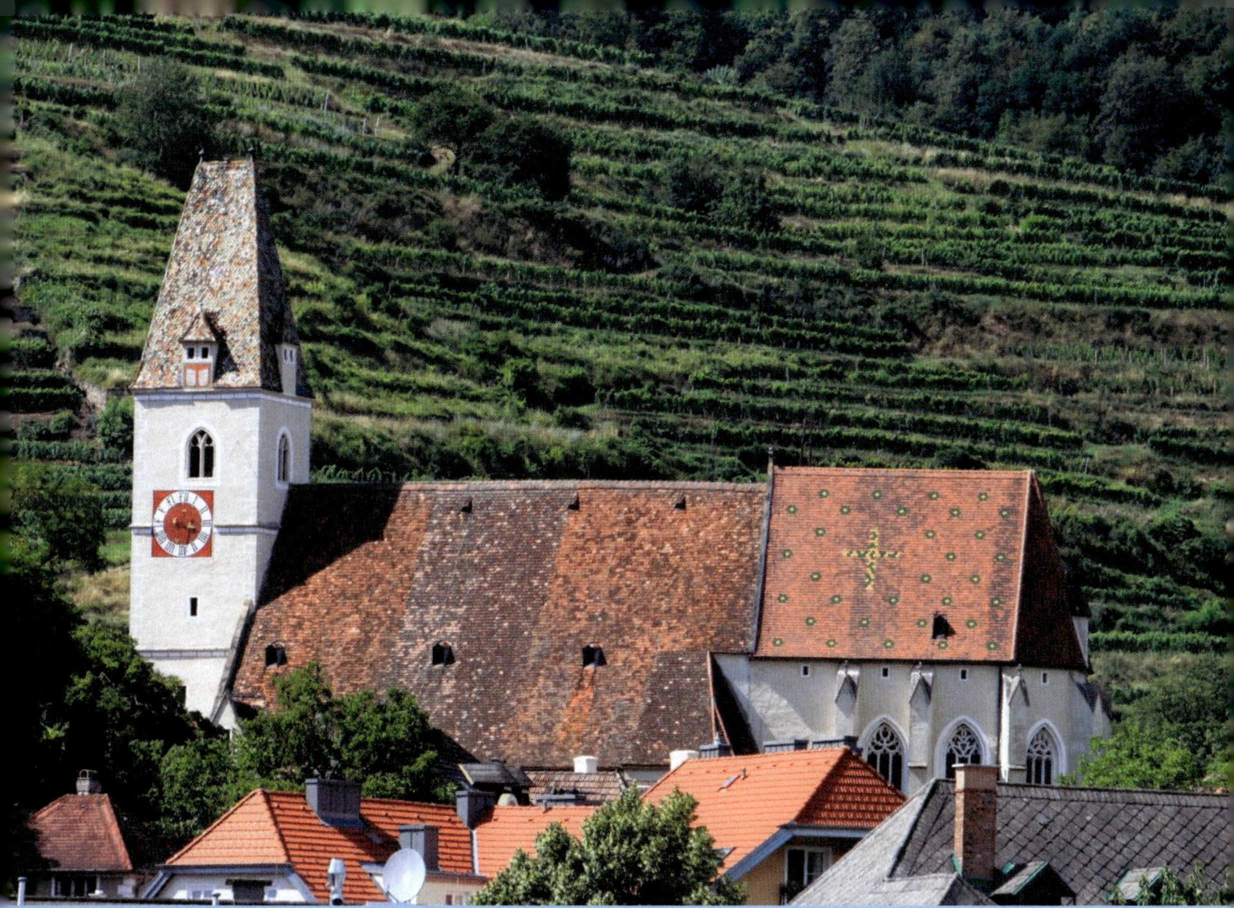

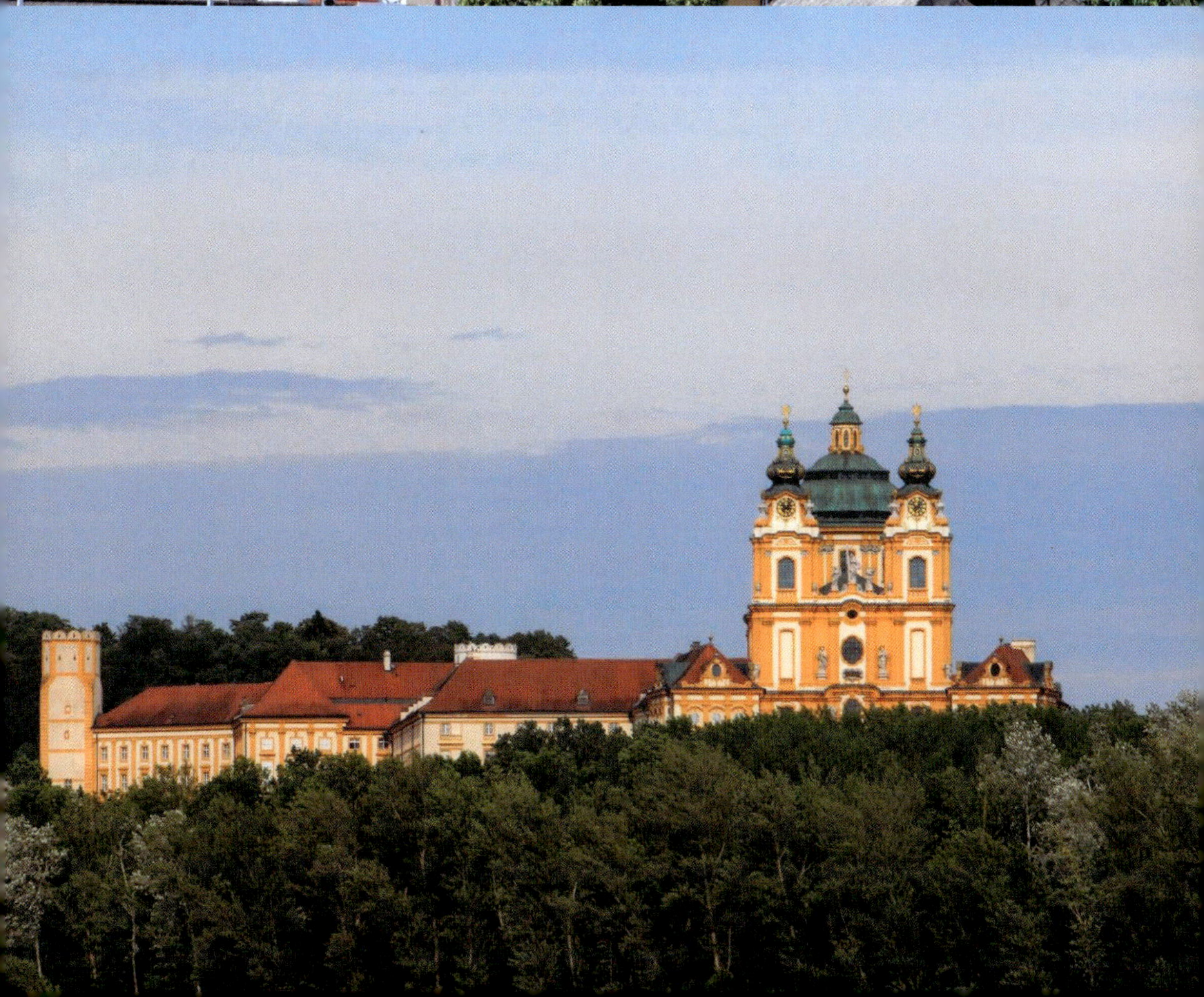

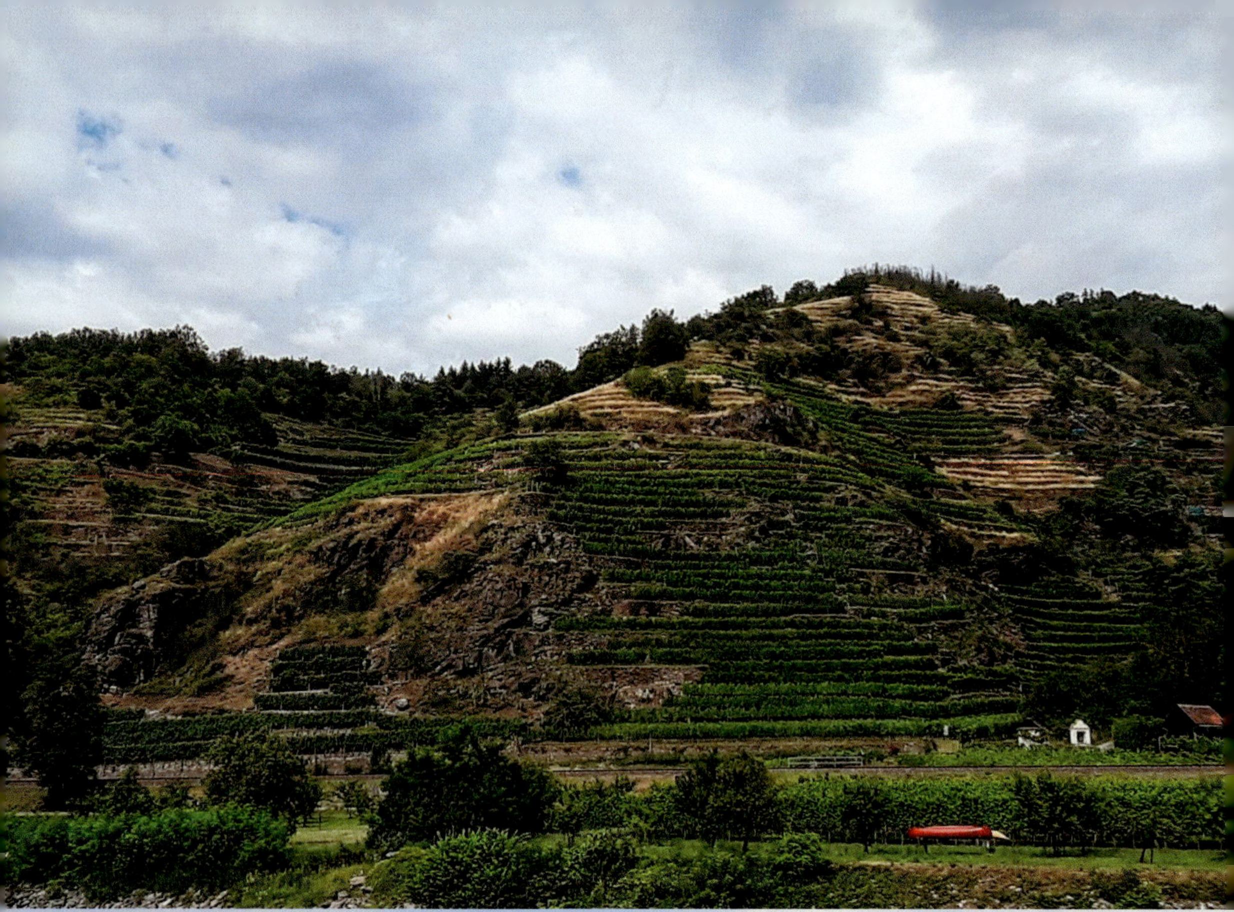

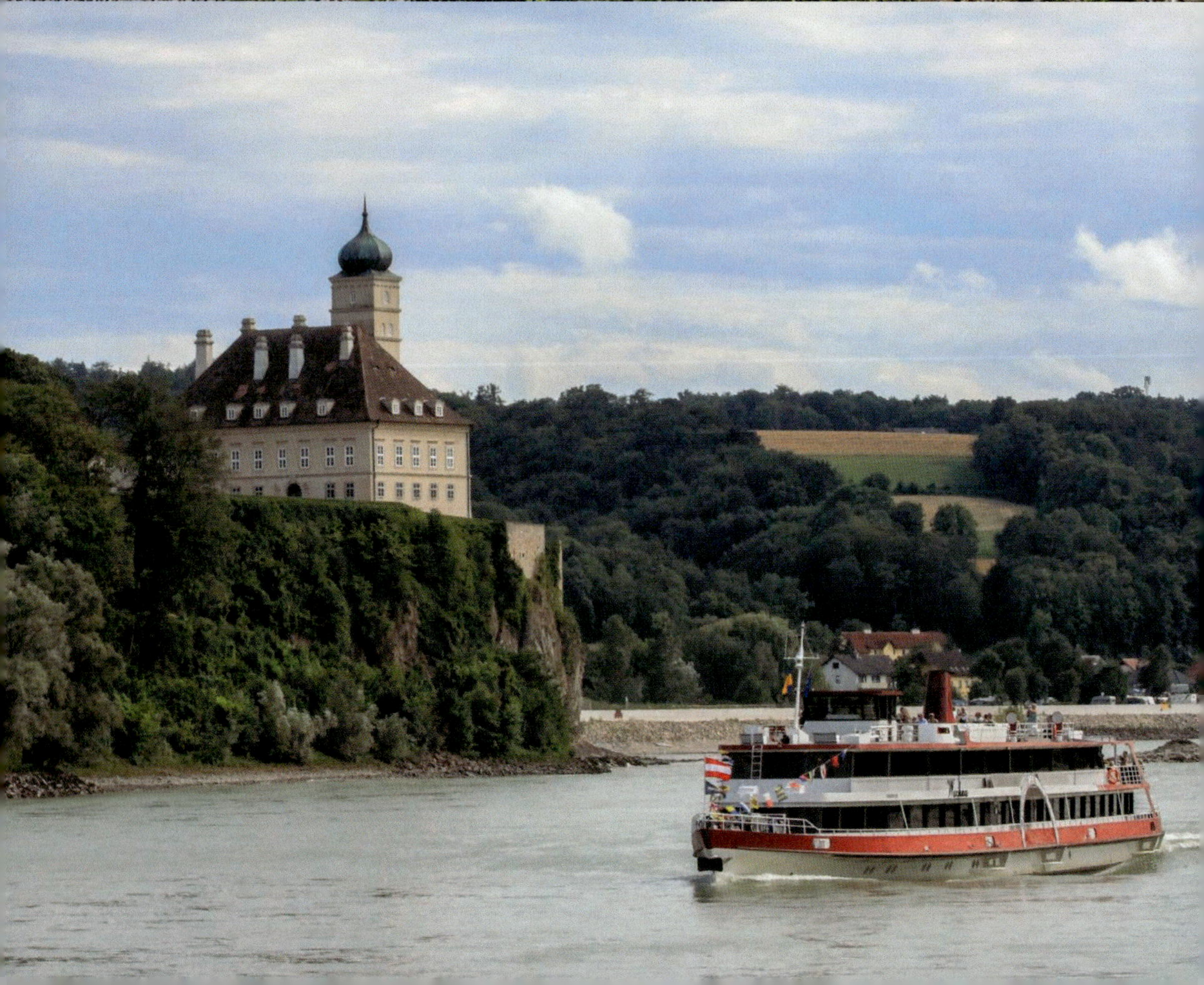

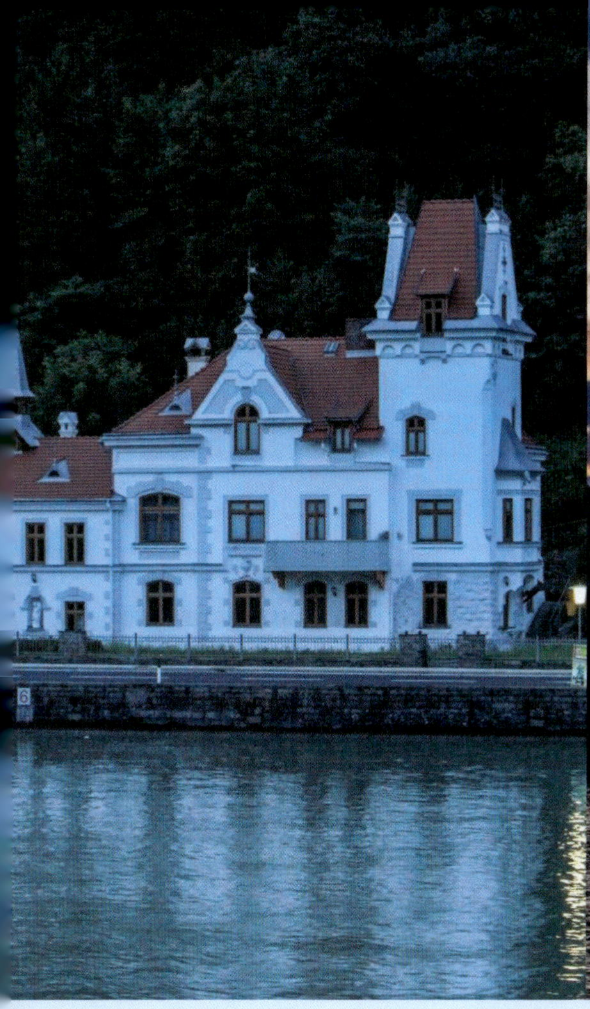

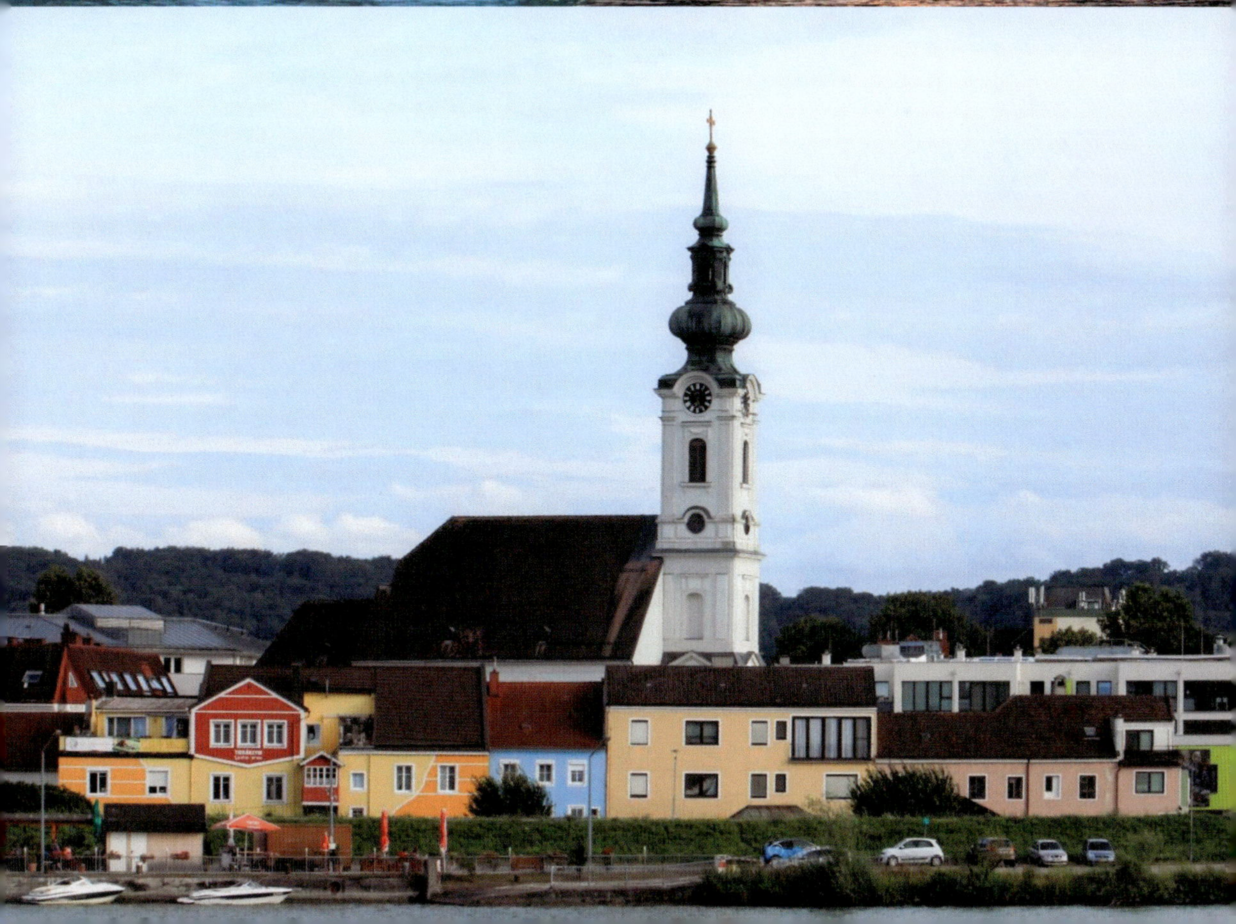

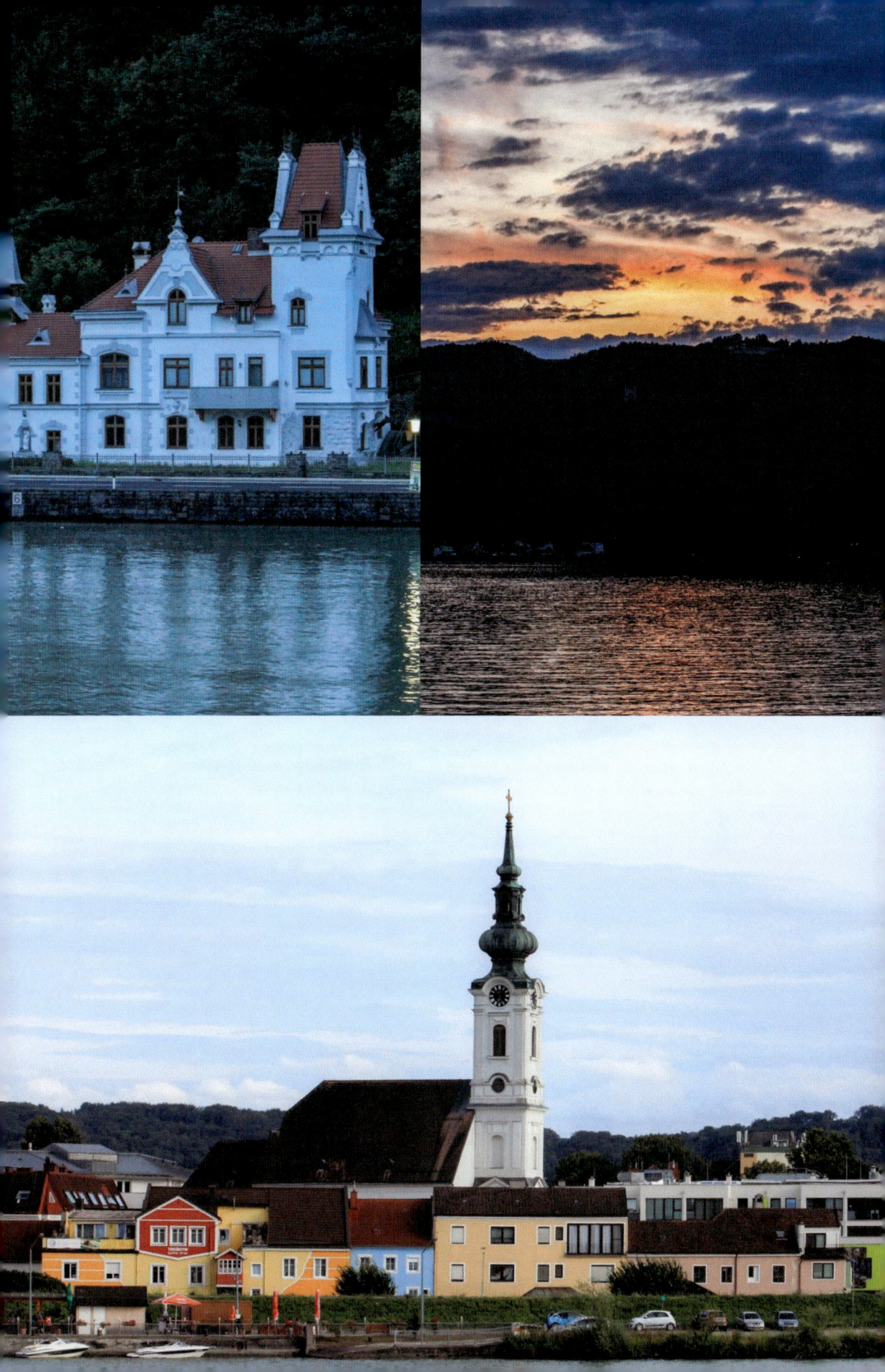

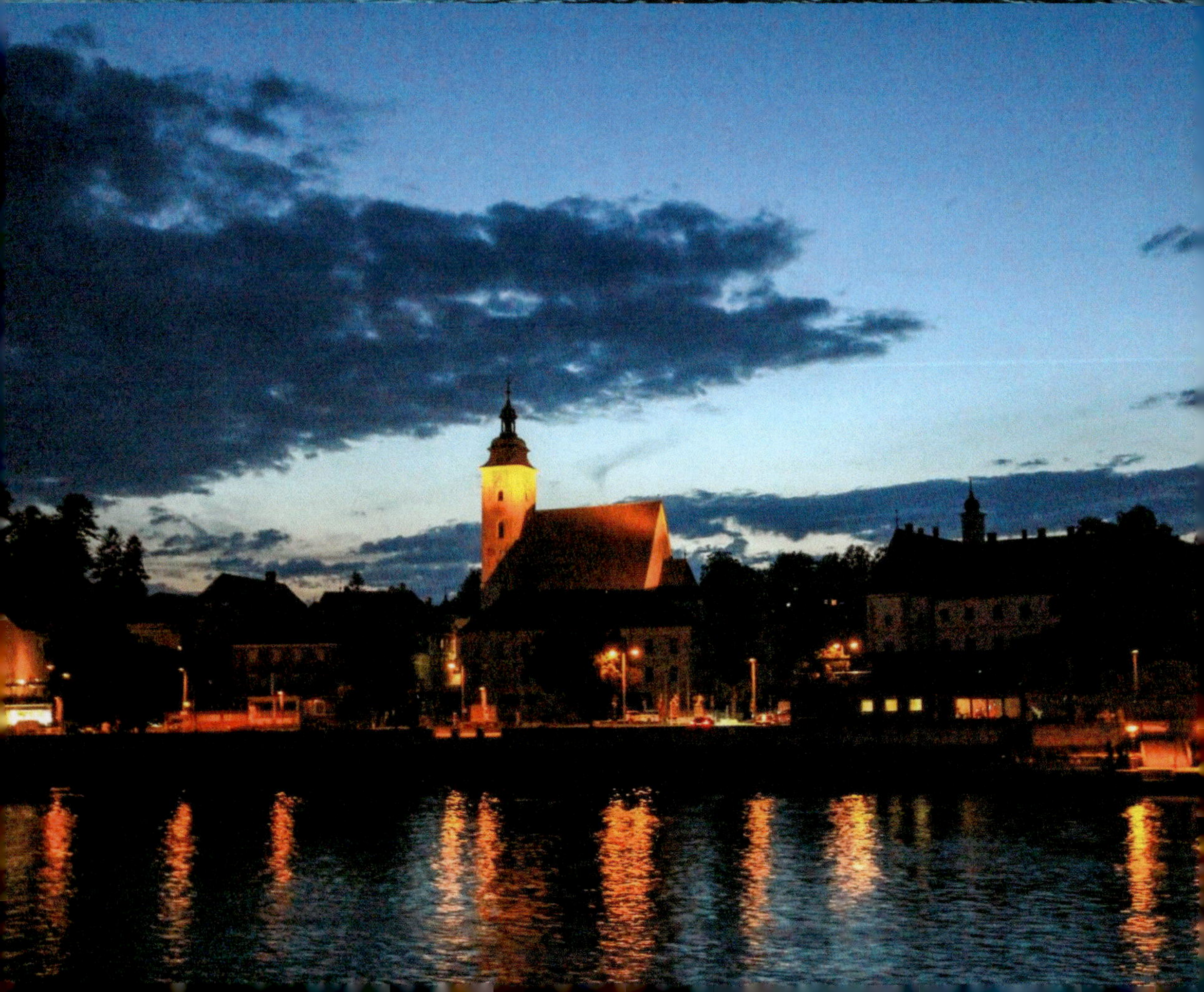

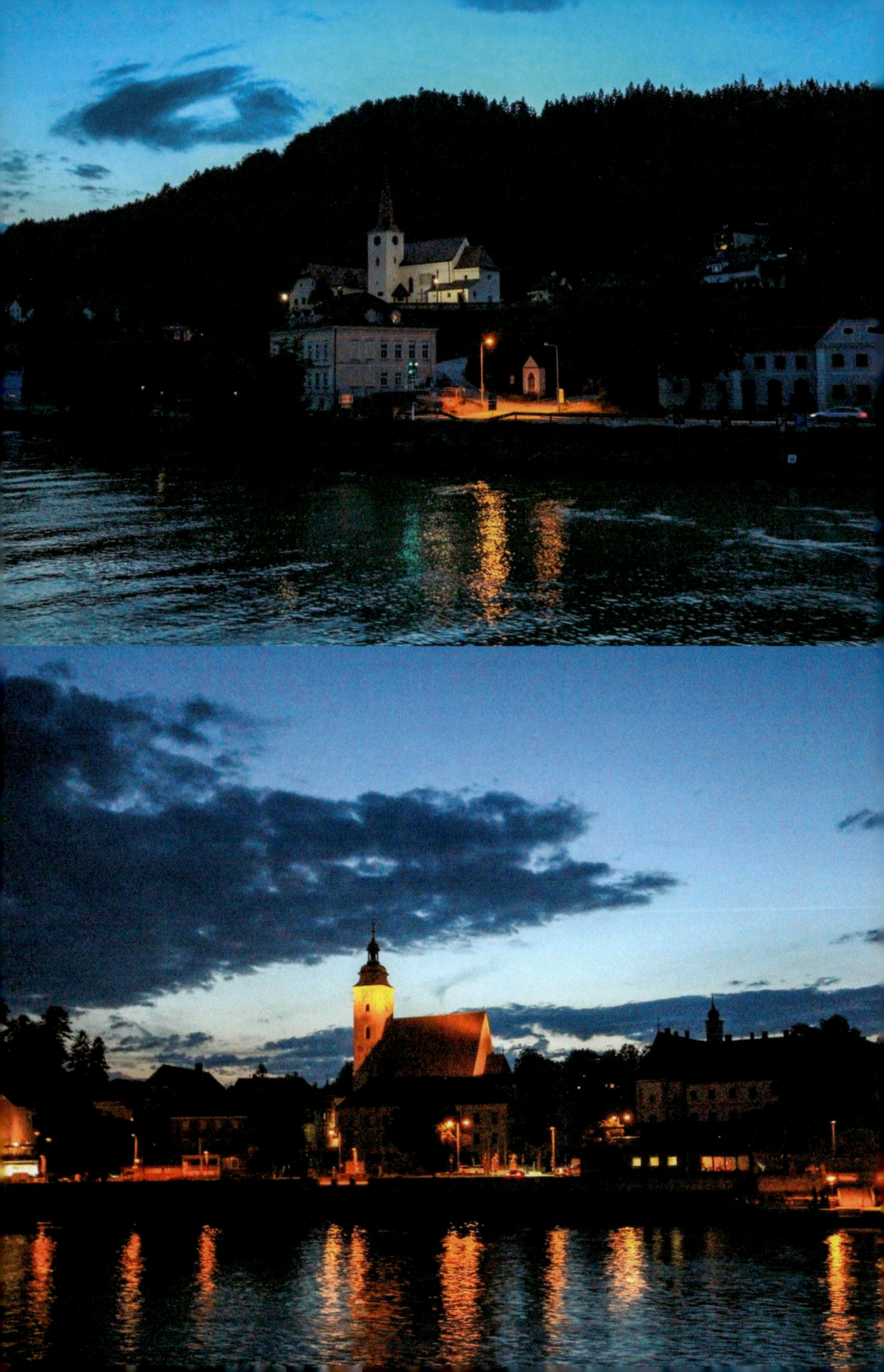

LINZ, AUSTRIA

Since we decided to take the day-long excursion to Český Krumlov, Czech Republic, we had little time to explore Linz. While it appeared to be a nice town, I didn't hear people exclaiming how quaint it was as they did with Český Krumlov. We walked around the pedestraian zone and stopped in a café for an espresso.

The town seemed well organized and the pedestrian zone was clean and had shops to explore. There were many beautiful flower beds around town.

The photo in this chapter of the advertisement on the front of a building indicates what I perceive to be a progressive-minded town. It would have been fun to explore more of the town.

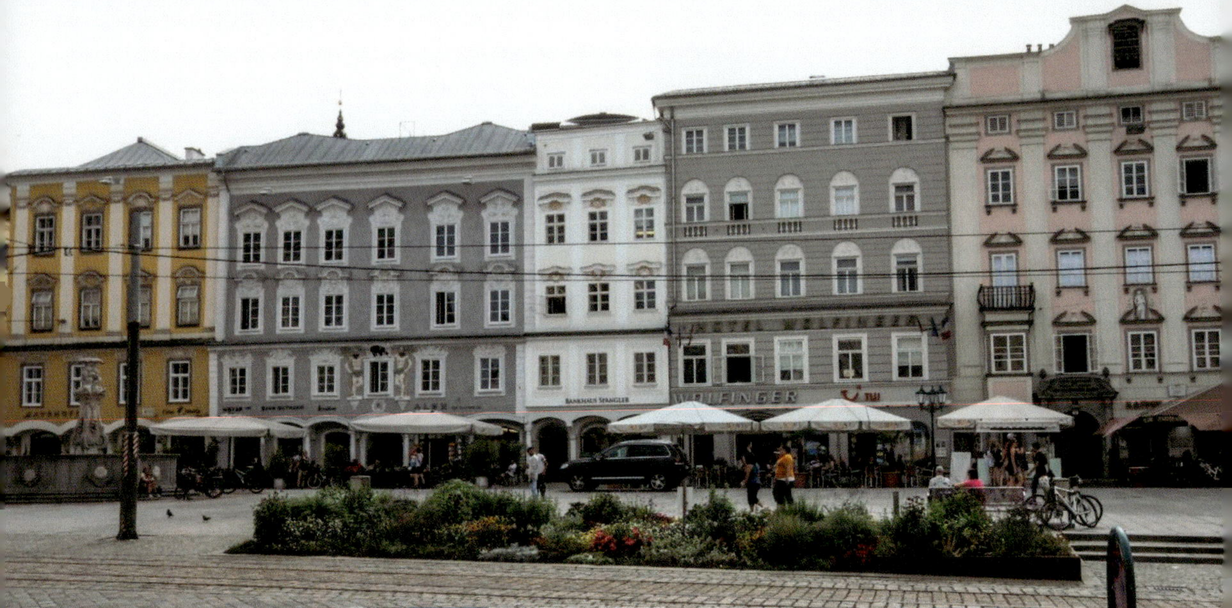
WOLFINGER

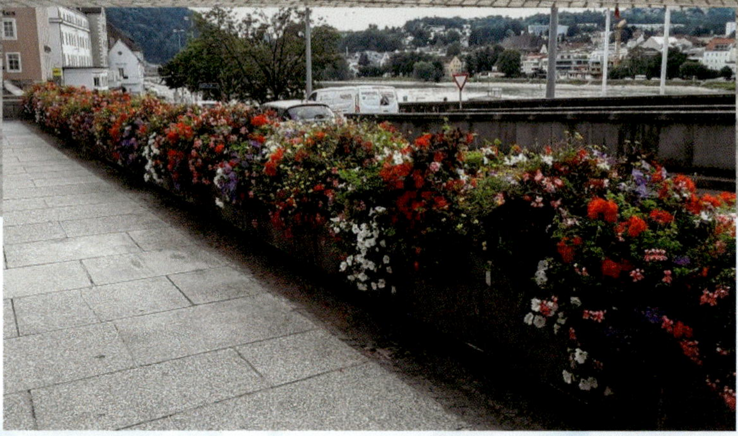

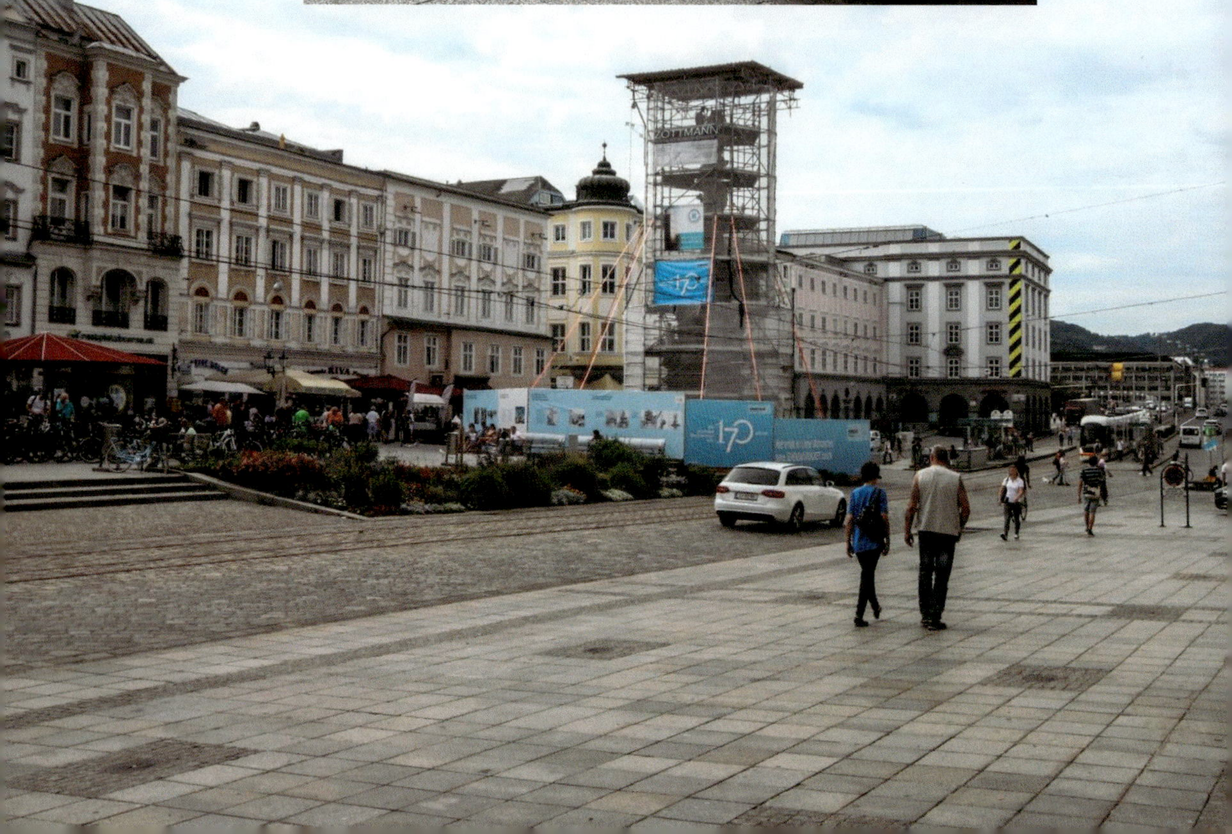
ZOTTMANN
170

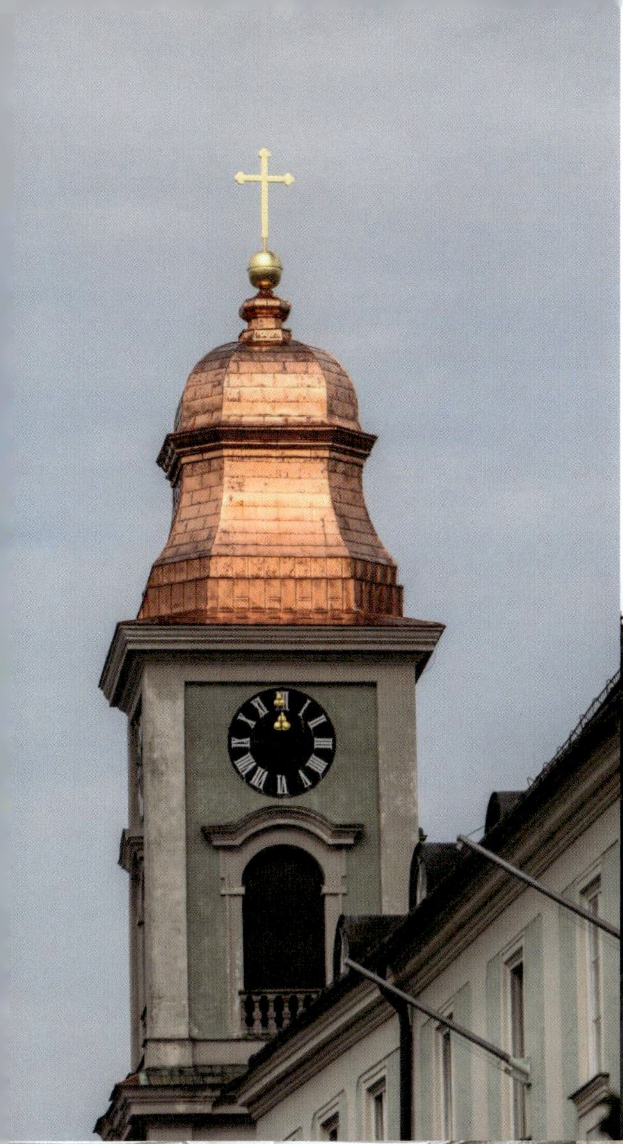

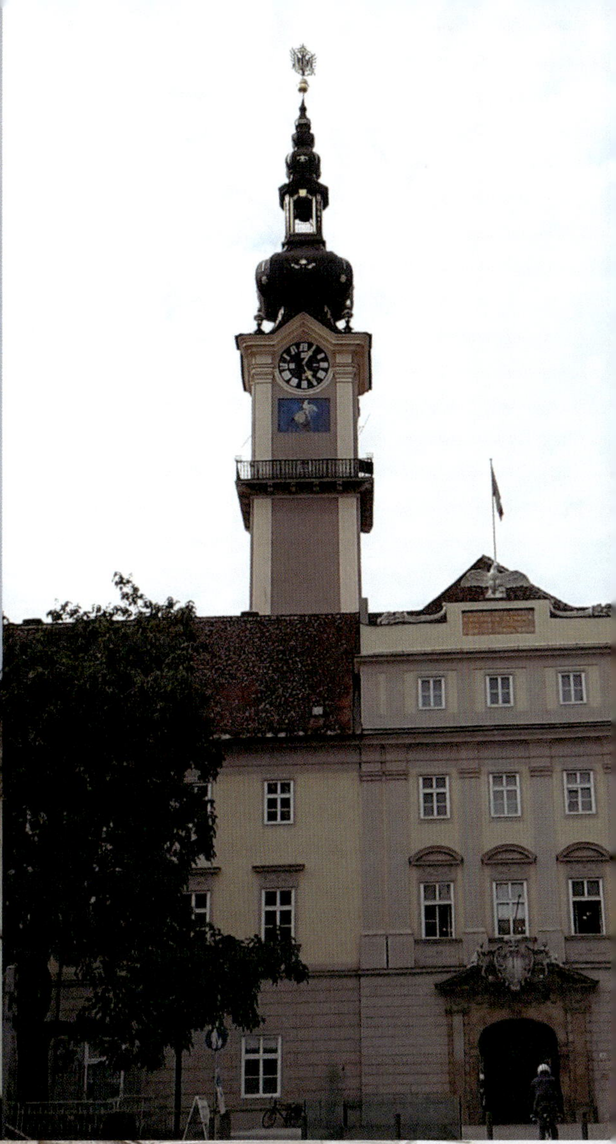

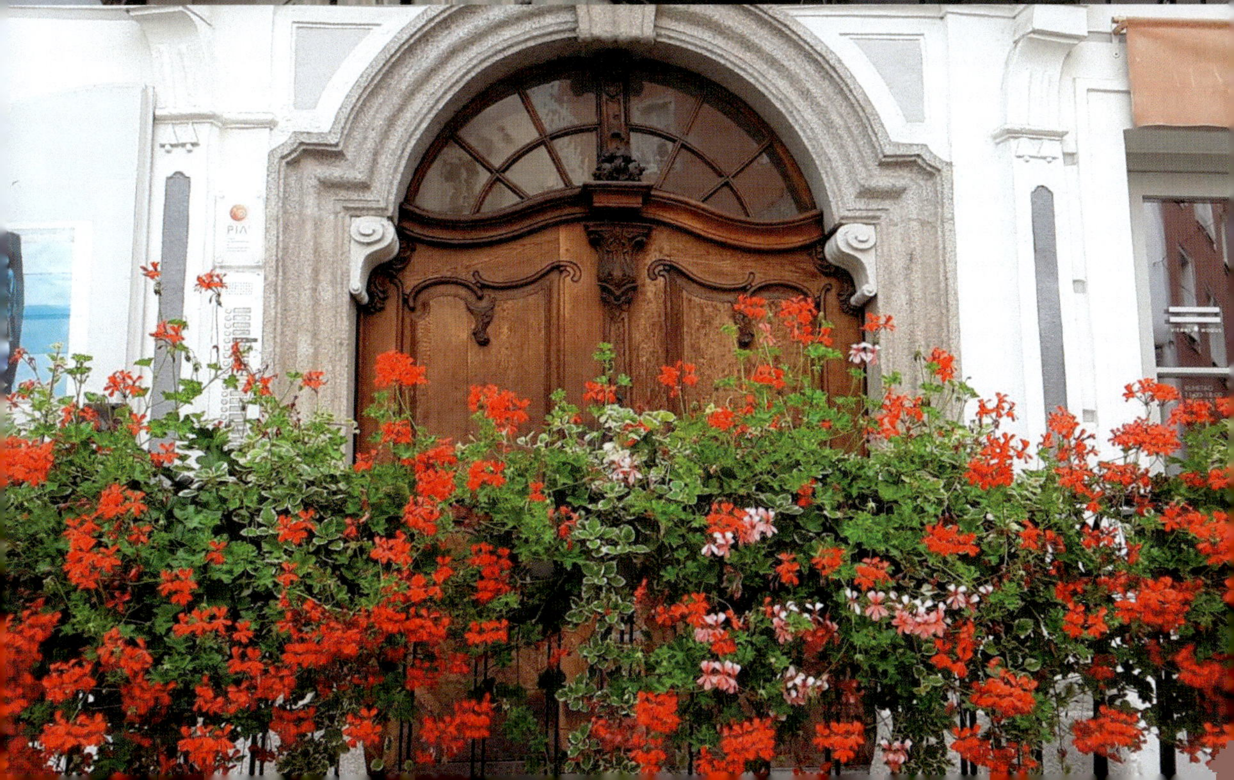
PIA

FLUCHTHELFER
DEIN PERSÖNLICHER REISEPARTNER

FLUCHTHELFER
DEIN PERSÖNLICHER REISEPARTNER

www.fluchthelfer.at

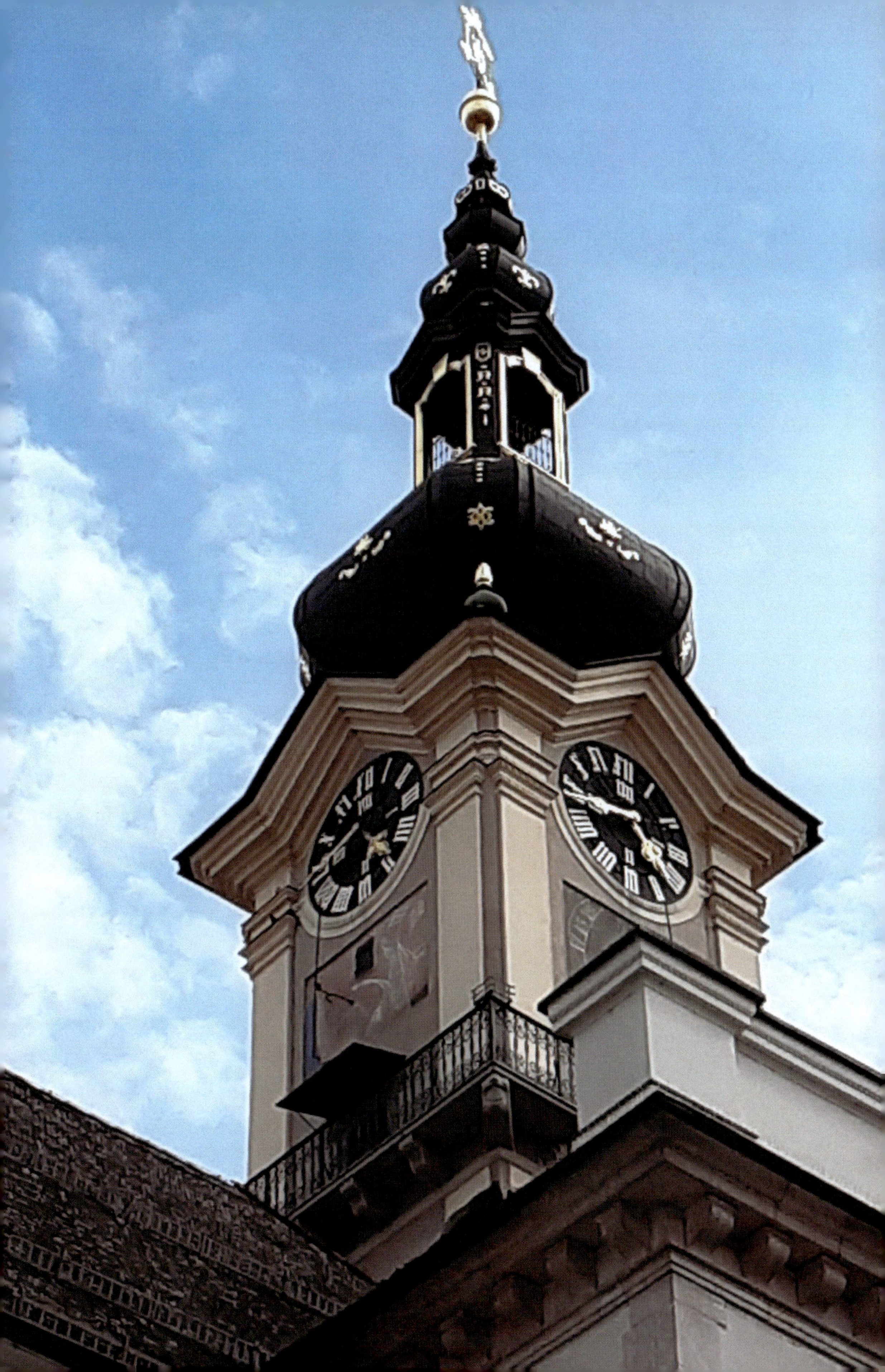

Český Krumlov, Czech Republic

We took an excursion bus on a two-hour ride from Linz, Austria to Český Krumlov, a cute town in the Czech Republic. On the trip our guide who grew up there spoke about growing up under communism. She was nearly in tears as she spoke about the pressure that the government put on her parents. At one point they were given three days to decide if they were going to stay in Český Krumlov or leave the country.

Český Krumlov was ignored and started to decay during communist rule. In the 1980's there were efforts to restore the town to its prior beauty. Those efforts have been successful and now the town is a tourist magnet. The view of the town, partially surrounded by the Vltava River, is awe inspiring.

We started at Český Krumlov Castle which was built in 1240. We didn't explore inside the castle; however, we enjoyed the views of the town and the river that surrounds most of the town.

One of our ship mates was excited to see the bears that are known to inhabit the moat that surrounds the castle (there is no water.) Prior castle residents wanted to align themselves with the Orsini family. Orsini is an Italian pun for the word bear (Orso.) However, when we looked down into the bear pit there were none to be seen. The enclosure was being cleaned out. Two of the bears died recently so there was only one left. Sad.

When we walked down the stairs from the castle we were in the old town where there were restaurants and shops. Our guide pointed out which shops were authentic, and which were simply tourist traps or filled with non-local gifts. She pointed out a restaurant near the steps at the bottom of the castle area that she recommended for lunch. That information was absorbed by my wife, however I missed it.

After the tour my wife and I walked around the town a little and then walked outside of the old town to see where we could have lunch off the beaten path, and away from the hordes of tourists. As we walked the streets just outside of the old town, we saw a young couple walking and asked them for restaurant recommendations. I explained that we didn't want anything in the old town to avoid the tourists. They had one recommendation; however, it was too far. The second recommendation was Švejk Restaurant. It so happens that was the same restaurant in the old town that our guide had recommended. The couple said it has good food at a fair price. While the staff was quite busy, they served us well and the food was great.

Once you get outside of the old town the area seems plain. The park just outside of the old town and the side streets were nice. We enjoyed walking through the park and watching people kayak in the river that surrounds most of the town.

The currency is the Czech koruna. You can pay in euros however your change will be in the Czech koruna. Be aware that you will need local currency (coins) to use the public restrooms.

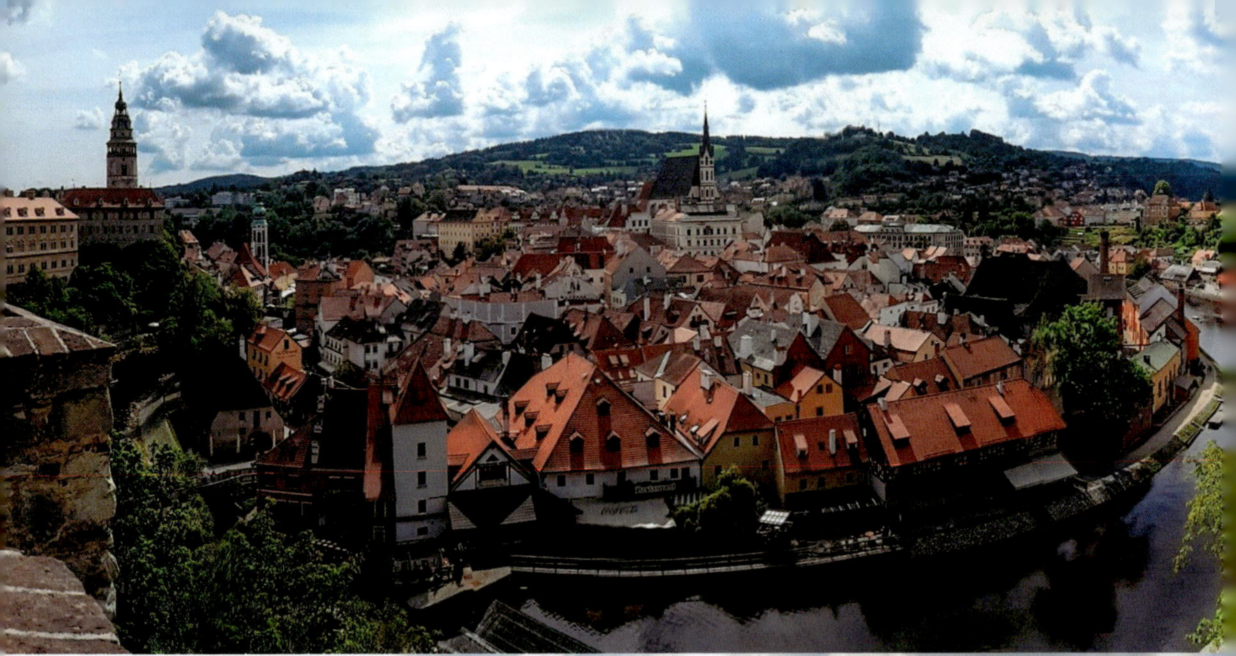

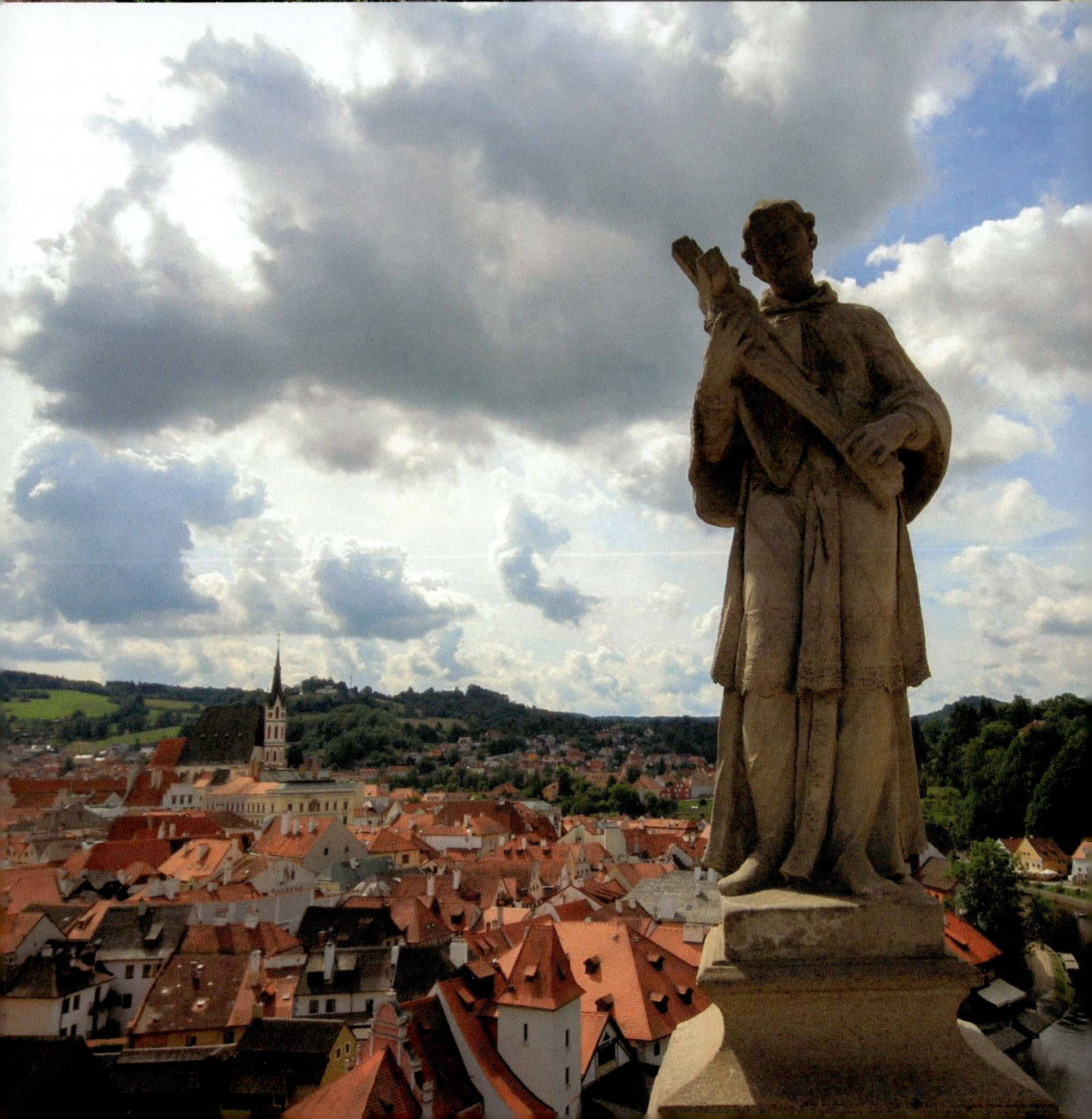

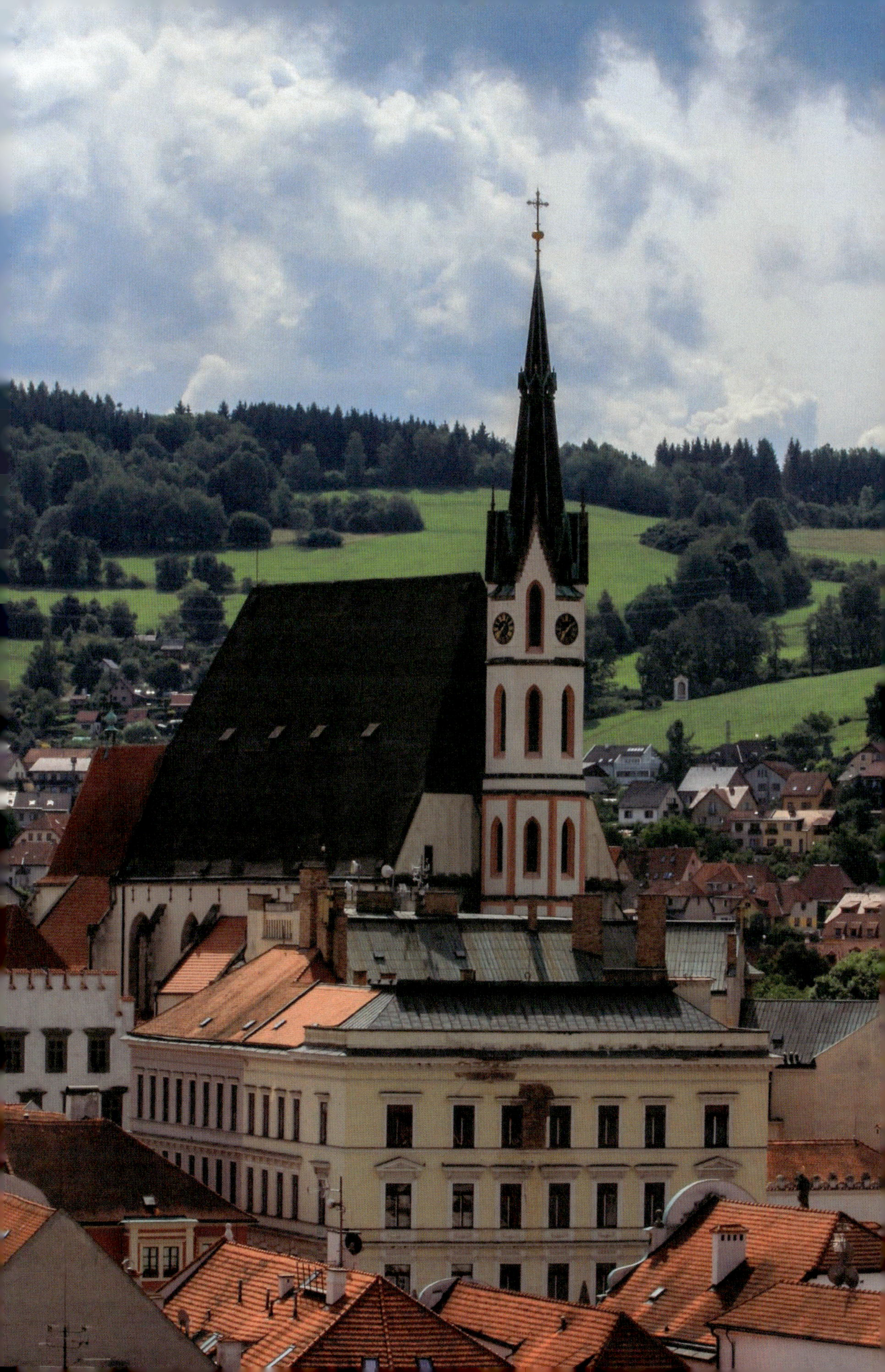

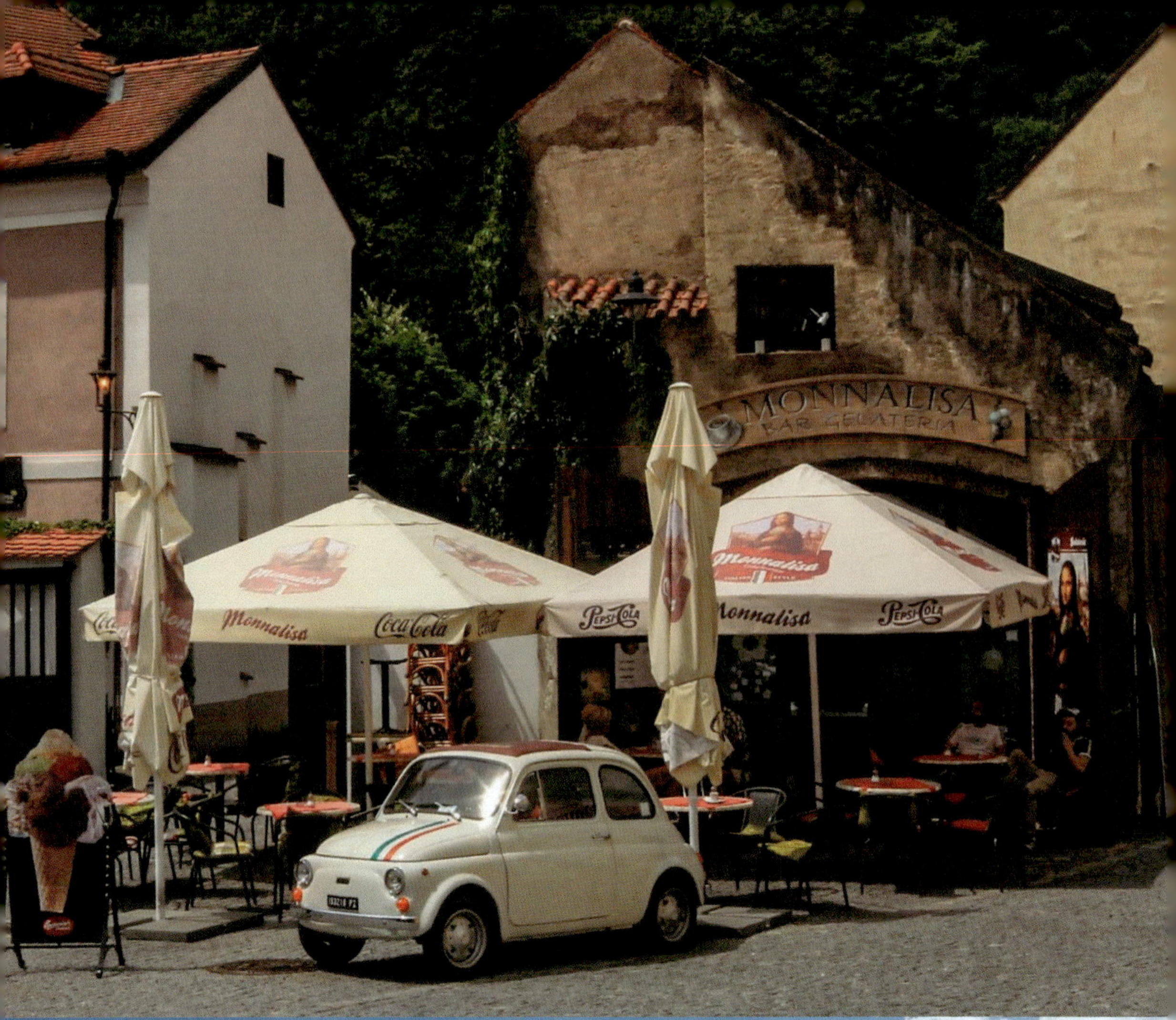
MONNALISA
BAR GELATERIA
Monnalisa
Coca-Cola
Pepsi-Cola

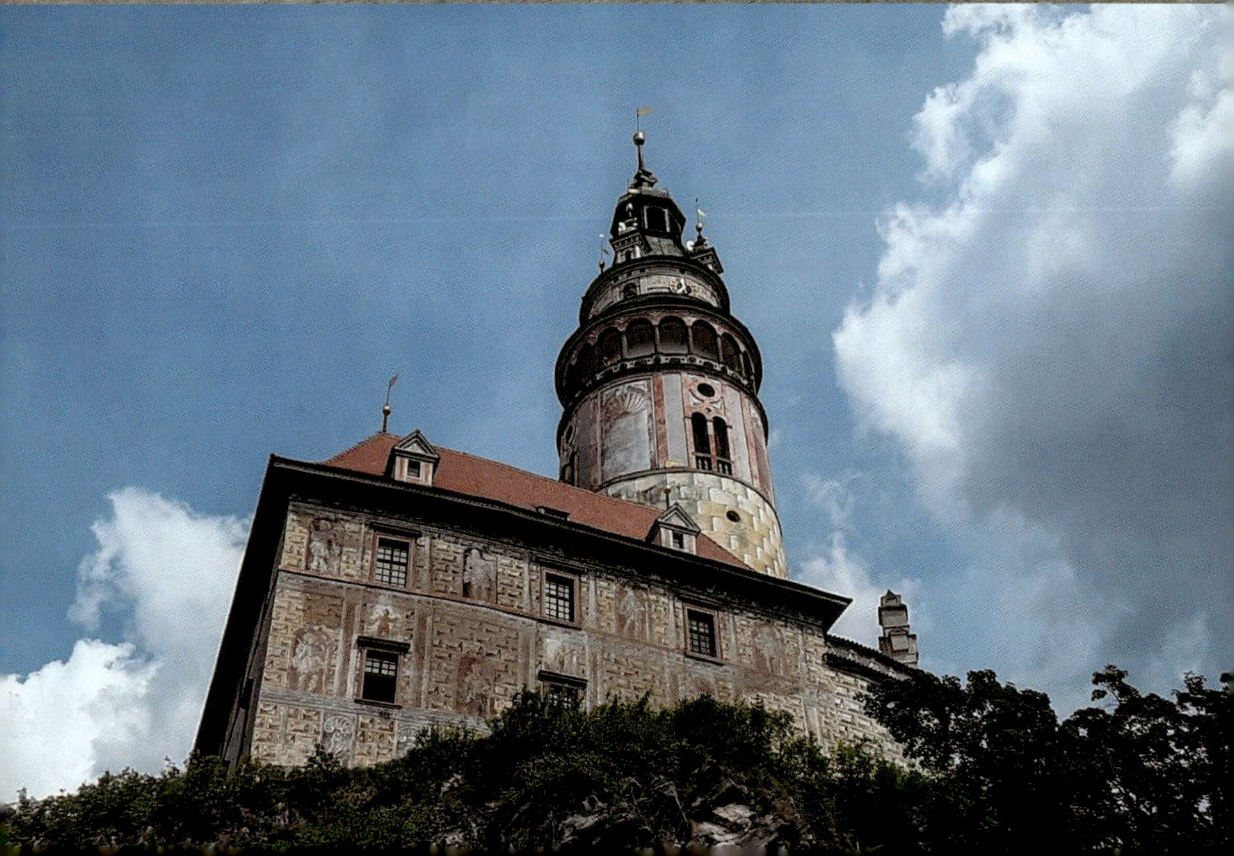

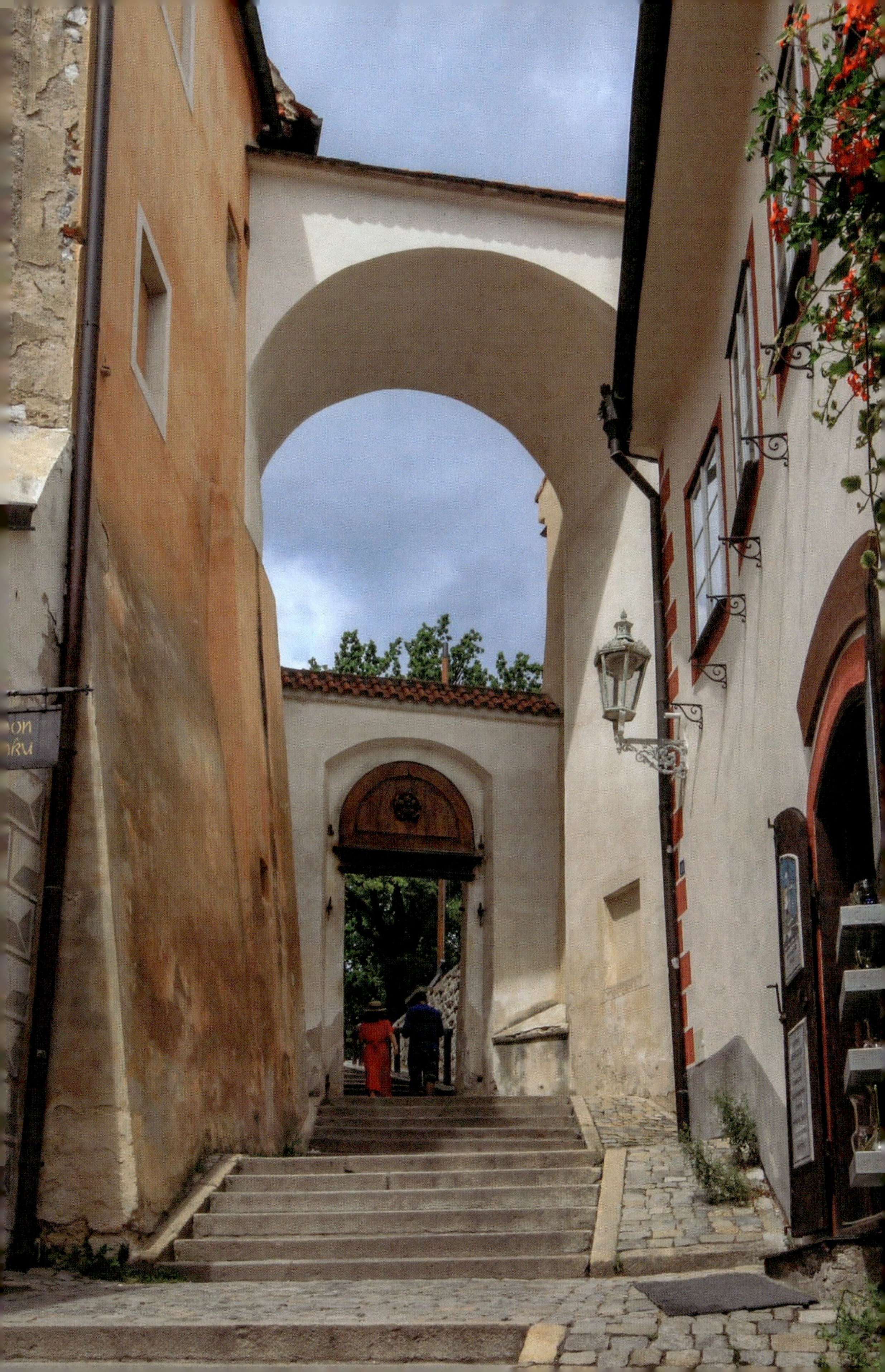

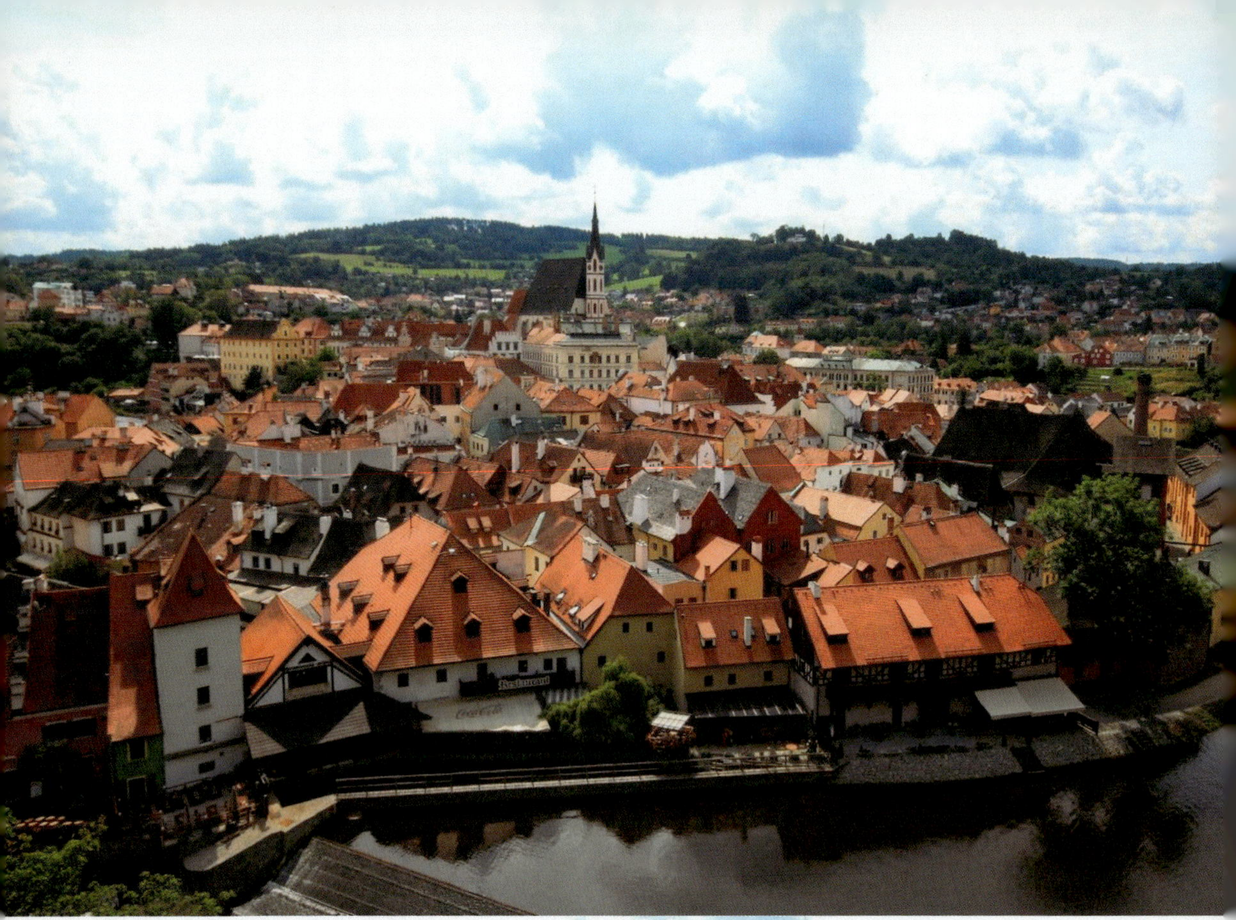

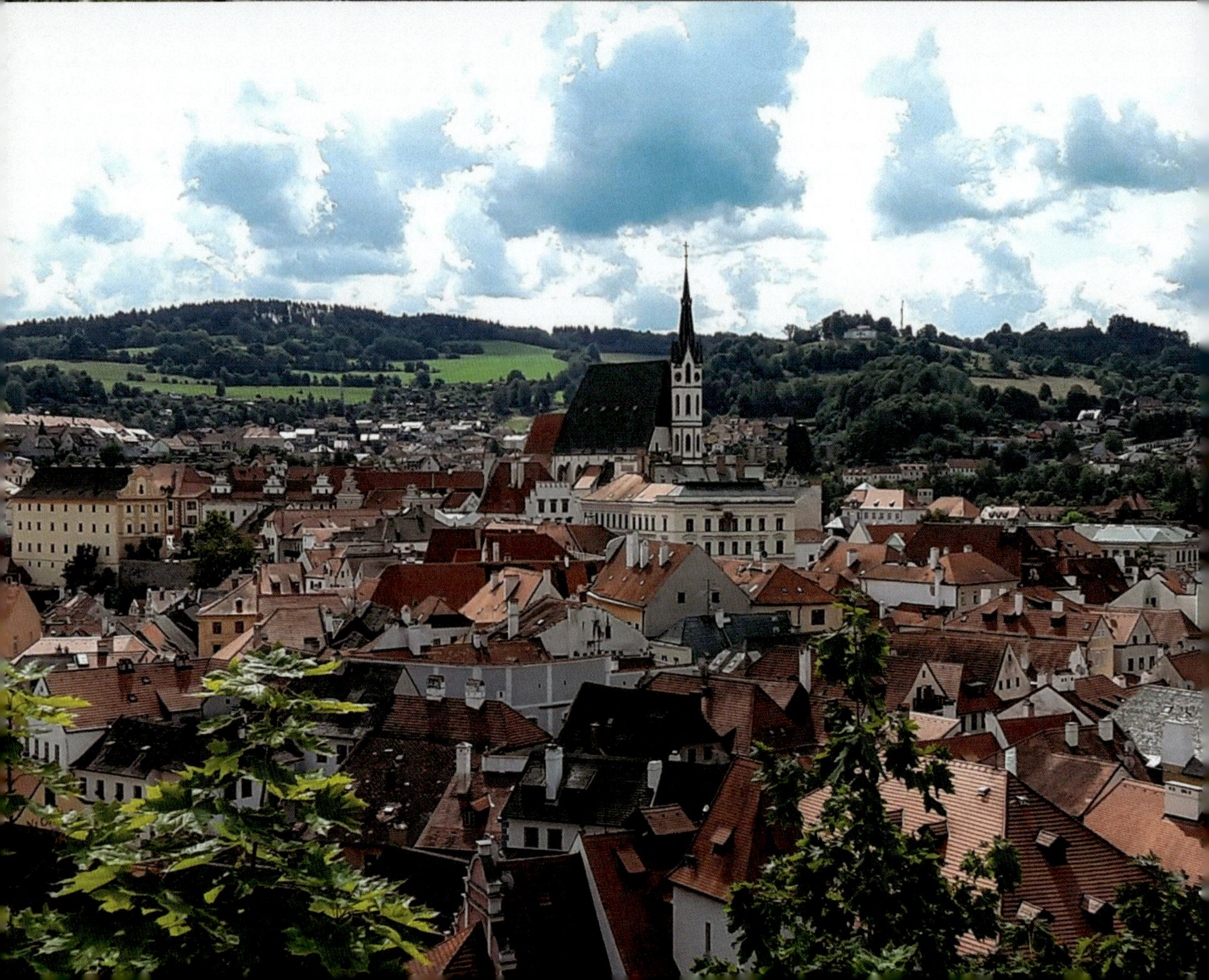

FÜRSTLICH SCHWARZENBERGSCHE SCHLOSS-APOTHEKE | KNÍŽECÍ SCHWARZENBERGSKÁ ZÁMECKÁ LÉKÁRNA

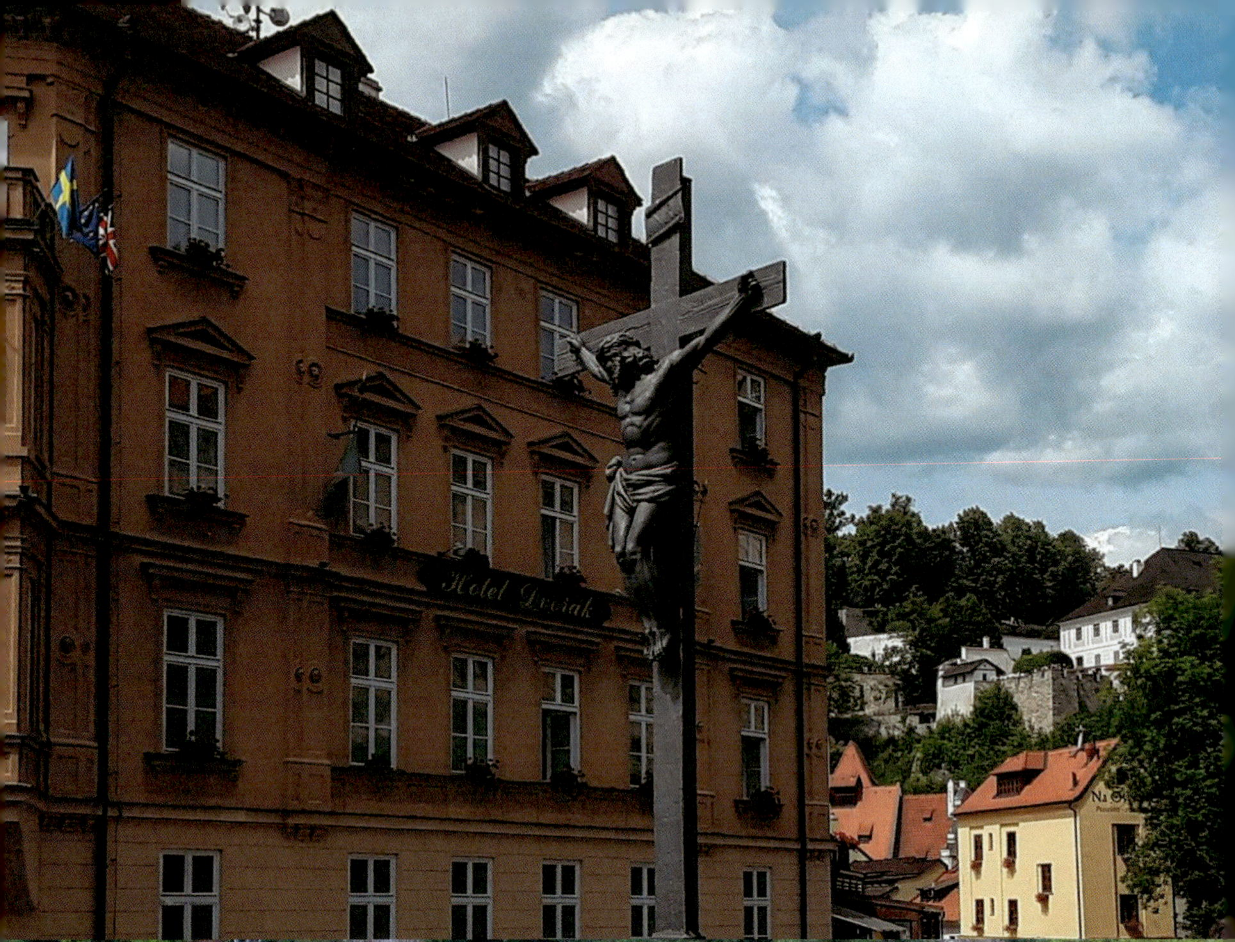
Hotel Dvorak

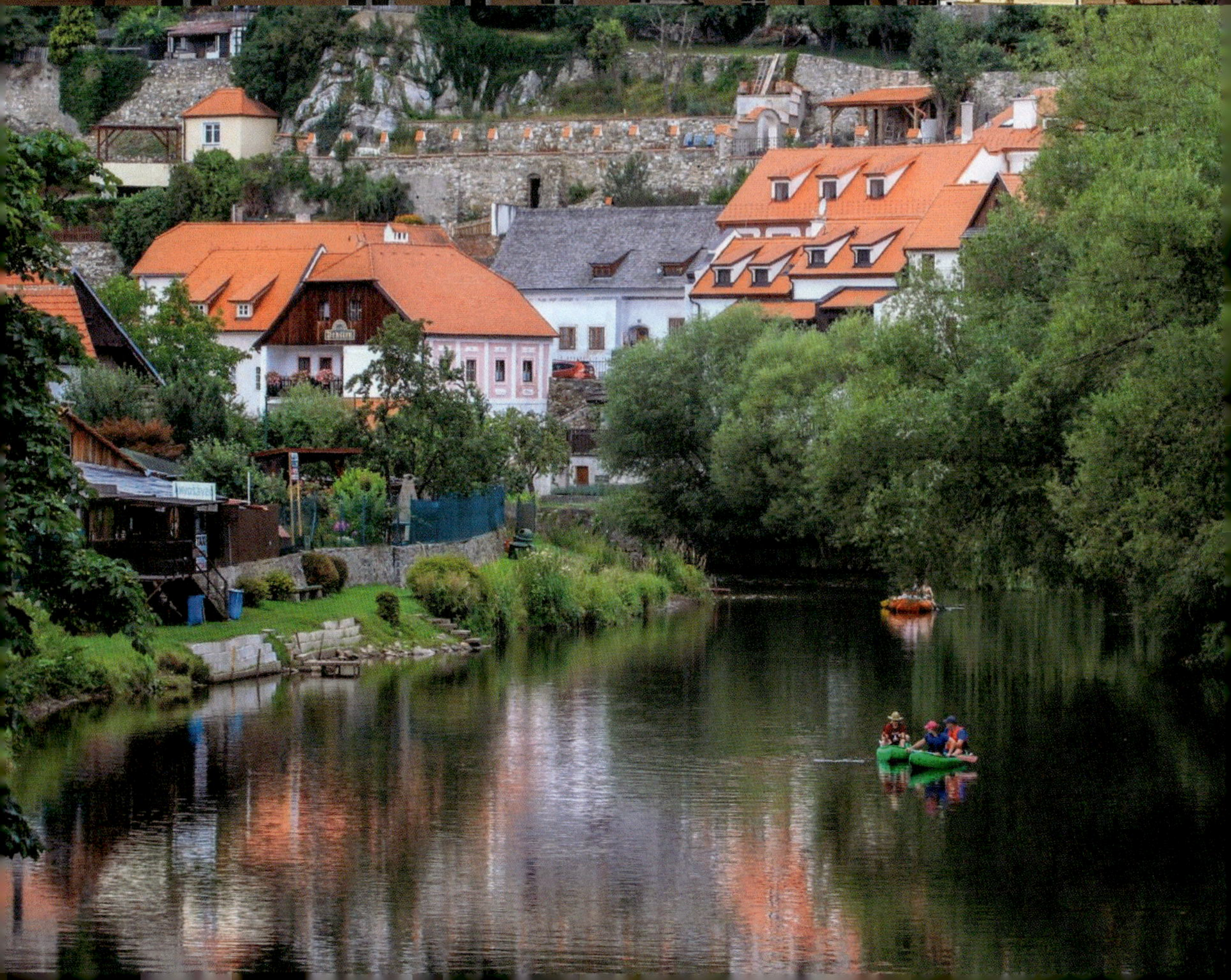

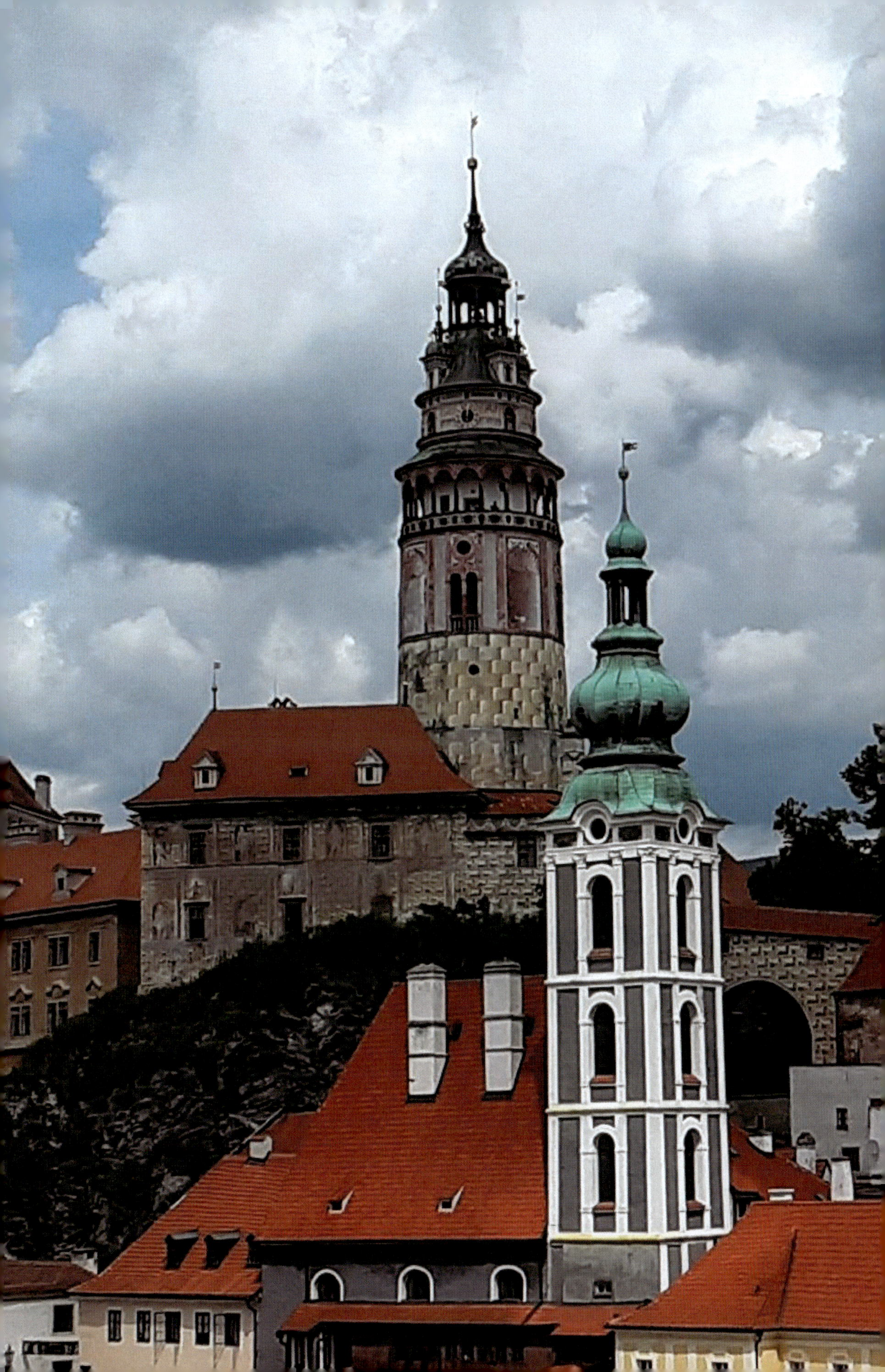

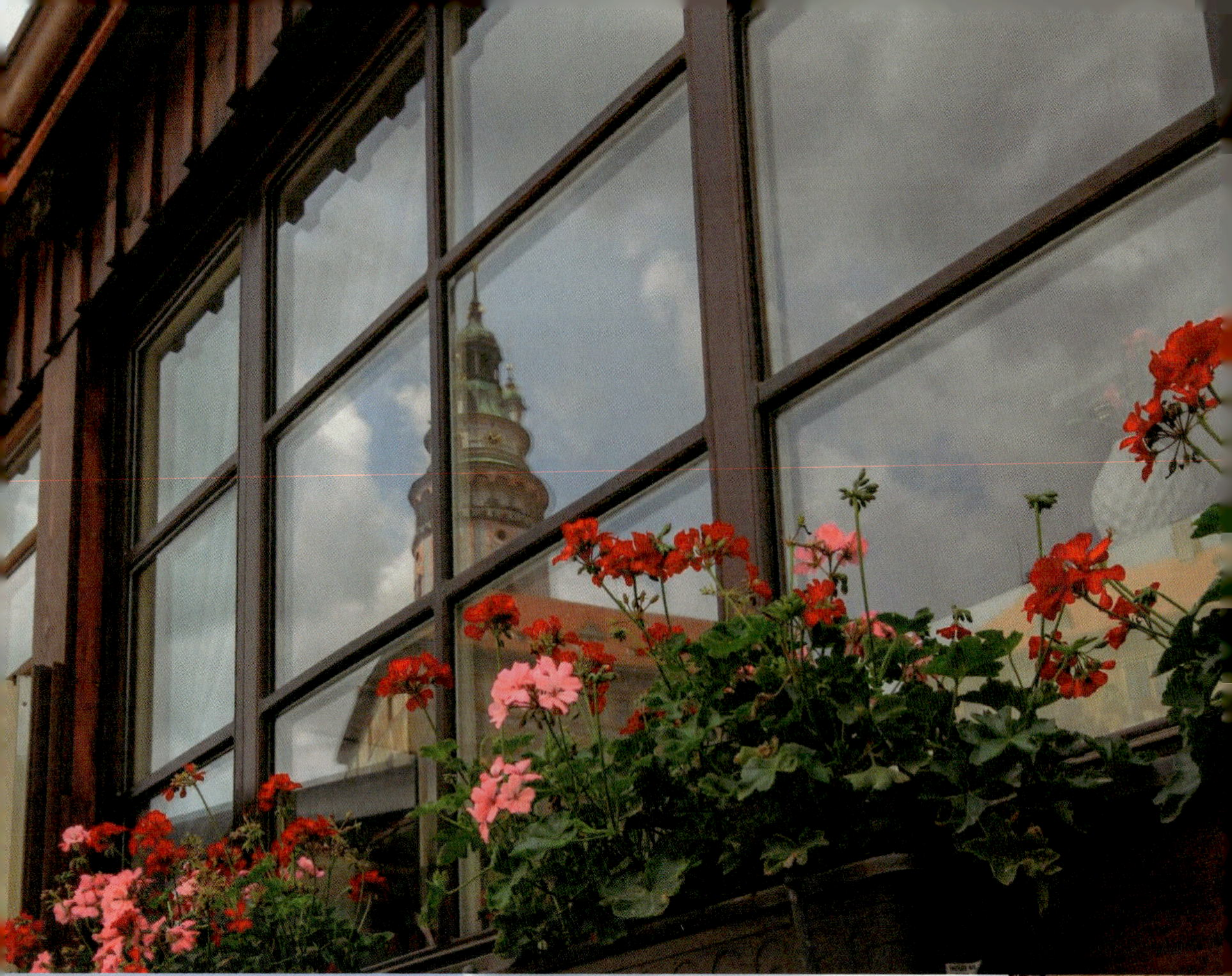
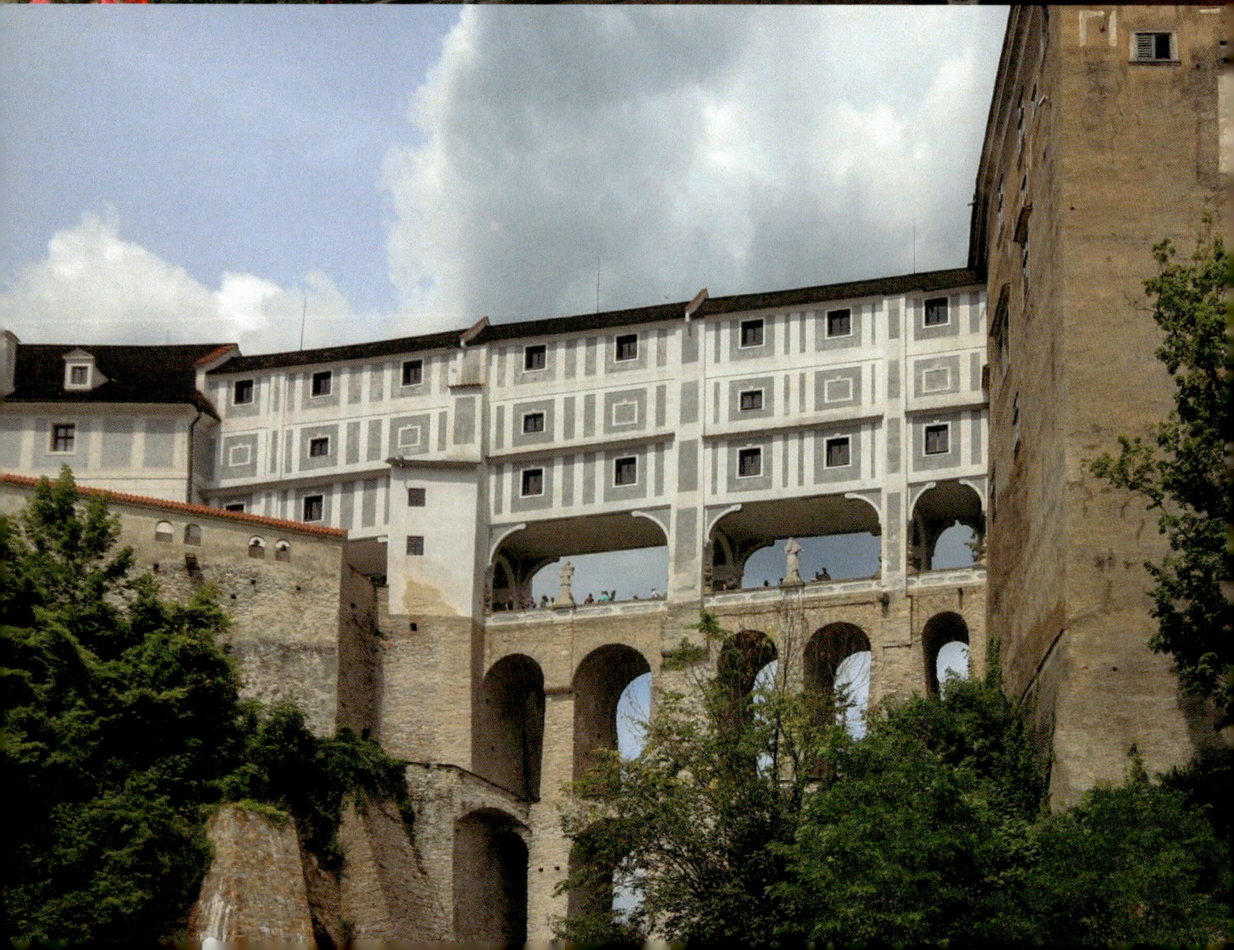

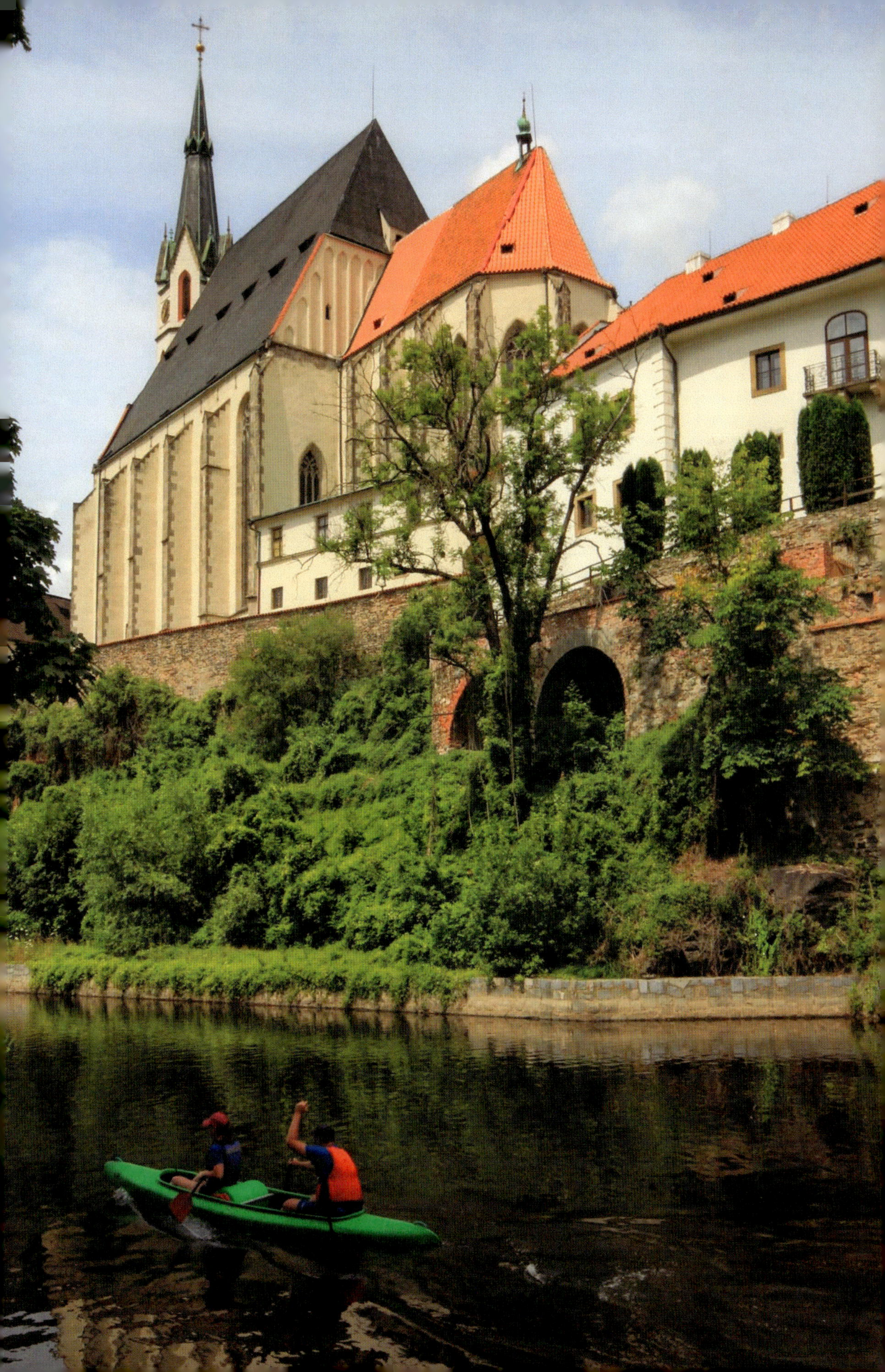

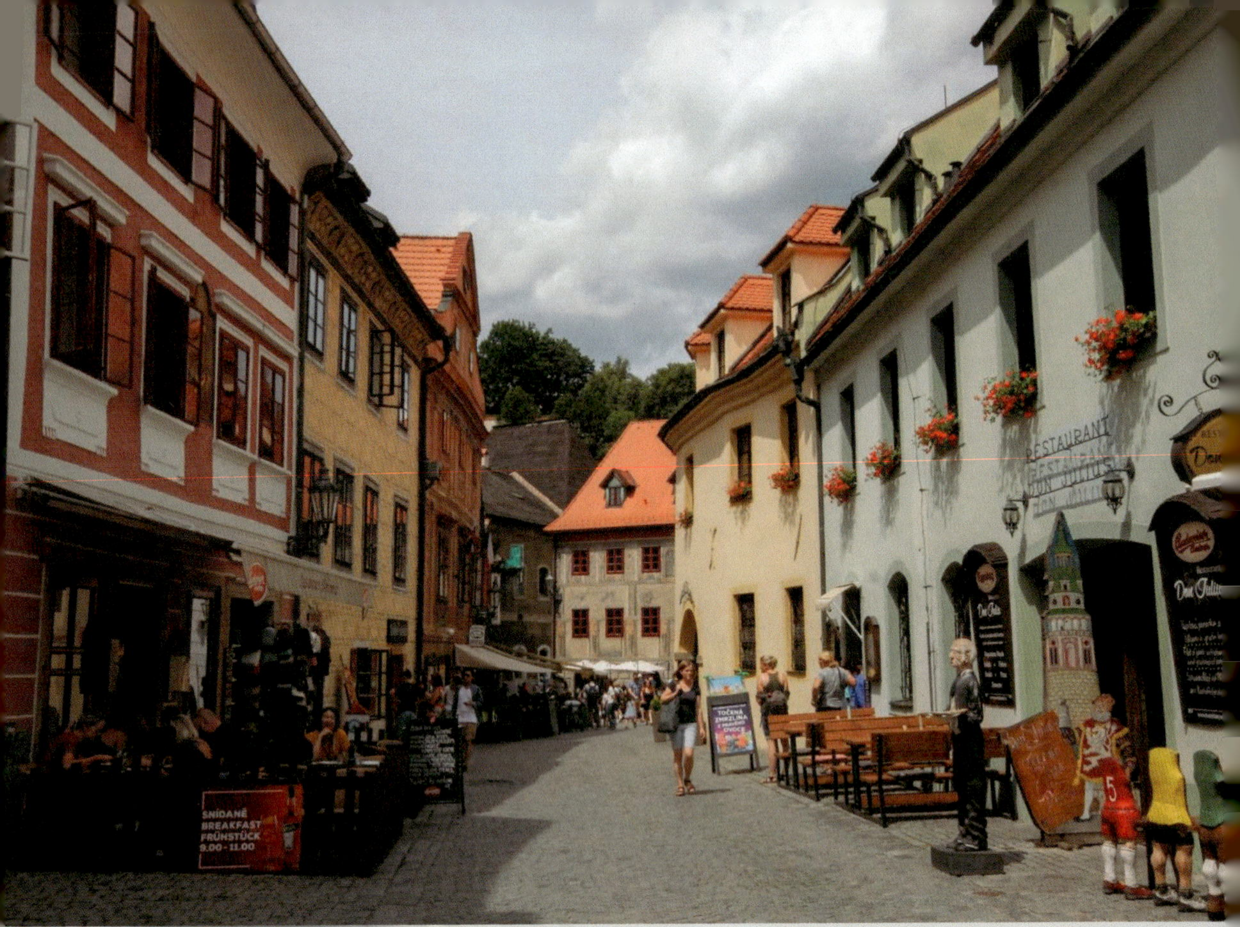
SNÍDANĚ
BREAKFAST
FRÜHSTÜCK
9.00 - 11.00
RESTAURANT

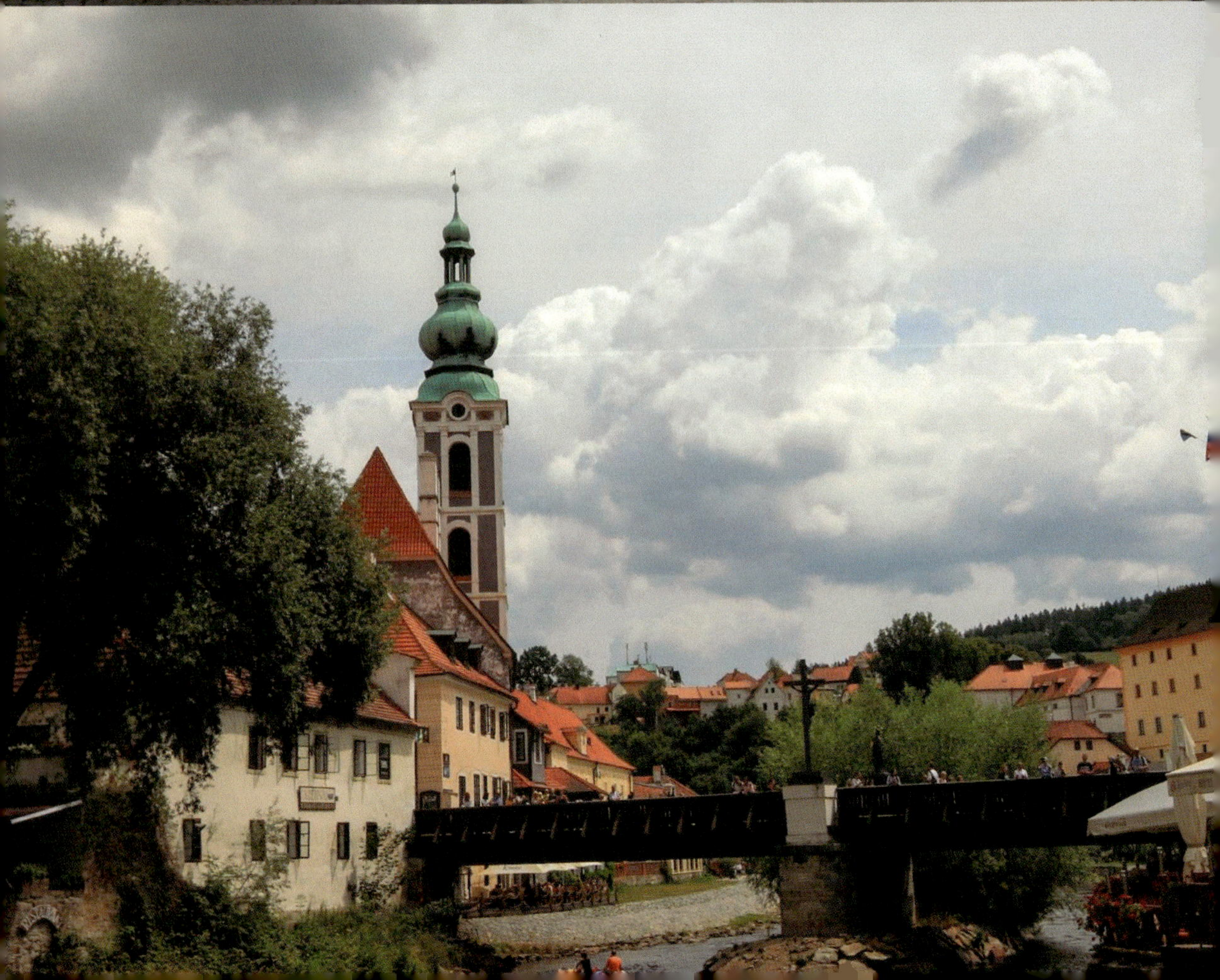

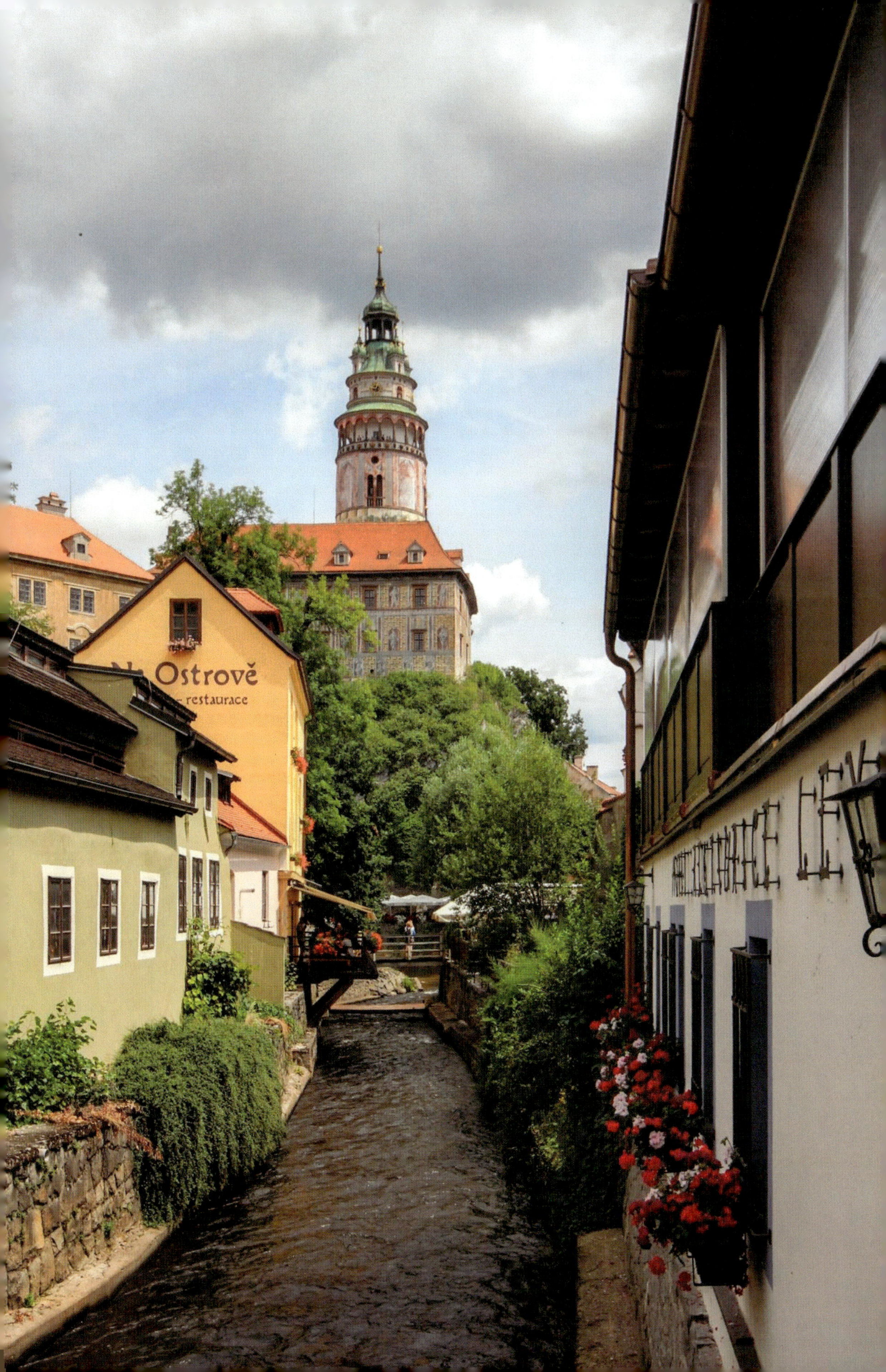
Ostrově
restaurace

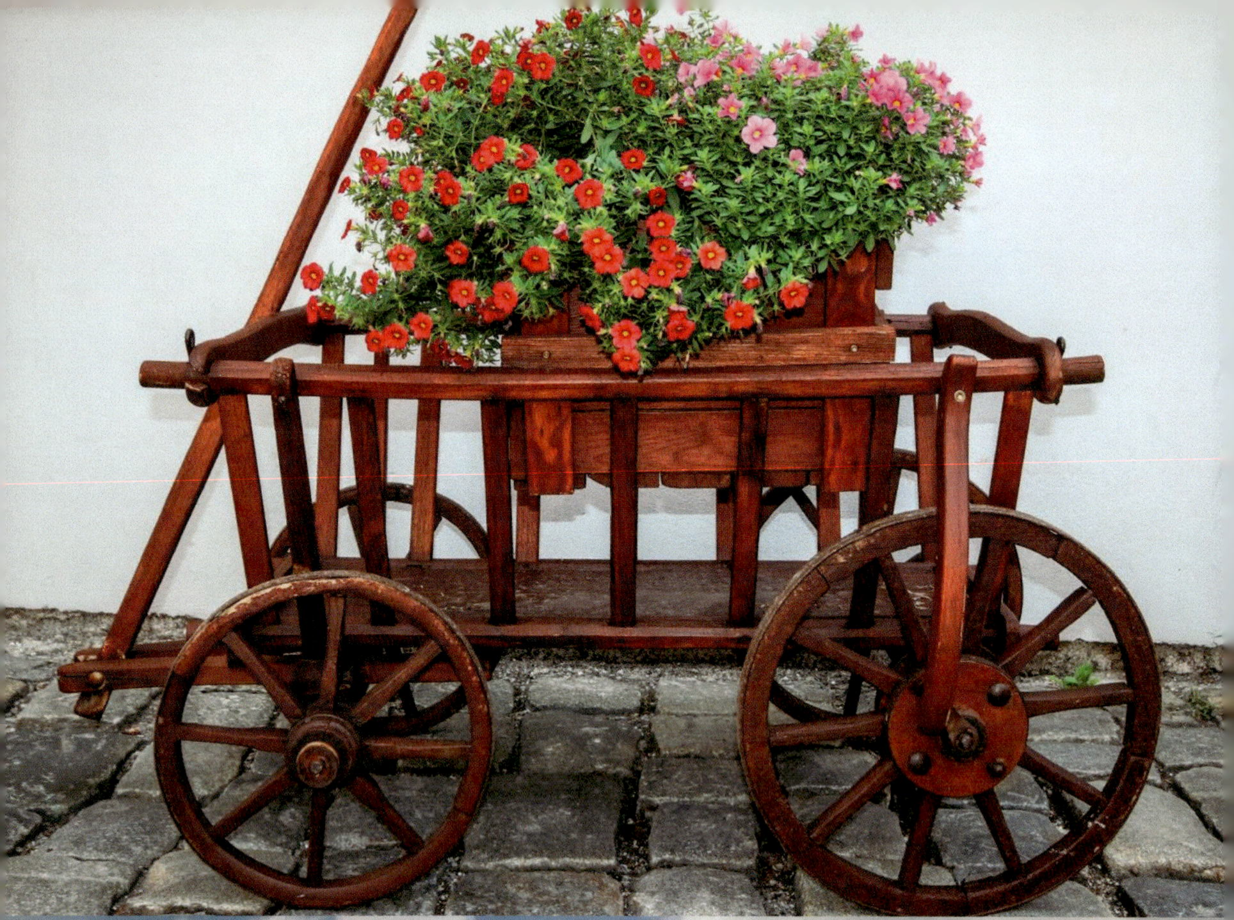

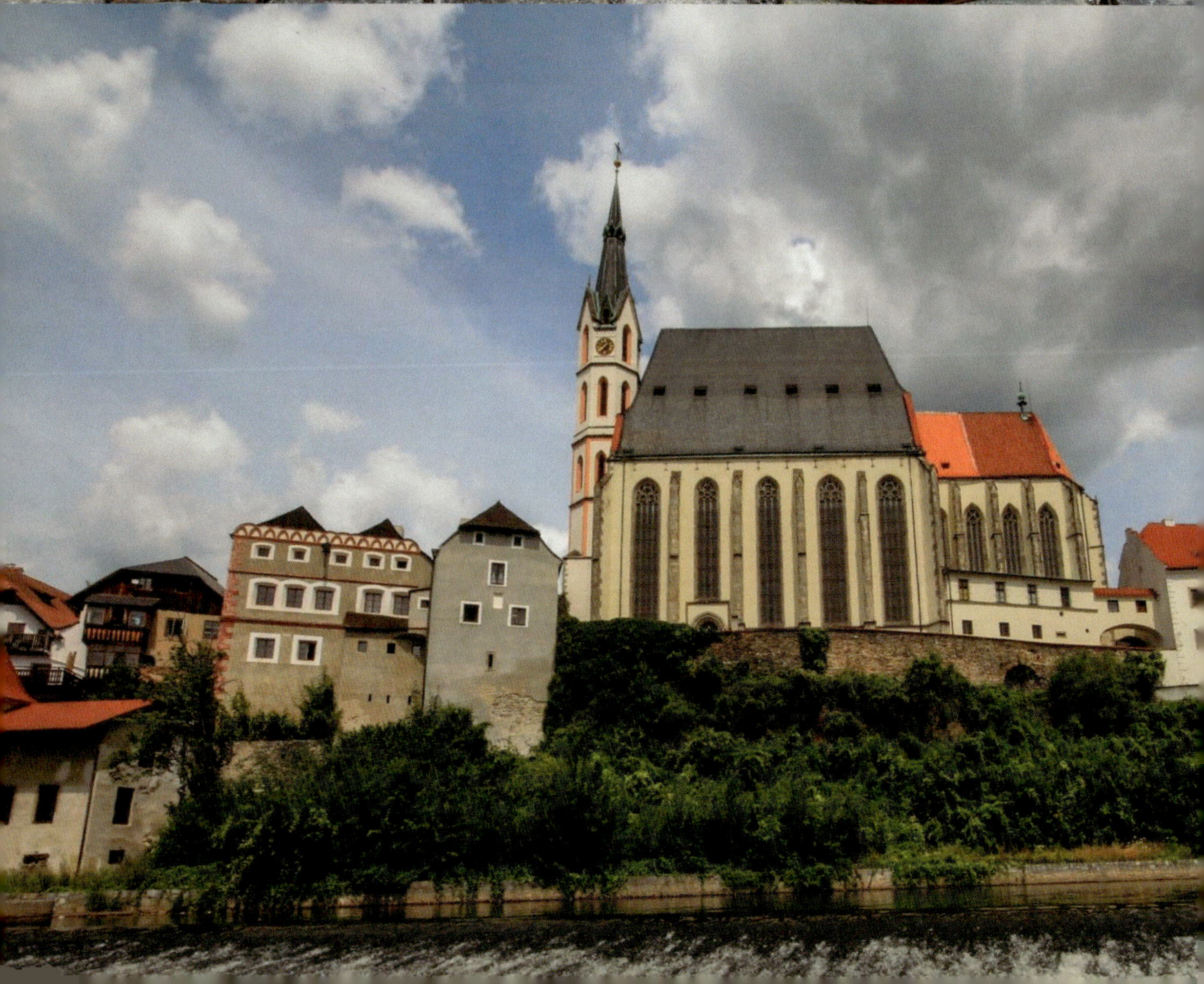

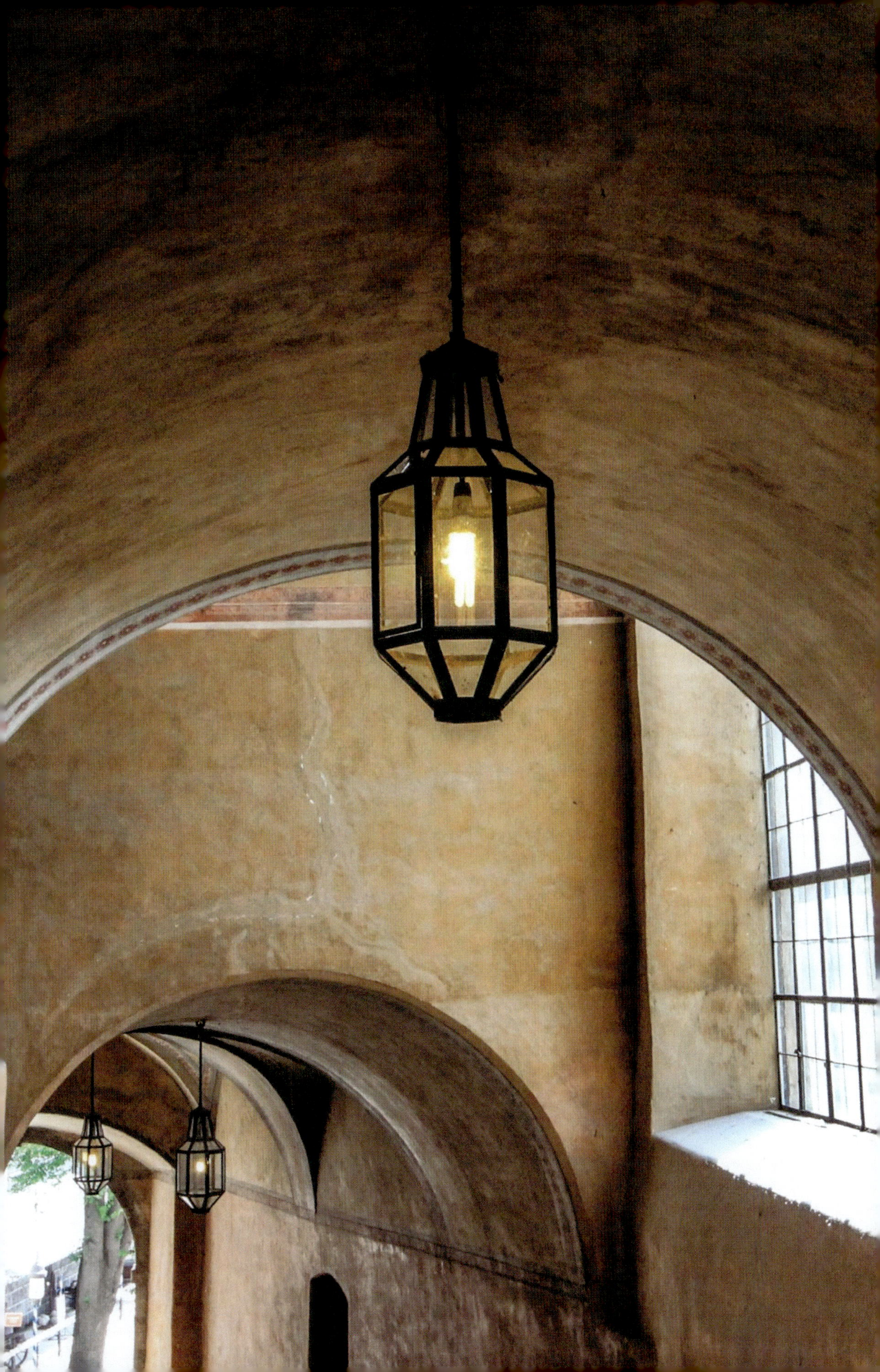

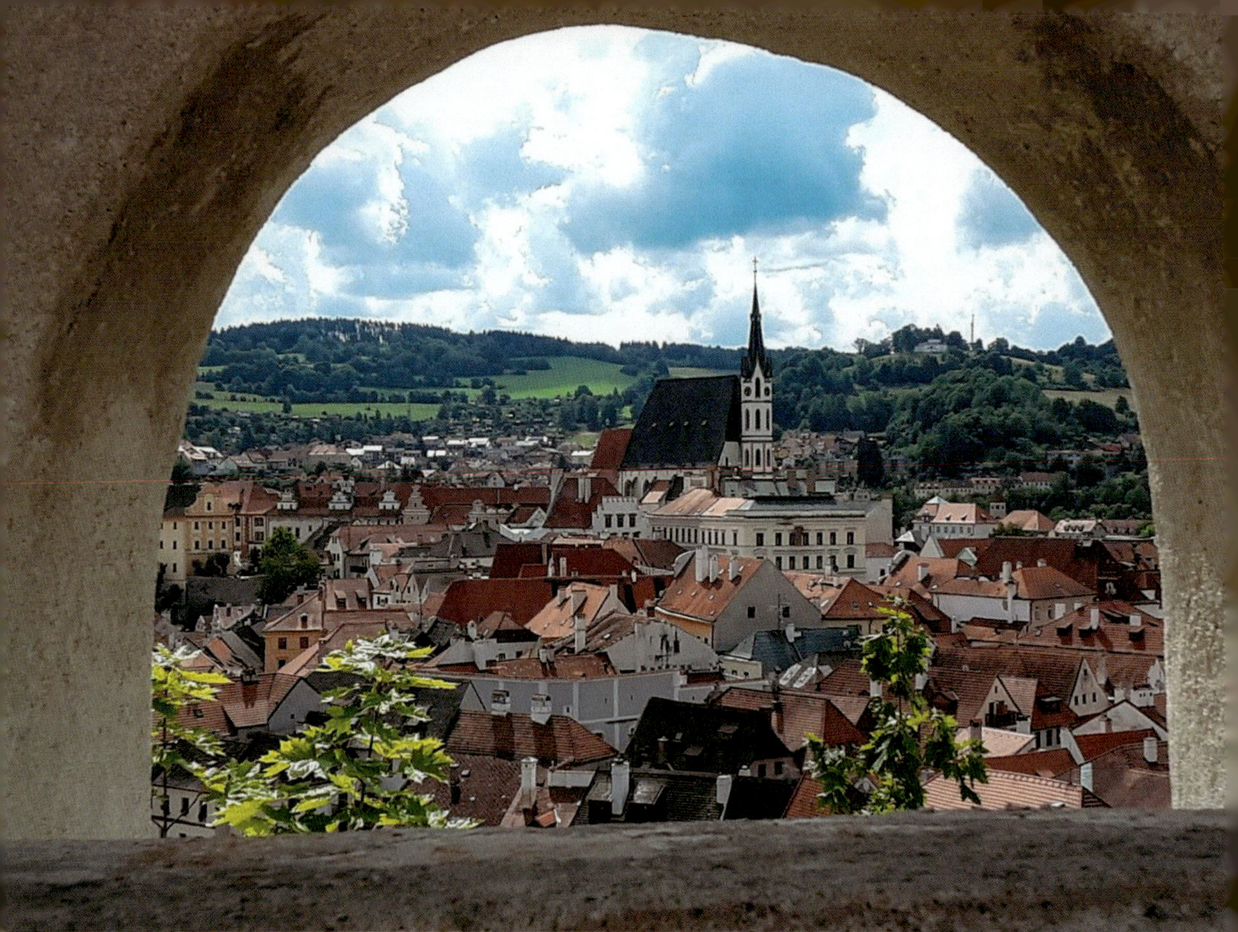
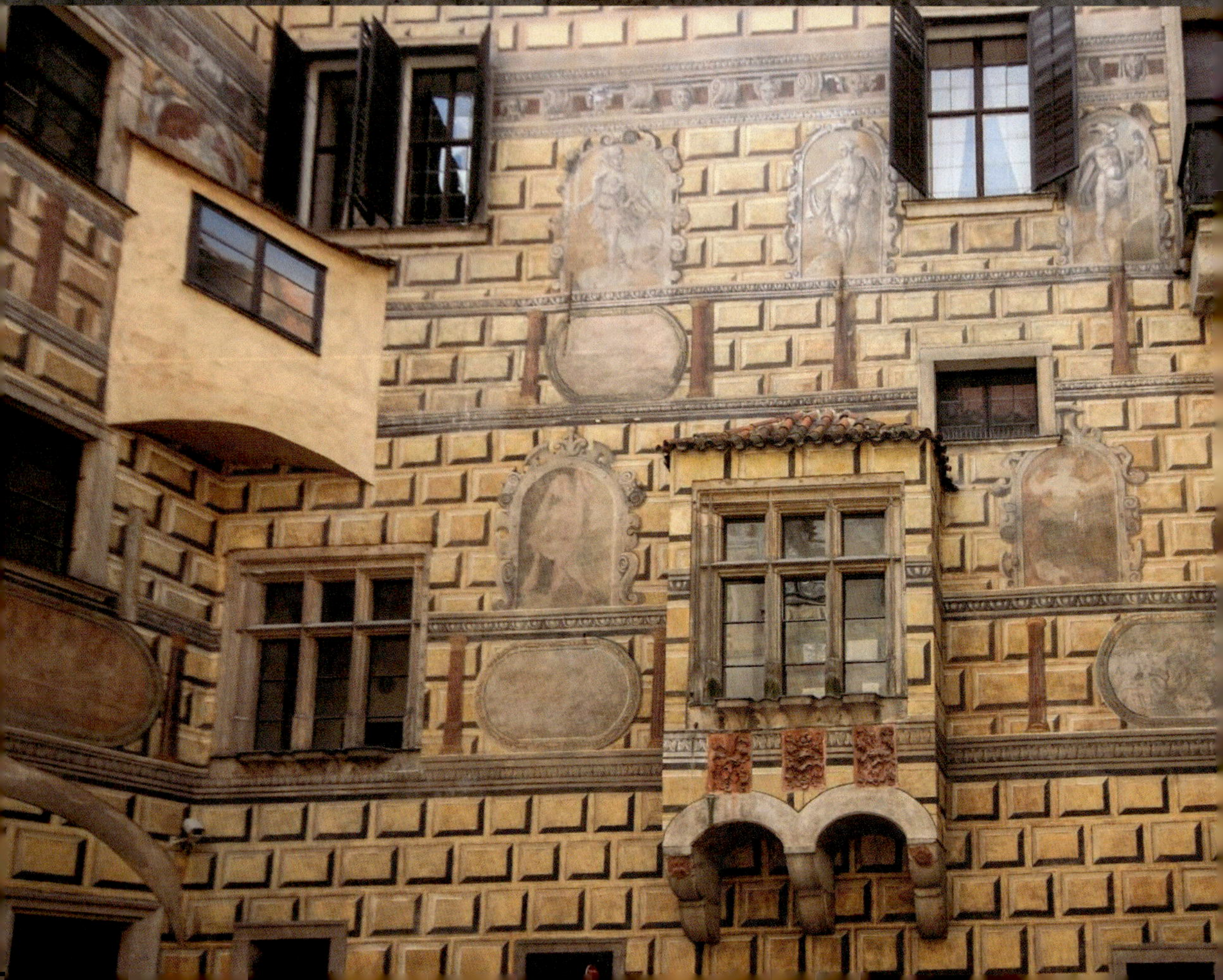

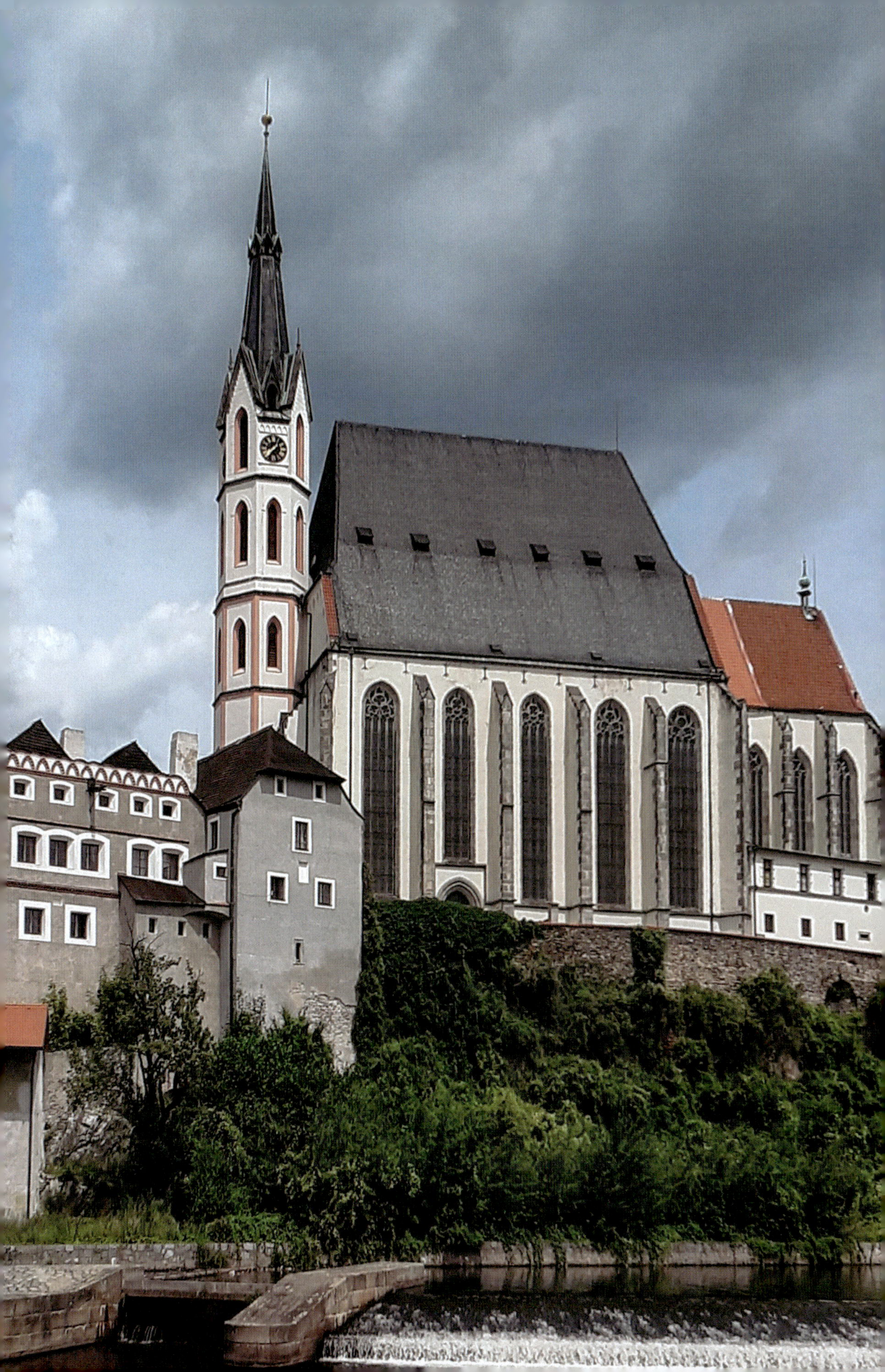

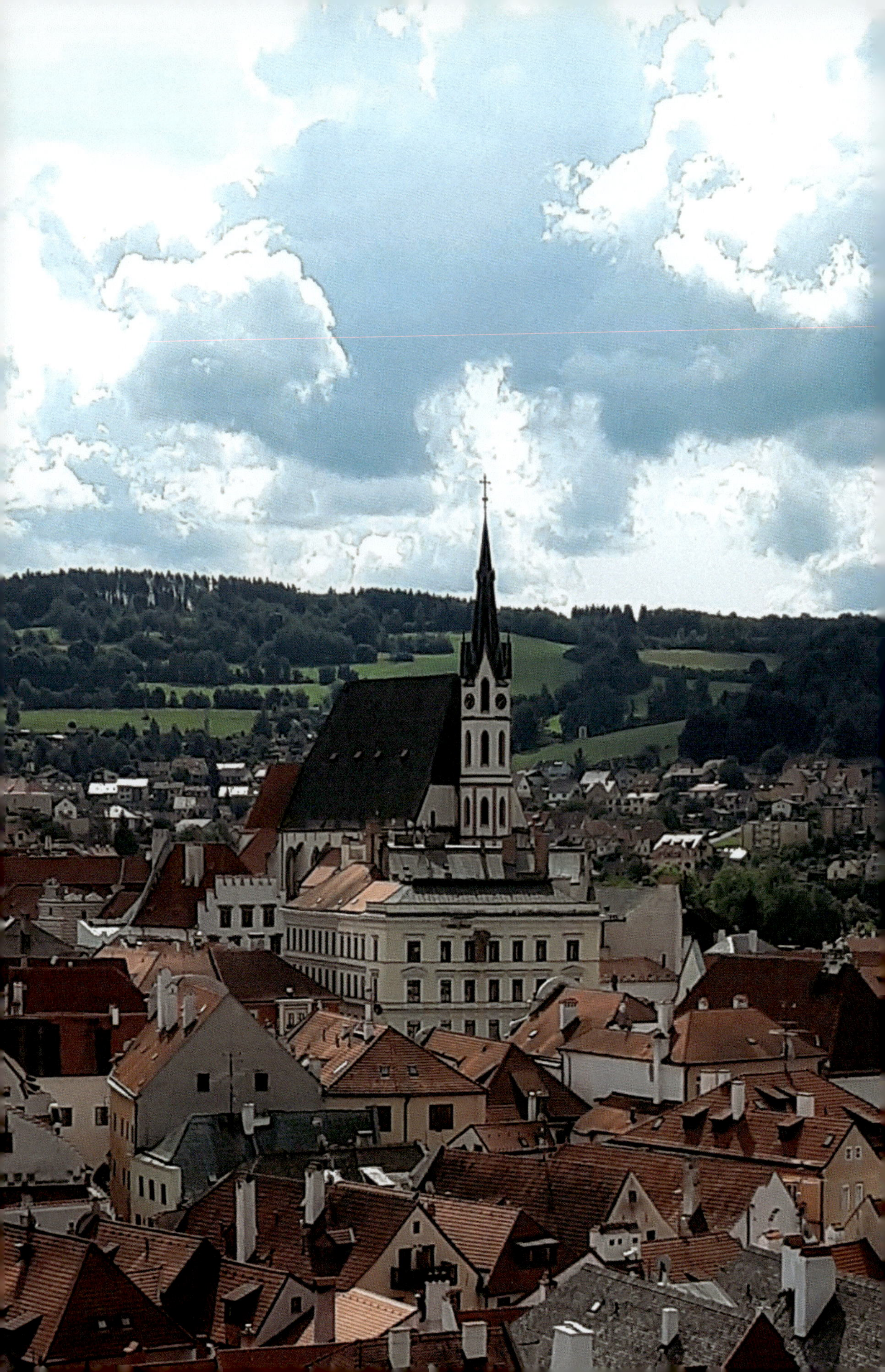

Passau, Germany

Passau is a beautiful and non-touristy town on the Danube where the Danube, Ilz, and Inn rivers converge. You can see in my photos two different river colors where the Danube and the Inn river meet. The Ilz river comes in at a different point on the landscape and isn't visible in the photos.

We followed our guide around part of the town, and he explained about the 2013 flood. The flood was the worst to hit in 500 years. Soldiers evacuated residents by using rubber boats. The river rose to more than 42 feet. and in its aftermath the town came together to throw drywall and other waterlogged materials into the Danube before they dried like concrete in the streets. It was impressive to hear how the community worked together to clean up the town.

We had time before our upcoming organ concert, so we stopped in a cute café for coffee and lemonade. I wanted to remember the name of the café so I could tell someone in our group who likes coffee about the place. I asked for something with the name. They didn't have any business cards, but I noticed that our server had a shirt with the name on the back. She agreed to a photo of the back of the shirt. (Minoo Café) As we walked to the concert, we saw a man playing the violin. Sitting in the violin case was an extremely well-behaved and cute dog. The dog was happy to sit, listen to the music, and watch people walk by.

We attended a 30-minute organ concert in St. Stephen's Cathedral, rebuilt in 1693 due to a fire. The concert was performed on the largest cathedral organ in the world. It has over 17,000 pipes. We read ahead of time about how loud the organ can be, so we brought ear plugs. Even with the ear plugs it was loud. I felt that 20 minutes would have been enough to get the impact.

After the concert my wife wasn't feeling well so I went out on my own to explore. My first stop was to revisit Schaibling Tower on the Inn river. In the 14th century the building was a fortified tower.

Eventually I walked up a steep hill to see the Veste Oberhaus castle. The castle was built in 1219. From the top of the hill I could see the countryside and the town of Passau below. I found the view so impressive and moving that I walked back to the ship and told my wife she had to come back with me. When I approached the ship, she was standing outside with the couple from Erie. The four of us went to the castle. I had found an elevator earlier, so we walked up to the lower level and then took the elevator to the top. They all agreed that the view was worth the trip. The next day we left to return to Philadelphia.

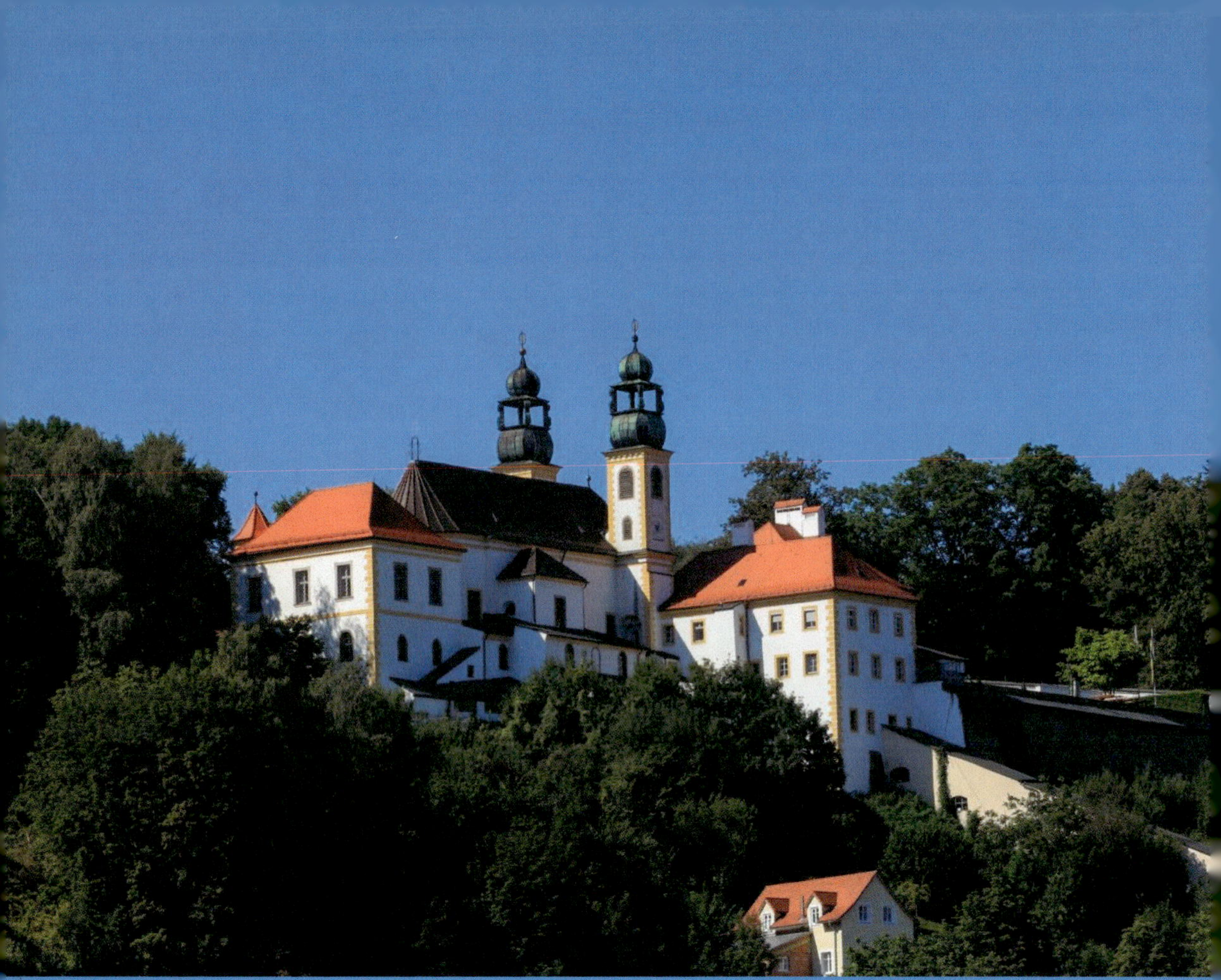

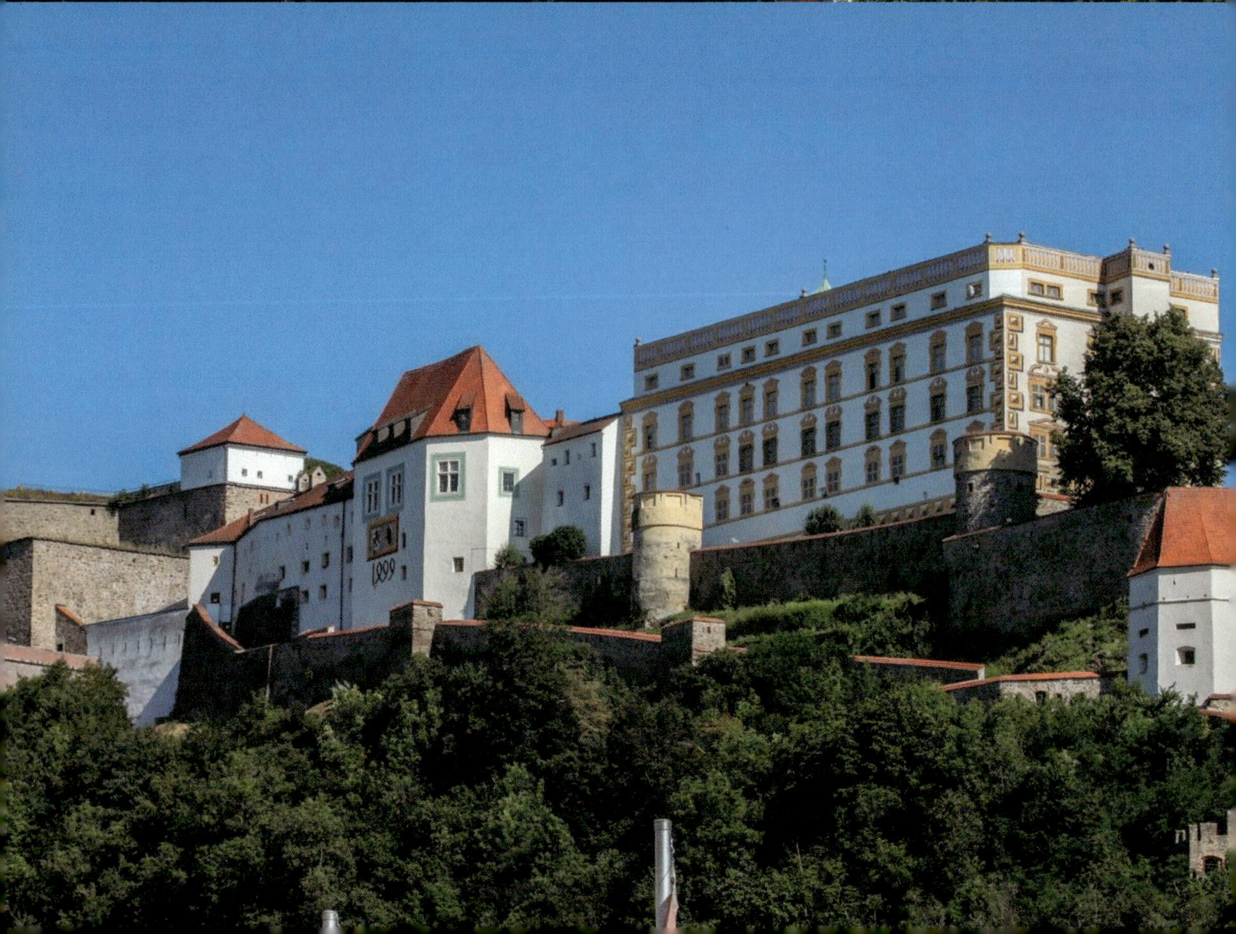
1999

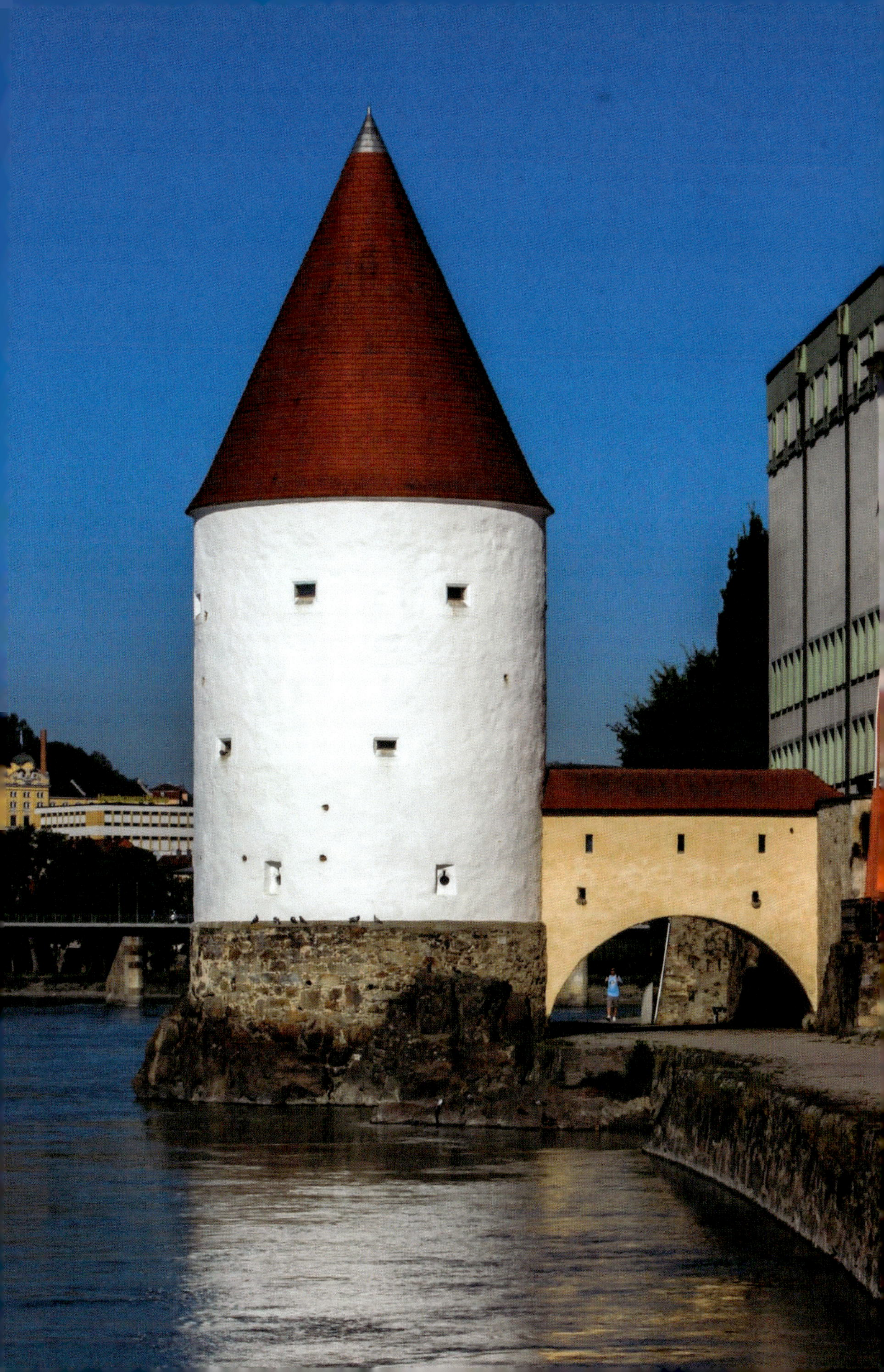

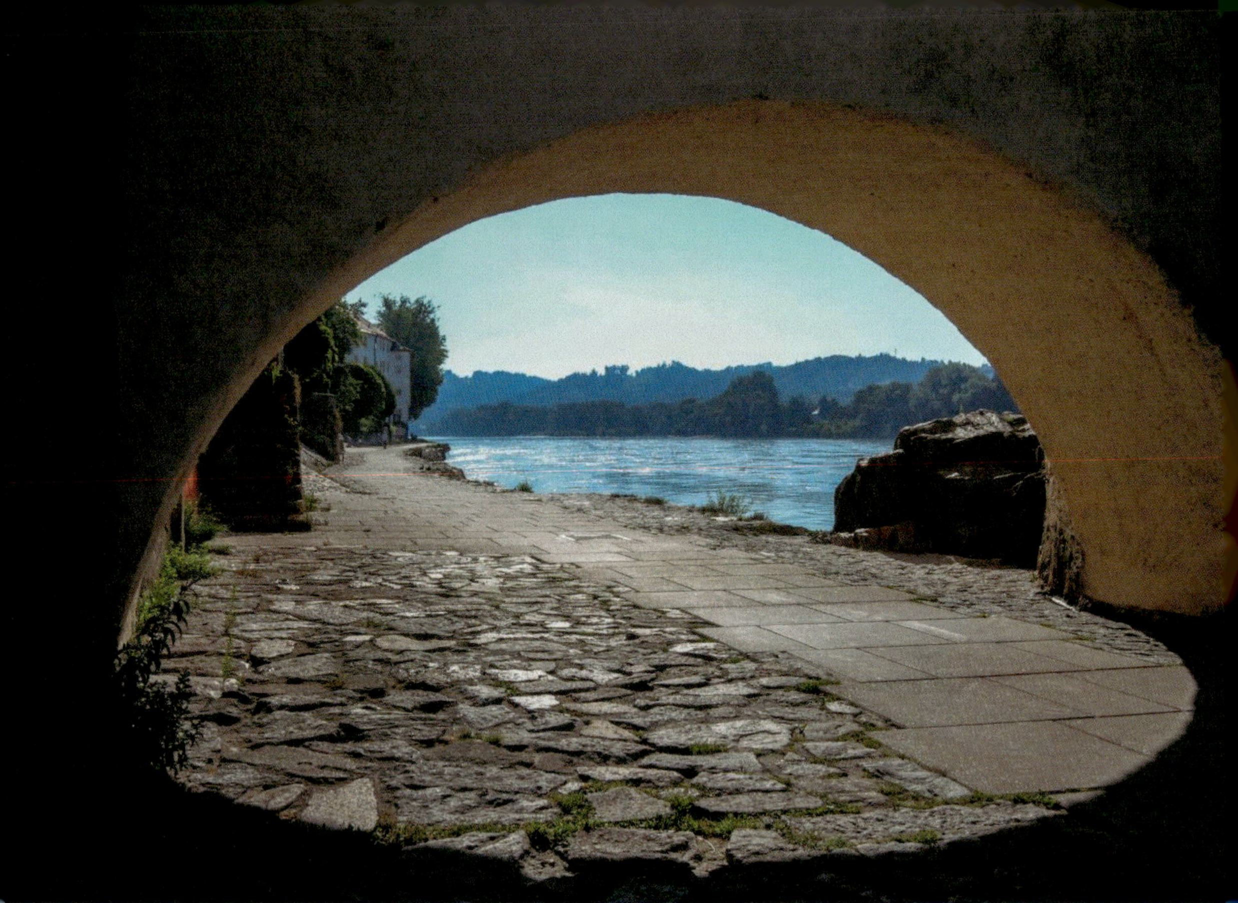

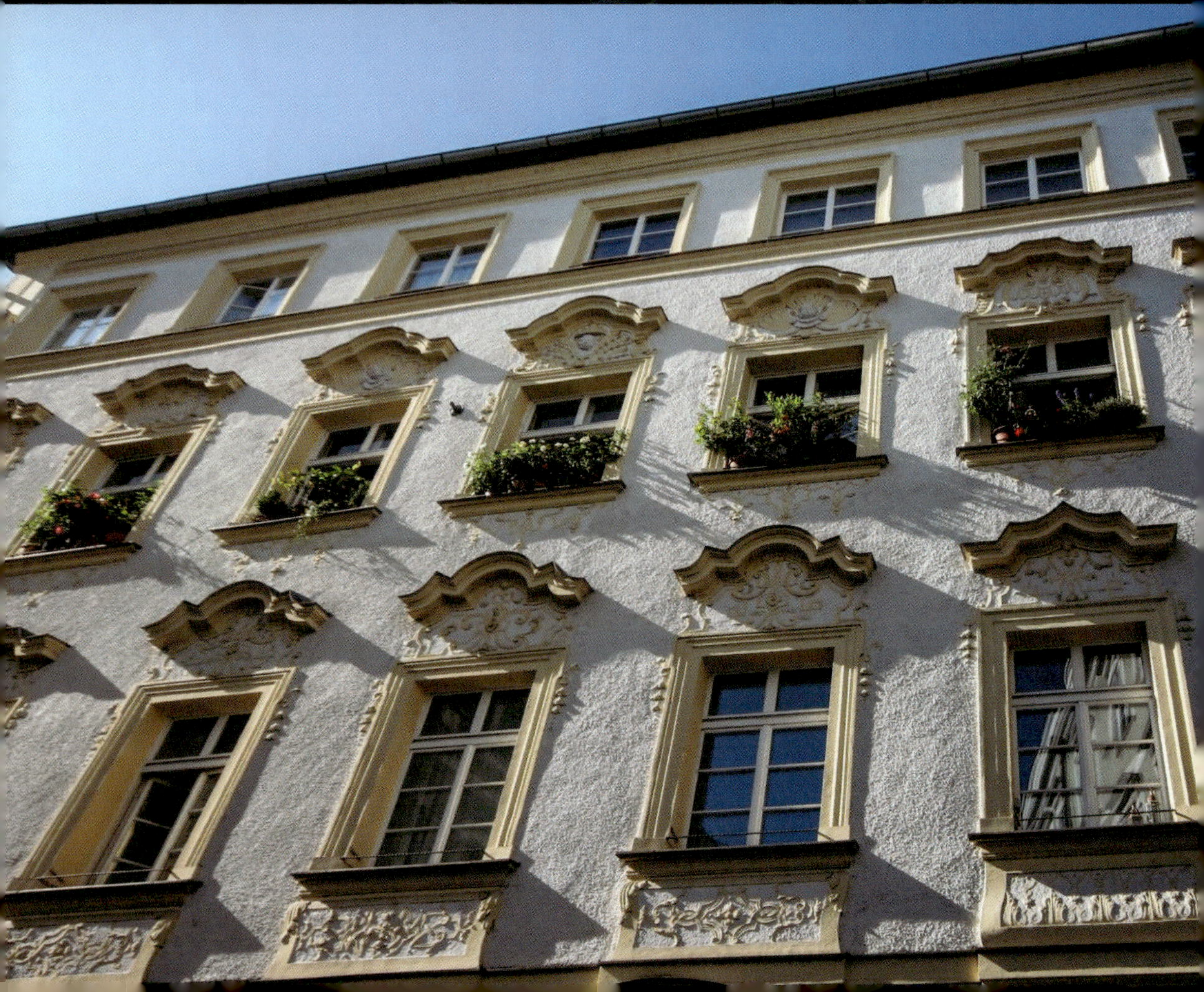

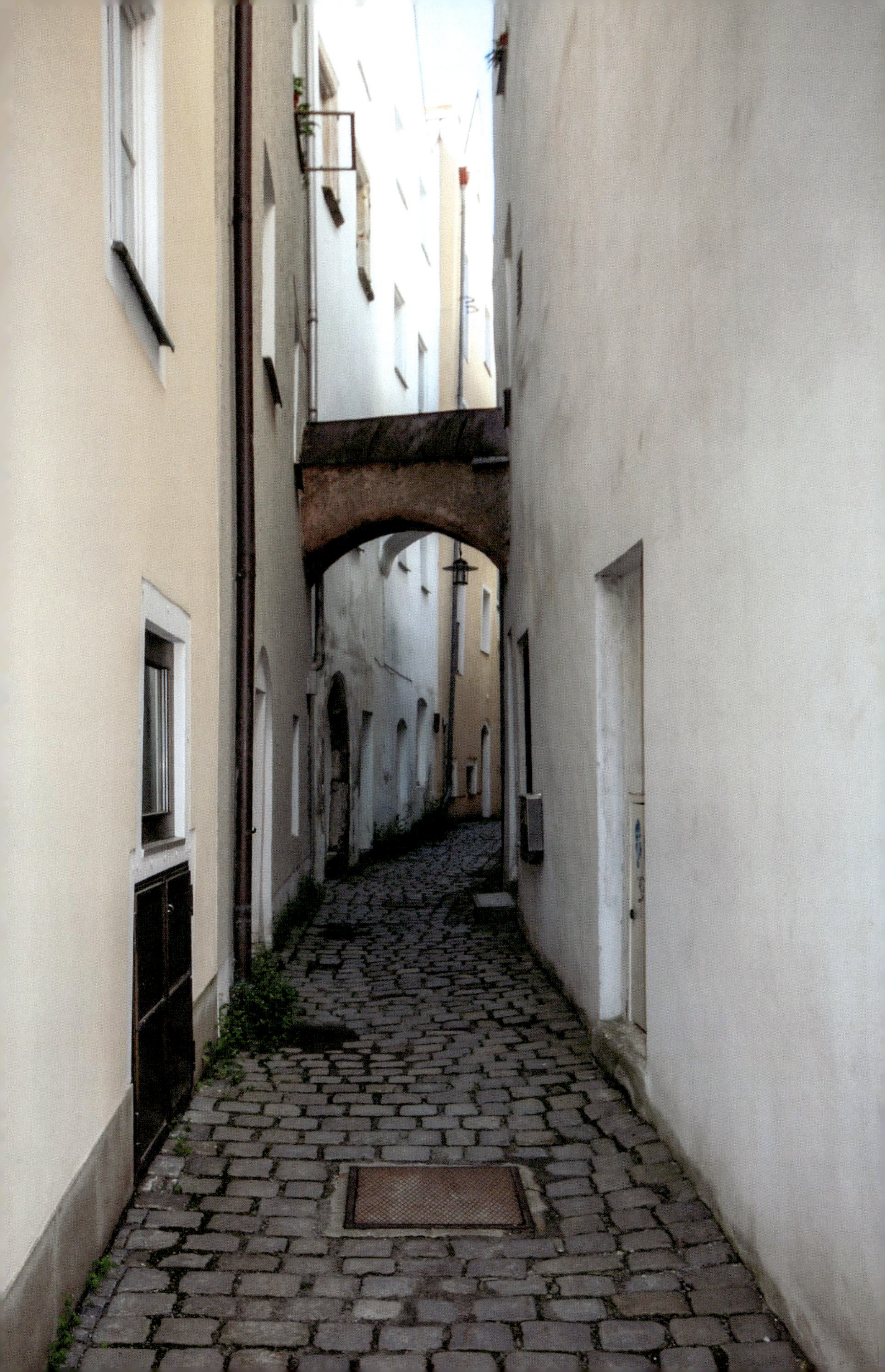

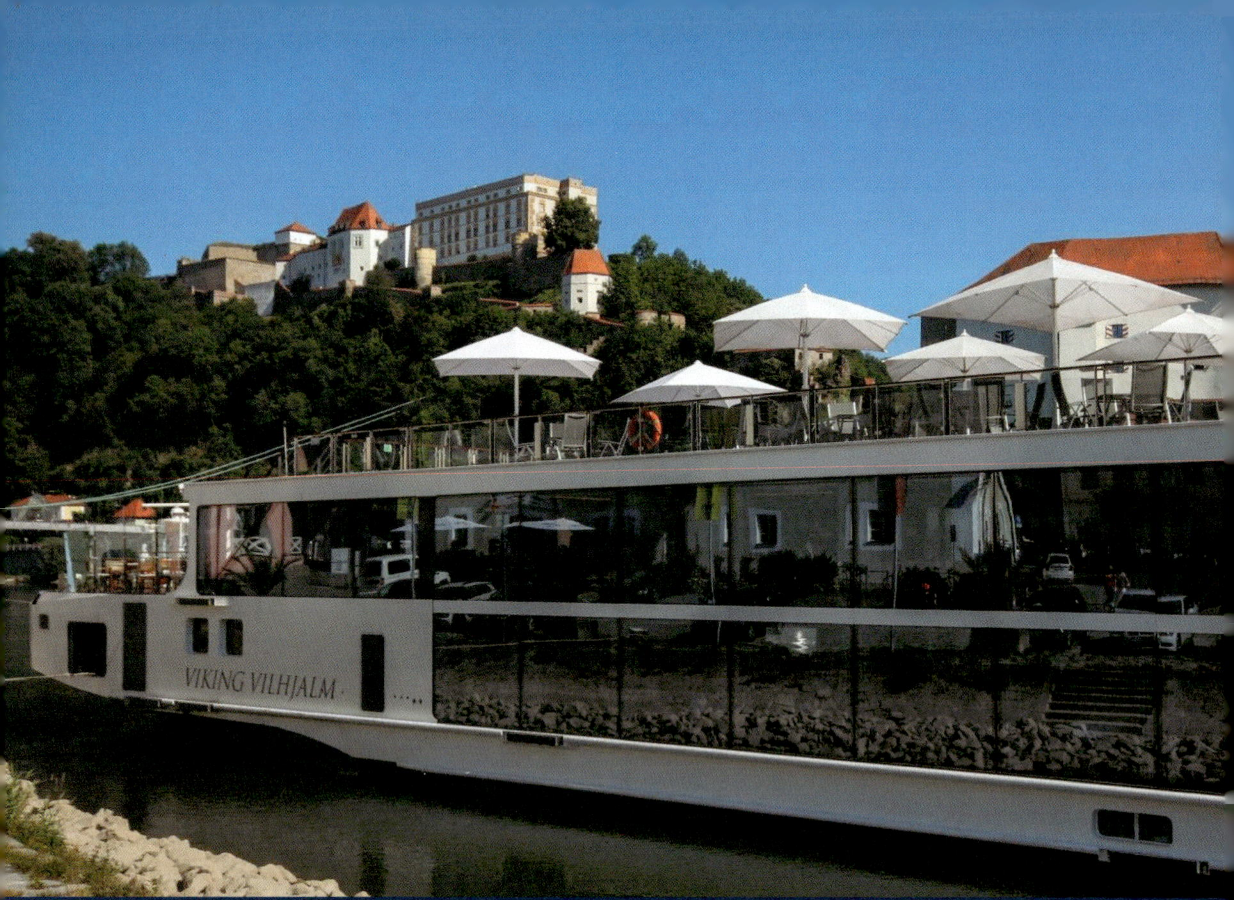
VIKING VILHJALM

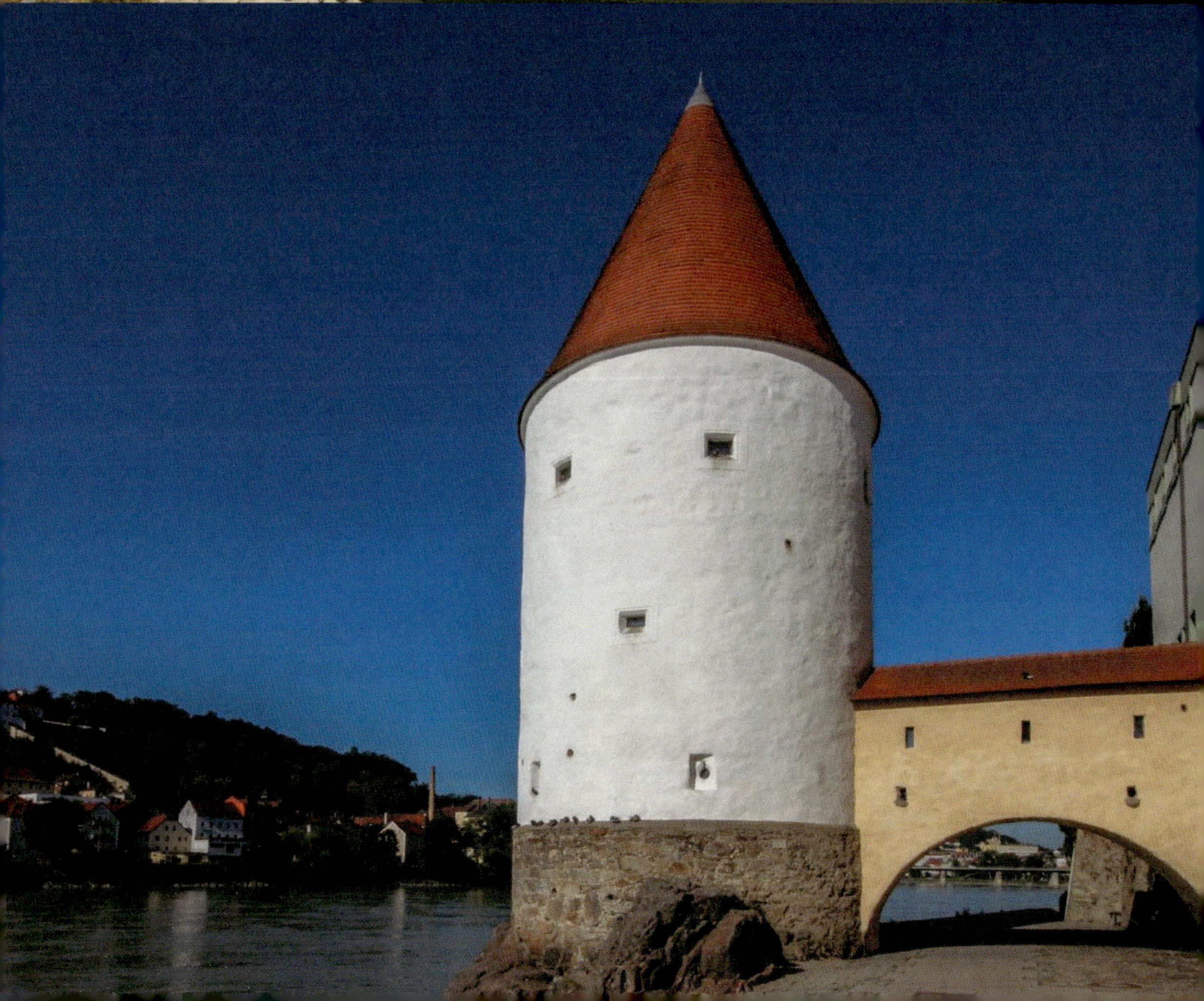

Künstlerwerkstatt

2a

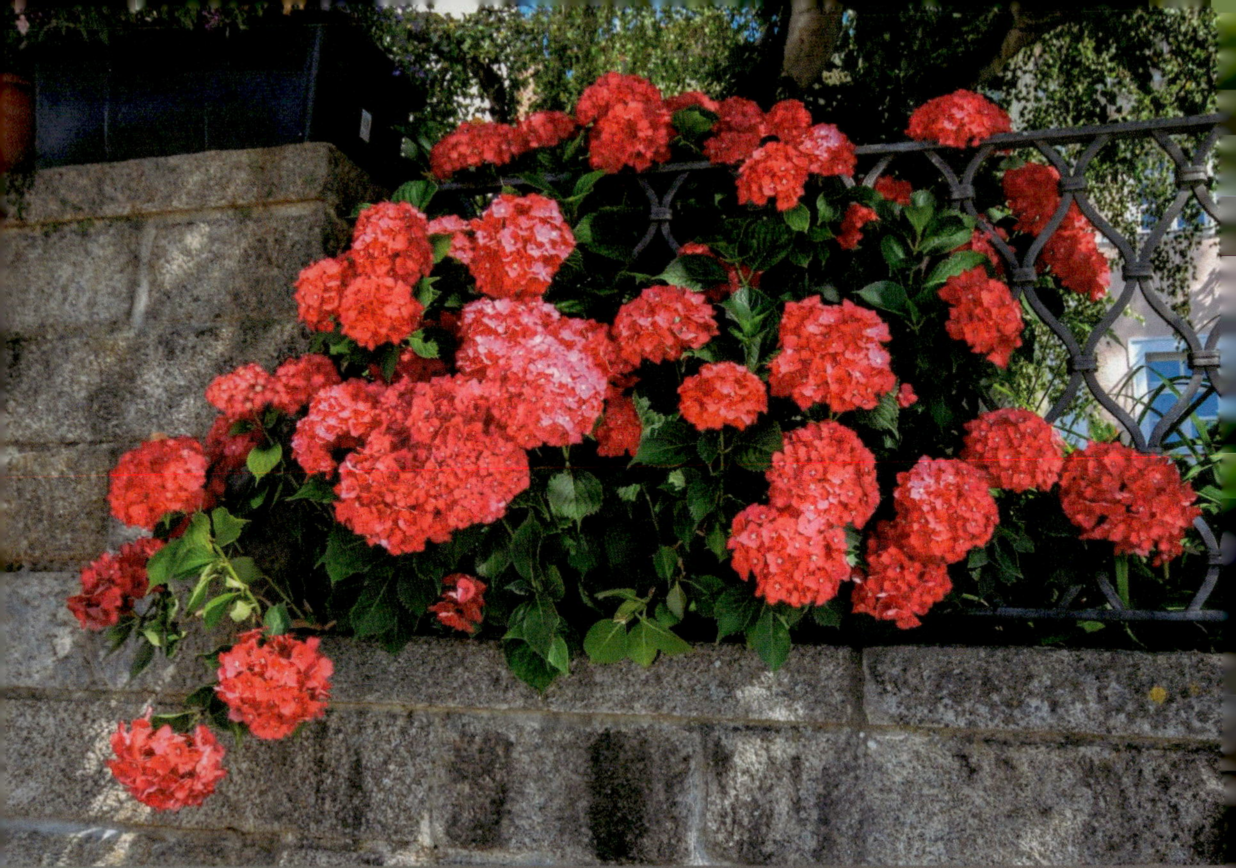
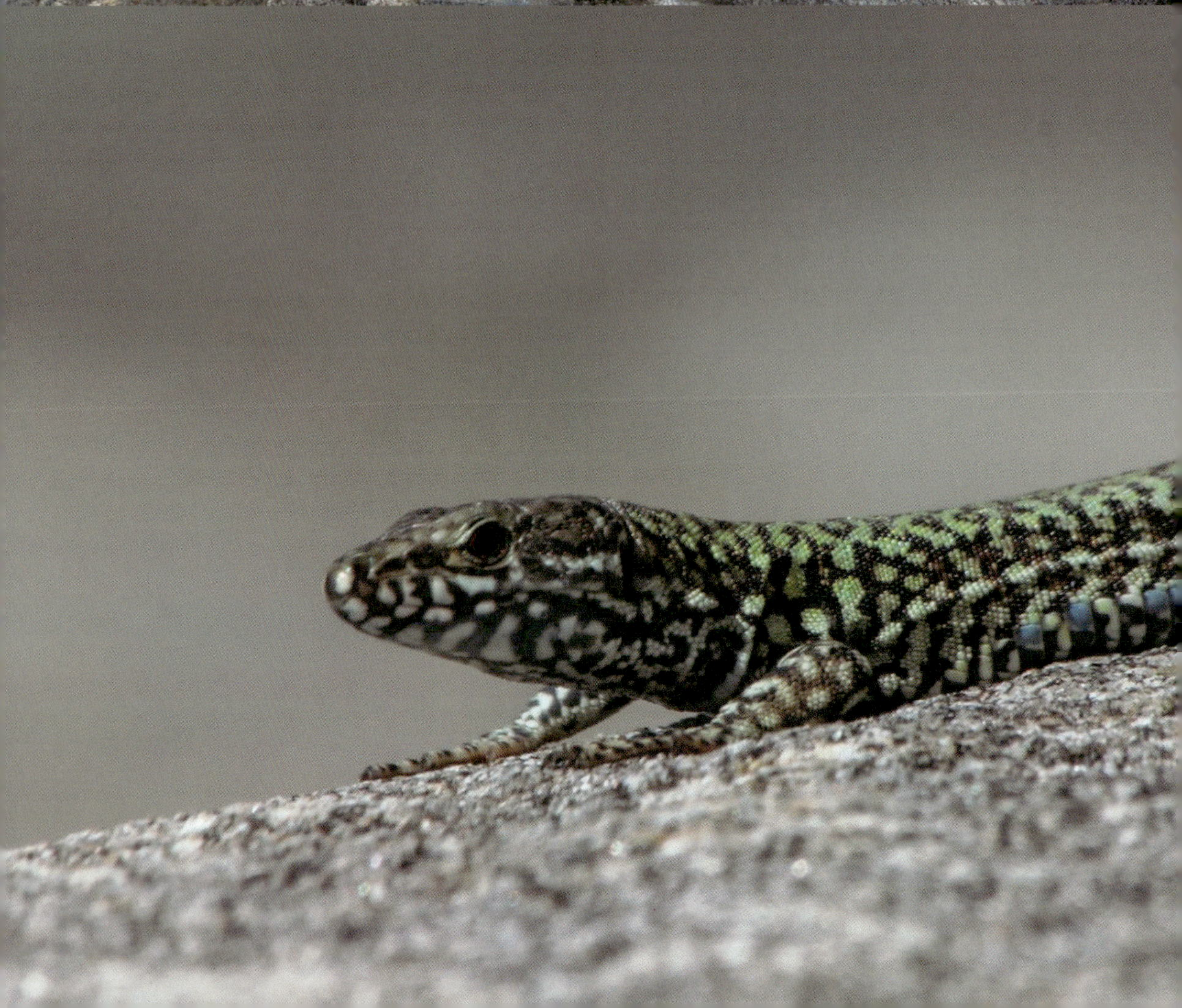

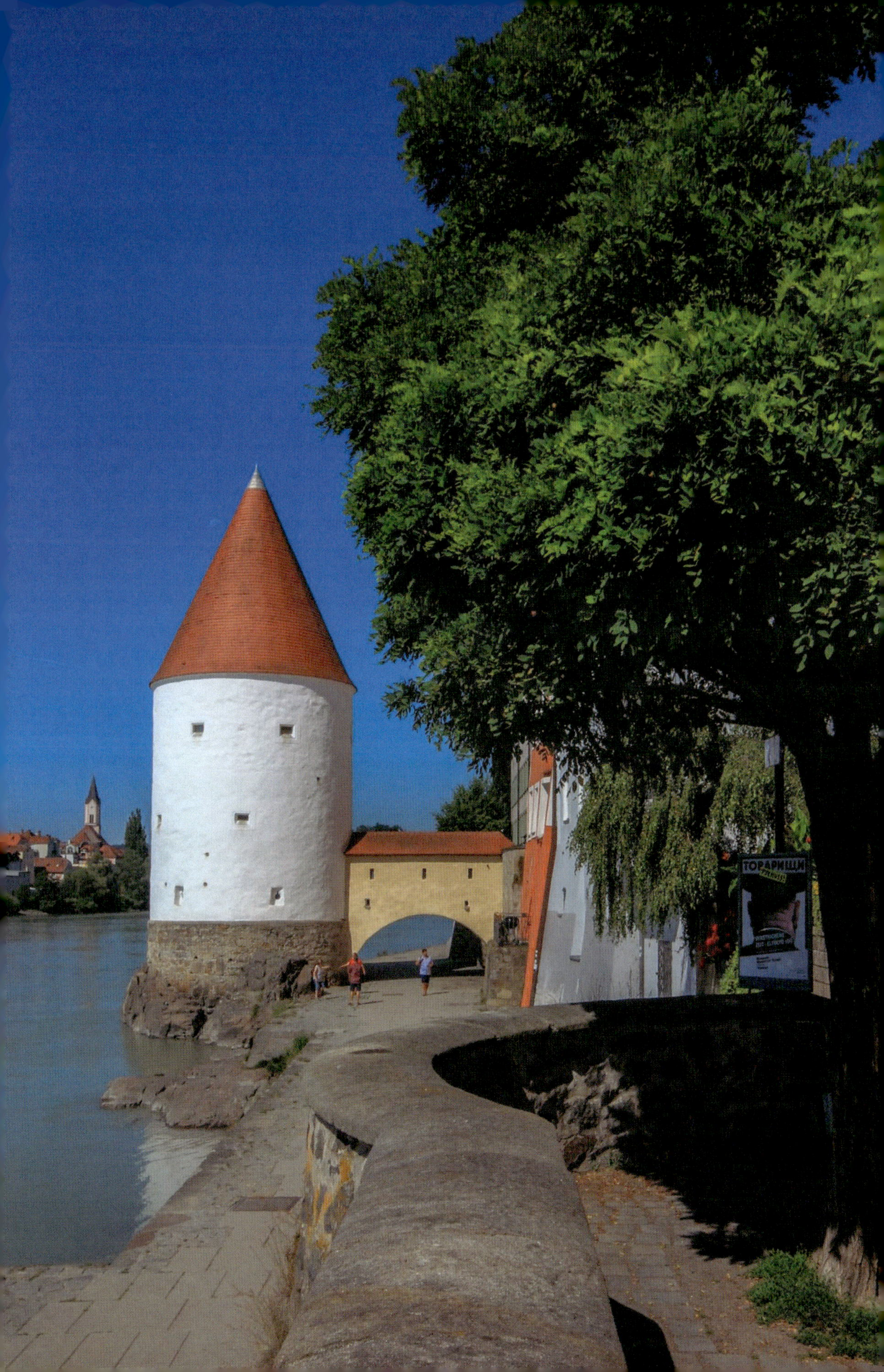

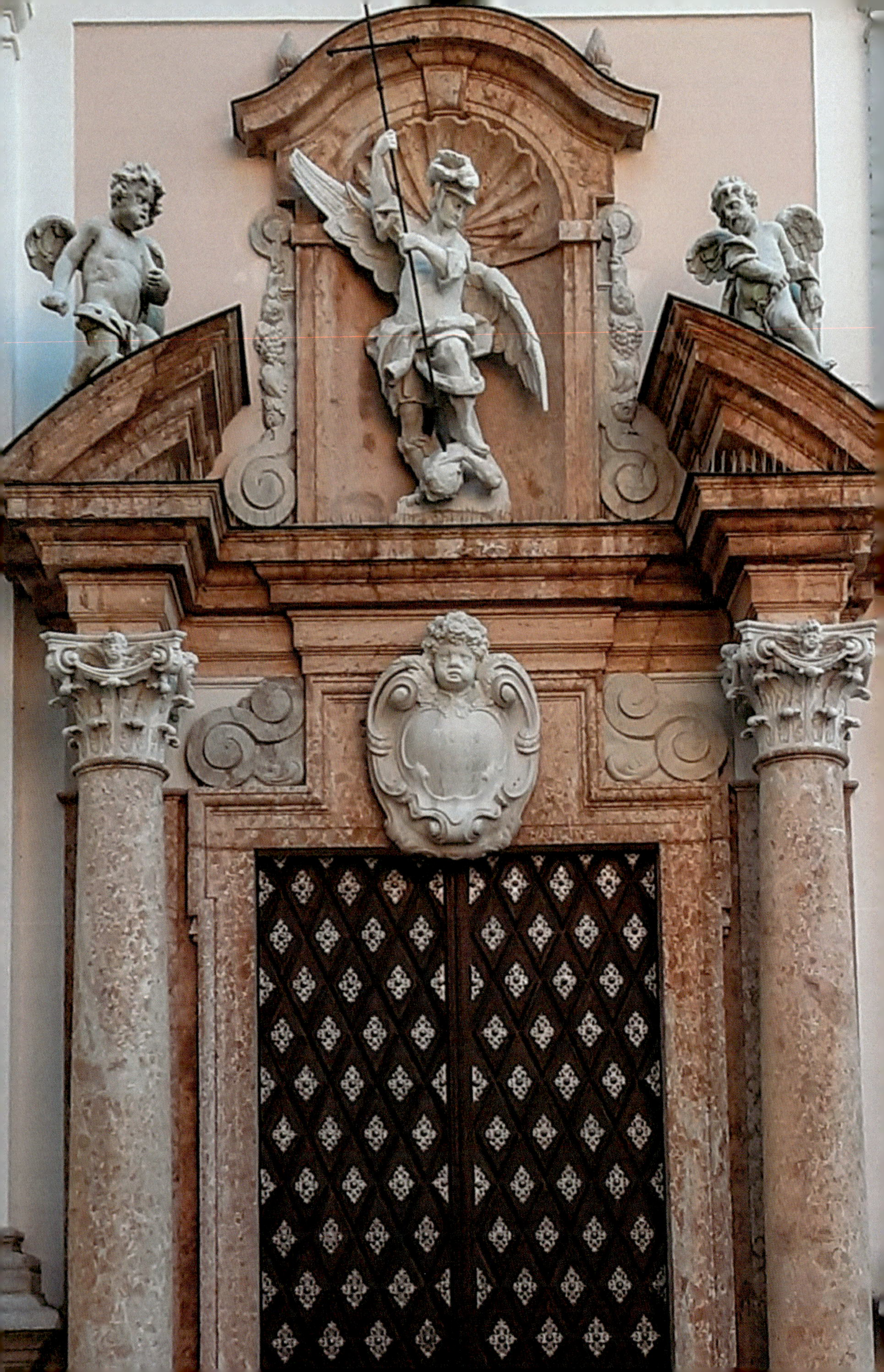

ScharfrichterHaus

IOANNES PHILIPPUS
D.G.EPISCOPUS PASSAVIENSIS
S.R.I. PRINCEPS EX COMITIBUS
DE LAMBERG
D.D.D.

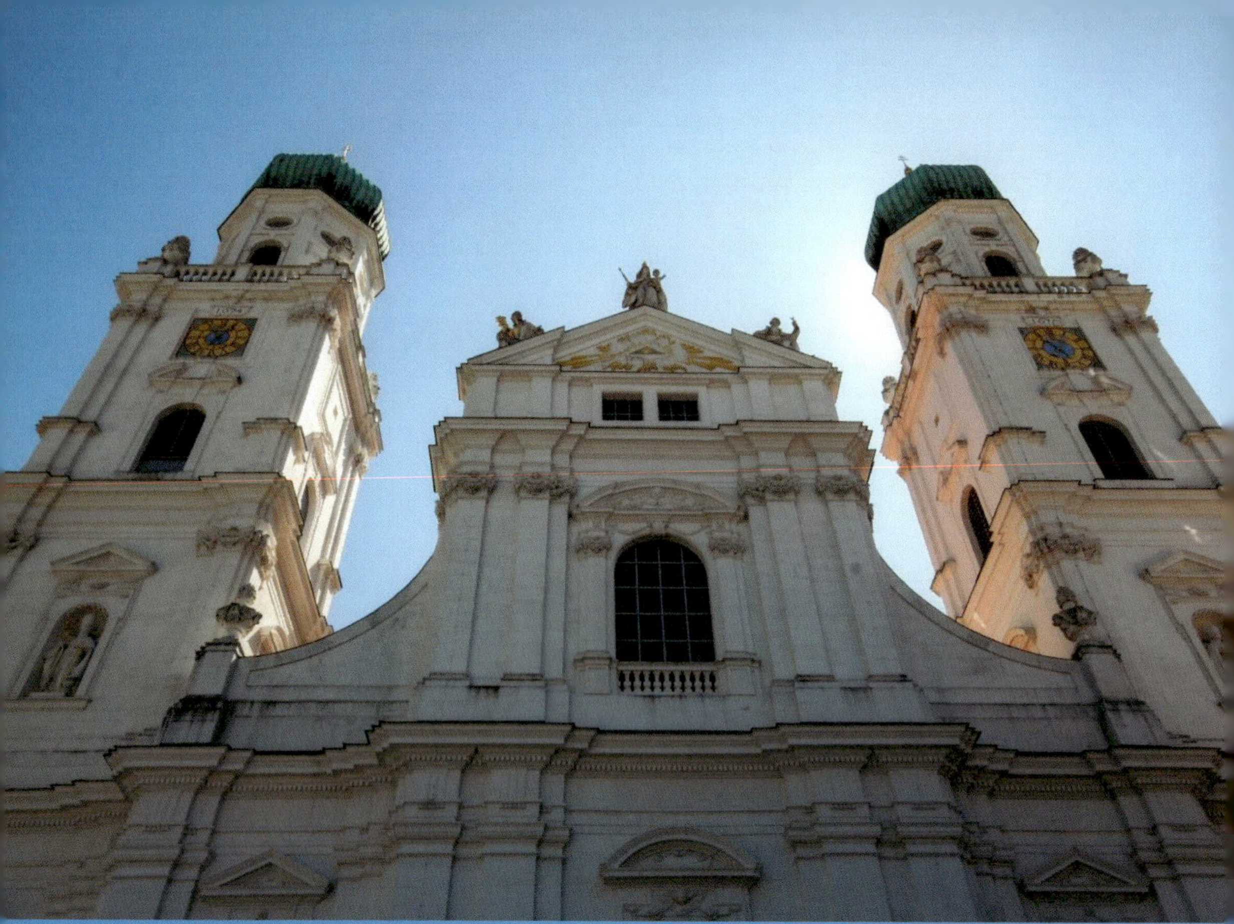

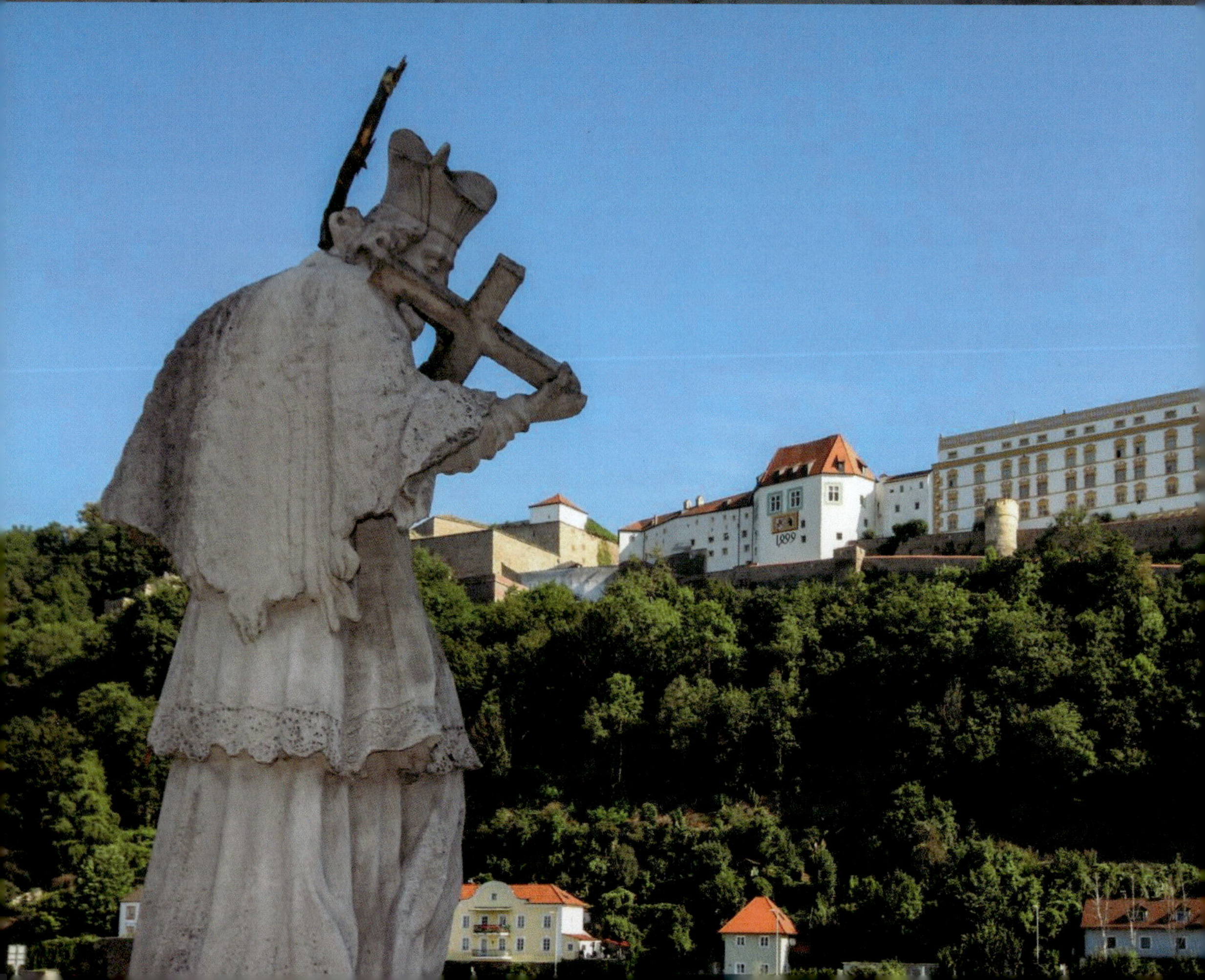

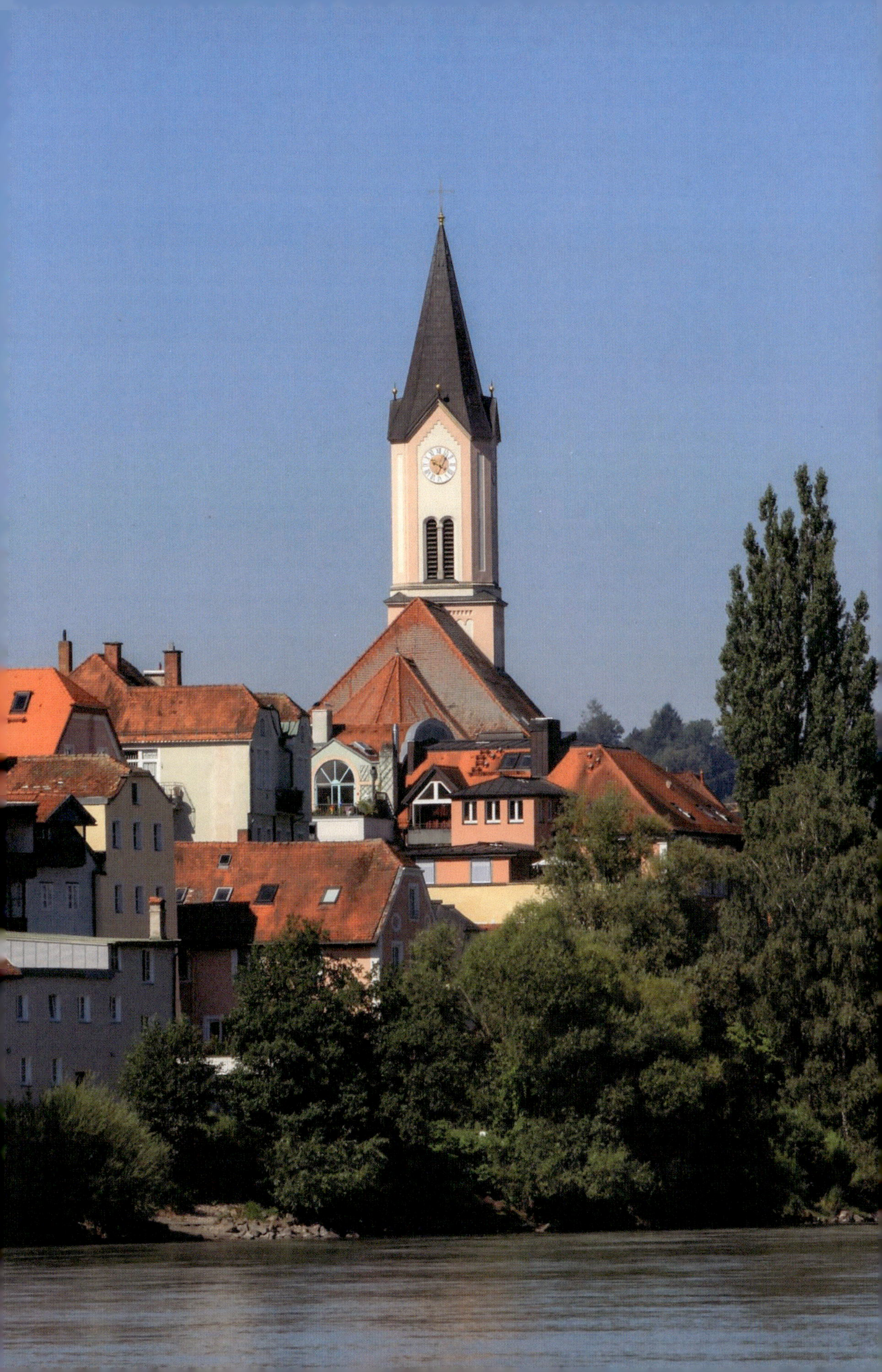

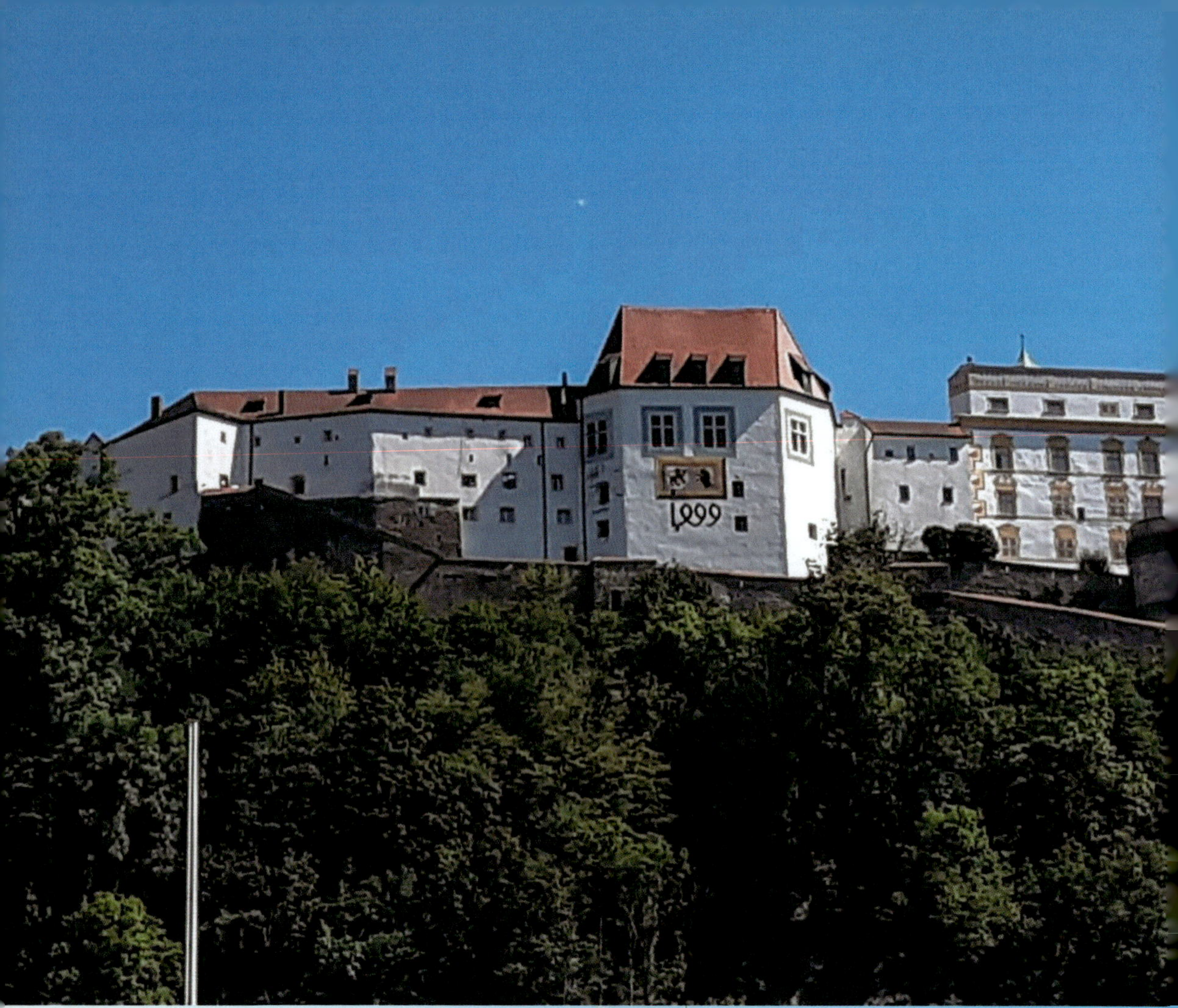

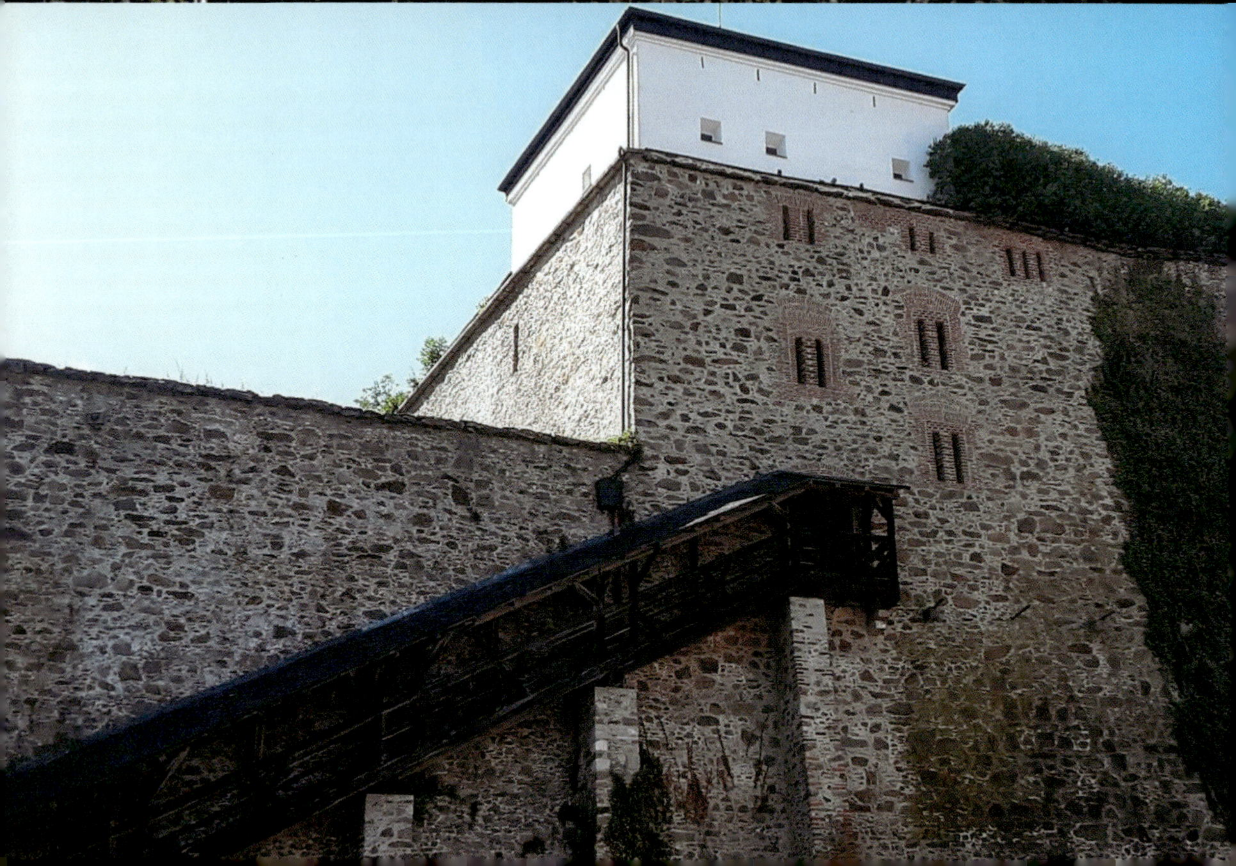

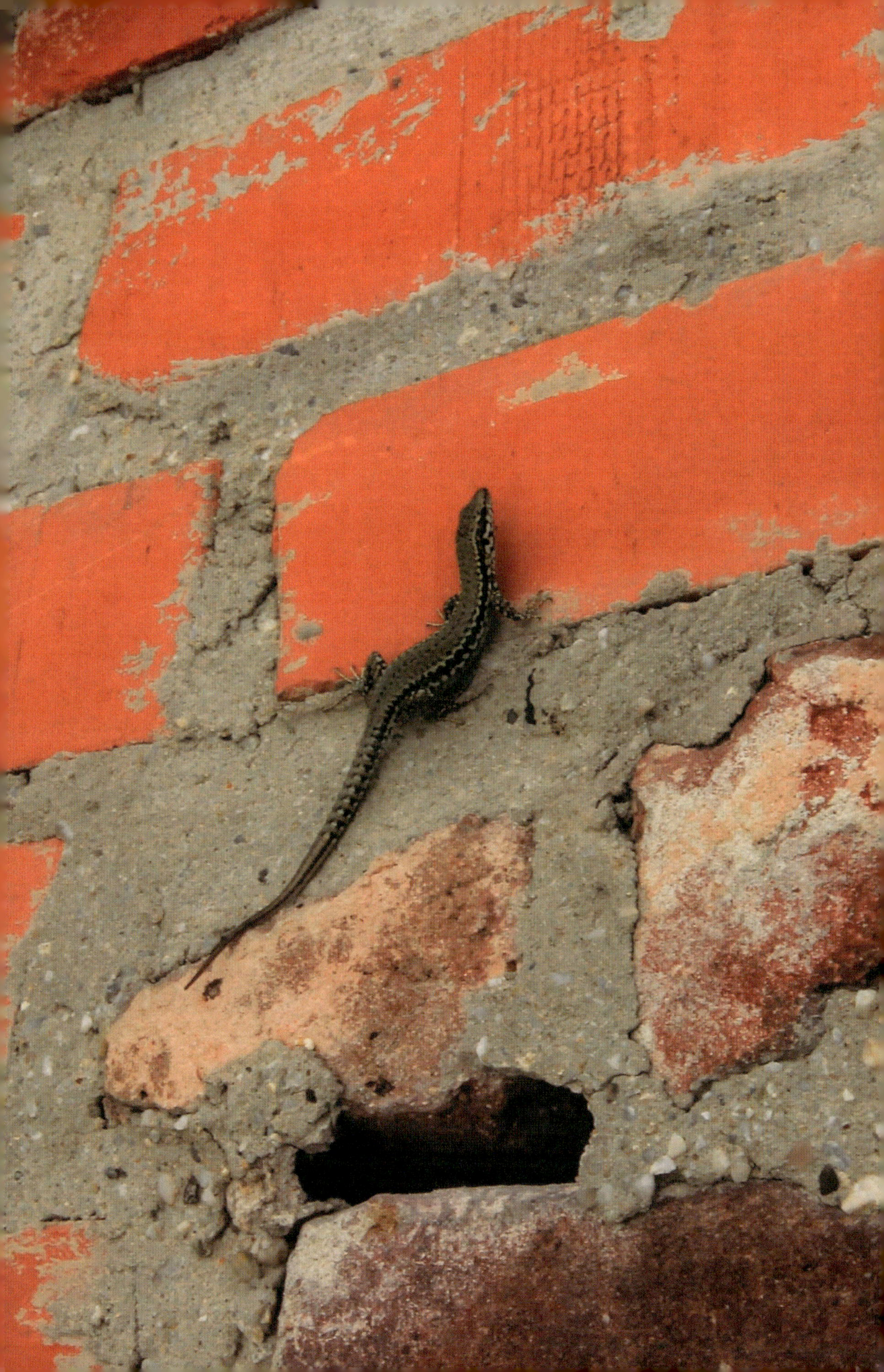

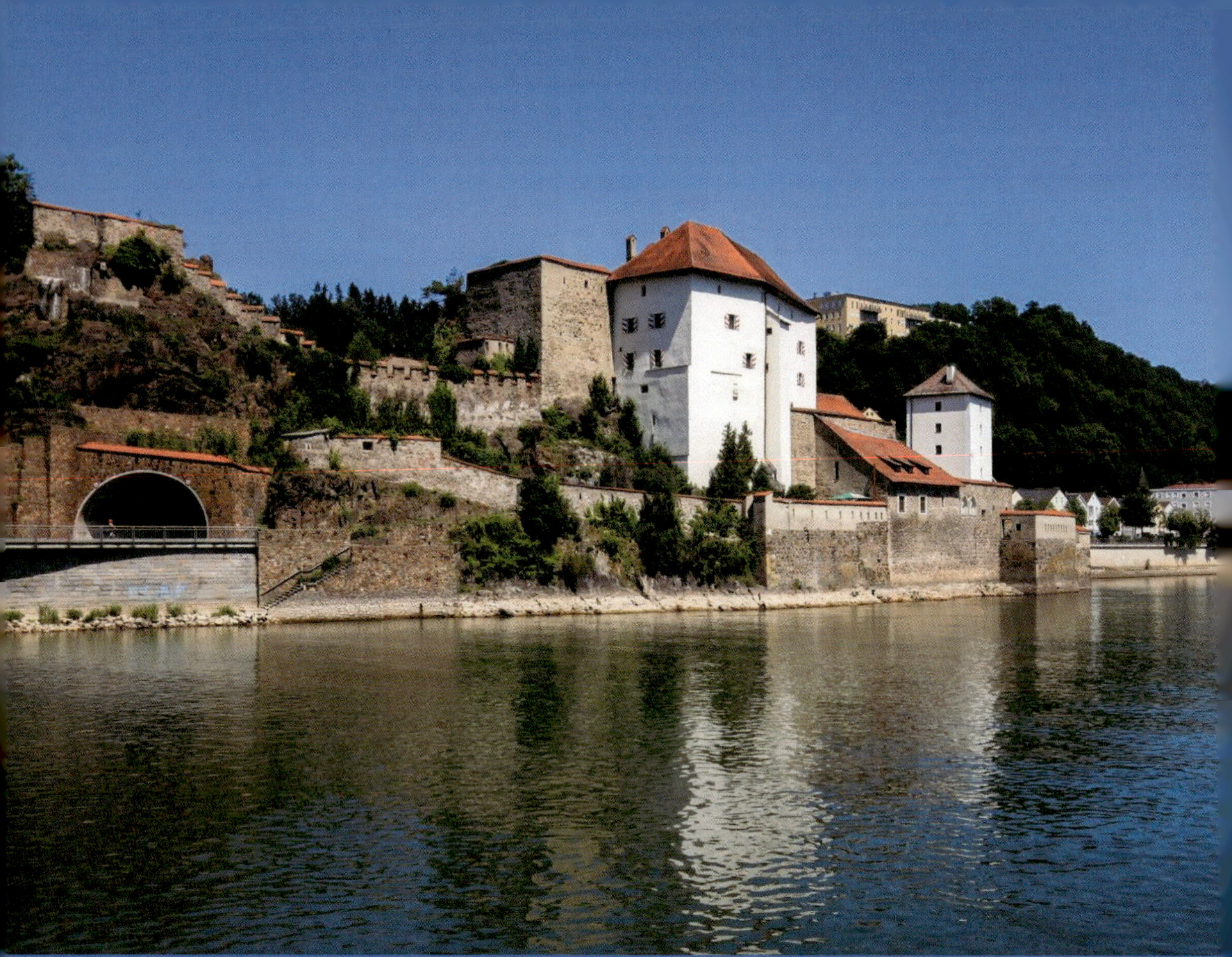
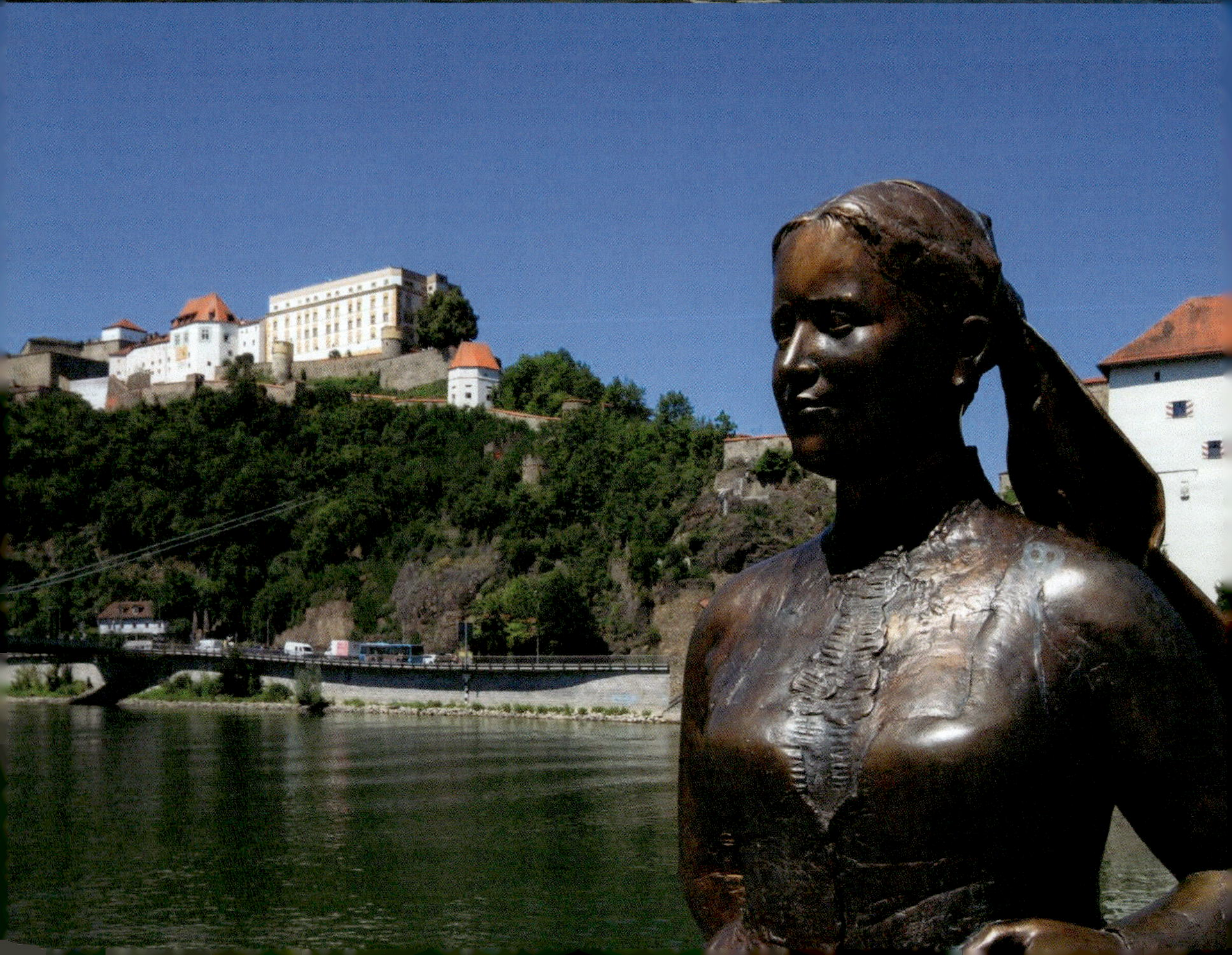

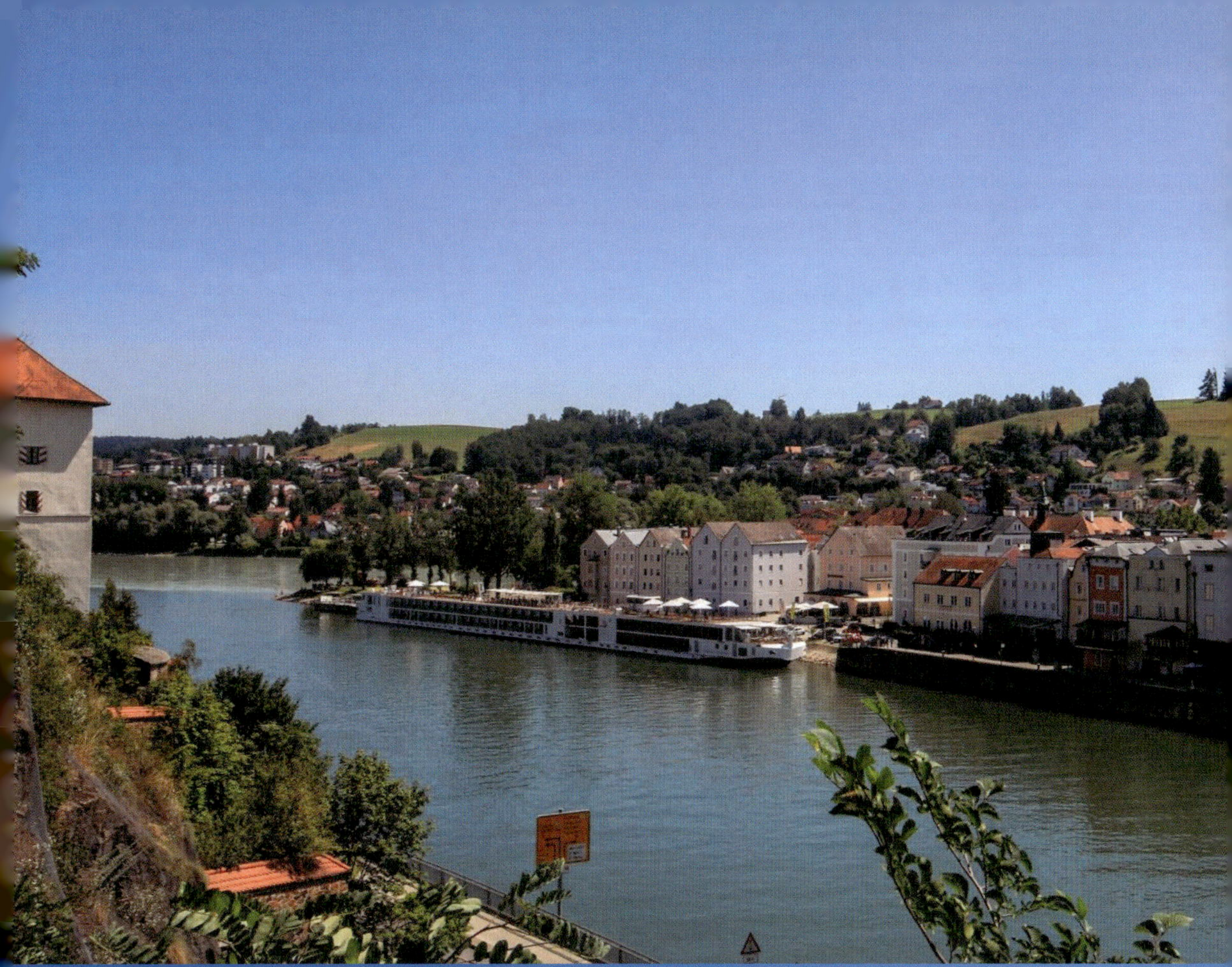

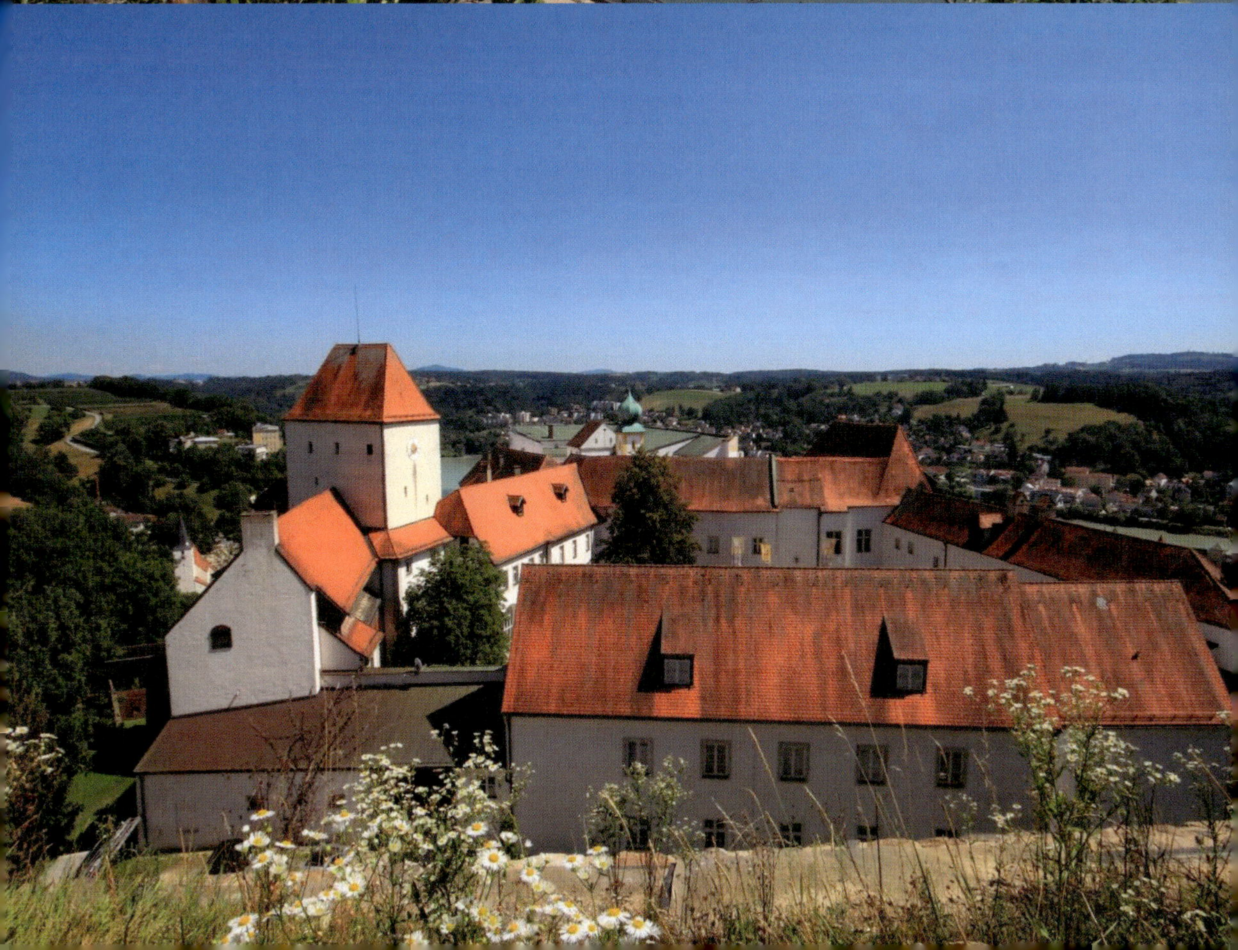

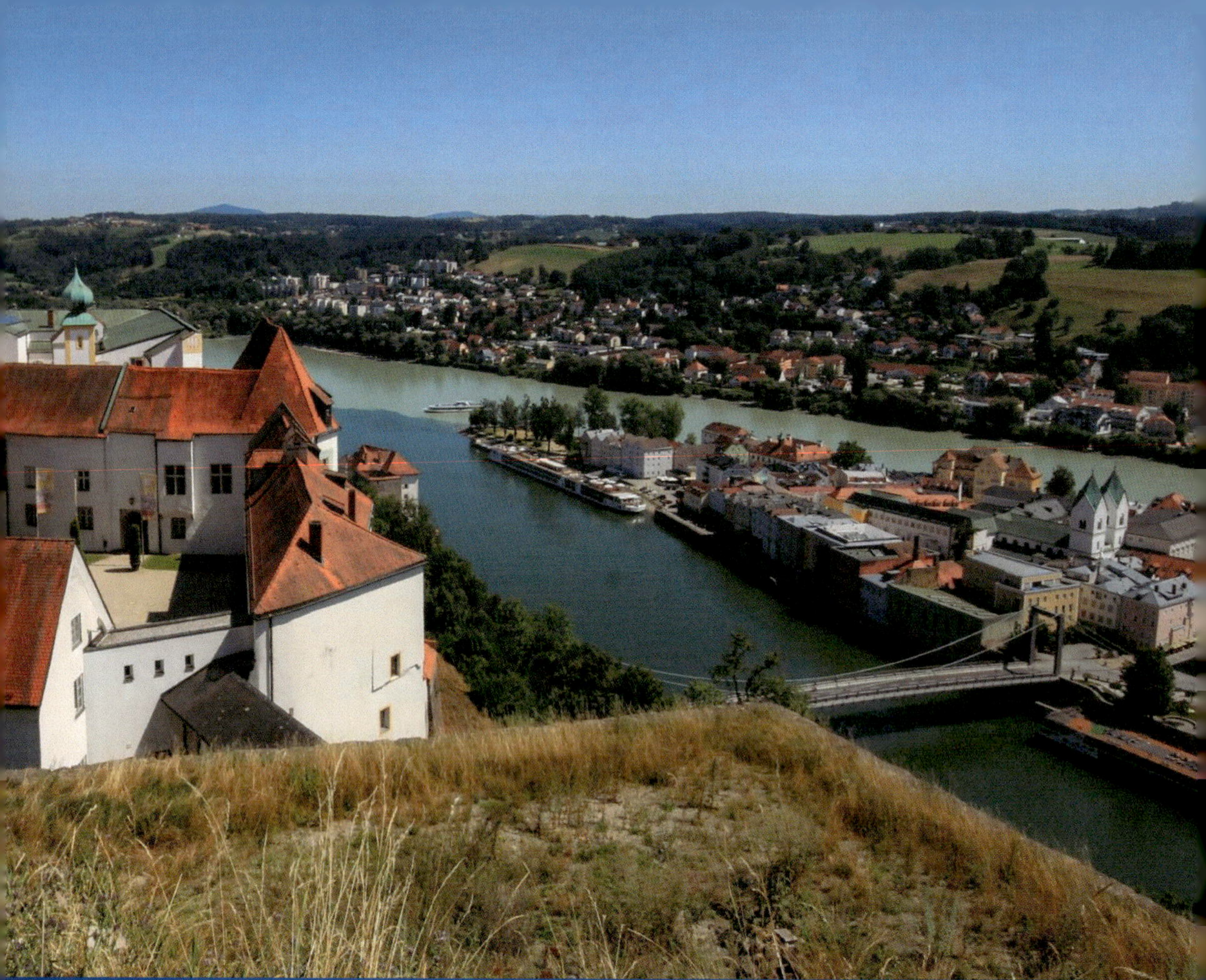

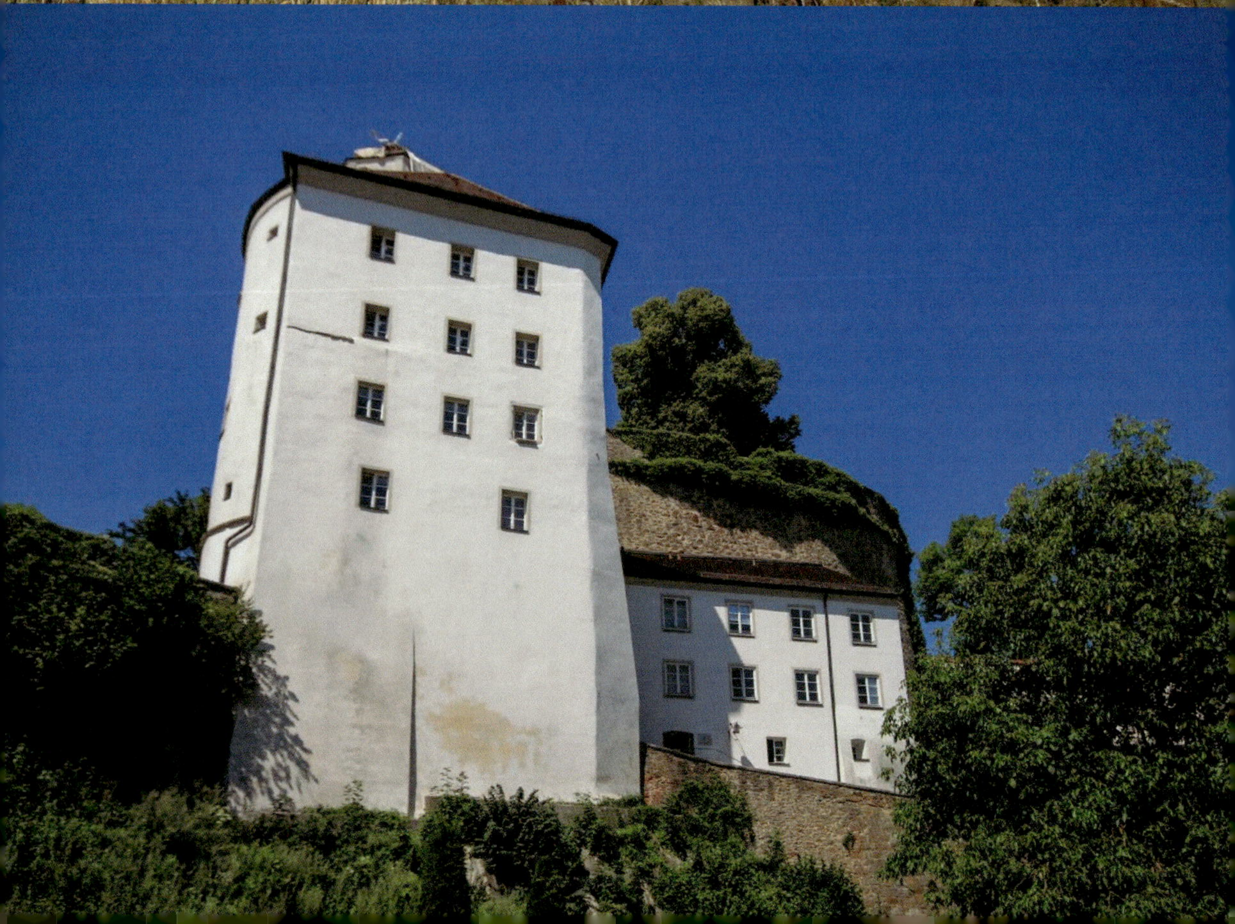

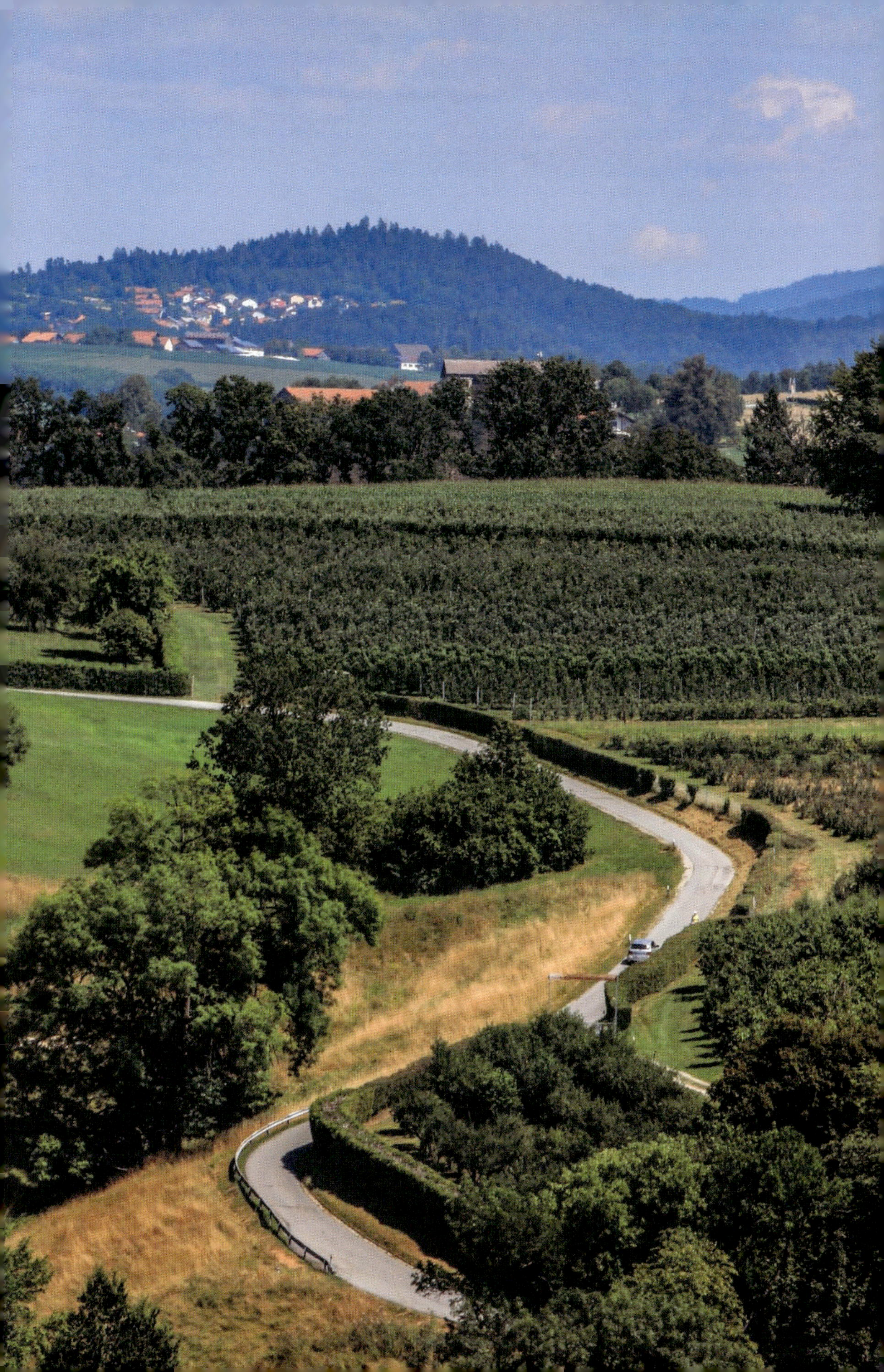

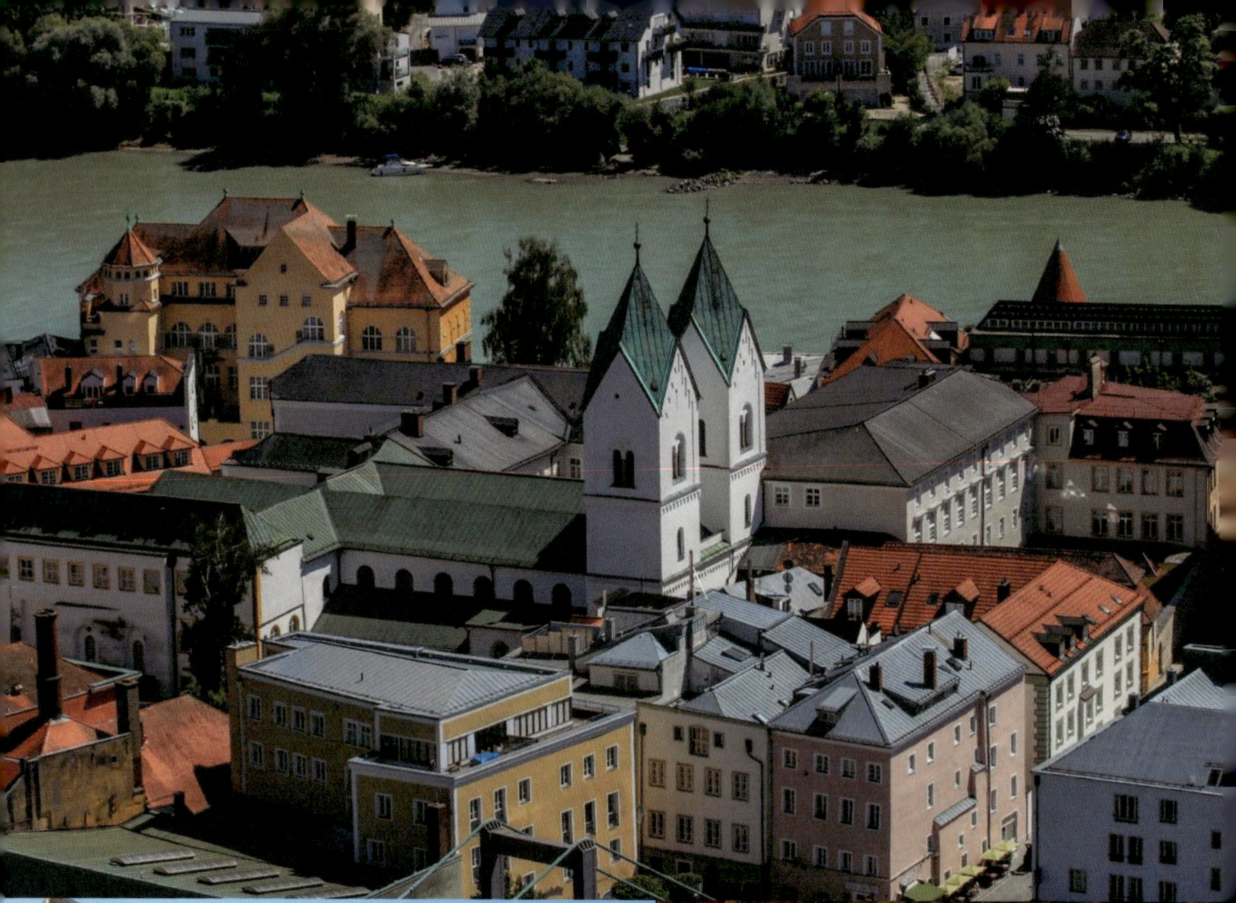

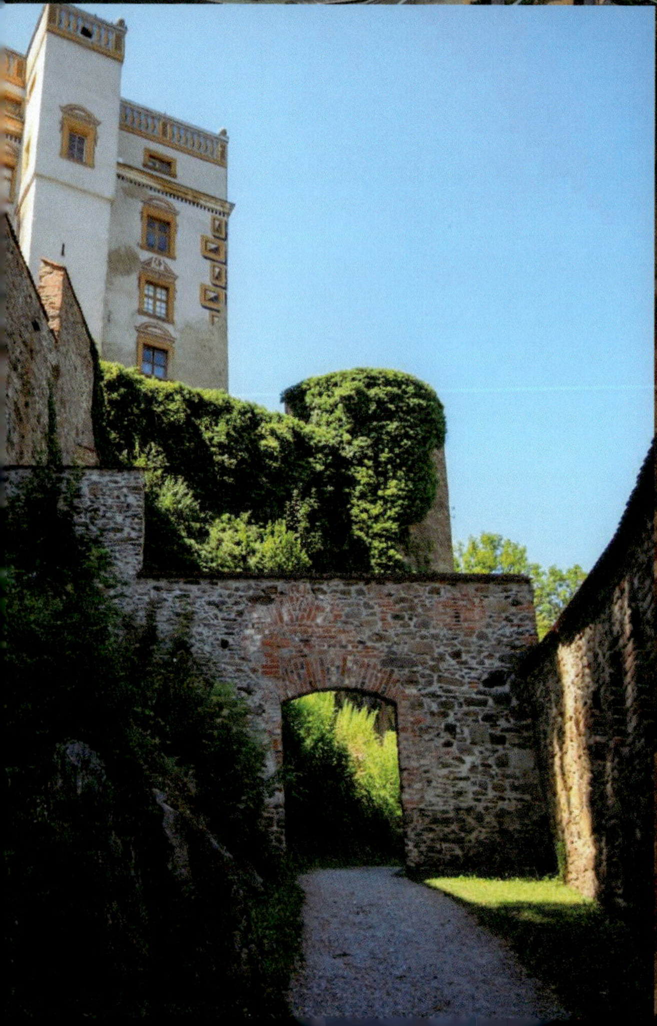

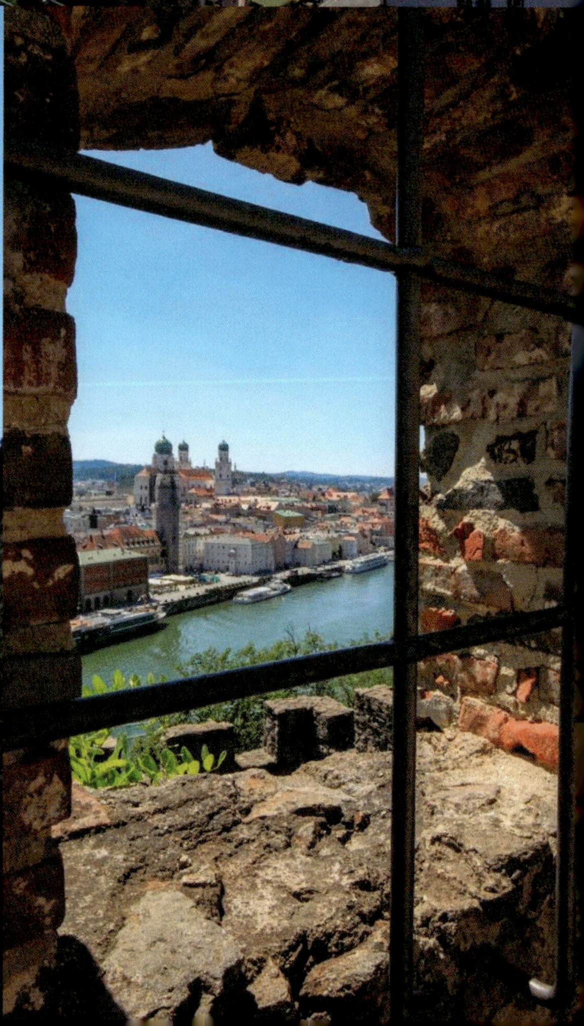

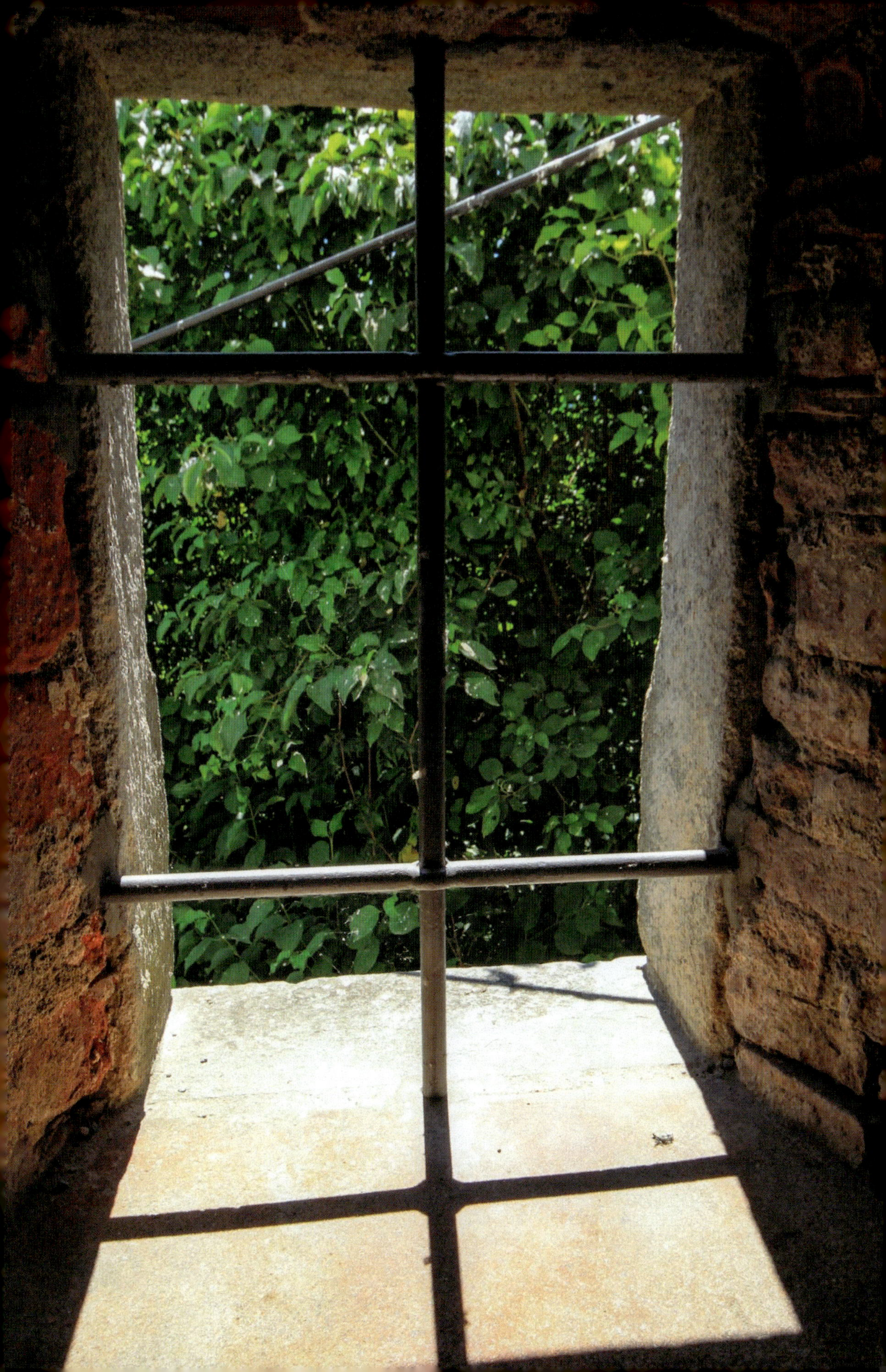

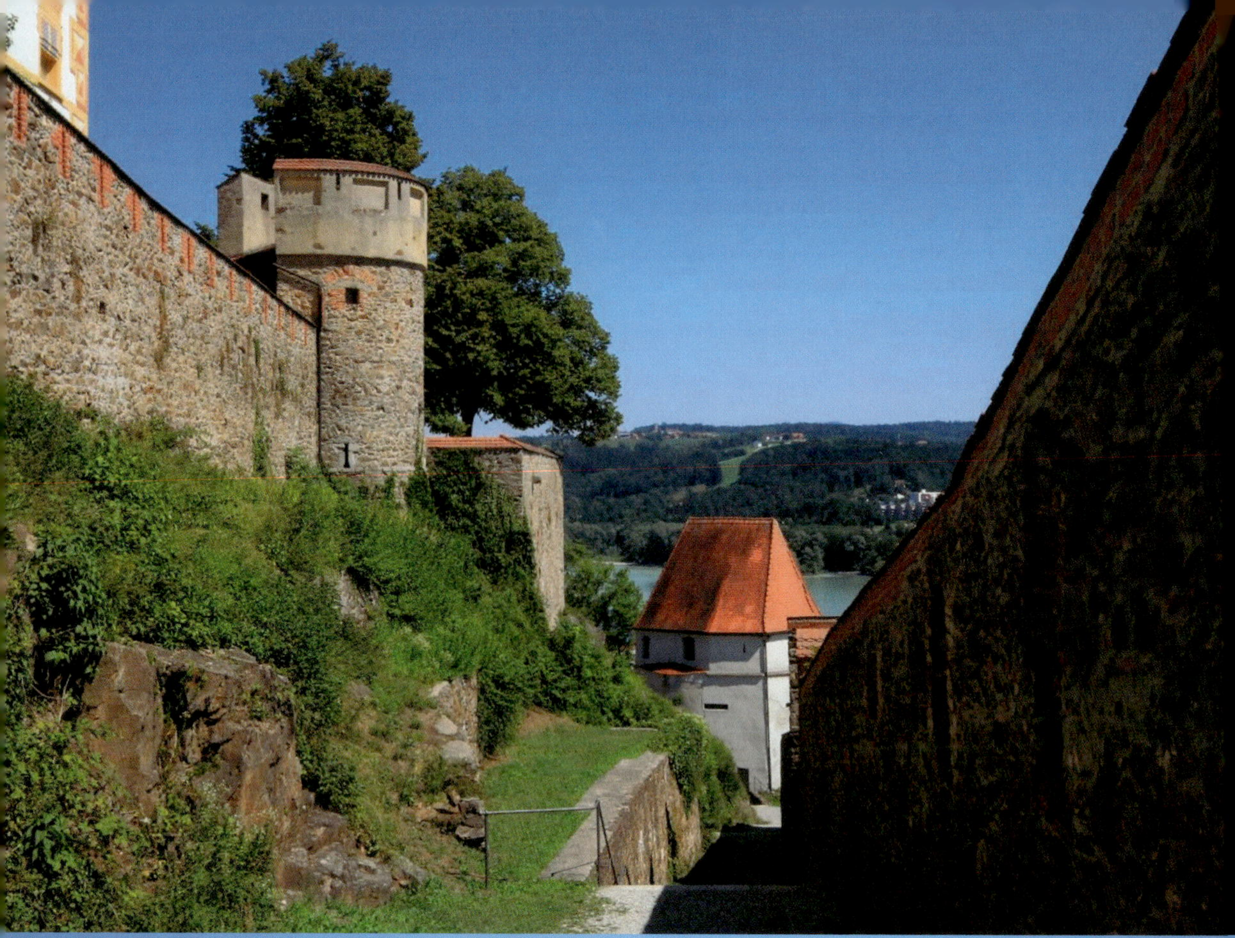

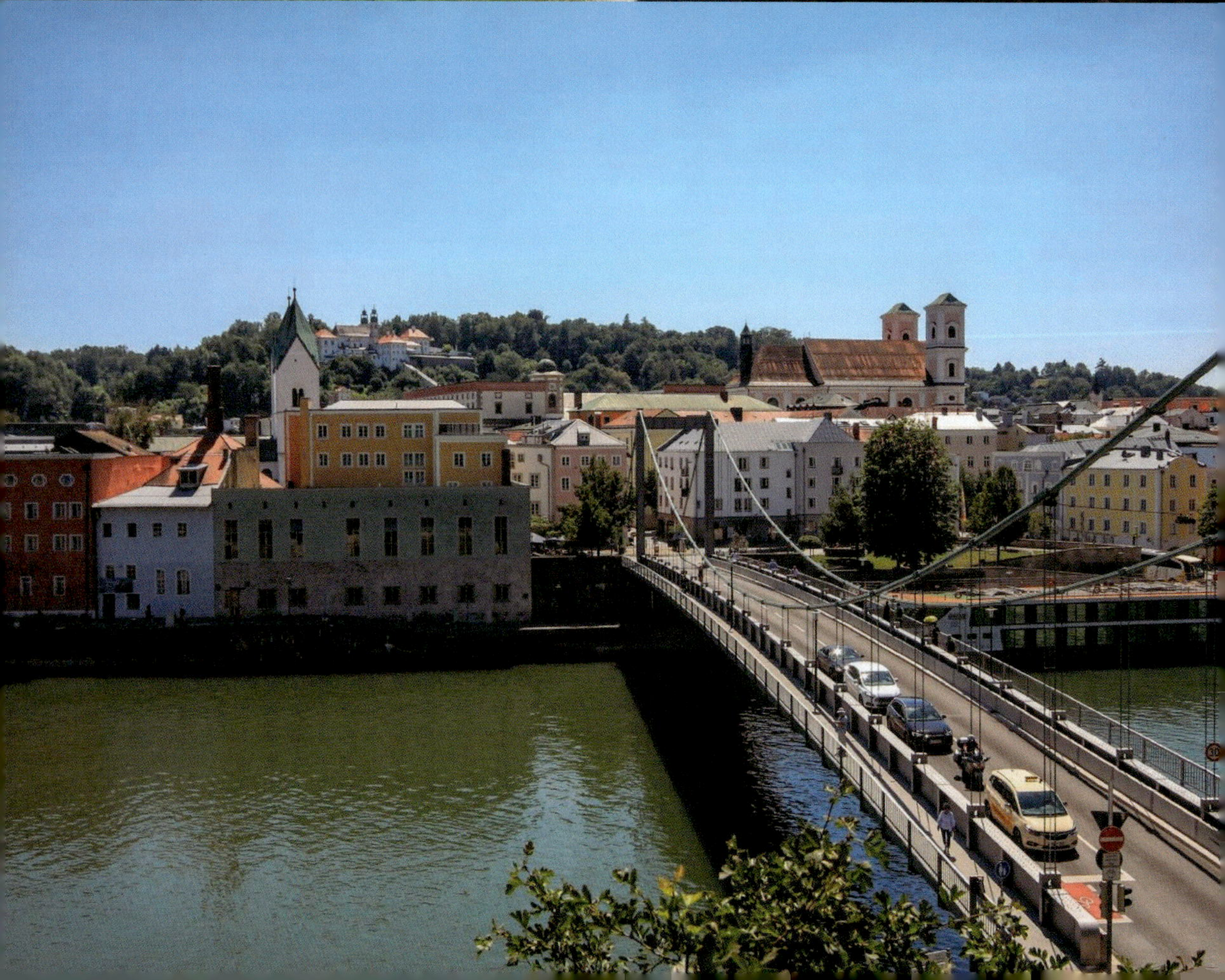

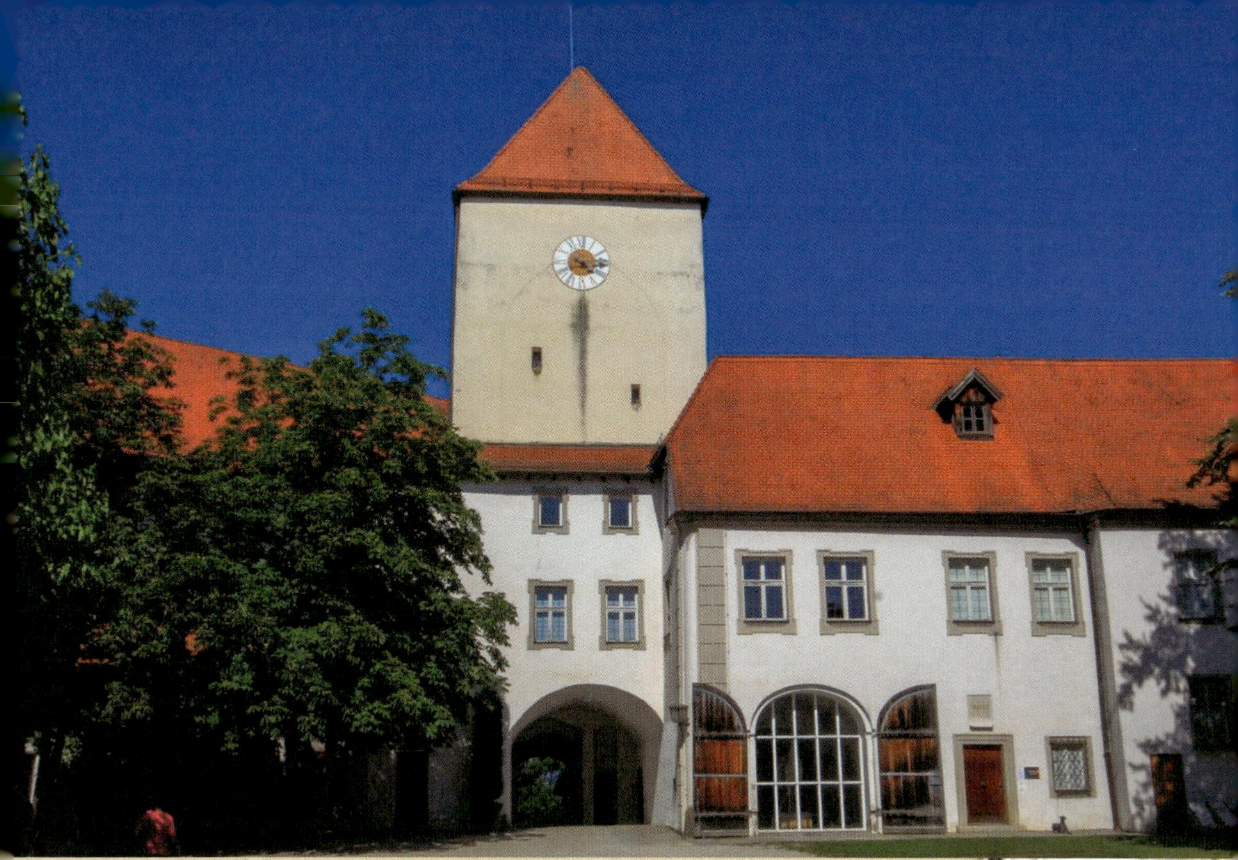

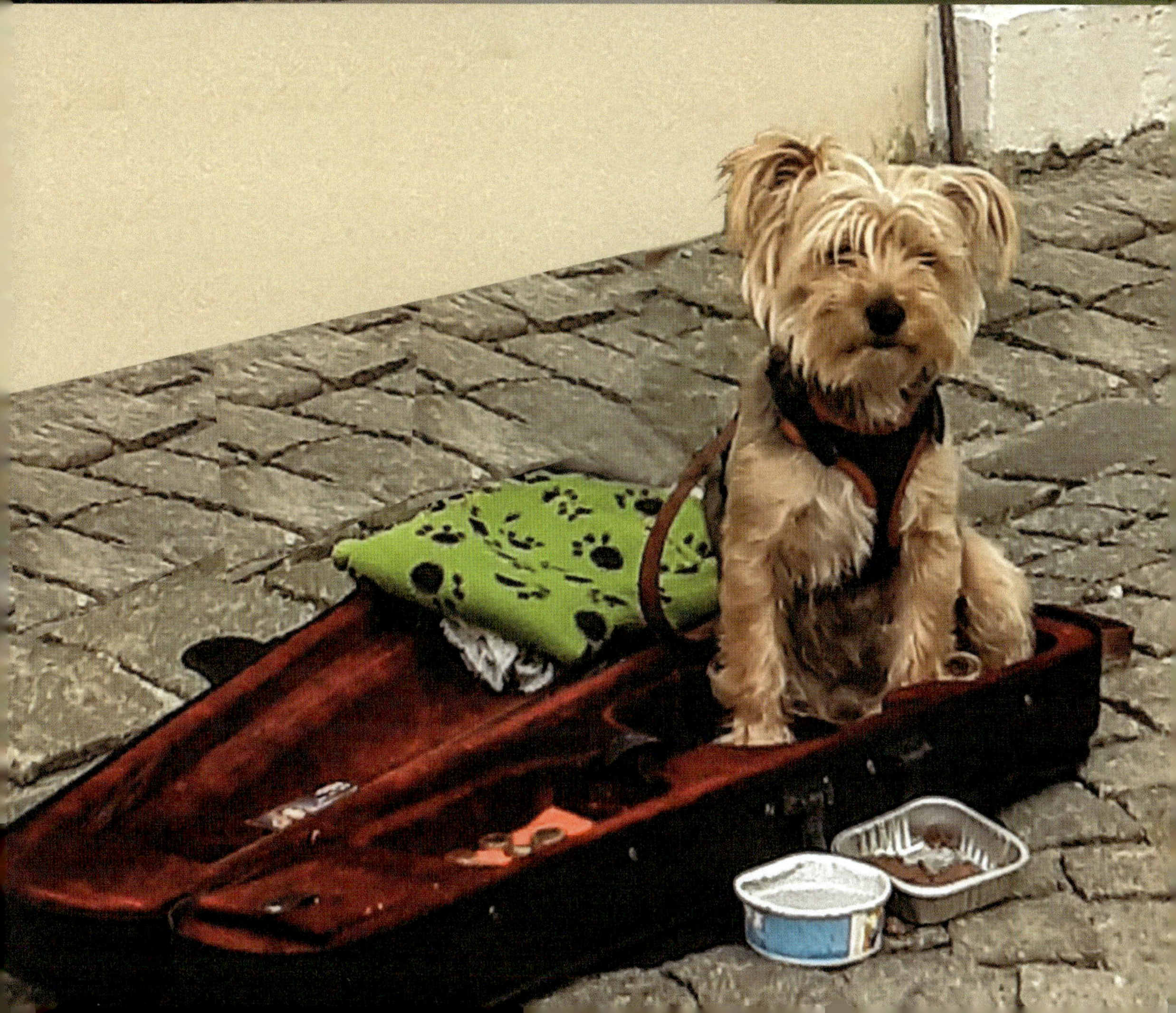

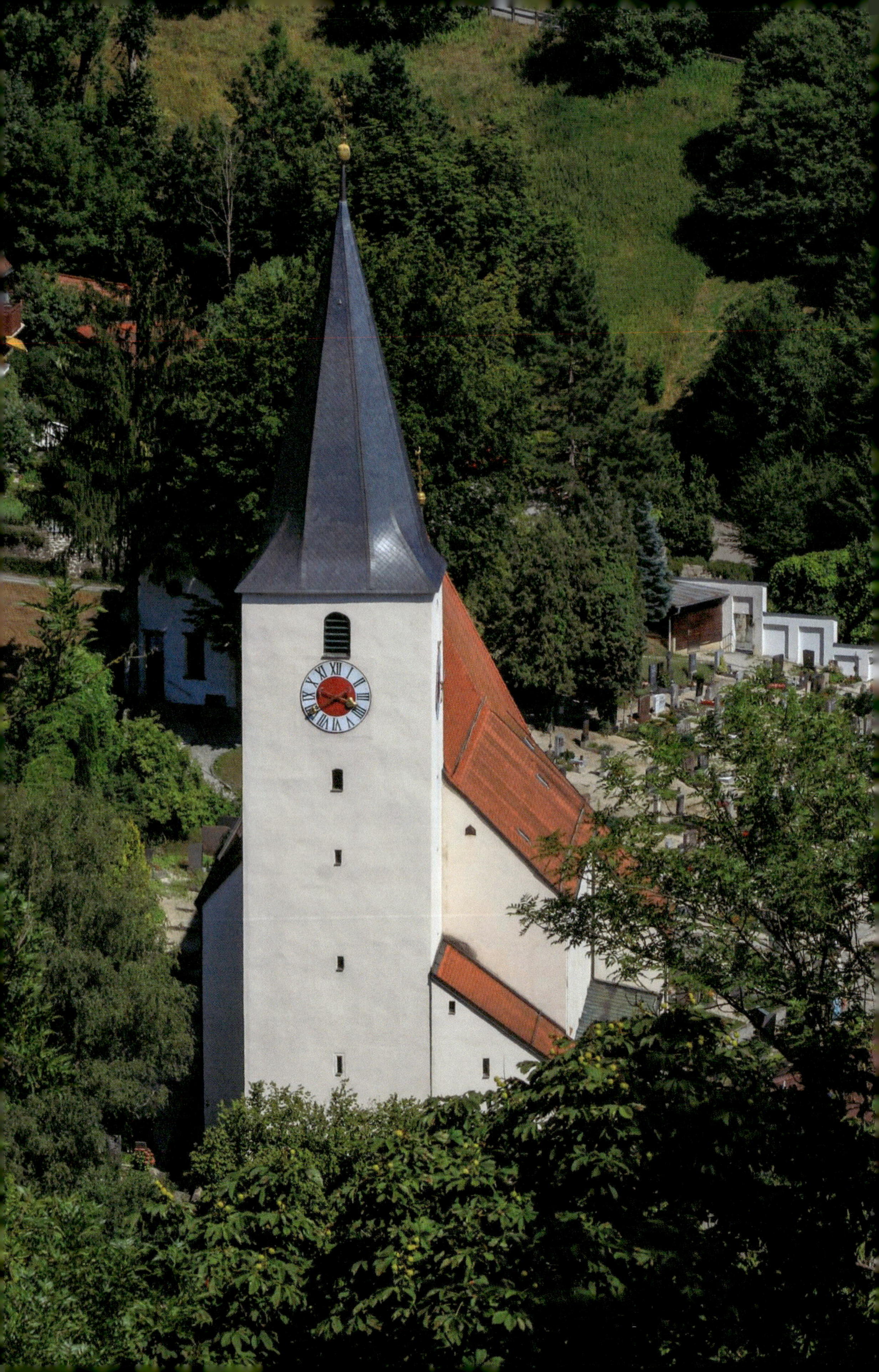

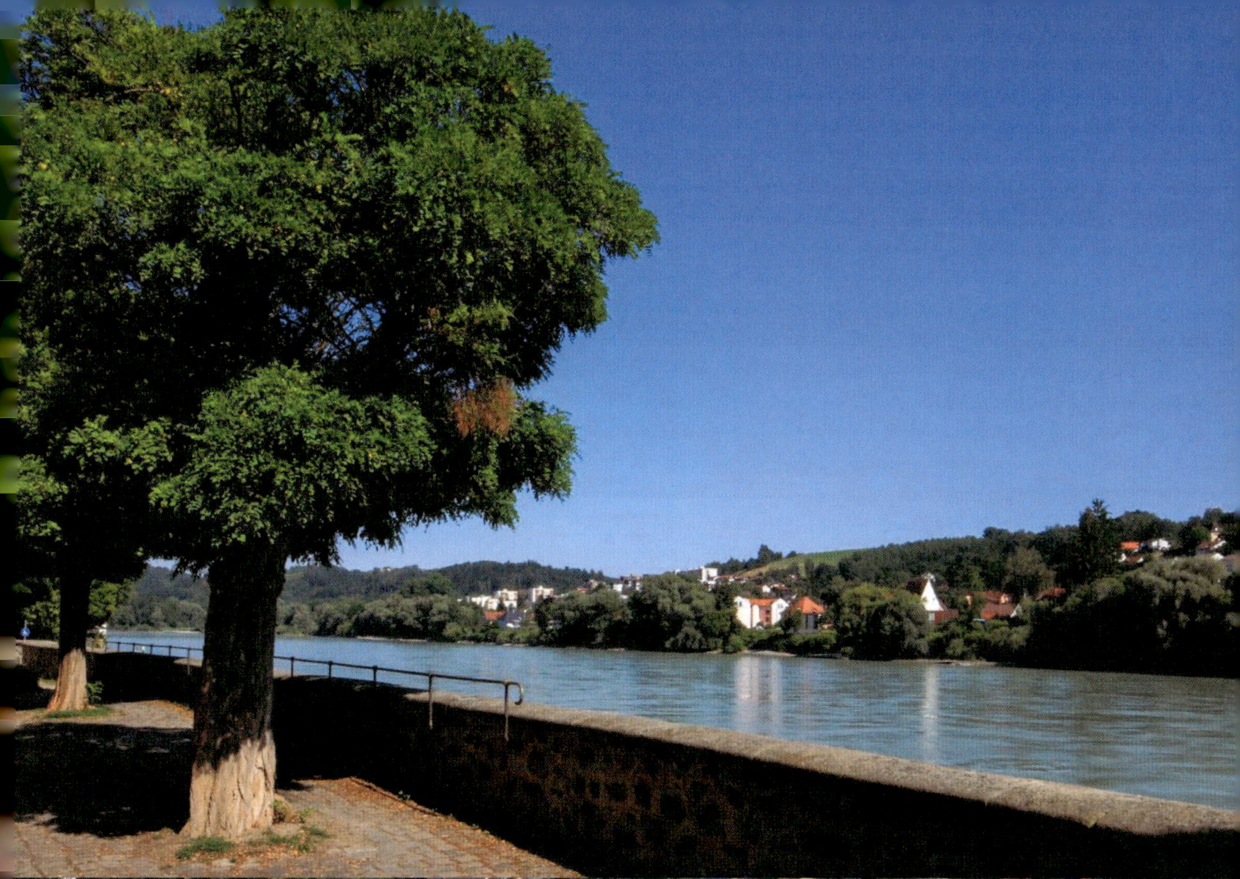

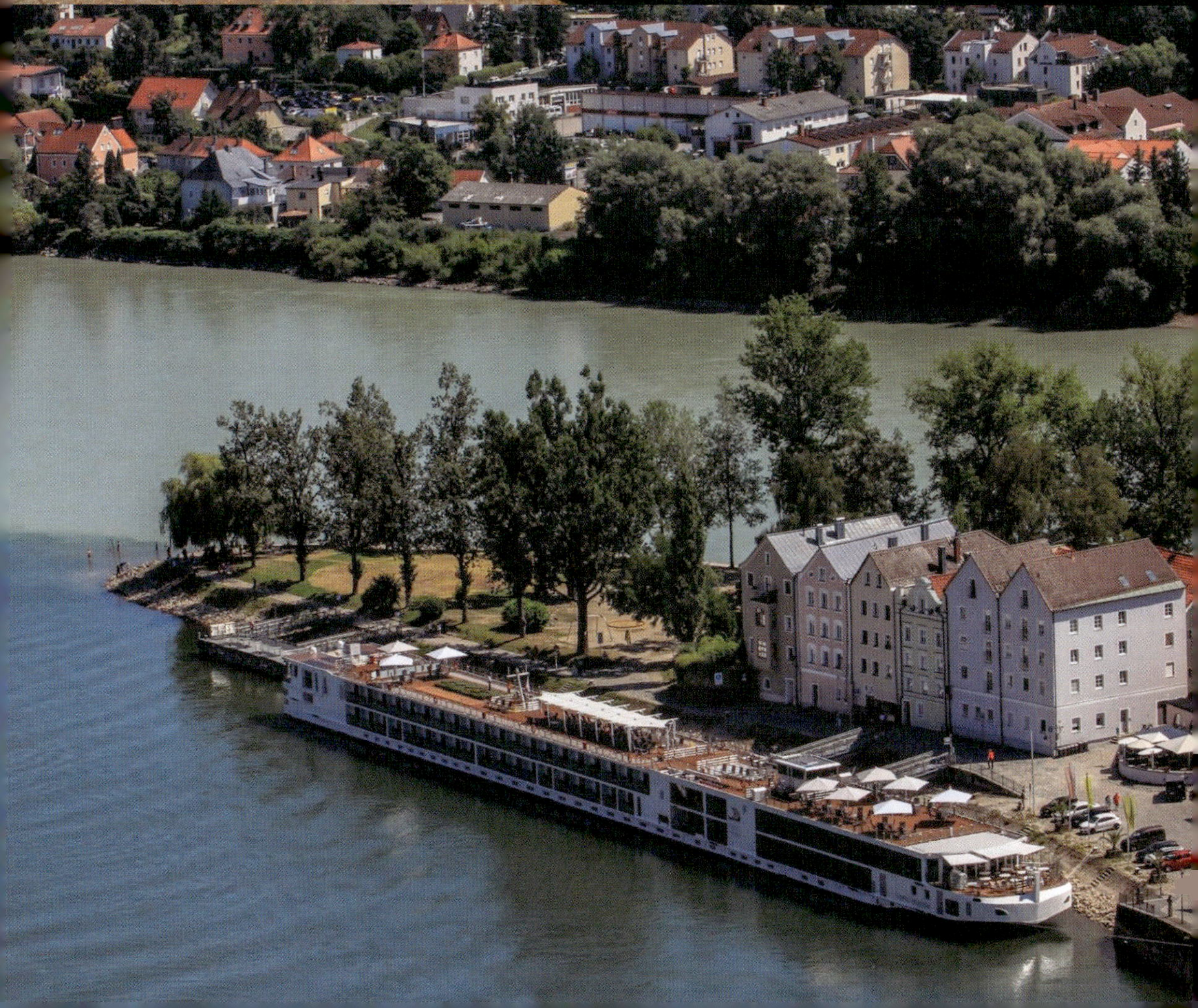

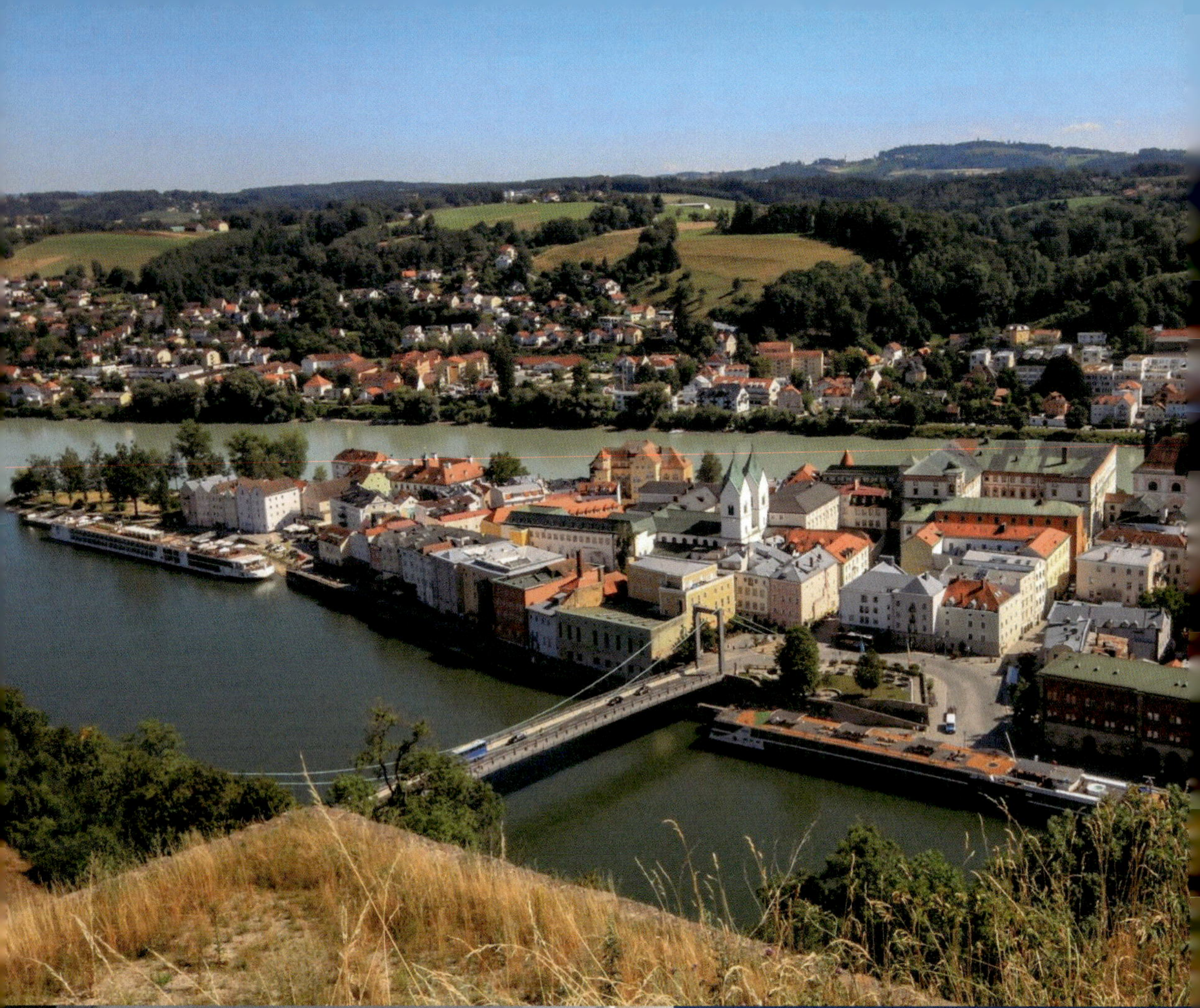
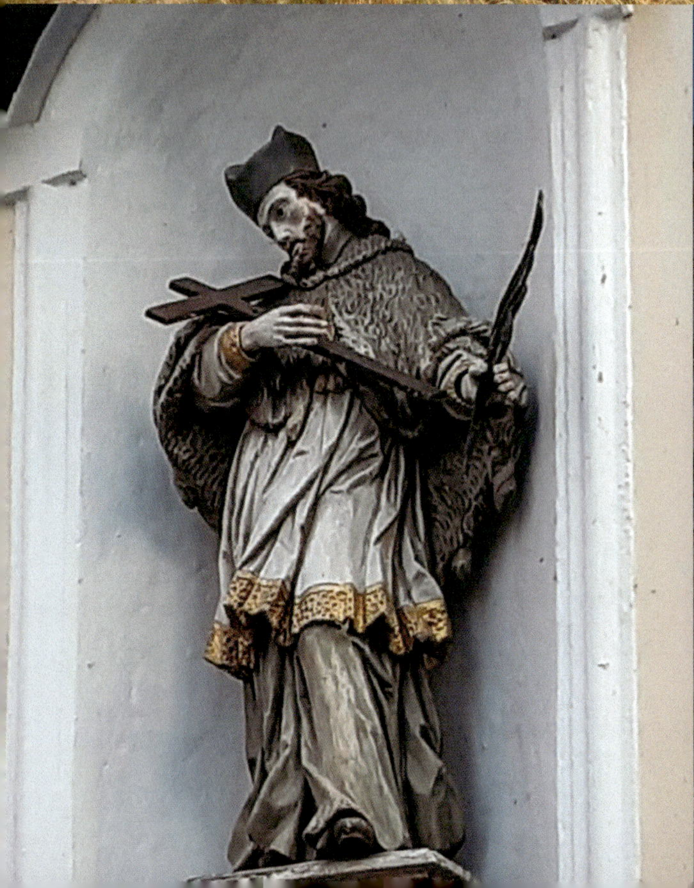
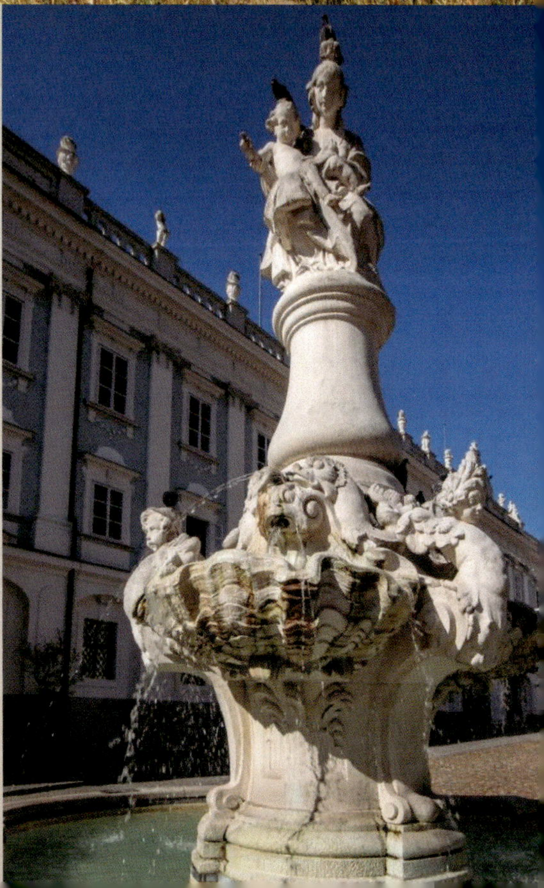

Český Krumlov

Printed in Great Britain
by Amazon